# Empire Jews

## Jewish Nationalism and Acculturation in 19th- and Early 20th-Century Russia

The New Approaches to Russian and East European Jewish Culture series aims to bring to the public the finest scholarship on Russian and East European Jewish culture. Drawing on Yiddish, Hebrew, and Slavic studies, the series emphasizes questions of the culture and intellectual history of the Jews in Russia and Eastern Europe. Of particular focus are the unexplored relationships between Jews and their neighbors and among Jews themselves. The editor hopes to publish works that challenge conventional or simplistic ideas regarding the role of Jews in the relevant literatures (Russian, Polish, Czech, etc...), cosmopolitanism and national identity, and the intersection of religious and secular conceptions of self. This series has the goal of becoming a central location for the development of new approaches, including work on the history of ideas, postmodernism, and gender issues.

*The New Approaches to Russian and East European Culture Series*

1. Ber Boris Kotlerman, *In Search of Milk and Honey: The Theater of "Soviet Jewish Statehood," 1934–49* (2009)
2. Brian Horowitz, *Empire Jews: Jewish Nationalism and Acculturation in 19th- and Early 20th-Century Russia* (2009)

Series General Editor: Brian Horowitz (Tulane University)

# EMPIRE JEWS

## JEWISH NATIONALISM AND ACCULTURATION IN 19TH- AND EARLY 20TH-CENTURY RUSSIA

### BRIAN HOROWITZ

SLAVICA

Cover: Exterior of St. Petersburg Choral Synagogue. Photo of William Craft Brumfield, courtesy of photographer.

Library of Congress Cataloging-in-Publication Data

Horowitz, Brian.
    Empire Jews : Jewish nationalism and acculturation in 19th- and early 20th-century Russia / Brian Horowitz.
        p. cm. – (New approaches to Russian and East European culture ; 2)
    Includes bibliographical references and index.
    ISBN 978-0-89357-349-2
    1. Jews--Cultural assimilation--Russia--History--19th century. 2. Jews--Cultural assimilation--Russia--History--20th century. 3. Jews--Russia--Intellectual life--History--19th century. 4. Jews--Russia--Intellectual life--History--20th century. 5. Jews--Russia--Identity--History--19th century. 6. Jews--Russia--Identity--History--20th century. 7. Jewish nationalism--Russia. 8. Russia--Ethnic relations. I. Title. II. Title: Jewish nationalism and acculturation in 19th- and early 20th-century Russia.
    DS134.84H66 2009
    305.892'404709034--dc22

                                    2009001202

Slavica Publishers
Indiana University
2611 E. 10th St.
Bloomington, IN 47408-2603
USA

[Tel.] 1-812-856-4186
[Toll-free] 1-877-SLAVICA
[Fax] 1-812-856-4187
[Email] slavica@indiana.edu
[www] http://www.slavica.com/

# Contents

## Jewish Writers between Two Worlds

## Conceptualizing a Nation Apart: Politics and Historiography

## Jews in the Russian Elite

# Introduction

The essays in this book are linked by two main themes: I investigate Jewish intellectuals in tsarist and early Soviet Russia who attempted to fashion a modern, secular, and nationally acute Jewish identity; and I study the contributions to Russian culture by Jews who participated as absolute insiders. Instead of repeating the conventional belief that Jews were marginalized in tsarist Russia, I have discovered that a number of them—many more than one might think—occupied positions in the epicenter of Russia's artistic and intellectual life. Moreover, as Jews became acquainted with Russia's world-class culture, they integrated its elements into Jewish life and into their artistic creations. Jews who joined the Russian elite brought with them a Jewish sensibility that permitted them acute insights into the Russian spirit. In both these cases, one finds an uncanny interpenetration of cultures, minds, and temperaments that was enormously productive for both Russian and Jewish cultures.

The hypothesis that Russian and Jewish cultures were mutually beneficial led me to question the simplistic views of earlier scholars who presented Russian Jews in one of four ways: either as backward and specifically Jewish Orthodox-religious, exclusively politically oppressed (victims of pogroms), Communist/Socialist, or Zionist. I examine the ineluctable fact that a large group chose a synthetic identity, Russian-Jewish, that emerged not in conflict, but in concert with modern Russian society. In many cases, one and the same person participated in two distinct circles. Maksim Vinaver, for example, was a leader both of the Russian Constitutional Democratic Party and of the Society for the Promotion of Enlightenment among the Jews of Russia. Shimon An-sky was an expert on Jewish folklore and a member of the Socialist Revolutionary Party. Similarly, in the cultural arena at least three generations of Jewish writers, considering themselves members of the Russian intelligentsia, struggled to create a specifically Jewish literature in Russian. Such names as Lev Levanda, David Aizman, Shimon Yushkevich, and Vasily Grossman come to mind.

Most of the essays in this book take up questions related to tensions implicit in modern Russian-Jewish identity. How should one resolve loving Russia as the source of one's personhood and creativity and hating its intolerant government and right-wing ideologies? Moreover, what seems most painful to me is that it might be impossible to untangle the positive and negative dimensions. Could it be that the good and the bad were mutually conditioned and inseparable, that at a fundamental level the amazing cultural blossoming of Jewish life at the turn of the 20th century was dependent in inexplicable ways on Russia's double-sidedness?

Even when Jews were divorcing themselves from Russian society, forming autonomous institutions to provide services the government refused to provide, such as schools and self-help organizations, they were engaged more than ever in a dialogue with it. For example, Russian radicals had a tremendous influence. Many Jews were attracted to the universal goals of a perfect society and moral justice expressed in the ideology of such radical thinkers as Nikolai Chernyshevsky, Nikolai Dobrolyubov, and Dmitry Pisarev. Jews joined the revolutionary parties in numbers that outpaced their proportion in the overall population.[1] At the same time, Russian dreams of *sobornost'* (absolute social harmony) and the *mir* (a pre-industrial collective community of peasants) paradoxically attracted urban Jews who were seeking a solution to economic displacement and social alienation. Such rural fantasies unexpectedly tantalized those who wanted to turn Jewish life backward to its agrarian beginnings and establish Jewish farming colonies in Russia, Argentina, Oregon, and Eretz Israel.[2] Even Jewish liberals were imbued with the idea of productivization—the view that only farming and crafts were morally justifiable occupations. Rare was the Jewish thinker with enough courage to defend capitalism or express the necessity of political stability above all else.

The most powerful work by Jews in the Russian elite during the fin de siècle was arguably in literary criticism and Russian thought. Such figures as Mikhail Gershenzon, Lev Shestov (Shvartsman), and Akim Volynsky (Flekser), were in the forefront of Russian philosophy. The study of the Russian national poet Aleksandr Pushkin—clearly a demonstration of one's allegiance to the national heritage—was dominated by Jewish scholars, starting with Semyon Vengerov, who converted to Russian Orthodoxy in the 1880s, and Nikolai Lerner, Pavel Kogan, Leonid Grossman, Yury Tynyanov, and Boris Eikhenbaum. As if to serve as a perfect symbol of the place occupied by Jews in the Russian elite, the head of the Russian collection at the Imperial Public Library in St. Petersburg was also a Jew, Aleksandr Braudo.[3] Because Braudo was a

---

[1] See O. V. Budnitskii, ed., *Evrei i russkaia revoliutsiia: Materialy i issledovaniia* (Moscow: Izd-vo "Gesharim," 1999); also Yuri Slezkine, *The Jewish Century* (Princeton, NJ: Princeton University Press, 2004).

[2] For a discussion of agricultural communities among Jews in late-tsarist Russia, see the first chapter of Jonathan L. Dekel-Chen's *Farming the Red Land: Jewish Agricultural Colonization and Local Soviet Power, 1924–1941* (New Haven: Yale University Press, 2005).

[3] L. Bramson, "Ob"edinenie russko-evreiskoi intelligentsii," in *Aleksandr Isaevich Braudo, 1864–1924: Ocherki i vospominaniia*, ed. Bramson (Paris: Maison du livre étranger, 1937), 7–22.

Freemason, he was well connected with the Russian nobility and trusted by radicals. In fact, Braudo played an important role in unmasking Evno Azef, the revolutionary who was supposedly a tsarist double agent.[4] These examples go a long way to show that at least some Jews were accepted as full members of the Russian intellectual elite.

In addition to Jews in Russian culture, I also focus my attention on liberals who strove to foster a distinct Diaspora nationalism. Liberals stood apart from radicals and Zionists because they put their hopes in a Russia that would be transformed and become a rule-of-law state. Like their Russian counterparts, Jewish liberals defended the principles of individual rights and democracy. They vocalized the need for minority rights, such as the right to autonomous Jewish cultural and political institutions funded through general, as opposed to Jewish, taxation.

Desiring neither full assimilation, as occurred in Western Europe, nor isolation, as some religious authorities advocated, Jewish liberals sought a third way. In order to foster Jewish national consciousness, they formed new institutions (voluntary societies) and remodeled old ones. For example, they revitalized the Society for the Promotion of Enlightenment among the Jews of Russia in the 1890s to serve the educational needs of the Jewish masses. Similarly, Jewish lawyers formed the Defense Bureau to use the tsarist courts as much as possible to protect Jewish victims of pogroms.[5] From the early 1880s until the end of the tsarist state, Jewish liberals tried to create a centralized Jewish administration, a new *kahal*, to satisfy the needs of Jewish communities throughout the country.[6] Bourgeois leaders such as Baron David Guenzburg and the lawyers Maksim Vinaver and Genrikh Sliozberg were involved in the Kovno Congress of 1908–09 and the Rabbinical Conference of 1910, where new political models were debated.[7]

It has often been argued that true Jewish nationalists spoke only Yiddish or Hebrew. However, as Jews began defining their own national culture in competition with Russian culture, they made use of the Russian language. For ex-

---

[4] Ibid., 112. Anna Geifman argues that Azef was neither a "provocateur" nor a "double agent." See Geifman, *Thou Shalt Kill: Revolutionary Terrorism in Russia, 1894–1917* (Princeton, NJ: Princeton University Press, 1993).

[5] See Benjamin Nathans, *Beyond the Pale: The Jewish Encounter with Late Imperial Russia* (Berkeley: University of California Press, 2002), 339.

[6] Jewish autonomous culture has its best definition in Simon Dubnov's collection of essays *Pis'ma o starom i novom evreistve* (St. Petersburg: Obshchestvennaia pol'za, 1907); the original essays were published between 1898 and 1906 in *Voskhod*.

[7] See the first two chapters in David E. Fishman's *The Rise of Modern Yiddish Culture* (Pittsburgh: University of Pittsburgh Press, 2005).

ample, starting in 1904, the official Zionist organization published a weekly newspaper in Russian, *Evreiskaia zhizn'*, to attract new readers. In 1909, after the famous weekly *Novyi voskhod* ceased appearing, three nationalist-leaning journals began to be published in St. Petersburg: a weekly, *Evreiskii mir*; a scholarly quarterly, *Evreiskaia starina*; and an annual, *Perezhitoe*. Thus, when nationalists in the Jewish Literary Society in St. Petersburg called for the exclusive use of Yiddish and Hebrew, Dubnov and An-sky rose up to defend Russian as a Jewish language.[8] Inevitably, in their demands to include Russian one can hear echoes from the Chernowitz Language Conference of 1908, in which Yiddish was acknowledged as a national language of the Jewish people.

Nevertheless, one also wants to ask: Why just Russian? What about Polish, Romanian, Ukrainian, Belorussian, Lithuanian, or any language spoken in those places where the Jews formed a sizeable minority? Here one already treads upon political turf. Jeffrey Veidlinger has noted, for instance, that the editors of *Evreiskaia starina* limited their interests primarily to the area of the Russian Empire (excluding Congress Poland) and seemed implicitly to accept the country's geographical borders as legitimate political and cultural boundaries.[9] In fact, one can make the case that many Jews imbibed some of the prejudices of Russian nationalists: Jews in Europe generally permitted themselves to be pulled into the intellectual orbit of the country in which they lived. Yet this attachment to the Russian borders is nonetheless difficult to fathom since it can be convincingly argued that East European Jewry formed a single people, despite being scattered across several countries.[10]

Regarding Russian, it is striking that even the greatest Yiddish writers, Sholem Yankev Abramovich (Mendele Mocher Sforim) and Sholem Aleichem, and the noted Hebraist and Zionist Ahad Ha'am, used the Russian language in their homes with their wives and children. Although this phenomenon deserves deeper investigation than can be provided here, one cannot help concluding that, if language models consciousness, Russian influenced the thinking of a number of Yiddish and Hebrew's greatest heroes of the 19th century.

The appearance of a Jewish cultural renaissance in fin-de-siècle Russia should not be surprising, since the soil had been prepared during the 19th century. Under Nicholas I (1825–55), Russia developed its own Haskalah (Enlighten-

---

[8] Dubnov and An-sky spoke out in favor of "tri-lingualism."

[9] Jeffrey Veidlinger, "The Historical and Ethnographic Construction of Russian Jewry," *Ab Imperio*, no. 4 (2003): 165–84.

[10] Yisrael Bartal makes this claim in *The Jews of Eastern Europe, 1772–1881*, trans. Chaya Naor (Philadelphia: University of Pennsylvania Press, 2005), 3–4.

ment) movement, out of which a secular Jewish intelligentsia, the so-called *maskilim*, was formed.[11] Nevertheless, it was Germany, not Russia, and the idea of *Bildung* that inspired this budding intelligentsia. More than education, *Bildung* signified a level of cultural achievement to which every human being should aspire. In particular, the person who had acquired *Bildung* gained self-respect and had reason to expect acceptance in the non-Jewish world.[12]

In large part these expectations for social acceptance and equal rights seemed to be fulfilled by the reforms of Alexander II, who included Jews in the great transformation of Russian society. Even before freeing the serfs, Alexander ended the most serious abuses of Nicholas's reign: for Jews it was the recruitment of cantonists—underage Jews who were enlisted for a 25-year term of service that began only after the recruit turned 18. Other decrees opened Russia to select Jewish habitation. The wealthy, the educated, useful artisans, and veterans of army service could now reside in St. Petersburg, Moscow, and even in Siberia. The government's positive treatment in the early 1860s awakened dreams of equal rights, inspiring loyalty among the Jewish elite.

Although the Russian-Jewish intelligentsia was optimistic that equal rights were close at hand, general emancipation never took place. As early as 1861, Osip Rabinovich felt profound disappointment when the governor general of the Southwest Province, Pavel Stroganov, threatened to close his newspaper, *Rassvet*, the first Jewish periodical in Russian, because "he suffered indigestion or felt bored," i.e., for no reason at all.[13] Menashe Morgulis and Ilya Orshansky, editors of *Den'*, a successor to *Rassvet*, were anguished by the pogrom in Odessa in 1871, which shattered their faith that Russian antisemites would not direct violence against those who wished to modernize and integrate. Petersburg's Jews also got their taste of pain in 1881–82, when they were widely blamed as helpless to stop the pogroms that broke out throughout the Pale. There could be no escaping the fact that pogroms appeared as a reaction to Jewish success, rather than to the failure of integration.[14] After

---

[11] The community in Shklov in the 18th century, which presaged the Haskalah movement in scope and numbers, does not deserve to be called a "movement." See David Fishman, *Russia's First Modern Jews: The Jews of Shklov* (New York: New York University Press, 1995), 46–63.

[12] George Mosse, "Jewish Emancipation between Bildung and Respectability," in *The Jewish Response to German Culture: From the Enlightenment to the Second World War*, ed. Jehuda Reinharz and Walter Schatzberg (Hanover, NH: University Press of New England/Clark University, 1985), 1–16.

[13] See S. M. Ginzburg, *Minuvshee: Istoricheskie ocherki, stat'i i kharakteristiki* (Petrograd: S. M. Ginzburg, 1923), 88.

[14] The government's first explanation was that the pogroms were the work of anarchists. Later, officials changed that and claimed that the violence was retribution for Jewish exploitation of the peasants. This version, while unfair and illegitimate—the

1882, most people had cast off the illusion that the government was a catalyst for positive change.

Elite Jews, however, faced a real dilemma because of increased antisemitism. Opportunities existed for individuals who wanted to participate in Russian culture as equals, but often at the cost of subordinating or even rejecting Jewish identity. Conversion, often only nominal, was prevalent, especially among those "in the professions," such as law or medicine, where opportunities contracted radically for Jews after 1887.[15]

It is important to recall that close interaction had a dangerous downside. Jews like Gershenzon and the painter Isaak Levitan were accused of perverting the Russian spirit.[16] Using arguments inspired by Richard Wagner's infamous diatribe against Jews in music, some Russians claimed that Jews were uncreative and could only imitate.[17] Moreover, it was claimed that by imposing themselves on Russian national culture, Jews had ruined it. The campaign against Jews reached a shrill note during the so-called Chirikov Affair of 1908.[18]

The affair was incited by a conflict between Jewish and Russian writers who were meeting together ostensibly to discuss literature, but also to show off their progressive attitudes. Acknowledging the success of Jewish authors in penetrating the Russian spirit, writers such as Evgeny Cherikov, Maksim Gorky, and Fyodor Sologub reacted indignantly when Sholom Asch complained that Cherikov, the author of a new drama, *Evrei* (Jews), had no right to treat the theme, since he was not Jewish and therefore unable to understand intimately what Jews experienced. Enraged, Cherikov complained that Jews had no right to censor Russians. Andrei Bely, the Symbolist poet, penned an anti-Jewish manifesto, and even the liberal Kornei Chukovsky argued against Jewish involvement in Russian culture.[19]

---

government exploited the peasants worse than anyone else—reflected the perception that Jews had become economic winners during the 1870s.

[15] Michael Stanislawski, "Jewish Apostasy in Russia: A Tentative Typology," in *Jewish Apostasy in the Modern World*, ed. Todd M. Endelman (New York: Holmes and Meier, 1987); also I. Cherikover, "Obrashchenie v khristianstvo," *Evreiskaia entsiklopediia: Svod znanii o evreistve i ego kul'ture v proshlom i nastoiashchem*, ed. L. I. Katsnel'son, Baron David Guenzburg, Simon Dubnov, and Albert Harkavy, 16 vols. (St. Petersburg: Obshchestvo dlia nauchnykh evreiskikh izdanii, 1906–13), 11: 884–95.

[16] Vasily Rozanov wrote an article entitled "Levitan i Gershenzon," *Russkii bibliofil*, no. 2 (1916): 78–81.

[17] Richard Wagner, "Das Judentum in der Musik," *Neue Zeitschrift für Musik* (1850).

[18] Ilya Serman, "Spory 1908 goda o russko-evreiskoi literature i posleoktiabr'skoe desiatiletie," *Cahiers du monde russe et soviétique* 36: 2 (April–June 1985): 167–74.

[19] Bely wrote "Shtempelovennaia kul'tura" (Culture with a Label) in 1909, while Chukovsky penned his "Evrei i russkaia kul'tura" (Jews and Russian Culture) in 1908. The gist of these articles was that Jews who participated in Russian culture were like a fifth column—they were harming Russia from within.

Surprisingly, elite Jews had mixed attitudes toward antisemitism. In fact, some members of the Jewish intelligentsia exonerated the Russian people, accusing the government alone of antisemitism.[20] Antisemitism arose, it was argued, from economic competition and had nothing to do with racial or religious discrimination. Although the argument was a hard sell, some Jews were unwilling to acknowledge that Russia might be inhospitable to Jewish habitation. They found political justifications for the hangings of Jews in the 15th century and the prohibition on any Jewish presence in Russia until the Polish partitions. The continued persecutions of Jews in the late 19th century were interpreted as incited by the government to deflect attention from its political failures.

I have divided the volume into three parts according to genre. In the first part I deal with creative writers and literary texts. In the second I treat historians and the way historiography was used to fortify Jewish nationalism. Finally, in the third part I look at Jewish thinkers in Russian culture and their experiences in formulating philosophies that crisscross Russian-Jewish boundaries. Chronologically, I deal with the period following the ascension to the throne of Alexander II until just after the end of tsarism in 1917.

In many of the articles I take a biographical approach, concentrating on an individual's life path. I do this because I am convinced that historical facts cannot be divorced from the people who experienced them. Biography permits one to get closer to the way people actually lived, to recover the ideas that motivated individuals in the past, and to view change through time. Nevertheless, sensitive to context, I choose often to write about secondary and little-known figures because they embody typical intellectual tendencies more vividly than more famous figures.

The articles themselves were written over a ten-year period in which changes in Jewish identity in Russia and the United States strongly affected my emphasis. When I first started this project, just after the fall of the Berlin Wall, Russian Jewry seemed more a literary trope than a living community. In Russia there were few scholars involved in this work and books were still packed away in "special collections" with limited access to readers. Since then, massive emigration from Russia to Israel has occurred, and Jewish communities in Russia and Ukraine have revived and even seem to be thriving. Similarly, there are serious Jewish Studies programs in Moscow and St. Petersburg and other cities of the former Soviet Union. Simultaneously, Jewish Studies programs are proliferating in American universities. This changed

---

[20] G. Sliozberg, *Pravovoe i ekonomicheskoe polozhenie evreev v Rossii (iz materialov po evreiskomu voprosu)* (St. Petersburg: Levenstein, 1907), 5.

political-academic atmosphere, accompanied by my own renewed personal commitment to Zionism, has inspired my studies.

The absence of religion and religious questions in the essays may strike one as odd in a book on Jews. In fact, the individuals I treat were almost exclusively secular. Nevertheless, in nearly all cases they were not iconoclasts or hostile to religion, or even active on behalf of religious reform. Therefore, although my work rubs against issues of religion, a reader may want to consult a different source for a close examination of Judaism in Russia.[21]

For the English-language reader, six of the fourteen articles have been available previously. Among the essays, two are appearing for the first time, while the rest have come out only in Russian and primarily in hard-to-find scholarly venues. It is my hope that bringing these works together will inspire greater appreciation of Russian-Jewish modernist culture.

---

[21] See Immanuel Etkes, *Rabbi Israel Salanter and the Mussar Movement: Seeking the Torah of Truth*, trans. Jonathan Chipman (Philadelphia: The Jewish Publication Society, 1993).

# Jewish Writers between Two Worlds

# Introduction to Part 1

In this section I focus on the relationship between literature and Jewish identity. Although some of the central writers, such as Shimon An-sky or Vladimir Jabotinsky, are well known, I also treat Lev Levanda, Leib Jaffe, and Shimon Frug, who have largely been forgotten today.

Scholars of Russian-Jewish literature have had some trouble defining it. Any definition, however, would have to include elements such as whether the author of a work was Jewish, who the audience was, and whether the content reflected "Jewish concerns."[1] However, the term "Jewish concern" is not at all clear. Could antisemitic literature written by a Jew belong to Russian-Jewish literature?

Although any definition would leave gaps, one thing is clear: Russian-Jewish literature is a hybrid. Jews in Russia, just like Jews everywhere in the Diaspora, used the literary and ideological resources around them. There is nothing strange about Jews in Russia writing in Russian, just as German Jews write in German or American Jews write in English. Even though Jews were an oppressed minority in tsarist Russia, it should not surprise us that Jews made contributions not only to their own Jewish culture, but to Russian culture as well.[2]

Criticism of Russian-Jewish literature has come not only from Russian nationalists, but from Jewish writers, too.[3] In his article in the *Jewish Encyclopedia* (1913), the Hebrew poet Saul Tchernychovsky viewed it as a sub-genre soon to be swallowed up by the voracious appetite and unifying trends of Russian literature.[4] There is more than a grain of truth to this idea. In subsequent generations, the great Jewish writers Isaak Babel, Osip Mandelshtam, and Boris Pasternak turned their backs on the sectarian world of Jewish culture and devoted themselves fully to Russian literature.

---

[1] Sh. Markish, "A propos de l'histoire et de la méthodologie de l'étude de la littérature juive d'expression russe," *Cahiers du monde russe et soviétique* 36: 2 (April–June 1985): 169–75.

[2] For a summary of these contributions, see G. Aronson, "Evrei v russkoi literature, kritike, zhurnalistike i obshchestvennoi zhizni," in *Kniga o russkom evreistve: Ot 1860-kh godov do revoliutsii 1917 g. Sbornik statei,* edited by Jacob Frumkin, Gregor Aronson, and A. A. Gol'denveizer (New York: Soiuz russkikh evreev, 1960), 361–99.

[3] M. Lazarev, "Zadachi i znachenie russko-evreiskoi belletristiki," *Voskhod,* nos. 5–6 (1885): 41–42.

[4] S. Chernikovskii [Tchernychovsky], "Russko-evreiskaia literatura," *Evreiskaia entsiklopediia,* 13: 640.

During the years before World War I, however, a full-bodied, serious, and lively literature in the Russian language for and about Jews came into existence. Russian-Jewish literature resembled Russian literature in many ways. For example, just like Russian literature, Russian-Jewish literature provided a mouthpiece for discussions of politics in the absence of other opportunities to publish. However, Jewish literature also bore the burden of expressing the experience of being members of a persecuted minority.

What is perhaps unique about the prerevolutionary Jewish culture in Russia is that it took place in at least three languages—Hebrew, Yiddish, and Russian (one could easily add a number of other languages). Although it is simplistic to connect language choice to a particular ideological affiliation—such as Hebrew with Zionism, Yiddish with Bundism, and Russian with the urge to assimilate into the larger society—nonetheless, people at the time did make these associations. The truth is that highly committed nationalists and Zionists also wrote in Russian; Vladimir Jabotinsky, Ahad Ha'am, Simon Dubnov, Ben-Ami, and many others published regularly in Russian. Beginning with the newspaper *Rassvet* in 1860, Russian developed as a language of, by, for, and about Russian Jews.

Because it was composed in Russian, this literature was involved more closely with Russian literature than writings in either Hebrew or Yiddish, which were read almost exclusively by Jews. Those who have read Frug's Russian can hear the rhythms of Pushkin; Levanda was known as the Jewish Pisarev, while An-sky is reminiscent of Gorky. More importantly, Jewish authors interacted with Russians and responded to their works with criticism and praise. One could even go so far as to say that Jewish writers expressed an "anxiety of influence" of Russian literature, its effect on their ideology and aesthetics. Aesthetically, Jews tried to reach the qualitatively higher level of their Russian teachers. Ideologically, the message of justice for the underdog and commitment to realize a better world inspired Jewish authors, although the din of contempt for Jews in the Russian press incited outrage and self-defense.

In the first part of the book, I probe the relationship between literary craft, literary life, and the social and economic position of the Jews—the "Jewish question"—from the 1860s to World War I. Although one may detect common threads, I see diversity and uniqueness in the way each author arrived at his or her views on the social, artistic, and religious problems of his age. Although one can downplay social trends, historical awareness, and sharp ideological positions, concentrating on aesthetic or creative choices that included not only selection of content, but also how to write, one cannot forget that these writers never entirely embraced the idea that art should have autonomy. Because of the political condition of the Jews in Russia, writers could only rarely throw off their obligations to serve as political spokesmen. In this constraint, Jewish writers once again resembled those among their Russian colleagues who wanted art to serve political ends.

# Chapter 1

# A Jewish Russifier in Despair: Lev Levanda's Polish Question

Lev Levanda (1835–88) is commonly regarded as a leading advocate of the Russification of the Jews of the Russian empire, but in fact his ethnic attitudes were far more complex and conflicting than this stereotype allows. One of the sources of conflict were his ambivalent feelings about Poland and the Poles— a people unwillingly subjected to Russian rule and, like the Jews, often the object of Russian state oppression.

Levanda's writings on Poland (four novels, one historical study, and more than twenty short essays) appeared after and, I believe, in response to major defeats in his Russification program.[1] They constitute a kind of literary wishful thinking. Unable to attain the goal of equal rights for Jews in the Russia of his time, Levanda searched into the region's past to find moments of harmony and integration between Jews and non-Jews. At the same time, he had a high regard for Polish literary culture, which had informed his development as a writer. His "Polish" texts are part of a dialogue with his other writings, providing idealistic visions of a world he dreamed of creating but was unable to realize.

Vilna, the capital of Lithuania, was Levanda's home for over 25 years; he lived there from 1859 until his death in 1888. In 1875 the city had a total population of 82,668, of which the 37,909 Jews comprised nearly 46 percent.[2] During the 1860s, Jews and certain non-Jews—mainly Lithuanian peasants, along with the smaller classes of Polish nobles and Russian administrators—were socially segregated. Contact was limited to business and administrative affairs. V. O. Harkavy, a Jewish intellectual, describes his experience as a youth in Vilna in the 1860s as follows:

> Jewish life was sheltered from the outside world and, thanks to the "ghetto," even physically. Of course, there were interactions between Christians and Jews in daily life, but they were often related to business, and, of course, were restricted to the public sphere by prefer-

---

[1] Between 1879 and 1884, Levanda published over 20 articles on Jewish life in Poland with the title "Privislianskaia khronika" in the weekly newspaper *Russkii evrei*.

[2] "Vilna," *Entsiklopedicheskii slovar'*, 82 vols. (St. Petersburg: Brokgauz-Efron, 1890–1905), 6: 381. For more on Vilna's Jewish life during this time, see Israel Cohen, *Vilna* (Philadelphia: Jewish Publication Society of America, 1943), 283–303.

ence. The Christian world appeared foreign and antagonistic, not so much because of the legal constraints upon us that emanated from it, but in particular because it threatened our spiritual world. Therefore, any novelty in dress or habits which came from that world seemed dangerous, and wearing German dress, a short frock, was considered a great sin and was permitted only to merchants who had business abroad and in Moscow.[3]

In this environment, for Levanda to write in Russian in itself implied various political and literary transgressions, symbolizing a conscious alliance with Russian power and with the goal of Russifying the peoples of the territory. In addition, if a writer identified himself as Jewish but wrote in Russian, he was inevitably marking himself out as a proponent of secular knowledge and an enemy of Orthodox Jews.

Thus, as can be imagined, during the Polish uprising of 1863, Levanda's views were considered dangerous; according to the historian Simon Dubnov they even drew death threats from "Polish spies."[4] However, by the 1880s the image of Levanda is that of a harmless eccentric—the object of gossip. We have this picture from Mordechai (Max) Rivesman, at the time an aspiring young writer:

> While he was getting shaved, he talked to the men waiting in the queue. He spoke in Polish, Russian, and Yiddish. He spoke really excellent Polish, or so it seemed to me at the time. I already knew that he wrote a column in *Vilenskii vestnik* and that people considered him a heretic [*apikoires*] and even … a Judophobe…. He earned that reputation after forcing the hero of his best novel, *Goriachee vremia*, to preach the need to destroy "the fig trees and vineyards" in order to "plant the seed of Russian enlightenment in their place."[5]

Like his contemporaries, later readers perceived Levanda as an ardent proponent of Russification.[6]

The Russification program in the northwest had begun in the 1840s, when the Russian government opened the first Russian-language schools. The state

---

[3] V. O. Garkavi [Garkavy], *Otryvki vospominanii* (St. Petersburg: Tip. I. Fleitmana, 1913), 7.

[4] S. Dubnov, *Kniga zhizni: Vospominaniia i razmyshleniia. Materialy dlia istorii moego vremeni* (Riga, 1934–35 [vols. 1–2] and New York, 1957 [vol. 3]; repr., St. Petersburg: Peterburgskoe vostokovedenie, 1998), 130.

[5] M. Rivesman, "Vospominaniia i vstrechi (1877–1915)," *Evreiskaia letopis'* 3 (1924): 74.

[6] The influential Lucy Davidowicz calls him a "Russian journalist and novelist who advocated Russification as the solution for Jewish problems." Lucy S. Davidowicz, ed., *The Golden Tradition: Jewish Life and Thought in Eastern Europe* (New York: Schocken Books, 1967), 31.

rabbinical seminary in Vilna was founded in 1847.[7] This policy of encouraging cultural life to flourish in the Russian language was designed to win over the political allegiance of the Jews to the Russian state. After the suppression of the 1863 Polish uprising , the question of what to do with the Jews of the northwest territories became more challenging. But their treatment was only one part of a broader policy toward the region as a whole.

In 1863 the Russian governor Mikhail Muravyov introduced policies designed to de-Polonize these provinces. Muravyov was extremely brutal in his methods and came to be known as "Muravyov the Hangman," recalling Muravyov the Hanged, the Decembrist who was executed in 1826. In addition to mass hangings, Muravyov exiled thousands of Polish noblemen to Siberia and confiscated their lands. Russian was established as the official state language. Although the Poles were the primary targets of repressive measures, the Jews of the northwest territories were also adversely affected; the government's policy brought more restrictions than privileges to the Jewish population.[8] Nevertheless, some influential Russian journalists and government officials viewed the Jews as a potentially pro-Russian force in the region and held out the possibility—albeit a slim one—of granting privileges to the Jews as a means of winning their affections.[9]

Levanda was not alone in siding with Russia. Many Jews in the 1840s and 1850s saw an opportunity for social advancement in the Russian educational system and little room for social mobility within Polish culture. Levanda, who was born into a poor family in Minsk in 1835, entered a state-sponsored school for Jews in 1846, the first year of its operation. Three years later he enrolled in the state rabbinical seminary in Vilna, from which he graduated in 1854. In 1860, while working as a teacher in Minsk, he was appointed to the position of "learned Jew" in the office of Vilna's governor-general, a position he held until his death. "Learned Jews" received a government salary and often acted as official censors. In general, they advised the tsarist government on policies toward the Jewish people and religion. Needless to say, their advice was not always heeded.

Levanda's literary career reflects his interest in issues of importance to Russian Jews. A key pioneer of the Jewish press in the Russian language, he was a major contributor to *Rassvet* (1860–61), the first Jewish newspaper published in Russian, and to *Sion*, the successor to *Rassvet*. During the 1880s he

---

[7] "Vilna," *Evreiskaia entsiklopediia*, 5: 588–90. Admittedly, instruction in the seminary was given in German until 1864, but the orientation was pro-Russian. For more on the seminary in Vilna, see Iu. Gessen, "Ravvinskie uchilishcha v Rossii," *Evreiskaia entsiklopediia*, 13: 258–63.

[8] John Klier, "The Polish Revolt of 1863 and the Birth of Russification: Bad for the Jews?" *Polin*, no. 1 (1986): 91–106.

[9] S. Tsinberg, *Istoriia evreiskoi pechati v Rossii v sviazi s obshchestvennymi techeniiami* (Petrograd: Tip. I. Fleitmana, 1915), 116.

wrote for *Russkii evrei*, the second *Rassvet* (1879–83), and *Voskhod*. He also published a large number of novels and stories, among which the best known are *Delo bakaleinykh tovarov* (The Grocery Affair, 1860–61), *Goriachee vremia* (Ardent Times, 1871–73), *Ocherki proshlogo* (Sketches of the Past, 1875), *Bol'shoi Remiz* (The Big Fraud, 1880–81), *Liubitel'skii spektakl'* (An Amateur Performance, 1882), *Gnev i milost' Magnata* (The Magnate's Anger and Mercy, 1885), and "Avraam Iezofovich" (1887).

At the beginning of his literary career, in the 1860s, Levanda ignored Poland and the Polish theme in his fiction and journalism. Absorbed by his political program of modernizing the Jews for integration into Russian society, he focused on criticizing Russian Jews for their backwardness and encouraged them to adopt the changes promoted by supporters of the Haskalah: to exchange the traditional Jewish kaftan for modern clothes, to reject the traditional *heder* and enroll in secular schools, and to use a "Western" language, preferably Russian or German. Simultaneously hoping for full emancipation for the Jews of Russia, he praised the tsarist government's first efforts in that direction.[10]

Levanda's first novel, *Delo bakaleinykh tovarov*, published in *Rassvet* in 1860–61, captures his views at the time.[11] The novel, which one critic has called "a textbook of the Haskalah," covers the cardinal principles of the movement.[12] Levanda uses the plot, which is loosely structured around the attempt of the hero, Arnold, to open a grocery store in the Belorussian town of N., exclusively as a forum for criticizing "Jewish vices"— arranged marriages, isolation from the non-Jewish world, and the greed that goes with speculation for profit. Arnold, by contrast, is the embodiment of progress. He has a German-sounding name, a European university education, modern clothing, and is clean-shaven. He promises to bring happiness to the town by offering good wages for all the workers, supporting secular education for young people, and fighting for marriage based on love. Levanda's explicit advice for Russia's Jews is for them to emulate Arnold, turning away from habits and beliefs characteristic of traditional Jewish life.

Surprisingly, Levanda does not criticize the government for limiting Jews' legal rights, including their rights to live outside the Pale of Settlement and

---

[10] In 1859, Alexander II permitted Jewish merchants of the first guild permanent residence in the capital, and in 1861 he extended this right to Jews who had graduated from institutions of higher education. From 1865, select categories of Jewish artisans were permitted to live within Russia proper. In his work on the reform period, Benjamin Nathans calls these reforms "selective emancipation." For more on the reform period and tsarist rule, see Nathans, *Beyond the Pale*, 17–24.

[11] The first installment of *Delo bakaleinykh tovarov: Kartiny evreiskogo byta v dvukh chastiakh* appeared in *Rassvet*, no. 10 (1860), and the last appeared in no. 12 (1861).

[12] Sh. Markish, "Stoit li perechityvat' L'va Levandy? Stat'ia pervaia: Posyl," *Vestnik Evreiskogo universiteta v Moskve* 3: 10 (1995): 101.

rights to land ownership. Apparently convinced of the validity of the so-called "emancipation contract," according to which the Russian government would extend full civil rights if the Jews modernized and integrated, Levanda concentrates only on the fulfillment of the Jewish side of the bargain. Admittedly, in the 1860s most modernized Jews were convinced of Russian assurances.

Levanda's earliest treatments of the topic of Poland were written in the 1870s in the context of growing Russian antisemitism. Although critics have perceived *Goriachee vremia* as an apology for his pro-Russian attitude, the author undercuts that viewpoint in the novel in various ways.[13] In particular, by showing the political failures of Sarin, the author's ideological mouthpiece, and by drawing the Poles as fully developed individuals as opposed to the one-dimensional Russians, Levanda subverts the positive message of Russification.

Set in Vilna in the two years before the Polish uprising of 1863, the novel presents the choice facing the Jews of Poland—to join the Poles, remain neutral, or support Russia.[14] While Polish nobles pressure Jews to join the rebellion, Arkady Sarin, a young Jewish intellectual, argues against any solidarity with them, claiming that the Poles have never fulfilled their promises. Sarin, apparently with the narrator's assent, proposes instead the Russification of the Jews. He is given such monologues as:

> We have thought it over and have decided to turn to the right and link ourselves with Moscow. Instinct, considered thought, and finally, the feelings of gratitude lead us there. We should never forget that barbaric Russia and not civilized Poland first began to worry about our education and development. We are obliged to Russia and not to Poland for the awakening of our self-consciousness.[15]

---

[13] A recent scholar, L. Salmon, wrote in 1997 that the book's "ideological direction is beautifully expressed with the words of the main hero, Arkadii Sarin: 'Our program consists of extricating our co-religionists from the vicious cycle in which unfortunate circumstances have squeezed them, and setting them on the path toward Russian citizenship. In brief: our program consists of making the Jews Russians.'" L. Salmon, "Krizis evreiskoi samobytnosti i romany-manifesty G. I. Bagrova i L. O. Levandy," in *Evrei v Rossii: Trudy po iudaike. Istoriia i etnografiia*, vyp. 4 (St. Petersburg: Peterburgskii Evreiskii universitet, Institut issledovanii evreiskoi diaspory, 1997), 287.

[14] A discussion of Levanda's treatment of the Jews' political views on the uprising can be found in S. Breimann, "Ha-mifneh bamahshavah haziburit hayehudit bereshit shnot hashmonim," *Shivat Zion* 2–3 (1952–53): 180–84; Yehuda Slutsky, *Haitonut hayehudit-rusit bemeah ha-19* (Jerusalem: Mosad Bialik, 1970), 95–96.

[15] The allusion is to the Russian government's creation of special Jewish schools, which were opened in 1844.

And:

> We should not concern ourselves with which civilization is higher....
> For us the issue is not about civilization, but about belonging to a
> people, i.e., about spirit and language. We live in Russia and there-
> fore we must be Russians.[16]

Despite such proclamations, a countervailing view manifests itself in the
structure of the novel itself—in the development of the plot, the characteriza-
tion, and the viewpoint of the narrator—casting doubt on the author's commitment to the program of Russification. For example, the fact that a Russian
official sentences Sarin to two months in prison raises questions about Levanda's attitudes toward Russian rule. In the early pages, when the narrator
asks Sarin what he will do if the Russians reject the Jews, Sarin does not answer directly, but reiterates that the Jews should prepare themselves for Russian citizenship.[17] And yet Levanda exposes the Russian officials' negative
attitudes toward the Jews and their hostile treatment of them. When Poles de-
nounce him to the Russian authorities, Sarin is jailed for criminal propaganda," that is, for speaking out in favor of the Russification of the Jews.
Sarin's offense, we learn, is related to his activity itself, not to its message. It
makes no difference that he supports the Russian effort; the fact that he acts at
all is suspect. The dialogue between Sarin and the Russian official reveals
Levanda's stark awareness of the distance between the Russian and Jewish
views:

> "Since when have the kikes started to worry about their usefulness to
> Russia?"
>    "Since the time when they stopped being kikes and started to feel
> like Russian citizens."
>    "*Citizens?*" the official became enraged. "There are no citizens in
> Russia, citizens, but there are subjects, do you understand? What did
> they imagine—citizens! Do we have a republic? We will beat that lit-
> erature out of your head. We do not need citizens, we need faithful
> subjects, and whoever does not understand this, we will make him
> understand; that is why we are the administrators, in order to make
> people understand."[18]

With this conversation Levanda outlines the conflict between Russian administrators and the Jewish intelligentsia. While the intelligentsia dreamed of
emancipation, with the same rights that Jews in the West enjoyed, the Russian

---

[16] L. Levanda, *Goriachee vremia: Roman iz poslednego pol'skogo vosstaniia* (St. Petersburg:
Tip. A. E. Landau, 1875), 77.

[17] Ibid., 78.

[18] Quoted in I. Sosis, "Period obruseniia: Natsional'nyi vopros v literature v kontse 60-
kh godov i nachala 70-kh godov," *Evreiskaia starina*, no. 2 (April–June 1915): 144.

government was not prepared to grant these rights.[19] In reality, participation in politics, while not forbidden, held certain dangers for Jews regardless of which side they took. For example, the newspaper *Rassvet* closed in 1861 after only a year because the content did not please Stroganov, the governor-general of New Russia.[20]

Although Sarin's prison term does not destroy his faith in Russia, it makes the reader wonder whether Jews would be able to make Russians love them. In truth, Sarin's experience demonstrates that Levanda was not sure whether Russians would treat Jews any better than the antisemitic Poles.

While he depicts Russians negatively, Levanda offers many positive figures among the Poles.[21] He has Sarin fall in love with the Polish aristocrat Julia Staszycka, the niece of Count Bolesław Tęczyński, the Polish rebel leader. Not only does she return his love, but she is also his equal in every way. Not just physically beautiful, she is morally courageous as well. Having discovered a plot by the Polish underground to kill Sarin, whom the Poles consider to be a Russian agent, she warns him of the danger. Although this might be interpreted as a betrayal of the Poles, the author justifies it as a sacrifice for the sake of love. Here Levanda clearly breaks away from the many novels of the period in which unrequited love develops between a Pole and a Jew. According to Israel Bartal and Magdalena Opalski, such a successful relationship is meant to symbolize the unity of the two peoples with regard to their cooperation during the uprising, despite their religious differences.[22]

---

[19] For more on the legal liabilities facing the Jews of Russia during the reign of Alexander II, see Iu. Gessen, *Istoriia evreiskogo naroda v Rossii*, 2 vols. (Petrograd: Tip. L. Ia. Ganzburga, 1916), 2: 156–201.

[20] Iu. Gessen, "Smena obshchestvennykh techenii," pt. 2: "Pervyi russko-evreiskii organ," in *Perezhitoe: Sbornik, posviashchennyi obshchestvennoi i kul'turnoi istorii evreev v Rossii*, ed. Saul Ginzburg and Israel Tsinberg, 4 vols. (St. Petersburg: Brokgauz-Efron, 1908–13), 3: 57–58.

[21] As John Klier notes, "For a novel devoted to the theme of Russification, Russians in the flesh play a very minor role ... and most of the Russian characters are negative ones. The exception is P. A. Dubov, a young idealist forced into a military career by family pressure, who dreams of devoting himself to public service. He is the only Russian who sees the potential of recruiting Jews to the Russian cause." Klier, "The Jew as Russifier: Lev Levanda's *Hot Times*," *Jewish Culture and History* 4: 1 (2001): 48.

[22] In their exceptional book on Polish and Jewish treatments of the Jewish issue, Israel Bartal and Magdalena Opalski point to the iconoclastic use of Polish symbols by Jewish authors. Moreover, they note differences in the use of romantic themes by Jewish and Polish authors. "Despite striking similarities in their treatment of secondary sociological and psychological detail, Polish-Jewish love stories, in both literary traditions, reflect conflicting worldviews. While the Polish romances are instrumental in illustrating the idea of brotherhood and providing an example of social relations in a more inclusive, democratic society, Jewish love stories focus on prejudice and deception. Whereas Polish authors elevate their Jewish heroes by assigning them a place in the

Nevertheless, Levanda reverses the schema. By having the Pole rather than the Jew sacrifice for love, he shows that a Jew, too, can inspire higher feelings.

In giving the Polish characters dramatic depth, Levanda invites the reader's sympathy for them. Even the negative Polish figures are depicted vividly. The dense descriptions of these characters can be juxtaposed with the portrait of Sarin, who comes across as little more than a mouthpiece for the author's propaganda. For example, one may contrast the depiction of Sarin with that of Stanisław (Stas), a Polish rebel and a common murderer. In love with the Princess Jadwiga, Stas had earlier seduced Martsisha, who is now pregnant and threatening to inform the Russians about his participation in the Polish underground government. Although Sarin mechanically utters his programmatic lines, Stas's psychology is depicted through his body language, snippets of consciousness, and sentence fragments.

> With his head lowered and his hands folded across his chest, Stas began to pace back and forth across the room, while Prakseda [a well-known salon hostess], bending over her favorite instrument, strummed several rich cords and started playing a song and then the hymn "Boże çoś Polske." Having finished the hymn, she rested a while, tuned her guitar, and again began to play, but Stas continued to pace the room. His face was pale, disappointed. It was clear that he was thinking, considering some weighty thought. "So," he said to himself. "So... Still, how can that be? Impossible... Meaningless! Stupid! And such self-importance!..." A moment later, "And of course... it's better, than... After all, the fatherland... the Count... Jadwiga..."[23]

I am not the first to notice the paradox that those characters who embody a pro-Russian ideology are poorly drawn in comparison with the Polish aristocrats. In his article on Levanda, written in 1913, the historian Yuly Gessen remarks, "Sarin is too schematic, but alongside him one finds in the novel living images—for the most part from Polish society."[24]

---

highly exclusive fabric of national history, Jewish writers use interethnic love stories to launch an attack on the romantic value system." Opalski and Bartal, *Poles and Jews: A Failed Brotherhood*, The Tauber Institute for the Study of European Jewry, no. 13 (Hanover, NH: Brandeis University Press, 1992), 96.

[23] Levanda, *Goriachee vremia*, 225.

[24] Iu. Gessen, "Lev Osipovich Levanda," in *Evreiskaia entsiklopediia*, 10: 61. In an article on the novel, Klier writes, "The Poles, in the midst of the preparations which will culminate in the 1863 uprising, are the most differentiated characters. They provide the most negative actors in the plot: an intolerant and hypocritical Catholic priest, Father Kwiencinski, who runs a home for orphans that supplies employees for a high-class brothel; a variety of debauched and arrogant aristocrats; flighty and dissolute Polish women; and a gallery of drunken and vicious commoners. These negative Polish characters are somewhat balanced by the portrait of the revolutionary circle, the 'National

While the contrast between the novel's message and the depiction of its characters does not require us to repudiate the traditional view that the novel is a defense of Russification, it does raise questions about Levanda's unconscious intentions. His individual treatment of Poles certainly reflects sympathy for and engagement with these individuals. Furthermore, by having Sarin fall in love with Julia Staszycka, Levanda shifts the novel's focus from its message that "we Jews must become Russians" to other issues such as love among enemies and the tragic fate of the Poles.

Why did Levanda undermine the main ideological message of the novel? An examination of the historical background against which the novel was written can help us to answer this question. Although the plot unfolds in the period of the Polish uprising of 1863, the novel first appeared in the first three issues of *Evreiskaia biblioteka* in 1871–73, and was presumably written around this time. In the years leading up to the novel's publication, Levanda had served on the Vilna Commission, which was set up to elicit Jewish reactions to Jacob Brafman's plan to turn the Jewish masses from urban dwellers into peasants. The commission submitted its final report in 1870, and, to quote John Klier, "with the governor-general's blessing, not only rejected plans to subordinate Jews to the peasant-village administration, but also sent a recommendation to the central government that the Pale of Settlement be abolished, and Jews permitted to reside throughout the Russian Empire."[25] Unfortunately, in the late 1860s and early 1870s the central government shifted its position from support for Jewish reform to open hostility to it, and the Ministry of the Interior rejected the commission's proposals.

Symptomatic of the change in policy was the government-financed publication of Jacob Brafman's anti-Jewish tract *Kniga kagala* (The Book of the Kahal), which went through four printings between 1867 and 1881. Arguing that the Jews had actually retained their *kehalim* (autonomous Jewish administrations), despite the fact that they had been abolished by tsarist law in 1844, Brafman claimed the Jews are bent on world domination. Furthermore, foreshadowing tragic times to come, the government did not provide aid to the victims of the Odessa pogrom of March 1871 or seriously pursue the culprits.[26]

---

rzad' and its members, Count Bolesław Teczynski, and his niece, Countess Julia Staszycka. The Count must pursue the Polish national goal with the assistance of the less than admirable agents described above. He does so with dignity and a modicum of honor, sincerely motivated by patriotism and love of the fatherland. In the mouths of other Polish characters, the expression 'love of the fatherland' acquires a satirical effect, being used a justify a whole range of heinous acts, including murder of a mistress and prostitution" (Klier, "Jew as Russifier," 19).

[25] Ibid., 25.

[26] See Steven J. Zipperstein, *The Jews of Odessa: A Cultural History, 1794–1881* (Stanford, CA: Stanford University Press, 1986), 114–15.

In this context, Levanda's contradictory treatment of the ideas of Russification and Russian antisemitism is understandable. While he still hoped for integration of the Jews into Russia society and gave Sarin the role of sermonizer, he was not blind to the obstacles. Moreover, it is worth noting that he already displayed admiration for various Poles, and that he invoked the Polish theme to outline the deficiencies in the Russian treatment of the Jews, as well as Polish shortcomings.

In his novel of 1880–81, *Bol'shoi remiz*, Levanda uses the Polish theme to criticize Jewish society in Russia. Setting the plot in the provincial Galician city of N, he chronicles a Jewish merchant's attempt to cheat his investors by falsely declaring himself bankrupt. The subplot, which becomes increasingly important, concerns Jewish-Polish relations and provides a moral antithesis to the primary story. Here we see the Jewish merchant's son—a violinist—fall in love with a Jewish innkeeper's daughter—a singer. They meet through the intercession of a music teacher, an elderly Polish aristocrat who embodies wisdom, dignity, and tolerance. Near the end of the story a younger, unscrupulous Polish nobleman tries to steal the innkeeper's daughter from the young Jew. It turns out that this nobleman had seduced her and feels that he has proprietary rights. The older Polish aristocrat intercedes and in a melodramatic confrontation demands that the rogue desist.

Although the characters of the nobleman and the music teacher are not of equal weight in the drama, and the subplot is set in the broader context of the community's economic ruin, Levanda's image of the Polish aristocrat is instructive. The values of culture, dignity, and honesty are embodied in the music teacher, who serves as a contrast to the greedy and heartless Jewish merchant, while in his dress and education the Polish rogue also represents high culture. The values of the dignified Pole win out in the end, and the teacher and his students leave for Western Europe, where they are certain to find artistic and financial success.

The novel, which was written in the late 1870s, touches on important issues concerning Russia's Jews at the time. Capitalism was taking hold in Russia, and Jews were among the most energetic businessmen in the country. Levanda condemned their swelling ambitions, fearing that their success would lead to increased antisemitism. In two of his other writings of the period, "Nashi domashnie dela (pis'mo iz severno-zapadnogo kraia)" (Our Domestic Affairs [Letter from the Northwest Territories], 1877) and the novel *Ispoved' Del'tsa* (Confessions of a Wheeler-Dealer, 1880), Levanda criticized the new Jewish youth, who, indifferent to morality, religion, and tradition, threw everything aside in order to become millionaires.[27]

Levanda's criticism of capitalism in *Bol'shoi remiz* can be found in his treatment of the Jewish merchant who seeks to become rich by defrauding his

---

[27] The first half of the novel was published with the title *Pokhod v Kolkhidu* [The Colchis Campaign], in *Evreiskaia biblioteka*, no. 7 (1879): 1–79.

fellow Jews. The author offers a positive alternative in his depiction of the two young musicians, who set themselves worthwhile goals. Significantly, the key to their successes hinges on the figure of the Polish teacher. The aristocratic Pole serves as a model for the two young Jews, who are encouraged to rid themselves of their provincial Jewish manners and become cultured. Strangely, the novel features no Russians. The Polish teacher fills the role of patron. Jewish artists, writers, and musicians needed the support of an aristocratic patron in order to succeed in Christian society; for example, in the cases of Mark Antokolsky or Anton Rubenstein, both were befriended and supported by Vladimir Stasov.

During the period of the pogroms in 1881–82 Levanda held up the Polish issue as a mirror to reveal Russia's deficiencies. When violence against Jews broke out in Warsaw in 1881, he wrote an article in which he contrasted the pogroms in southern Russia with the recent pogrom in Poland.[28] Although he was enraged by the violence in Russia (which the government defended as an expression of the people's wrath against Jewish exploitation), he was somewhat heartened by the condemnation of the violence in the Polish press. The Poles, he wrote, behaved "in knightly fashion, refusing to kick a man when he was down or to applaud bestial behavior." One could live in such a society, he claimed. As for Russia, he wondered whether one could "live in a society whose chance leaders and self-proclaimed councilors, dressed in a triple armor of lies, deception, and unbounded arrogance, overturn the most elementary rules of honor, conscience, justice, and human community, taking this for a highly patriotic feat."[29] Levanda's conciliatory attitude toward Poland did not last long, however, for in Poland, just as in Russia, the Jews continued to be blamed for the violence directed against them.

The change in Levanda's attitude toward Poland after the pogroms of 1881–82 can be seen vividly in his shifting views of the writer Eliza Orzeszkowa.[30] Before the pogroms Levanda heralded Orzeszkowa's novel *Eli Makower* as:

[T]he first attempt in Polish literature to depict a Jewish character, Jewish daily life and the attitudes of Jews toward the peoples among whom they live, without the conventional prejudices of Polish criticisms or contempt for the humiliated and oppressed person of the Jew, but seriously, objectively, and with a very noble aim. This goal is

---

[28] L. Levanda, "Pis'mo iz provintsii," *Russkii evrei*, no. 3 (January 15, 1882). The pogrom occurred as a result of events that took place in Warsaw's Holy Cross Cathedral on Christmas Day 1881, when someone falsely cried "Fire!" causing a stampede and leading to several deaths. The event was blamed on the Jews, and the Poles took revenge by creating a pogrom that lasted two days. It appears that pickpockets committed the act in the hope of practicing their craft during the commotion.

[29] Ibid., quoted in Klier, "Jew as Russifier," 28.

[30] Eliza Orzeszkowa (1841–1910).

the reconciliation of the two peoples by means of common understanding and respect, the reconciliation of equals with one another
not in the name of some archaic tendencies or illusions, but in the
name of a more rational economic modus vivendi...[31]

Orzeszkowa's achievement was all the more startling, Levanda writes in his
introduction to his own translation of the last part of *Eli Makower*, because the
conventional treatment of Jews in Polish literature was so stereotypical.[32]
Every Polish author, Levanda lamented, felt the need to include at least one
Jew, either a moneylender, an estate manager, or a tavern-keeper. Even the
great Mickiewicz could not resist inventing Jankiel, "whom he remembered
suddenly in the last minute of his wildest leap onto his unbridled Pegasus
who, it seems, had no head or legs, but only wings."[33] Levanda claims that
Jankiel was merely an artistic inspiration, a symbol that never came alive as a
full character. Orzeszkowa, however, was a happy exception.

Levanda's positive attitude toward Orzeszkowa evaporated after the
publication in 1881 of her article "O żydach i kwestyi żidowskiej" (On Jews
and the Jewish Question).[34] Although Levanda conceded that her proposal
that Jews and Poles be forced to study together and ultimately intermarry
was not objectionable in itself, he was angered at her accusation that educated
Jews were responsible for the failure of Jewish integration.[35] He could not
help noticing a paradox: Only a few decades earlier, when Jews had resisted
integration, they were left alone. As soon as they responded to the call to integrate, the violence began. This paradox revealed the real attitude of Christians
toward the Jews.[36] But, writes Levanda, Jews should not be fooled by these
accusations and threats:

> They are false threats aimed at scaring us off the common path ... so
> that we will crawl back into the nooks and crannies from which we
> emerged when we became attracted to the rays of light that have also
> shone upon us. This only proves that the alarmists are hardly ac-
> quainted with the natural history of our tribe. It is a fact that we are
> made up in such way that we can only move forward, not backward,
> and for their part it would be a great deal more sensible if they would
> reconcile themselves to the indisputable fact of the weakening of our

---

[31] Levanda serialized his translation of part of *Eli Makower* as "Tri pokoleniia," in
*Russkii evrei*, nos. 1–4, 6–8, 11–12 (1880). Orzeszkowa's two Jewish novels are *Eli Makower* (2 vols., 1875) and *Meir Ezofowicz* (1878).

[32] Levanda, "Tri pokoleniia," *Russkii evrei*, no. 1: 32.

[33] Klier, "Jews as Russifiers," 31.

[34] Published as a pamphlet (Vilna, 1882).

[35] L. L. [Levanda], "Privislianskaia khronika," *Russkii evrei*, no. 48 (1881): 1906–09.

[36] Ibid., 1909.

tribal isolation and acculturation to the civilized world, for they will not achieve their aims: we will not crawl back into our abandoned nooks and crannies no matter what you do, whether you attack us or not![37]

In Levanda's view, Orzeszkowa revealed the same callousness as those who were openly hostile to the Jews. Although she encouraged tolerance, she refused to countenance real Jewish equality; she called instead for further concessions from the Jews as a condition for their becoming full citizens. Levanda's polemic against Orzeszkowa did not end here, however, as we shall see.

Indisputably, the pogroms of 1881–82 led Levanda into an ideological cul-de-sac. In many articles after 1881 he lambasted Russia for its treatment of the Jews and for refusing to accept them as equal citizens. At times his articles became highly emotional. For example, in 1882 he wrote, "The fact is that now our enemies do not demand any proof [of our allegiance], they demand our lives. We are Semites, and with this enough has already been said to justify our death sentence."[38] At the same time he began to rethink his views of Jewish integration in Russia. In particular, he was dismayed by the moral disaffection brought out in the younger generation through the achievements of integration.

In the education of our children we have straightforwardly pursued a single aim: let our sons become doctors, lawyers, and engineers.... We see how the organic bonds tying our children to us and the [Jewish] people become weaker every day.... There will come a time, and it is not too far away, when these attenuated homemade bonds will break entirely. Then our children, these cherished, doted-on, and pampered doctors, lawyers, and engineers, for whose education we have worked so hard, given up nights of sleep and crumbs of food, our children, you will see, will become alienated and distant, and will reject us as "kikes" with whom they do not have or want to have anything in common. In truth, what binds our children to us? Religious tradition? They are certainly unacquainted with it. The historical past? But they live in the present, imbued with brilliant hopes for the future. Our experience of suffering? But they haven't suffered at all and do not suffer. Solidarity with the people's interests? They are privileged doctors, lawyers, and engineers, and we are uneducated

---

[37] Ibid.

[38] L. Levanda, "Fel'eton," *Rassvet*, no. 52 (1882): 2031. This article was written in response to the first international antisemitic conference, which tool place in Dresden that year; quoted in Markish, "Stoit li perechityvat' L'va Levandy?" 125.

"kikes"; it follows, therefore, that there cannot be any talk about a unity of their interests with ours.[39]

Such reflections on the flaws of integration and the permanence of anti-semitism propelled Levanda toward a nationalist position in which Jews would not turn to the Russian government for help in solving the Jewish question, but look to themselves for succor. Levanda expressed his new views in an article in *Palestina*, a "volume of articles and information about Jewish settlements in the holy land," which appeared under the editorship of Vasily Berman and Akim Flekser in 1884.[40] In "Sushchnost' tak nazyvaemogo 'palestinskogo' dvizheniia (pis'mo k izdateliam)" (The Essence of the So-Called 'Palestine' Movement [Letter to the Editors]), Levanda expressed his attraction to the proto-Zionist movement, seeing in it a "practical solution" to a "vicious cycle." In fact, he explained that the movement made perfect sense in its historical context as "a natural consequence of the preceding causes," and as a "symptom, demonstrating that the process of resolving the so-called Jewish question is entering a new phase."[41]

But Levanda wavered in his commitment to the nationalist position. Perhaps Palestine appeared too far away or the possibility of colonizing the land with millions of Russian Jews seemed implausible. In any case, ultimately he refused to surrender his ideal of the cultured Jew who combined secular and traditional qualities, hoping against hope that the Jews could find a homeland in the Diaspora. "Jewish nationality ... is such a unique phenomenon in history that, in contradiction to logic and theory ... a definite territory would likely be more harmful than useful. The Jewish nationality began to harden and crystallize exactly at that moment when the Jewish people lost their territory."[42]

In the 1880s, for him a period of ideological disappointment, Levanda wrote extensively on the Polish theme. He wrote three novel-length prose narratives and a short history of Poland. As Russia showed itself unwilling to give the Jews the rights of citizens (as they were understood in Western Europe), he looked to Poland's past for a model of relations between Jews and non-Jews. Furthermore, in his fiction he depicted an image of the past in which Jews lived happily in a Polish society that, while deeply flawed, re-

---

[39] L. Levanda, "Russko-evreiskoe religioznoe obrazovanie," *Russkii evrei*, no. 11 (1880); quoted in B. A. Gol'dberg, *L. O. Levanda kak publitsist (po sluchaiu sorokoletniago iubileia vozniknoveniia russko-evreiskoi pechati)* (Vilna: Tip. D. i Kh. Ialovtser, 1900), 28–29.

[40] L. Levanda, "Sushchnost' tak nazyvaemogo 'palestinskogo' dvizheniia (pis'mo k izdateliam)," in *Palestina: Sbornik statei i svedenii o evreiskikh poseleniiakh v sviatoi zemle* (St. Petersburg: Tip. Lebedeva, 1884), 5–19.

[41] Ibid., 9.

[42] L. Levanda, *Nedel'naia khronika Voskhoda*, no. 38 (1885): 1023; quoted in Markish, "Stoit li perechityvat' L'va Levandu?" 135.

flected the humanist sensibility that was absent in Russia. At the same time he created positive Polish characters—representatives of virtues such as sensitivity to culture, kindness, and lack of prejudice. Equally striking is the absence of Russian figures endowed with these same qualities.

In 1882, Levanda published *Liubitel'skii spektakl' (vospominaniia shkol'nika piatidesiatykh godov)* (An Amateur Performance [Reminiscences of a Student in the 1850s]).[43] In what is apparently a *roman à clef*, he features a first-person narrator who closely resembles himself as a young man. In fact, the author emphasizes that the story is indeed based on fact, recalling events from his own life.

In chronicling events surrounding the illegal performance of a student play written by the narrator, Levanda presents a broad description of life at the Vilna Rabbinical Seminary. The government of Nicholas I opened this seminary, along with its sister institution in Zhitomir in 1847, as an alternative to the traditional Jewish yeshiva. The goal of these schools was to create modern rabbis who would spread enlightenment in the Jewish communities. Although unsuccessful in meeting their narrow practical goal, the institutions played a vital role in the formation of a Jewish intelligentsia that would struggle later for equal rights for the Jewish people in Russia.[44]

In the novel the narrator confesses that Polish literature serves as the inspiration for his own development as a writer. He praises the senior supervisor of the seminary, a "veteran of the former Polish army" who is "considered the best teacher of Polish language and literature" in the city. Although receiving high fees for teaching in the girls' boarding school and in the foremost aristocratic homes, the senior supervisor teaches the hero these subjects "gratis and with remarkable zeal," granting "free access to his rich Polish library, which he treasures like the apple of his eye."[45]

When the authorities find out about the play, the hero is summoned to the senior supervisor. Giving little thought to his own fate, the hero worries about having harmed the one person who taught him to love Polish literature as native Poles love it.

---

[43] The first installment of *Liubitel'skii spektakl' (vospominaniia shkol'nika piatidesiatykh godov)* appeared in *Russkii evrei*, no. 11 (1882), and the last appeared in no. 23 (1882).

[44] Michael Stanislawski, *Tsar Nicholas I and the Jews: The Transformation of Jewish Society in Russia, 1825–1855* (Philadelphia: Jewish Publication Society of America, 1983), 102–05. For information on the Vilna Seminary, see Verena Dohrn, "Das Ribbinerseminar in Wilna (1840–73): Zur Geschichte der ersten staatlichen höheren Schule für Juden in Russischen Reich," *Jahrbücher für Osteuropäische Geschichte* 45 (1997): 379–400; and Verena Dohrn, "The Rabbinical Schools as Institutions of Socialization in Tsarist Russia, 1847–73," *Polin* 14 (2001): 83–104.

[45] Levanda, *Liubitel'skii spektakl'*, no. 23, 888.

Twice a week I was *obliged* to come to his home, where I was received in his family as if I were one of them, a member of the family—an honor not accorded to any other student. Usually we greeted one another like relatives, i.e., he kissed me on the forehead and I kissed his hand. Just a few days before, he had gone quite out his mind and wept like a child, almost crushing me in his embrace, when I, wanting to give him a surprise offering as my benefactor and knowing what a passionate Polish patriot he was, had recited by heart in front of his family two long passages from Mickiewicz's *Konrad Wallenrod* and Malczewski's *Maria*. But now, despite what our relations had been, he had to reprimand and judge me, and for my part, I felt that I was almost the chief cause of the danger that was threatening my benefactor! You can easily imagine what we both must have felt on that occasion![46]

While the performance is ultimately written off as a harmless prank, the hero's acknowledgement that writing the play contributed to his literary progress makes the story an example of the genre "a portrait of the artist as a young man." If we recall that the story was based on fact, we can imagine the powerful effect that Polish literature as introduced by his Polish mentor had on Levanda's development as a writer.

In 1885, Levanda published *Gnev i milost' magnata* (The Magnate's Anger and Mercy). Setting the story in eastern Poland in the middle of the 18th century, he focuses on the life of Jewish peasants living on the estate of the Polish Prince Radziwiłł. Although Levanda does not give the prince's full name, he resembles Karol Stanisław Radziwiłł (1734–90), who was one of the wealthiest landowners in the Polish-Lithuanian Commonwealth. In Levanda's story the Jews of the region have been suffering through an economic depression brought about by the fact that the magnate has not visited the town for more than two years. The Jews pray for their benefactor to come with his court and make merry, since his revelries stimulate the local economy.

The magnate's visit, however, yields mixed results. For example, Radziwiłł orders his chief of police to have him transported to his castle on a sled, although it is the middle of summer. The Jewish leader and the magnate's bailiff, Rabbi Sakhno, devises a plan to make a road of salt on which the sled can be pulled, and it succeeds. However, things go very badly when the Jews fail to greet Radziwiłł on his arrival because they are praying in the synagogue. The magnate calls for the death sentence for those responsible. But Radziwiłł has another reason for enacting this extreme measure. Having discovered that the government in Warsaw is planning to interfere with his absolute control over what he considers his Jewish property, he is prepared to demonstrate his unlimited power.

---

[46] Ibid., 889.

The story, however, has a happy ending. Not only does the magnate spare his Jews, but in the novel's final scene, amazed at the beauty of Rabbi Sakhno's daughter, he also offers to grant any wish she makes. Instead of asking for money, she asks only that the magnate come to her wedding. Radziwiłł, touched by her devotion and respect, agrees to come with his entire court.

Rather than focusing on the horrible examples of the magnate's cruelty, the omniscient narrator emphasizes his mercy, as shown in this dialogue between Radziwiłł and his servant, mediated by the narrator:

> "And here's another thing," added the Prince, already taking up his hat, "in the evening send Tramontano to the square with his musicians, actors, magicians, bears, and all the rest of those devils. Let them give a performance under the open sky and let the Jews enjoy themselves, watch, and have fun. Do you hear?"
>
> "I hear, your highness."
>
> "And tell them that, just as before, Radziwiłł will be their lord in the future. A better lord they will never have forever and ever. I'll tell those upstarts from Warsaw where to go and they won't touch my Jews. Let the Jews live in peace until they die a natural death..."

Here the narrator joins in with an allusion to the Book of Esther: "And everything was done as it was supposed to be. 'The Jews became bright, happy, joyous and solemn'" (Esther 8:16).[47]

The reader cannot help but be struck by the idyllic tone of the ending. Such language conveys the view that this is a harmonious world. To be sure, there is a hierarchy, with the magnate at the top, but it is one each member willingly accepts. At the same time one recalls that the hierarchy consigns the Jews to a low status, their very lives and livelihood fully dependent on the goodwill of a capricious landowner. Moreover, it is striking that Levanda wrote *Gnev i milost' magnata* in the year after the publication of *Palestina*, the collection of articles in support of proto-Zionist ideas in which he spoke out in favor of plans to transfer the Jews to Palestine. The use of the genre of *byl'*, which is characterized by a mock-epic language, to describe Jewish life in prepartition Poland seems entirely out keeping with any proto-Zionist leanings.

*Gnev i milost' magnata* reflects Levanda's historical nostalgia. He gave his imagination a choice and it chose to go back to a time when Poland was independent, and the Polish aristocrats and the Jews lived in a kind of symbiosis. He seems to be saying that Polish rule was better than Russian, because, although Jews were not always treated well, they nevertheless felt happy and were fully aware of their privileges and liabilities in traditional Polish society.

---

[47] L. Levanda, *Gnev i Milost' magnata: Byl' XVIII stoletiia* (Odessa: Odesskie novosti, 1912), 74.

Although it might seem paradoxical, Jewish authors of the 19th century often depicted the Polish nobleman in warm and sympathetic tones. According to Israel Bartal, the nobleman, despite his wantonness, might be treated positively as a friend of Jewish enlightenment and as an instrument for good.[48] In fact, the Polish nobleman's excesses are actually two sides of a single coin; the arbitrariness and caprice that presage misfortune in one instance can also bring them salvation in another. According to Bartal, the positive depiction of the nobleman apparently emerges from the Jews' need for an ally in Polish society.[49]

A year after the publication of *Gnev i milost' magnata* Levanda continued his ruminations on the history of the Jews in the region with his "Sud'by evreev v pol'skoi Rechi Pospolitoi (istoricheskii ocherk)" (Fates of the Jews in the Polish Commonwealth [A Historical Sketch]).[50] Dividing Jewish history in Poland into three parts corresponding to three different sources of power, he describes the reign of the powerful kings, the rule of the Sejm, and the dominance of the Catholic clergy. In the first period he features the kings' extensions of "special" privileges to the Jews. In the second, he describes the rule of the Sejm, lauding this parliament of nobles for its heightened sense of humanism. Finally, he outlines the increasing domination of the Catholic clergy, who manage to roll back the rights and privileges that the Jews had acquired.

But this is not an objective history. At several points Levanda's description becomes an anthem of praise. For example, of the Jewish reforms of the Four-Year Sejm he writes that this was "the first legislative act in modern Europe that in principle claimed for the Jews civil and political rights equal to those of the country's other subjects. This reform preceded by several years the great French Revolution, which one usually credits with first proclaiming the equality of all creeds before the law and in the state."[51] In addition, Levanda acclaims the original privileges granted by Kazimierz the Great, who "in his enlightened tolerance and amazing humanism was far ahead of his time."[52]

---

[48] Israel Bartal, "The *Porets* and the *Arendar*: The Depiction of Poles in Jewish Literature," *Polish Review* 32: 4 (1987): 357–58. Bartal writes, "Along with a sense of alienation from and revulsion due to the licentious and violent behavior associated with Polish nobility, one also finds strains of identification with this economic and political class with which the fate of the Jews was linked. Thus, one finds side-by-side deep fears of violence and persecution, and a feeling of affinity and even desire to assimilate to some of the traits of the nobility. Other social classes in the Polish state were not the object of such bonds" (357).

[49] Ibid., 366.

[50] L. Levanda, "Sud'by evreev v pol'skoi Rechi Pospolitoi (istoricheskii ocherk)," *Voskhod*, nos. 9–12 (1886).

[51] Ibid., no. 11, 57.

[52] Ibid., no. 9, 174.

What is surprising is not Levanda's tone but his value system. While Dubnov and other Jewish nationalists glorify the system of Jewish self-rule in Poland—the Va'ad Arba Aratsot and the efficient local *kehalim*—Levanda is largely indifferent to internal Jewish life.[53] He focuses rather on examples of the successful integration of the Jews and on displays of tolerance and generosity on the part of Poland's rulers. It is not a coincidence that the goal of integration, which is embodied in this perspective, is the original aim of his modernization program for the Jews of Russia.

Levanda saves his most biting criticism for the clergy, who, although they were rulers neither in name nor in law, began to wield decisive power as early as the 17th century. Levanda notes sadly that, while the politics of the Sejm and the Crown "more or less strove for the integration of the Jews with the Polish people, [the clergy] pursued a diametrically opposite aim: synodal regulations simply struck down the royal and Sejm statutes."[54] With the clergy antagonistic to Jewish emancipation, the Jews were ultimately left as alienated and isolated from Polish society as they had been when they first arrived in the 13th century.[55]

The Polish theme becomes the backdrop for Levanda's last work of fiction, "Avraam Iezofovich," which deals with the growing influence of the clergy in Poland.[56] Apparently written at the same time as his historical sketch (it appeared a month later, in January 1887), this novella provides a realistic depiction of Polish rule in the early 16th century, at the height of Polish prosperity and might. Avraam Iezofovich, a young and talented Jew, is invited to serve as the king's financial adviser on the condition that he convert to Catholicism—which he does. The conversion creates an uproar among the Jews of Kraków, who send Moshe Halevi Lando, the chief rabbi of the city and previously Avraam's personal teacher, to beseech him to return to Judaism. During the conversations between the two men the story takes a psychological turn. Avraam begins to understand what he has forsaken and feels the need to return to the religion of his fathers. Deciding to live in effect as a *marrano*, he appears to everyone as a good Christian, but in the privacy of his home he secretly performs the Jewish rites.

With Passover nearing, Avraam prepares his home for the *seder* dinner. The local Catholic clergy, who have been jealous of his success from the very beginning, decide to unmask him. Learning of their intention, he and his brothers succeed in removing any sign of Jewish affiliation before the king

---

[53] See S. Dubnov, "Avtonomizm kak osnova natsional'noi programmy: Pis'ma o starom i novom evreistve," *Voskhod*, no. 12 (1901): 21–24; reprinted in Dubnov, *Pis'ma o starom i novom evreistve.*

[54] Levanda, "Sud'by evreev v pol'skoi Rechi Pospolitoi," *Voskhod*, no. 11, 65.

[55] Ibid., no. 12, 15.

[56] L. Levanda, "Avraam Iezofovich: Istoricheskaia povest' pervoi poloviny XVI-go veka," *Voskhod*, nos. 1–2 (1887).

arrives. Soon after, he resigns his post and goes to Germany to live openly as a Jew. Sadly, he does not find peace there either, but dies of a tormented conscience. The key passage explaining Avraam's worldview lies in his repentance of his conversion:

> Ever since I betrayed the holy faith of our fathers, I have not had a peaceful minute. I do not sleep at night, my conscience troubles me, and I am not happy with life. All the honors that have been showered upon me by the king gave me no satisfaction; they burn me and I am ready any minute to give up everything and run to the ends of the earth. One should remain in the religion of one's birth until one's last breath. In betraying my religion, I made a mistake for which I will repent till my grave. Here Satan meddled and clouded my reason. And therefore I have to correct what I mistakenly did in an unfortunate hour. Otherwise it would be better not to live at all.[57]

While the story can certainly be read as a protest against the phenomenon of religious conversion from Judaism, which had grown to serious proportions in Russia, Levanda underscores the dilemma facing the Jew who seeks integration.[58] Forced to choose between assimilation and his religion, Avraam makes the fateful choice that leads to his death. At the same time, the image of Poland is ambiguous at best. While Levanda exonerates the king of antisemitism, he portrays the Catholic clergy as an evil force. Pressuring the king to force Avraam to convert, the clergy persecutes him, seeking his downfall at every turn. Not surprisingly, the situation portrayed in the novel corresponds exactly to the views about the clergy that Levanda expresses in his article "Sud'by evreev v pol'skoi Rechi Pospolitoi."

The character of Avraam in many ways resembles Levanda himself. Desiring acclaim at the highest level of his adopted society, Levanda also encountered resistance because he was Jewish.[59] He understood that his literary success would be enhanced if he converted, as did his colleague Grigory Bagrov.[60] Clearly the psychological dilemma Avraam experienced was one that Levanda could easily imagine.

---

[57] Ibid., no. 2, 48.

[58] Conversions from Judaism were rising in the 1880s. For a short description of this phenomenon, see G. Sliozberg, *Dela minuvshikh dnei: Zapiski russkago evreia*, 3 vols. (Paris: Komitet po chestvovaniiu, 1933), 2: 94.

[59] Levanda did not have any of the requirements to gain the right to live outside the Pale of Settlement.

[60] In letters from 1878 Bagrov advised Levanda to move to St. Petersburg and write on general themes for a Russian audience—and thereby escape the unpleasantness associated with journalism on the Jewish question. See Gol'dberg, *L. O. Levanda kak publitsist*, 19–20.

It is also likely that Levanda wrote his novel in response to Orzeszkowa's historical epic *Meir Ezofowicz* (1878), since Levanda had good reason to want to correct aspects of her portrayal, especially in light of the fact that Orzeszkowa's novel had come out before the pogroms and was widely seen as a realistic portrait of Polish Jews. It may be for this reason that Levanda gave the hero of his novel the same surname as Orzeszkowa's hero. Although the stories treat different historical periods—*Meir Ezofowicz* takes place in the early 19th century—the issue of integration with the host nation is the main theme in both. Orzeszkowa's hero, Meir, is punished with a *herem* (excommunication) by the narrow-minded religious obscurants who keep the people in poverty and ignorance. In her account the religious fanatics are responsible for hindering the Jews' progress toward integration.

In opposition to Orzeszkowa, who contrasts progress with obscurantism, Levanda treats the issue of Jewish identity in subtle and troubling ways. Instead of progress versus obscurantism, Levanda juxtaposes self-realization and loyalty. Although Avraam would like to be of use both to Poland and to its Jewish citizens, the conditions of his service, set by the Poles, prohibit him from serving without betraying Judaism. In addition, even after he has converted to Christianity, he is still an object of persecution. Thus, it is not the Jews who need to change but the Poles. Polish intolerance harms not only Avraam but also the interests of the Polish state, since it causes Avraam to leave his position in the chancellery, where he managed to revive the economy.

Although Levanda does not give us a consistently positive image of Poland, it seems safe to say that Levanda's engagement with Poland as a literary theme in the last years of his life reflects his search for a time when the Jews of Eastern Europe were integrated, happy, and well treated. Having rejected Palestine as a potential home for the Jews, Levanda needed something to believe in, somewhere to build a future for the Jewish people. Although this ideal could not be contemporary Poland, as his debate with Orzeszkowa shows, he emphasized the few happy times in Polish history—inevitably contrasting them with the unhappy situation in contemporary Russia.[61]

It is important to consider, however, that Levanda needed to stretch the truth in various ways to interpret Poland as he did. After all, Karol Radziwiłł was in fact one of the most rapacious noblemen in a period famous for aristo-

---

[61] Levanda expressed his dismay at the situation of the Jews in Russia following the pogroms in a series of articles published in *Voskhod* and *Nedel'naia khronika Voskhoda* in 1881 and 1882 under the titles "Mimokhodom (letuchie mysli nedoumevaiushchego)" and "Mimokhodom (skromnye besedy o proshlogodnem snege)."

cratic excesses.[62] Moreover, the Polish reform of the Four-Year Sejm, so exalted by Levanda, died stillborn, incapable of overcoming the resistance of the Catholic clergy. And even that poignant image in *Bol'shoi remiz* of two Jewish musicians leaving Galicia with their Polish teacher to begin brilliant careers in Western Europe is hardly credible. In a study of Levanda's fiction Akim Volynsky notes ironically: "For double effect the intrigue begins with cruel violence against a Jewish girl who, from a tavern buffet, later lands on a concert stage and wins abundant laurels."[63] But it is impossible entirely to consider Levanda an incorrigible idealist. After all, he wrote "Avraam Iezofovich" exactly to show the difficulties of achieving Jewish equality in medieval Poland.

Although Levanda tried to create various positive images of Poland, the modern reader will probably find "Avraam Iezofovich" the most realistic depiction of all. And precisely because Levanda's images diverge from reality, they provoke questions about his motives. If he really felt close to Poland, why did he not write in Polish, a language that he spoke fluently, and devote his efforts to achieving equal rights for Jews there? Or, conversely, why did he not move to St. Petersburg and set himself up as a model of integration, depicting in his fiction images of Jews successfully living together with Russians?[64] Why did he write in Russian for a Jewish audience about a Poland that no longer existed?

Although it is impossible to be sure, the chronology suggests that in the 1860s Levanda was convinced Russia would embrace its Jews, granting them equal rights. When that did not occur, he turned to historical Poland as a model for relations between Jews and non-Jews. In the Poland of the past he discovered some moments when Jews lived in harmony with Poles—although he was careful not to overlook the times of persecution. He also expressed his admiration for Polish mentors, such as the senior supervisor in *Liubitel'skii spektakl'* and the music teacher in *Bol'shoi remiz* who supported and encouraged Jews in their desire to become creative artists. Similarly, he expressed a love of Polish literature, considering it more highly developed than either the Russian or Jewish literature of his day.

In many ways Levanda's evolution makes sense in the context of his political program. His indifference to Poland before 1870 is justified by his faith

---

[62] According to Jerzy J. Lerski, "[B]asically uneducated and an excessive drinker, [Karol Radziwiłł] found a place in the Polish national tradition as a symbol of the backward and corrupt magnates who brought about Poland's destruction." Lerski, *Historical Dictionary of Poland, 966–1945* (Westport, CT: Greenwood Press, 1996), 493–94.

[63] A. Volynskii, "Bytopisatel' russkogo evreistva: Kriticheskii obzor beletristicheskikh proizvedenii L. O. Levandy," *Voskhod*, no. 1 (1889): 25.

[64] See the 1861 letter from his friend and the former editor of *Vilenskii vestnik*, M. F. de-Poulé, to Levanda, published in Gol'dberg, *L. O. Levanda kak publitsist*, 31–32.

in Russia. We recall that the promise of Alexander II's Great Reforms had a spellbinding effect on the Jews. It also makes sense that when the Russian government turned to reaction Levanda retreated into history after expressing his anger in a few articles following the pogroms. In the Polish past he discovered unrealized possibilities for relations between Jews and non-Jews. At the same time, he saw much that was worthy of acclaim in contemporary Polish culture and its representatives. By telling stories about near misses in the past, and consoling himself with depictions of Polish Judophiles, Levanda tried to lessen the weight of the obvious failure of his political program—a failure that, according to witnesses, ultimately caused his death.[65]

---

[65] "The patriotism of Lev Levanda and many other Jewish 'Russofiles' significantly grew cold [after 1881]. One has to consider that the crack in his argument in favor of 'unity' with the Russian people, who were moaning under the yoke of autocracy, shook his whole spiritual world, and he even became a proto-Zionist, dying from a serious mental illness at age 53" (Rivesman, "Vospominaniia i vstrechi," 75). Dubnov affirms this view with his own description of a mentally broken Levanda awaiting death in a mental asylum in Vilna (*Kniga zhizni*, 131).

## Chapter 2

## Pacifism and Aggression in
## Shimon An-sky's Spiritual Evolution

The zigzag trajectory of Shimon An-sky's life has propelled scholars to view him as plagued with paradoxes. One cause for this perception is his shifts in ideology. Before 1905 he defended armed revolution, then turned to pacifism and folklore studies, and then returned to support revolution. It can be shown, however, that these apparent swings, rather than signs of eccentric indecision, reflected An-sky's coordination with mainstream thinking in Russian and Russian-Jewish society. In particular, An-sky was deeply affected by the Revolution of 1905 and the ideological changes that occurred following it. His literary works, civic activism, and folklore expeditions all reflect the rejection of revolution that became part of the general *Weltanschauung* of Russian society after 1905. Similarly, An-sky's change to support revolution and militancy during World War I and in 1917 also links him with a society that was equally infected by a sharp turn toward aggression.[1] Finally, his turn to folklore reflects a Jewish sensibility that was engaged in increasing degrees with the Jewish past and the culture of the Jewish people, as opposed to its elite.

Despite the external changes in his life, a persistent feature of An-sky's works is the striving for utopia. An-sky's work in the Socialist Revolutionary Party (PSR) and his Jewish ethnographical studies were paradoxically motivated by a single fundamental desire to transform the world. Even when he rejected revolution as the most effective means to achieve utopia, An-sky proposed cultural projects that nevertheless encouraged the struggle for change. In fact, although his folklore studies may seem apolitical, in his treatment he did not just describe (as would a scholar), but attempted to give the Jews a new Torah. This new Torah was supposed to bring about a reconciliation of Orthodox and secular Jews and transform Jewish society.[2]

Another characteristic of An-sky's life and works, especially after 1905, is his attempt to bring Russians and Jews closer together. He claimed that their

---

[1] R. N. Ettinger, *Roza Nikolaevna Ettinger* (Jerusalem, 1980), 21.

[2] As the historian and critic Israel Tsinberg [Zinberg] put it, An-sky felt that "everything on which until now Judaism rested—religion, Torah, Talmud—has fallen, is destroyed. And now we, Jewish writers, try to create something new that, exclusive of religion, would unite the people into a single whole." Tsinberg, "S. An-sky," *Evreiskaia entsiklopediia*, 2: 618.

political interests and spiritual origins paralleled one another's and they were both "chosen" peoples. Trying to synthesize elements from the Jewish and Russian traditions, An-sky wrote stories, practiced journalism, and engaged in political projects that benefited both Russians and Jews.

To understand An-sky's unique synthesis of Russian and Jewish elements, I use as a key marker An-sky's famous essay "Jewish Folk Art" ("Evreiskoe narodnoe tvorchestvo," 1908).[3] This article was not only one of the most innovative and weighty of all his contributions to a modern conception of Ashkenazi Jewish culture, but also represented a pivotal moment in An-sky's evolution. Paradoxically, "Jewish Folk Art" provides unlikely support for the claim that An-sky sought a Russian-Jewish synthesis, since in that essay he drew a vivid distinction between Jewish and non-Jewish cultures.

An-sky argued that, as opposed to Christian nations that had their origins in paganism and subsequently praised military prowess, the Jews were different. Their folklore, he contended, reflected the spiritual origins of Jewish culture. Established on the grounds of ethical monotheism, the Jewish religion encouraged the Jewish people to disregard, even scorn military might. According to An-sky, the Jews were exceptional as compared with all other nations, because they possessed exclusively spiritual values. Concentrating on Torah, Jews devoted their lives to study, moral contemplation, and theological inquiry. In theory, they ignored the external aspects of life and mined the riches of their own internal depths, which found tangible form in folk creations: legends, plays, songs, jokes, and religious artifacts.

In "Jewish Folk Art" An-sky offered more than merely an expression in modern form of ideas that traditional Jews had been saying about themselves for centuries. Rather, by viewing the life of *shtetl* Judaism as the source of Jewish creativity, An-sky expressed some important tenets of Diaspora Jewish nationalism. Traditional Jews were not fanatics, inclined to isolation, ignorance, and poverty, but, by seeking spiritual as opposed to material riches, they composed a unique, contemplative religious-ethnic nation. And the Jews were a genuine nation with its own folk culture—the expression of the nation's experience during its long journey to the present.

To understand how "Jewish Folk Art" reflects An-sky's conception of synthesis, we should examine two critical themes that run through the essay and reflect a departure from An-sky's earlier worldview: his idealization of physical weakness and positive reevaluation of traditional Jewry. For example, only three years before, during the Revolution of 1905, An-sky vaunted physical strength. As a leader of Russia's most important revolutionary party, the Socialist Revolutionaries, An-sky insisted that might offered the sole means of removing the tsar and bringing about a better society. Similarly, after 1905, in both his Russian and Jewish writings, An-sky reached out to

---

[3] S. An-skii, "Evreiskoe narodnoe izkusstvo," in Ginzburg and Tsinberg, eds., *Perezhitoe*, 1: 276–310.

groups he had either ignored or condemned earlier. In his civic activism and fiction regarding Jewish life he demonstrated his respect for the idea of *klal yisroel*, a love for all groups in Jewish society. Indeed, in contrast to previous criticism of Orthodox Jewry, now he extolled traditional Jewish texts, including the Bible, Talmud, and Hasidic folktales and songs. In his Russian writings he did something similar, attempting to reach out to groups in Russian society that he had ignored earlier, such as the bourgeois intelligentsia.

To understand An-sky's evolution, it is necessary to perceive his desire for synthesis.[4] While his essays on the Russian peasant reader, written in the early 1890s, demonstrate his early association with Russian Populism, An-sky remained committed to the Russian radical movement even in the years when he became active as a Jewish nationalist. For example, in 1907 An-sky published an anthology entitled *Chto takoe anarkhizm?* (What is Anarchism?), in which he made available for the Russian reader selections from the writings of William Godwin, P. J. Proudhon, Max Stirner, Mikhail Bakunin, Petr Kropotkin, and Lev Tolstoy.[5] In 1909 he compiled *Vsiudu zhizn'* (Life is Everywhere), a volume of parables, stories, and poems by Lev Tolstoy, Vladimir Korolenko, Vsevolod Garshin, and Nikolai Nekrasov that were meant to edify

---

[4] We should disclaim the idea that An-sky repudiated his work as a Russian radical. Although An-sky made a speech in 1910 at the 25th anniversary of his literary career in which he claims exclusive fidelity to Jewish national causes, his subsequent actions contradict such a view. I have to recognize the pioneering and brilliant work of David Roskies, who recovered Shimon An-sky after more than a half-century of scholarly neglect. In a superb and more comprehensive essay, Roskies precedes me in reaching the conclusion that An-sky's creative contributions emerge directly from his work in the Russian Populist movement. Roskies writes, "Instead of a bifurcated life, half of which was lived in error, the other half in a state of grace, Ansky's career was a four-act drama. First came the break with Jews and Judaism, accompanied by the total embrace of Russian radical culture. Then came a series of jolts—political, cultural and, if the tale of conversion has any validity at all, spiritual—that awakened in him a longing for what he had left behind…. But the very culture that seduced him away provided him with the rationale for the means of retrieval. It was as a Russian Populist that Ansky took the critical next step toward a creative, dynamic appropriation of the East European Jewish past. He did not renounce his modernism or his radical faith in order to become a good Jew; he acted upon that faith and reinvented Jewish culture accordingly. He turned the disparate remains of Jewish folklore and folk life into an all-embracing Oral Torah." Roskies, "S. Ansky and the Paradigm of Return," in *The Uses of Tradition: Jewish Continuity in the Modern Era*, ed. Jack Wertheimer (New York: Jewish Theological Seminary of America, 1992), 260.

[5] S. An-skii, *Chto takoe anarkhizm?* (St. Petersburg: Zhivoe slovo, 1907). An-sky published the work under his own name—Shimon Akimovich An-sky—and included in parentheses his birth name (Rappoport).

the Russian lower classes.[6] Furthermore, in 1914, at perhaps the high point of his participation in Jewish national culture, An-sky published a collection of articles on the Russian peasant reader with the new title *Narod i kniga* (The Folk and the Book).[7]

Because An-sky was active in Russian intellectual life during the period of his main contributions to Jewish culture, one might consider the degree to which the Russian context influenced his conceptions of the Jewish people. To understand how An-sky arrived at his idea of Jewish spiritual might and his reassessment of the relations between Orthodox and modern Jews, we have to consider the Revolution of 1905 as a catalyst that drastically changed An-sky's worldview. Just as did many Russian radicals, An-sky reexamined his ideological principles following the failure of the Revolution.

During 1905 An-sky had supported the PSR, even entering in early 1906 into a heated polemic on the pages of the Jewish newspaper *Voskhod* with the Jewish historian and leader of the Folkspartei, Simon Dubnov. Taking a strictly nationalist perspective, Dubnov argued that during the pogroms that started in October, the Jews were attacked solely due to their status as Jews and not as revolutionaries.[8] As a result, by siding with the Revolution, by renouncing national interests, the Jews were akin to "slaves in revolution." Aiming to discredit the Jewish revolutionaries with this term, Dubnov advocated a defense of national interests, which supersede class identity. In response An-sky attacked Dubnov, claiming that the Jews had their best chance for liberation by joining with Russian radical parties to achieve the overthrow of tsarism. At that time An-sky maintained the theoretical validity of the class struggle and believed it should be applied to Jewish society.[9]

The failure of the Revolution of 1905 was a traumatic experience for revolutionaries. The lack of will to continue the struggle among both workers and peasants after the announcement of the October Manifesto in 1905 pointed to a tragic disparity between dream and reality. The peasantry, it turned out, was not a revolutionary element in society, but for the most part a conservative stratum loyal to the tsar. As a result of the failure of the Revolution, many Russian intellectuals repudiated their commitments to radicalism and sought more promising avenues for their political energies, such as support for the Duma and participation in the growing civil society. Some even made peace with the tsarist government itself. The example of Pyotr Struve is especially

---

[6] S. An-skii, comp. and ed., *Vsiudu zhizn'* (St. Petersburg: Razum, 1909).

[7] S. An-skii, *Narod i kniga: Opyt kharakteristiki narodnogo chitatelia* (Moscow: Universal'-noe knigoizdatel'stvo, 1914).

[8] S. Dubnov, "Uroki strashnykh dnei," in *Pis'ma o starom i novom evreistve (1897–1907)* (St. Petersburg: Obshchestvennaia pol'za, 1907), 294–329.

[9] S. An-skii, "'Uroki strashnykh vekov' (Po povodu stat'i S. M. Dubnova 'Uroki strashnykh dnei,'" *Voskhod*, no. 8 (1906): 8–9. An-sky's article appeared in issues 8, 9, 10, 11, 13 (February–April).

revealing in this regard, since he put aside the revolutionary goals of the liberation movement, which he led, to become a major activist in the Kadet (Constitutional Democratic) Party.[10] Another monument to the change in viewpoint is *Vekhi* (Landmarks, 1909), a volume that sold out five editions in a year. In that slim tome, seven Russian writers addressed the revolutionaries, asking them to seek more profound avenues for their energies, namely the gradual education of society as a whole and deeper spiritual understanding of the self.[11]

An-sky was politically to the left of the writers of *Landmarks*, but he too drew similar lessons from the failed revolution. In *What is Anarchism?* An-sky added a postscript in which he described his own views on political action. Although he was not a member of any anarchist syndicates, he began to see the logic of such thinkers as Leo Tolstoy that an immediate and broad revolution was not the answer. Instead, An-sky located the site of revolutionary change in the individual. Comparing the power of education to the effect of microbes, which can produce enormous change in society, An-sky wrote:

> Just as microbes invisible to the naked eye destroy the quiet course of life in entire countries, so too the ideas of anarchism little by little gain possession of minds, enter into an irreconcilable struggle with thousand-year-old prejudices and finally lead humanity to the true path of historical development. This development, an improvement in social forms, will occur in connection with the inexorable amelioration [of reality] for the individual's own benefit.[12]

Previously convinced of the efficacy of revolution, by 1907 An-sky had changed his mind. Instead of an immediate political upheaval on the horizon, An-sky put his faith in the gradual political maturation of individuals, who inexorably would bring about the transformation of society. Anarchy, working like powerful microbes, held the answer to political change, but results would appear only among future generations. The 1909 volume *Life is Everywhere* had a similar purpose. While the ultimate goal was to radicalize the reader, the selected parables and stories were intended to bring about the individual's gradual change in consciousness.

For many Russian and Jewish intellectuals, the idea of power began to have negative associations after 1905. After all, physical might had put down the Revolution and had shown that might is stronger than right. Furthermore,

---

[10] Richard Pipes, *Struve: Liberal on the Right, 1905–44* (Cambridge, MA: Harvard University Press, 1980).

[11] M. Gershenzon, ed., *Vekhi* (Moscow, 1909). For more on the positions of the writers of the writers in that work, see Brian Horowitz, "Unity and Disunity in *Landmarks*: The Rivalry between Petr Struve and Mikhail Gershenzon," *Studies in East European Thought* 51: 1 (March 1999): 61–78.

[12] An-skii, *Chto takoe anarkhizm?* 85.

after the defeat, it was now better to speak about the moral superiority of society. But the rejection of revolution did imply a positive conception of society. Instead of basing his hope on a war between classes, An-sky's new conception involved the healing of society and a belief in the harmonious unity of its members for the good of the whole. These ideas of gradual improvement reflect a new sympathy with society as a whole that surpasses An-sky's previous fixation on the struggle of the workers and peasants led by the revolutionary intelligentsia.

In setting off in a new direction, An-sky was in good company among his Jewish colleagues. A glance at other Jewish Diaspora nationalists of the time shows that Simon Dubnov, Henrik Sliozberg, Maksim Vinaver, and Aleksandr Braudo were also deeply skeptical of military might after 1905. In his writings about 1905, Vinaver speaks of the "moral struggle" to fight the closing of the First Duma on July 8, 1906, a struggle that he hoped the Vyborg Declaration would introduce.[13] Certainly scholars are aware of this change in attitudes. Perhaps less known is the fact that such a conception of power influenced the kind of Jewish historical and folkloric research that took place in pre-World War I Russia. If we take a look at *Perezhitoe* (Experience), the four volumes issued in St. Petersburg between 1909 and 1913 devoted to historical studies of Ashkenazi Jewish society, in which An-sky's "Jewish Folk Art" originally appeared and on whose board of editors he sat, we see to a certain degree a focus on subjects that feature powerless Jews.

In these volumes one finds a surprising interest in Jewish passivity. We encounter articles on the struggle with the government concerning Jewish dress by Yuly Gessen and an article on the folk songs about the slaughter of Jews by Cossacks in 1648. We also find a celebration of earlier, supposedly ineffectual, sources of Jewish power, such as the *shtadlanut* in Henry Sliozberg's article on Baron Horace Guenzburg and An-sky's own treatment of the legend of the Mstislav Affair of 1843–44.[14]

The title of the journal metaphorically underlines the editors' emphases on offering studies of what today we would call a history of daily life, rather than the traditional subjects of historical investigation, such as politics, law, and military events. For example, in the introduction to the third volume, the

---

[13] M. Vinaver, *Istoriia vyborgskogo vozzvaniia (vospominaniia)* (Petrograd, 1917), 34–36.

[14] *Shtadlan*, plural *shtadlanim*, refers to a "representative of the Jewish community with access to high dignitaries and legislative bodies." According to the *Encyclopedia Judaica* (14: 1463–63), the *shtadlan* had "to combine the roles and abilities of diplomat, advocate and intercessor." To this description we may add that the *shtadlanim* were often referred to as "court Jews," and their representative role for the community was largely based on their enormous wealth, in addition to purported moral qualities.

editors wrote, "In the combination of various sources and facts on which the study of the past is based, there are no materials that are bereft of decisive meaning; every line, however unimportant it might seem, every outline, however insignificant, has value in the general picture of the reconstructed [*vossozdavaemoe*] past."[15] History, as the editors envisioned it, consisted of the subtle, quotidian, and seemingly hidden and insignificant.

In his treatment of the altercation in 1843 between the Jews of Mstislav and Russian soldiers, in which a Russian was killed, An-sky chose to highlight that version of the legend that reflects admiration for Tsar Nicholas I. The story that An-sky relates tells how the Jews of Mstislav sent a wealthy representative, Itsele Monastyrshchiner, to St. Petersburg to win a reprieve from the tsar's harsh punishment. With the help of a Jewish magnate in the capital, Itsele gains an audience with the crown prince. Unnerved by fear and intense reverence, he faints. Waking up unconscious later, Itsele is told that he has been successful in saving the Jews of Mstislav because his fainting was taken as a sign of sincere devotion, and it convinced the tsar of the Jews' innocence.

In telling the story, An-sky gives an idealized, colorful treatment of royal majesty. Led into a large hall, Itsele is waiting for the prince with the rabbi of St. Petersburg:

> The rabbi nodded his head in confirmation. Itsele also began to read prayers of mercy, "Confession" [*Vidui*].[16] And he had barely finished his confession, when the door immediately opened. And behind this door, on the other side in the next room another door opened and then further a third door, and a fourth. And altogether twenty doors opened one after another. And at every door two soldiers stood with their swords exposed. And when the twentieth door opened, the crown prince himself appeared. He was dressed from head to foot in a golden robe, a crown on his head, and his whole figure shone.
>
> And the crown prince walked with a measured step through the long, long row of rooms, approaching the hall where Itsele and the rabbi stood. At first he seemed small, but as he approached he became larger and larger, taller and taller, more and more terrible. "Reb Itsele! He doesn't touch the ground..." Reb Itsele suddenly heard the rabbi's whisper. And he himself saw that the crown prince was walking, his feel not touching the ground. Itsele's heart froze, his eyes turned dark. And the prince moved closer, closer, closer.[17]

---

[15] Ginzburg and Tsinberg, *Perezhitoe*, 3: viii.

[16] "Vidui," signifies confession, a prayer that is recited on Yom Kippur.

[17] S. An-skii, "Iz legend o mstislavskom dele," in Ginzburg and Tsinberg, *Perezhitoe*, 3: 254.

An-sky transforms his scholarly article into an opportunity to recount the entire story, transposing into Russian the intonation and structure of an authentic Yiddish folktale. He uses the literary devices typical of folktales: the excessive number of doors and rooms, 20 in all; word repetitions (such as *dlinnyi-dlinnyi riad* [long-long row]), repetitive constructions (such as *stanovitsia vse bol'she, vse vyshe, vse groznee* [larger, taller, more terrible]); and *i* (and) at the beginning of every sentence. His artistic rendition is surprising, because this version confirms the Romanovs' divine legitimacy—they walk on air—and extends particular praise to Nicholas I for withdrawing his evil edict. Recall that this same Nicholas was responsible for the evil recruitments of cantonists; Jewish boys as young as 9 and 10 were taken from their homes to serve in the army for 25 years.

In "Jewish Folk Art" An-sky arrived at a new conception of religious Jewry. His views were formed from his folklore studies in which he wanted to reconnect modern and traditional Jews regardless of class. This new view can be seen in both his fiction and his civic activism. In 1908, for example, An-sky became a strong advocate of Jewish solidarity, revealing his perspective on the question of a Jewish national language. At a time of heated battles among Yiddishists, Zionists, and integrationists, and just a few months after the Chernowitz language conference, in which Yiddish was acknowledged as "an" official Jewish language along with Hebrew, An-sky defended trilingualism. At one of the first meetings of the newly established Jewish Literary Society in St. Petersburg, An-sky demanded equal status for Jewish literature written in Hebrew, Yiddish, or Russian. According to Dubnov, this position actually caused quite a scandal, and the society had to hold a series of evenings to debate the reasons to include Russian.[18] An-sky's positive attitude toward religious Jews in Jewish Folk Art had an echo in his folklore studies, especially his recounting of Hasidic legends.[19]

This new esteem, however, contrasts with his earlier position, especially as it was expressed in his fiction, which had been overwhelmingly negative. Having broken with religious authority early in his life, his fictional sketches of Jewish life in Russia reflected ambivalence toward religious Jews. In an early story from 1892, "Mendel Turk" (Mendel the Turk), An-sky featured a young enlightened Jew's perceptions of *shtetl* life in the period of the Russian-Turkish War. While the first-person narrator paints the Hasidic world in romantic hues, the character of the Hasid Mendel is depicted in all its short-

---

[18] Dubnov, *Kniga zhizni*, 297. An-sky's speech was entitled "Ravnopravnost' iazykov v evreiskoi literature" (Equality of Languages in Jewish Literature). For more on this, see Serman, "Spory 1908 goda," 167–74.

[19] See S. An-skii, "Narodnye detskie pesni," *Evreiskaia starina*, no. 3–4 (1912): 6–8.

comings. Mendel is shown as superstitious and intolerant. Although he has
no reliable information, Mendel uses the Hasidic method of *gemetria* to pre-
dict that the Russians will lose the war. Furthermore, Mendel is unkind, refusing to greet the narrator in public because he has contempt for an *apikoyres*
(religious heretic). Because the narrator admires and feels repulsion toward
pious Jews, the reader is left undecided about the author's judgment.

Similarly, in works from the first decade of the 19th century, such as
"Pervaia bresh': Iz epokhi 70-kh godov" (First Breach: From the 1870s; 1903),
or "Pod maskoi: Rasskaz molodogo maskila" (Behind a Mask: A Story of a
Young *Maskil*; 1909), the negative depiction of religious Jews has its mirror
image in the moral lassitude of enlightened Jews. By criticizing both groups,
An-sky emphasized the difficult historical circumstances that did not permit
the health and well-being of Russia's Jews either in rigid traditional communities or the circles of militant secularists. Although his novel, *Pionery*
(Pioneers; 1905), has a slightly different emphasis, since the *maskilim* in that
novel are depicted in far more positive colors, ambivalence toward religious
Jewry remains. While the progressive *maskilim*, represented by the character
of Mirkin, remember with affection their earlier experiences as students of
Talmud in *heder* and synagogue study rooms, they nevertheless struggle
against religious Jews, considering them a scourge they must defeat.

In his fiction, even after 1905, for example in "Under a Mask," An-sky's
negative treatment of religious Jewry, it can be noted, has a parallel in his ambivalence regarding young Jewish adherents of the Haskalah. It is possible,
therefore, to interpret his criticism of Jewish religious figures as something
other than a blanket condemnation of traditionally religious ideology and behavior. An-sky condemned the cleft between religious and secular Jews and
perhaps even before 1905 lamented this state of affairs. Such an interpretation
of the paradoxes in viewpoint allows us to see even in An-sky's early fiction a
presentiment of the reconciliation of religious and secular Jews that he would
depict later.

In fact, An-sky depicted such a reconciliation in *V novom rusle* (In a New
Way; 1906), the novel that one critic has called a "snapshot of the Revolution
of 1905."[20] In that work, An-sky underscores the moral and political unity of
traditional Jews and their radical children. A monologue by a pious Torah
scribe, the father of a member of the Bund's politburo, reflects the new
solidarity:

> Three months ago a man from Homel was here. He recounted how
> the Christians had attacked the Jews and wanted to brutalize and
> slaughter everyone, men, women and children, just as in Kishinev—
> but God the all-merciful saved us. And the man told us that young

---

[20] Mikhail Krutikov, *Yiddish Fiction and the Crisis of Modernity, 1905–1914* (Stanford, CA: Stanford University Press, 2000), 137.

Jews interceded ... from among those they say are not Jews, the apostates, those who have lost the divine spark.... They interceded and saved the entire Jewish community from destruction, defended women and children, and many of these youths died a cruel death.... For forty whole years I copied the scrolls of the Torah, I copied as God ordered, with trepidation, repentance and pious thoughts. Each time, before setting the name of God on the parchment, I washed in the "mikvah" (ritual bath). During my life, without compromising as much as possible, I fulfilled all the commands exactly, but the Lord did not honor me with the heroic deed of praising His name ... the defense of his scrolls! But He honored them.... I was a scribe my entire life, but did not inscribe anything in the great book. But they, in a single moment ... [were] inscribed.[21]

Although the novel ends on a negative note—a group of Cossacks ride into the town to put down the uprising—the Jews have attained a huge internal victory. They have soldered the cleft between secular intellectuals and pious traditionalists that had opened with the arrival of the Haskalah at the start of the 19th century. By depicting the ideological unity between generations, An-sky emphasizes the reconciliation of families and, by analogy, the entire nation under the leadership of the Bund, i.e., politically radical Jewish nationalists.

Although in real life An-sky resisted joining the Bund himself, remaining in the PSR, he admired the Bund's national program. Therefore, he did not hesitate to write two songs for the Bund, "Die Shvue" ("The Oath") and "Tsum Bund" ("To the Bund"); the former became its anthem. Nevertheless, as a disciple of Pyotr Lavrov and loyal to the idea of the role of the conscious intellectual in history, An-sky could not accept the Bund's Marxism, especially the idea that the revolutionary struggle followed impersonal laws.[22] Instead of joining the Bund, An-sky hoped, albeit unsuccessfully, to create a Jewish national group within the PSR.[23]

His positive attitude toward religious Jewry visualized in his depiction of harmony between religious and secular Jews reflects a desire to heal wounds caused by decades of antagonism. Just as the failure of the Revolution of 1905 led An-sky to see the need to reach out to larger groups in Russian society, so

---

[21] S. An-skii, *Sobranie sochinenii*, 3: 88–89.

[22] An-sky was Lavrov's secretary in Paris from 1894 to 1900.

[23] V. M. Chernov and Viktor Shulman, *Yidishe tuer in der Partay Sotsyalistn Revolutsyonern: Biografishe eseyen* (New York: Grigori Gershuni Brentsh, 247 Arbeter Ring, 1948), 87. For more on An-sky's attitudes toward the Bund, see Jonathan Frankel, "'Youth in Revolt': An-sky's 'In Shtrom' and the Instant Fictionalization of 1905," in Gabriella Safran and Steven J. Zipperstein, eds., *The Worlds of S. An-sky: A Russian Jewish Intellectual at the Turn of the Century* (Stanford, CA: Stanford University Press, 2006), 137–63.

too he realized that the health of Jewish society depended on full social cohesion and solidarity.

In his memoirs Dubnov describes the process by which An-sky shifted his viewpoint toward Jewish nationalism. Reflecting years later on their polemic in 1906, Dubnov wrote:

> During an argument An-sky confessed to me that when reading several parts of my article he was touched to tears, but still he was going to challenge me in *Voskhod*, especially with regard to the chapter "Slavery in Revolution." This chapter apparently wounded him as a member of the Russian Party of Socialist Revolutionaries. But already then I noticed that in An-sky's soul the Jewish revolutionary spirit [*evreiskii revoliutsionizm*] was struggling with the Russian. In general he had more of a political temperament than a fixed ideology; in a few years he entered our "Folkspartei," and later drew closer to Zionism.[24]

An-sky's shift in thinking emerged from factors other than just his psychological makeup; he also encountered actual events and people that affected his worldview. Given a position in 1906 as a journalist for the new PSR newspaper *Syn otechestva* (Son of the Fatherland), An-sky had a free assignment. He could travel where he wanted and write about what he wanted. As one might imagine, he spent a good deal of time in areas with a high concentration of Jewish residents. In his travels through a Russia he had not seen since the early 1890s, An-sky documented the physical ruin of Jewish life and the simultaneous blossoming of Jewish culture.[25]

What amazed An-sky most was the ardent passion for knowledge among young Jews. He writes, "Really, you know it is something striking, unbelievable! Literally all the young people, every one of them, spend their days and nights reading books and textbooks. They take pleasure in serious books; some of them are preparing for entrance exams somewhere. And it is both boys and girls, everyone. Poor, hungry, exhausted, they do not care about anything but intellectual interests and metaphysical questions [*prokliatye voprosy*]. It is really amazing!"[26]

These travels through the Pale of Settlement were truly an inspiration to An-sky. Surprised at the obsession with intellectual matters, An-sky claimed that Jewish essence was still alive in the *shtetlech* he visited. Although young Jews were not occupied with Torah, nevertheless their contempt for the physical side of life, the engagement of all their energies in spiritual growth, re-

---

[24] Dubnov, *Kniga zhizni*, 275.

[25] These writings were published in a single volume as S. An-sky, *Iz putevykh zapisok*, vol. 4 of *Sobranie sochinenii*, 5 vols. (St. Petersburg: Prosveshchenie, 1911–13).

[26] Ibid., 4: 252.

vealed the "same orientation as the ancient national creativity." In "Jewish Folk Art" he writes:

> Contemporary Jewish folk culture has not only mastered biblical forms, images and terms, but is also entirely suffused with the same orientation and basic tendency as the ancient national creativity, and it is namely this: that spiritual perfection, the good life, and, above all, intellectual development are identified with the study of Torah. It is the natural aim of life and the highest good of a person in this world, and such perfection gives a person universal strength, raises him to a divine level, and brings to its knees the most powerful material, physical force, which is a synonym for crudeness and stupidity. In original tales and songs, just as in other works of folk art, the heroic element is entirely absent, motives of struggle on the basis of material, physical force are absent.[27]

In his conception of old and new Jews, An-sky noted a parallel between the biblical Jew, strong in his faith before the manifold destruction of Jewish life, and the modern Diaspora Jew, spiritually uplifted by his own powerlessness. By connecting a Jewish essence across time boundaries, however, An-sky removed the difference between sacred and profane, theological and secular. Refusing to recognize the specifically religious context of ancient Jewish texts, An-sky viewed Jewish creativity in any form as an expression of "Jewishness." Thus, secular Jews, such as An-sky himself, were every bit as Jewish in their study of folk culture as traditional rabbis or Hasidic *zaddiks*. Although the disregard for differences in religious feeling and observance was bound to lead to mistakes in understanding, it did have a pragmatic aim. One of the goals of An-sky's folklore studies was to rescue Judaism and the Jewish people for a modernity that was hostile to religion.

Although it would be easy to view An-sky's ideological transformation as emerging from the Jewish tradition and opposed to his work as a Russian revolutionary, that is not the case. In fact, An-sky's identification with Russian culture led him to attribute to the Russian people the same superlative qualities as the Jews possessed. In 1914, when publishing new essays about the peasant reader, which he had written since 1900, An-sky added a new article entitled "Narod i voina" (The Folk and War). Claiming that the Russians too were characterized by spiritual values and that their folklore was spiritual in nature rather than material, An-sky cleansed the Russians of any military inclinations. He writes:

---

[27] S. An-skii, "Evreiskoe narodnoe tvorchestvo," 1: 291.

The Russian people were not notable for their bellicose nature, did not look at war as an aim of life or a permanent activity and did not give it a halo of moral qualities. The ancient Slavs did not have their own "God of war." And if we turn to the works of poetic folk culture—that honest expression of folk views, thoughts and strivings—we will not find there either military poems similar to "Chansons de Geste," or songs which emerge from the sweat of battle and which could incite military enthusiasm.[28]

The contents of this essay from 1914 closely resemble the viewpoint An-sky expressed about the Jews in 1909. The idea of a spiritual Russian people certainly resembles the ideas of the Slavophiles, perhaps retouched here and there by An-sky's contemporaries Vladimir Solovyov, Nikolai Berdyaev, Sergei Bulgakov, and Pavel Florensky.

Although Slavophile conceptions probably influenced An-sky, one must regard as absolutely irresponsible the assertion that the Russian people have no sagas or heroic stories, since the "Lay of the Host of Igor" contradicts this claim, as do many examples of epic *byliny*. The *byliny* are all about battles with Tatars; all the Russian folk heroes—Ilya Muromets, Alyosha Popovich, Dobrynya—are fighters. In addition, it is absurd to say that the Jews seek only spiritual enrichment. The stories of Joshua, Saul, David, the Maccabees, and Samson contradict such claims. Under the likely influence of Lev Tolstoy's ideas of non-resistance to evil, An-sky willfully misread the histories of these two nations. He made Jews and Russians into ideal nations, spiritualist as opposed to materialist. These two nations, morally superior to others, were linked not only by geography and history, but by temperament as well. For An-sky the Jews and Russians were obviously meant to join together, perhaps for some important purpose as yet unknown to both nations.[29]

It might seem surprising to discover a link between An-sky's Jewish and Russian writings, especially in 1914, when An-sky was engaged in his Jewish ethnographic expedition, but the two orientations are actually intertwined. The anti-materialism and idealism of his writings after 1905 show the influence of the Russian religious renaissance. Writers and thinkers associated with Symbolism expressed ideas about the spiritual essence of man and the mystical fate of nations. Moreover, An-sky himself was close to the epicenter of literary modernism. He was friendly with the Symbolist writer Fyodor Sologub, he was criticized by the poet Mikhail Kuzmin, and he contributed to *Russkoe bogatstvo* (Russian Wealth) at a time when the journal was veering

---

[28] S. An-skii, "Narod i voina," in *Narod i kniga*, 209.

[29] Interestingly, Heinrich Heine held a similar view with regard to Jews and Germans.

away from the literature of Populism and publishing writers associated with Symbolism.[30]

Yet it seems strange to find "The Folk and War" in a single volume with articles about teaching the peasant reader to read. After all, the difference between An-sky the Populist and the An-sky of 1914 could not be starker. The An-sky of 1914 was a Jewish nationalist, ethnographer, and writer associated with Symbolism, while the earlier An-sky had been a convinced Populist, devoted exclusively to the liberation of the Russian peasantry.

For Jewish intellectuals of An-sky's generation the connection between Russian Populism and Jewish nationalism was actually entirely understandable. As a populist devoted to working on behalf of the Russian people, once An-sky realized the Jews too were a nation, he easily transferred his emotions from the Russian folk to the Jewish folk. Maksim Vinaver summarizes this view when he writes that

> An-sky's entire life was the best example of this. The same passion, the same ceaseless energy that he showed in his work on behalf of the Russian people was apparent in his attitude toward the Jewish people. Here was the same faith in the people as a kind of embodiment of absolute truth, goodness and beauty, the exact same love for this supra-rational entity.[31]

Changes in his worldview also affected An-sky's attitudes toward ethnography. Instead of regarding revolution as the motor of Jewish salvation, An-sky believed in the promise of ethnography. Convinced—and he was probably right—that many modern Jews were alienated from religion and community, An-sky believed folk culture could have the same anthropological function as the Torah had had in earlier times. That is, folklore could serve as the spiritual source, the glue—so to speak—keeping the Jewish people together and giving them a vision of the ideal that Judaism can be. Although such an idea was blasphemy, An-sky was convinced of its certitude. Moreover, since folklore was not exclusive to one nation, An-sky believed that it could draw other nations closer to the Jews.

When World War I broke out, An-sky repudiated the spiritual values he had articulated from 1908–14, sanctioning physical strength as a useful means of self-defense. In selections from his unpublished diary, An-sky speaks constantly and with considerable verve about forming a Jewish legion to liberate

---

[30] A depiction of An-sky reading "The Dybbuk" to an audience that included Fyodor Sologub can be found in An-sky's unpublished diary, located in the Central State Archive of Literature and the Arts (TSGALI) f. 2583, op. 1, d. 6, ll. 21–40. I want to thank my esteemed colleague Mikhail Krutikov for making these papers available to me. Mikhail Kuzmin's review appeared as " Zametki o russkoi belletristike," *Apollon*, no. 9 (1911): 73–75.

[31] M. Vinaver, *Nedavnee: Vospominaniia i kharakteristiki*, 3rd ed. (Paris, 1926), 288.

Palestine, ostensibly with the goal of establishing a Jewish homeland.[32] In fact, he spoke out in favor of a Jewish army at public meetings in St. Petersburg in 1916. His change of mind emerged from his work as a first-aid worker on the front lines in Russian-held Galicia, Bukovina, and Poland, where he witnessed the senseless and murderous persecutions of Jews, mainly by the Russian Army.[33] Realizing that both the German and Russian sides had Jewish soldiers who were perpetrating violence on their own brethren, An-sky became convinced of Zionism's validity. In Zionism he discovered an ideology that stood up for Jewish interests first and foremost, as opposed to the other pro-Diaspora political ideas that asked the Jews to compromise political and national sovereignty in exchange for acceptance in a multinational state.

Both sides of An-sky's identity became active in the last years of his life. When the Revolution of February 1917 caused the downfall of the Romanov dynasty and brought the Provisional Government to power, An-sky quickly went to work on behalf of the PSR. He was elected as a representative to the Petersburg Soviet and played a not too insignificant role in October 1917 by attempting to convince the Bolshevik representatives in the Soviet not to monopolize power as a result of their successful coup. He remained in St. Petersburg during the winter and was elected as a representative to the ill-fated Constituent Assembly, which Lenin never permitted to open. When an order was issued for his arrest, An-sky, dressed as a Catholic priest, escaped to Poland, where, in the final days of his life, he was occupied with organizing a Jewish historical society in Warsaw, to match the one just established in Vilna.

Although in these final years he never returned to the dichotomy of spiritual versus material peoples, the ideas he expressed between the Revolution of 1905 and 1914 proved exceptionally useful for his creative activities. He was extraordinarily productive in that period, writing important stories such as "The Sins of Youth," "Behind a Mask," and "Go Talk to a Goy," plus articles on Jewish folklore such as "Children's Folksongs" and "Incantations against the Evil Eye, Sickness, and Misfortune," and such plays as *In a Conspiratorial Apartment*, and his major achievement, *The Dybbuk*. He also organized and carried out the Jewish Ethnographic Expedition. Inspired by a rarified view of the Russian and Jewish people, An-sky could discover what was ideal, profound, and unique in both peoples. Although he could not ultimately retain these views permanently, nevertheless they enabled him to have insights that, when translated into texts or cultural activity, created entirely new categories for understanding Ashkenazi Jewish history and society.

---

[32] An-sky, "Unpublished Diary," RGALI, II. 28–32. Incidentally, in these same documents An-sky spoke of his admiration for Vladimir Jabotinsky and his attitude toward Jewish power.

[33] An-sky described his experiences in his Yiddish memoirs of World War I, *Der yiddisher khurbn fun Poyln, Galitsye un Bukovine fun togbuch 1914–17*, which appeared in vols. 4–6 of his *Gazamlte shriftn*, 15 vols. (Warsaw: S. An-ski, 1920–25).

**Chapter 3**

# Poet and Nation: Fame and Amnesia in Shimon Frug's Literary Reputation

Shimon Frug, the Russian- and Yiddish-language poet and Jewish nationalist, was apotheosized in his own time. But he was loved more for reasons having to do with the specific needs of his contemporaries than for the aesthetic quality of his poetry. Moreover, Frug's enormous reputation in his own time has not carried over to the present. Juxtaposing these two conditions—his enormous popularity in his own time and the nearly total amnesia today—one may ask why the gap between these two features was so large.

Frug was something of a cult figure in tsarist Russia. Reports have it that when he died in 1916, 100,000 people followed his coffin along the streets of Odessa. Indisputably, he had a strong and devoted readership. In his life, ten editions of his poems were published in Russian, Yiddish, and Hebrew, he was praised by Aleksandr Skabichevsky, the Russian Populist, and esteemed by Simon Dubnov, the historian and Frug's close friend. In addition, although Frug was not a Zionist, such luminaries as Hayim Nahman Bialik, Yosef Klausner, David Frischman, Mordechai Spector, and Yehoshua Ravnitzky came to his funeral. In the Zionist paper the day after the funeral Leib Jaffe wrote these lines:

> Different times will come. Our people will live, free and revived in their old and reborn fatherland. We will resurrect [Frug], the genius of the people, who having lived in slavery, will begin again to weave the broken thread of his art, the indestructible and still unintelligible testament. It will be like the dawn of a future free life; when darkness covered the land and ignorance shrouded the peoples, he will become a "light of nations."
>
> At that time the Jewish nation will recall with love and gratitude this poet, who in the darkest years of the people's life, under the thunder of a storm and in impassable fog, lonely and sad, sang a new song of Zion to the people....[1]

---

[1] L. Jaffe, "S. G. Frug," *Evreiskaia zhizn'*, no. 39–40 (25 September 1916): 11.

The sad new song of Zion refers to Frug's *Sionidy* (Songs of Zion), his long narrative poem. Jaffe's point is that in the future Eretz Israel Frug will acquire the significance he deserves.

The Hebrew writer Micha Joseph Berdyczewsky wrote about Frug in a different way, conflating his poetry with the *Mahzor*, the high-holiday prayer book: "[W]hen one reads one of Frug's verses and then another, one hears in them the voice of a living Jew. But as one reads more and more it turns out that they are psalms, the poetry of the High Holy Day service. They are not verses and also not songs of the people. They are really prayers, genuine prayers from the *Sidur* [prayer book], and every Jew should sing the *brukhot* [blessings] and not understand, and even more they should *daven* [pray] and sing Frug. I mean this in fact."[2]

Berdyczewsky's claim would seem ironic or, at the minimum, strange, were it not that other readers have emphasized the connection of Frug's verse with the part of the Bible known as Prophets, especially Jeremiah. Moreover, because of Frug's *Sionidy*, sympathizers have compared him to Yehuda Halevi, whose verses were incorporated into the liturgy. Nevertheless, Berdyczewsky goes beyond what critics usually say by imploring Jews to sing Frug's verses as part of the Jewish prayer service.

In addition to Zionists, the writer Reuven Brainin used the thickest hyperbole to describe Frug. In the 1910 essay that appeared in Frug's three-volume collected works in Yiddish, Brainin writes:

> Poetry in our *Mama-Loshen* [Yiddish] has its own special world, its own sky, own earth, unique idea of beauty. Yiddish poetry has its own fiddle, entirely its own flowers, even its own angels. In its little world laughter contains some crying, lamenting, and moaning. Its flowers are somewhat poisonous and deathly pale. Its sky is always somewhat thick with lead, cloudy, and overcast. Its stars are veiled and dark, its angels are strict, old, gloomy, and serious spirits. Yiddish poetry gets its strength and syrup, its deep meaning and its human sorrow, first of all from our time, the poets that we have, and our *Mama-Loshen*, which has never let us down. And one of our greatest and best folk poets is Shimon Shmuel Frug.[3]

This evaluation is particularly astounding since Frug wrote most of his poems in Russian and contributed only a few original works to Yiddish. Moreover, he wrote a scathing criticism of Yiddish in 1899 in which he repeated stock arguments about Yiddish being a jargon and an unworthy vehicle for real literature. The Yiddish writer Mordechai Spector responded angrily to Frug that

---

[2] Quoted by Reuven Breinin in "Vorrede" [Introduction] to S. Frug, *Ale Shriften* (New York: Hebrew Publishing Co., 1910), 1: iv.

[3] Ibid., 1: v.

Yiddish had come a long way and a genuine literature had emerged thanks to such talents as Mendele Mocher Sforim, Itzak Peretz, and Sholem Aleichem.

Praise for Frug was not limited to Jewish circles. Aleksandr Skabichevsky, the Russian critic, wrote about Frug: "He does not occupy a central place in Russian poetry, will not create any school, will not force his contemporaries nor future poets to sing in the same manner. But that does not prevent him from being one of the most sympathetic, honest, and, most importantly, genuine poets. The lack of pretentiousness and extravagance, simplicity, clarity, distinctiveness, and the harmony of a bold and energetic verse, a rich form, and personal warmth are the irrevocable virtues of Frug's poetry."[4] Skabichevsky valorized Frug's non-didactic poems, in which he found embodiments of intimate genres.

The fact that in his day Frug was beloved by thousands of readers and the finest Jewish writers in Hebrew, Yiddish, and Russian prompts one to ask: Why did writers from such different literary camps equally idealize Frug? Why have we forgotten him now, and what were his true contributions to Jewish literature in Russia? What can explain the unbridgeable gap between his reputation yesterday and today?

Frug's fame in his lifetime reflects a complicated cultural phenomenon. For one group, he was a Jewish populist, for another he was a brilliant representative of folk (Yiddish) culture, and finally he was a hero to Zionist writers. Nevertheless, it is fair to say that his talent as a writer did not warrant his popularity. Frug belonged squarely to the populist poets of the 1880s, an age that D. S. Mirsky, the author of the standard history of Russian literature, viewed as the absolute low point in Russian poetic culture of the 19th century. Frug can be compared to his teacher Semyon Nadson, about whom Mirsky wrote that his poetry was "inspired by the impotent desire to make the world better by the burning consciousness of his own impotence."[5] A famous verse, often quoted as proof of his role, reveals, I think, the distinction between his importance as a Kulturträger and his failings as a poet.

> Everything around is bent low, lifeless,
> As if in the wilds of a desert valley.
> If only someone would boldly sob!
> If only someone would groan aloud!
> These nights without stars or storm,
> These days without shade or azure—

---

[4] A. M. Skabichevskii, *Istoriia noveishei russkoi literatury, 1848–1903 gg.*, 5th ed. (St. Petersburg: Obshchestvennaia pol'za, 1903), 499.

[5] D. S. Mirsky, *A History of Russian Literature*, ed. F. J. Whitfield (New York: Knopf, 1960), 345–46.

My people, how like they are
To your mournful years![6]

The lines embody a particular relationship between author and reader. While they perhaps do not make for great poetry, Frug's verses were closely associated with the intellectual atmosphere following the pogroms of 1881–82, serving as a mouthpiece for Jewish anger and suffering. Frug penned lyrics that upheld Jewish dignity, reproaching Russia for its mistreatment. That service alone earned him the loyalty of a generation of Jewish readers.

The Jewish public was apparently also thrilled to be able to identify a real Jewish poet who showed non-Jews that Jews deserved a place in the pantheon of cultured peoples. The Zionist Ben-Ami (Mordechai Rabinovich) expressed joy as a young man at discovering Frug. "I do not recall that I found any particular literary merit in his first poems. We did not look for it and did not even think about it. It was enough that at the time of the epidemic flight from Judaism there suddenly appeared poems that were saturated with ardent love for Judaism. It made a huge, unforgettable impression precisely because it was associated with moral issues."[7] By "moral," Ben-Ami means that Frug was not cut off from the Jewish people.

Born in 1860 in a Jewish family in the farming colony of Bobrovy Kut, located in the district of Kherson in the Ukraine, Frug had an atypical childhood. Growing up in an agricultural colony and not a shtetl, he was closely acquainted with nature. Nevertheless, he did not forego a *heder* education, although he also studied in a government school. At age 16, he moved to the city of Kherson, where he served as secretary to a "state" rabbi. Early on he became a *maskil*, an Enlightener, and believer in general education, secularization, and modernization for Russia's Jews. He published his first poem in 1879 in the St. Petersburg Jewish weekly *Rassvet*. Soon after, Frug went to live in Petersburg, where he became a regular contributor to Alfred Landau's newspaper *Voskhod*. He published his first book of poems in 1885 and his second in 1888. His major work on Zion, *Sionidy*, appeared in 1901.

Jewish writers loved Frug because he contributed to the development of a powerful lyric poetry, particularly in Hebrew and Yiddish, helping to introduce a Romantic aesthetics into Jewish literature. He modernized Jewish poetry stylistically and linguistically. He offered a new treatment of biblical themes, employing folk motifs, including legends, stories, and events from

---

[6] Quoted in S. Dubnov, *Evrei v Rossii i zapadnoi Evrope v epokhu antisemitskoi reaktsii* (Moscow-Leningrad: L. D. Frenkel', 1923), 67–68. Warmest thanks to Hugh McLean for the translations of Frug that I use here and throughout this chapter.

[7] Ben-Ami, "Frug (Vospominaniia)," *Rassvet*, no. 10–11 (September 20, 1917): 16.

Jewish history.[8] He presented himself as the Jewish national poet. Although many of his verses were stylizations or prose renditions without much artistic merit, his verse influenced such Hebrew poets as Hayim Nahman Bialik, Saul Tchernychowsky, and Uri Nissan Gnessin, as well as the Yiddish writers Mani Leib and Mordechai Halpern.

The poetry of the Jewish Enlightenment dominated the scene when Frug emerged as a young poet. Dan Miron describes it this way:

> [Judah Leib] Gordon's success, and he was the dominant Hebrew poet of the period, only emphasized the distance of that time's Hebrew poetry from a will and ability to express individual life. Gordon's success stemmed from his identification with a collective, non-individualist poetry, a poetry of learning, not metaphor, in short, a poetry that did not speak the feelings of modern man, tied to a mental zimmer-frame that European culture had ditched a hundred years earlier with the "Age of Reason."[9]

Similarly, Enlightenment poetry featured an image of the artist, who, although identified as a spokesman of the people, was not a particular or unique individual. He was knowledgeable, of definite opinions, and even charged with a mission, but his own personal experience was secondary. The timeless message, and not the means or the specific literary context, transmitted core meaning.

Frug broke decisively with the Enlightenment tradition and with the orientation toward Germany (Gordon looked to Germany for his literary models). Instead of trying to convince with the help of reason, Frug used the power of feelings. He proclaimed the beauty of nature and treated topics from the Bible in a sentimental fashion that, although out of sync with the Haskalah, approximated trends in Russian literature of the first half of the 19th century. Frug employed the genres of elegy, ballad, and historical poem, including folk songs and legends. He combined emotional lyrics on the subject of personal resignation, disappointment, and loss with the theme of the rebirth of the Jews as a people. Frug's achievement was to present the Jewish

---

[8] Hebrew poetry clearly developed under the influence of Russian literature, according to Hamutal Bar-Yosef, who writes, "In spite of the national differences and the achievements of each culture in isolation, we cannot deny the obvious facts: in the nineteenth and the second half of the twentieth century the majority of Hebrew-language writers were born in Russia, the Russian language was their first language, and sometimes their only language, and Russian literature was their main 'window' onto European literature and literature in general. In such circumstances an influence is unavoidable." Bar-Yosef, "Vliianie russkoi literatury na stanovlenie i razvitie novoi literatury na ivrite," *Vestnik evreiskogo universiteta v Moskve* 2: 15 (1997): 114–15.

[9] D. Miron, "Introduction," in *Songs from Bialik: Selected Poems of Hayim Nahman Bialik,* ed. and trans. Atar Hadari (Syracuse, NY: Syracuse University Press, 2000), xvii.

poet as a particularized self and romantic individual, who appeared as sufferer, prophet, and representative of the people.[10]

Perhaps in the same way that Nikolai Karamzin brought the new aesthetics of Sentimentalism to backward Russian literature at the end of the 18th century, Frug brought the advanced aesthetics of the age of Pushkin to backward Jewish literature in Russia of the second half of the 19th century. It did not matter that Frug wrote in Russian, as opposed to Hebrew or Yiddish. According to Bialik, Frug's Russian had the sound and intonation of Hebrew.[11]

At the same time, Frug also penned political poems in the spirit of Nikolai Nekrasov. Although it might seem paradoxical that he was influenced by such seemingly antagonistic trends as Romanticism and Realism, in fact the period of the 1880s was marked by eclecticism. The work of his mentor, Semyon Nadson, reflects the aesthetics of the period, characterized by an incongruent combination of internal psychological confession and criticism of the general political order.[12]

In his political poems Frug employed the theme of the prophet because it corresponded to his idea of the poet as a messianic figure, a messenger to the people. In the poem "Videnie proroka Isaii" (The Vision of Isaiah the Prophet), Frug depicts the prophet's vision of God, a vision which caused him to imagine the revitalization of the Jewish people and, furthermore, the ultimate victory of universal peace and brotherhood. Frug's portrayal of the prophet as a fiery critic of political power underscored the symbiotic relationship between the poet and the people.

The relationship between poet and people was deepened by Frug's use of Jewish legends, Midrashic stories, Talmudic disputations, and Jewish history. While making stories or poetry from Jewish religious material is not in itself unique—Hasidic masters fashioned the same material—Frug, along with Itzhak Peretz, was a pioneer in employing Jewish folklore for secular, aesthetic purposes. It is interesting to recall that Frug's use of such themes coincided with the rise of Jewish nationalism and that previously secular Jews had been hostile to Hasidic mysticism.

In the poem "Sozdanie cheloveka" (The Creation of Man), based on the Talmudic passage in *Bereshchit Rabba*, XII, Frug describes God's creation of

---

[10] Certainly there is no need to exaggerate the influence of Frug's Romanticism; Hamutal Bar-Yosef's point that Jewish readers perceived Romantic literature, such as Pushkin and Gogol, realistically is well taken. Nevertheless, this insight does not invalidate my claim that Frug modernized Jewish literature by introducing genres and devices from the Romantic cannon. See Bar-Yosef, "Vliianie russkoi literatury," 122–23.

[11] Quoted in *Biographical Dictionary of Modern Yiddish Literature*, 8 vols. (New York: Congress for Jewish Culture, 1956), s.v. "S. Frug," 7: 238.

[12] G. A. Bialyi, "Vstupitel'naia stat'ia," *Polnoe sobranie sochinenii S. Ia. Nadsona* (Leningrad: Sovetskii pisatel', 1962), vi–viii.

Adam as the joining of heaven and earth. The only problem is that man has forgotten this unity and leans to one or to the other direction exclusively. In still other poems, the forefathers, Abraham, Isaac, and Jacob, are portrayed as living and human men, while King Saul, David, and Solomon are portrayed in prosaic situations, either as children or engaged in mundane activities.[13] Similarly, Frug has poems devoted to such Jewish holidays as Lag ba-Omer, Tisha be-Av, Hanukkah, Purim, and Pesach, among others.

Of course, one could easily argue that Frug's humanistic treatment of Jewish themes reflected universalism and that he suppressed the conflict between national and universal interests. Inculcating pride among a Jewish elite that was growing more and more estranged from Jewish religious and ethnic identity, Frug stylized Jewish folk culture, weaving it into high culture. He showed that one could be advanced culturally and a proud Jew at the same time.

One may conclude, nevertheless, that Frug was not a creator of new values, but was in fact conservative, since he actually valorized the reigning literary hierarchies. His Romanticism, for example, was primarily rhetorical. Paradoxically, he shared this feature with the poetry of the Enlightenment; his poems feel less from the soul than from the mind, and even his poetry about Jewish revitalization seems not to touch real living beings, but mirrors instead an abstract nationalist discourse. Moreover, in his conception of Jewish nationalism Frug was not ahead of his time. Hibbat Zion and the cult of yearning for Zion, rather than political Zionism, shaped his views. For example, Frug lauded Jewish agricultural activity in Palestine. In "Seiateliam" (To the Sowers) Frug describes how the difficult efforts of farming in Palestine will bring results in the future and the sufferings of today will not be forgotten tomorrow. Similarly, in *Sionidy* we find a number of optimistic pronouncements about Jewish settlement.

> Sow with buoyant hands
> Sow with a clear soul,
> And in the gloom of bad weather
> These grains of power and freedom
> God will help to grow!
> Sow in cold and bleakness,
> Our sun, our happiness,
> Our harvest lies ahead![14]

Even before the rise of political Zionism, Frug was enthusiastic about Palestine, especially as a site for the advancement of Jewish labor. Frug was proud of Jewish farmers, especially of their capacity for suffering.

---

[13] See Frug, *Polnoe sobranie sochinenii*, 1: 43–44 ("Saul i David"); 1: 35–36 ("Videnie Saula"); and 1: 240–44 ("Smert' Samsona").

[14] Ibid., 6: 99.

Despite his love of Jewish farming, nonetheless he was not optimistic about Zion. Like many others, he could not imagine establishing a Jewish state in Palestine; the whole endeavor seemed unrealistic. Despite his desire to see Jewish success, he felt ambivalent about Jewish return to Zion, the culture of the Diaspora, and the purpose of Jewish life itself.

Perhaps the single theme that stands out in all Frug's works is the theme of suffering. In his magnum opus, his long narrative poem *Sionidy*, he gives full voice to his ideas of Zion, the *Galut*, Jewish history, identity, and poetry. The poem has 24 parts with such titles as "The Western Wall," "The Golden Calf," "Pesach," "A Hymn of Zion," "Four Cups," and others. The poem is complicated and ultimately not entirely intelligible, since the poet's ultimate viewpoint and message are left unfinalized.[15]

*Sionidy* opens with the poem "Credo," in which Frug claims that Zionism "is equally beautiful and short-lived." After a short time, he relates, it will "burn out in the darkness of the night." Despite the optimism of various parts, memorably those in which he describes the First Zionist Congress and the Passover Seder, other parts are deeply pessimistic.

The final chapter, for example, paints a grotesque picture. Entitled "Griadushchee" (The Future), Frug describes a wild and beautiful bird with a woman's face. The horrors of the world appear before her and leave her disfigured. She hides in a grove of trees, and tears flow from her eyes unseen by anyone. The poet writes that his heart is also a wild prophetic bird. Nevertheless, thinking about the future, the poet recalls the past in peacefulness; happiness fills his heart. The poem ends this way:

> We go on living, growing, and nurturing two life-giving
> Forces. One great force is knowledge,
> But the greatest is faith. Engendered by them,
> O future, you must be bright and splendid![16]

The poem nevertheless is enigmatic. What is the meaning of the bird? If his heart is also a wild bird, is it disfigured? The bird certainly represents the Jewish soul, but it may also signify the *Shekhinah*, the divine spirit, which in the form of a bird protects the Jews from danger.

In the chapter entitled "The Ninth of Av," Frug describes a Jewish soldier who has gone insane after the destruction of the temple. This soldier shouts, "There is no altar and no motherland." The narrator comments:

---

[15] *Galut*, Hebraic for "diaspora," i.e., geographically any place other than Eretz Israel.

[16] Ibid., 6: 113.

Worthless slave! Will the heavens save you
When people begin to drive you from the threshold with a stick
And then once again lure you with a bone, like a dog?
"Neither altar, nor motherland" — as an echo
Sounds among the squares covered with corpses.
And the burst of our enemies' laughter
Blends with the cracking of whips and the jangle of chains.[17]

This dramatic enactment of Jerusalem in flames is mediated by an acknowledgment, apparently from the poet, that God is merciful and good. But one may be left unconvinced because the depiction of the physical action appears more powerful than speech about God's promises.

Frug also gives us disturbing images in other poems. In "The Golden Calf" he describes the site where the golden calf stood, and the poet imagines what it was like at that time. Then the narrator switches again to *medias res*, describing the priests, whom the narrator calls "Aarons," "openly and shamelessly" "bending over the calf and singing and burning incense and kissing the golden hoof."[18] The poem ends with night covering the desert, a hyena squealing, and a star falling. The final line states, "Someone wept silently in the distance." Finally, in "The Western Wall" we have another frightening image. A ghost comes out of a coffin and curses the Jews. "Get away you despised stranger, go away by the will of olden days, damnation to the chosen tribe." Frug adds two more lines, "At that time the prodigal son will recall the remains of the Western Wall."[19]

In contrast to these depictions of suffering, Frug also portrays the quiet happiness of a family during Passover.[20] In addition, he describes the joy of the spring during Purim and a father introducing his son to the pleasures of Torah during Shavuos.[21] These depictions of Jewish religious ritual in a family represent the positive aspects of Diaspora Jewry. The only other optimistic moments are linked with Herzl and the Zionist movement. Frug writes:

Didn't a miracle really occur
Before our eyes?
—Who are they,
In whom a passionate heart beats,
Torches that light the way for us
Quickly lit up in the night's shadow.
He who is inspired by youthful strength,

---

[17] Ibid., 6: 101.

[18] Ibid., 6: 94.

[19] Ibid., 6: 93.

[20] Ibid., 6: 106–07.

[21] Ibid., 6: 109–10.

Invites with ardent triumph:
"Come, you who are lost, into the paternal home!
Come up, my light, the dawn of Zion?...[22]

The question mark seems somewhat misplaced, as though Frug were not sure whether he meant it as a real plan or a wishful fantasy.

Although the poem has the title *Sionidy* and includes some discussion of the theme of Zion, it probably does not belong to the genre of "songs of Zion," at least as defined by the scholar of Hebrew and Russian poetry Zoya Kopelman. Kopelman writes, "In all languages poems which are called 'songs of Zion,' have been published which are not 'Songs of Zion.' [Among them] are verses that lament the bitter fate of the Jewish people-eternal wanderer and often begin sadly 'on the rivers of Babylon...,' and verses about the bright and proud pages of the national history."[23] In her view, in order for a poem to belong to the "songs of Zion" genre it must deal primarily with the positive attributes of Zion and the author's yearning to go there.[24] In his poem, Frug devotes most of his energies to describing life in the Diaspora, its suffering, joy, and purpose.

*Sionidy* appears impossible to understand as a composite whole. Perhaps it is not even meant to make sense logically, but rests on an emotional or rhetorical appeal. It is not a narrative poem with a single narrator, united by a hero and a story, as is Samuel Taylor Coleridge's *The Rime of the Ancient Mariner* or T. S. Eliot's *The Wasteland*. The parts of *Sionidy* do not fit together easily. But if one can identify one unifying aspect it is the image of the Jew that Frug invents in the poem. This Jew, aware of his origins, understands that identity is connected to history, to the rituals, memories, and values Jews have shared for centuries. Of course many of these memories touch upon raw pain, but consciousness dialectically links suffering in the past with identity in the present.

Thematically the images of Jews in *Sionidy* do not differ from Frug's treatment of them in other poems. Palestine was just another locus of pain and suffering, sources of intense Jewish consciousness. Zionism gave Jews dignity, identity, and purpose, but Frug did not attribute to Zionism any particular superiority. He was impressed by the Zionist dream, but it seemed unrealistic, too far away; close by were Russia and Russian Jews. Their experiences, struggles, and suffering composed the subject of his writing and helped form his personal identity. In the autobiographical fragment he wrote about Russia,

---

[22] Ibid., 6: 96.

[23] Zoia Kopel'man, "Sionidy—palomnichestvo dushi (k dinamike zhanra)," *Vestnik Evreiskogo universiteta v Moskve* 6: 24 (2001): 136–37.

[24] Ibid., 138. In her article, Kopelman describes the revival of the "songs of Zion" genre in the early 1880s with the rise of the Hibbat Zion movement.

Frug expresses his love for the places of his youth where his relatives and friends are buried.

> The old cemetery, covered over with thick grass, chamomile, and dandelions, lay before me. Here and there shady acacia trees rose up over the blackened gravestones, and a low-lying hazelnut tree extended its prickly dark branches. The evening dew whitened on the fragile and straight stems of grass on which I walked, climbing between the humps of the graves. Many names familiar to me were written on the stones, many faces, figures, and situations arose before my eyes. And how small and also how fine these people were![25]

This passage epitomizes Frug's attitude toward his home and homeland. Despite his anger, Frug made his peace with Russia because in her graveyards and nature he found a landscape that preserved the memories of people and experiences that had made him who he was. Frug was therefore unable to negate the *Galut*, as Ahad Ha'am recommended, since the *Galut* represented a source for his poetic inspiration and ideological foundation.

We should now turn to the question of why Frug was so popular. In addition to his role as a poet, he raised awareness of the need for Jewish rights. He was one of the original activists who rallied for the establishment of a Jewish emigration society during the pogroms of 1881–82, supporting emigration to Zion and the Hibbat Zion group. Nonetheless, it must also be acknowledged that in the years before his death he sold his talent to the Russian gutter press, prostituting his talent and ideals out of economic need.

Skabichevsky, as a representative of the progressive intelligentsia, eagerly praised those Russian-language writers from among the national minorities who were critical of the government. By esteeming minority writers, Skabichevsky showed off the tolerance of Russian culture, which, in opposition to the government, was open to the participation of all, even Jews such as Frug.

For Dubnov, himself an advocate of Diaspora Jewish nationalism, Frug expressed the voice of Diaspora Jewry. Comparing Frug to Judah Halevi, who reflected the spiritual achievements of the Diaspora and the ability to create in the language of the majority people, Dubnov expounded:

> Frug was an atavistic partner of the best creators of our "Selikhot" and "Kinot" [medieval religious poems], which have an elegiac beauty that only a few contemporary historians can appreciate.... In him lives the vigorous soul of a "Salakh," the bard from the wonderful Sephardic school of Moses Ibn Ezra, but he managed to reach the

---

[25] Frug, *Polnoe sobranie sochinenii*, 3: 1–2.

poetic pathos of Judah Halevi.... Frug wrote primarily in Russian, masterfully using the Russian poetic language, but nevertheless remained a Jewish national poet—this is his main characteristic and huge advantage. He stood on the border between two literatures— Jewish and Russian—and if he occupied himself solely with presenting general, I mean, exclusively poetic themes, he could occupy a central place in the "Russian Parnassus," where many people situated him.[26]

Dubnov praises Frug, arguing that he successfully synthesized two cultures and created masterpieces in the language of the host nation. His proof—a syllogism: just as Jews in Muslim Spain contributed to the larger culture, so too Frug contributed to Russian culture.

For Yiddish critics such as Brainin or David Frischman, Frug represented stylistic modernization and cultural advancement, and thus deserved lavish praise. Frug apparently not only invigorated Yiddish poetry with his European aesthetics, but also contributed to the victory of syllabo-tonic prosody in Yiddish, although perhaps unintentionally, since Frug merely adopted the syllabo-tonic meters that he borrowed from Russian.[27]

The reasons why Zionist writers lauded Frug are more complicated. Of course such writers as Yehoshua Ravnitzky and Hayim Nahman Bialik followed Frug's footsteps in their treatment of Jewish legends and stories (see their book *Sefer ha'aggadah*; 1908–11). Moreover, Bialik himself learned a good deal from Frug.[28] For example, Hamutal Bar-Yosef has argued that Frug preceded Bialik "in the adoption of the persona of the poet-prophet. For example, the creative prophetic source partially comes from the Russian poetic tradition in the nineteenth century in poems like Pushkin's 'The Prophet,' Lermontov's 'The Prophet,' and Tiutchev's 'The Vision,' which was written in 1829, and 'The Dreams of Our Time' by Nadson, etc...."[29] At the same time, Bar-Yosef shows conclusively that Bialik, especially as he grew more confident of his talent, felt uncomfortable with the influence of Frug and distanced himself from it either by mocking Frug's aesthetics or dispensing with the latter's Romanticism and Sentimentalism altogether.[30]

But Zionists also liked Frug for other reasons. In his pride and love for the Jewish people, Frug showed himself to be a comrade. In fact, he seemed to share a theodicy with Zionists. The early Zionists explained Jewish suffering

---

[26] S. Dubnov, "Vospominaniia o S. M. Fruge," *Evreiskaia starina*, no. 4 (1916): 447 and 448.

[27] Conversations with Dov-Ber Kerler, Bloomington, Indiana, November 14–15, 2005.

[28] Hamutal Bar-Yosef, *Maga'im shel dekdens: Byalik, Berdits'evski, Brener* (Bersheva: Ben Gurion University, 1997), 54.

[29] Ibid.

[30] Ibid., 55.

in *Galut* as inevitable. Any national group living under the physical and spiritual yoke of a foreign power was bound to suffer. Of course such pain would disappear when Jews lived in their own country. Suffering in *Galut*, therefore, had a positive aspect, because it reminded Jews that they were not at home, but merely guests. Frug's cries of pain conformed to this paradigm.

At the same time Frug's image of the prophetic national poet paralleled the ideas of those Zionists who regarded the poet as a messianic figure. Incidentally, both Zionists and Frug based their overall conceptions of the world on Pyotr Lavrov's notion that consciousness makes individuals historical agents capable of willfully shaping history. Frug's poetry, Leib Jaffe considered, was supposed to stimulate a change in behavior and lead to the creation of a new world. Zionists could not help but see a parallel between their activist positions on Jewish history and Frug's use of the topic as a means for teaching lessons about our own day. However, since Zionists were fully engaged in a reevaluation of Jewish history, celebrating figures of strength and power such as the Macabees or the martyrs of Masada, they diverged from Frug.

Regarding Frug's idea of suffering, it is impossible not to feel that the poet admired Dostoevsky and the so-called Russian national idea, based as it is on the Christian tradition. For Dostoevsky suffering is salutary because it deepens consciousness, making one aware of the need for redemption. Frug hints at this and suggests that suffering is redemptive, although he does not disclose what it means for the Jewish people. Nonetheless, the depiction of unredeemed suffering weighs on readers, leaving them wondering about whether there really is a purpose to suffering either for the nation or the individual.

Although some Zionist writers did not forget that Frug had ambivalent feelings toward Zion, that fact did not extinguish their admiration for him. The debates over Jewish life in Palestine or in *Galut* were living issues in those days and have remained so in our own day. Even among Zionist writers, Frug's ambivalence would not have been unfamiliar or necessarily elicited opposition.

At the time of Frug's death, Dubnov predicted that the poet would be read by generations.

> For a long time in the future those with a sentimental heart will "weep over his poisoned verses." For a long time the images of his Biblical and Talmudic legends will illuminate the minds of thousands of children, placing into that young spirit the seed of love for the eternal nation. And for an even longer time Frug's inspired elegies, in which one can hear the "echo of the people's pain," will serve to

measure the depths of the tragic experience of Judaism at the end of the nineteenth century.[31]

Why didn't it happen? Perhaps it was a problem of readership. Jews who read Frug in Russian were bound ultimately to discover the best Russian authors and turn away from Frug. Similarly, the Diaspora Jewish nation in Russia that Dubnov predicted would form and which would celebrate Frug as the national poet never took shape, as Jews opted for integration under Soviet rule. Today, Frug remains little known. Despite several publications of his works in recent years, the gap between his popularity in his own time and the nearly total amnesia about Frug today remains to be explained.

History has been both kind and unkind to Frug. His struggle to become Russian Jewry's national poet was crowned with success. Skabichevsky was wrong: Frug's contemporaries and even his descendents paid him full homage. But posterity has not treated him gently. Despite his enormous role in developing Jewish literature in Russia, the best anyone can say nowadays is that his work satisfied the needs of a particular time and place, but has not been able to go beyond the borders that separate timeless from time-bound writing. Although being remembered is a rare feat, it seems that posterity has little use for writers who can say of themselves only that

> For long I shall be held endeared to the mortals
> For kindness that my lyre was often to unfold,
> Because in our cruel age I've shown freedom's portals,
> For pardon to the fallen called.[32]

---

[31] Dubnov, "Vospominaniia o S. M. Fruge," 458.

[32] From Aleksandr Pushkin's "Exegi Monumentum," trans. Boris Leyvi, http://spintongues.msk.ru/pooshkin.html (accessed September 26, 2006).

# Chapter 4

# Russian-Zionist Cultural Cooperation, 1916–18:
## Leib Jaffe and the Russian Intelligentsia

In 1916, Leib (Lev) Jaffe, the editor of the Moscow Zionist weekly printed in Russian, *Evreiskaia zhizn'*, devoted a double issue of the newspaper to the 25th anniversary of Hayim Nahman Bialik's literary career. Emboldened by the issue's popularity, in 1917 Jaffe decided to bring out a volume of Hebrew poetry in Russian translation under the title *Evreiskaia antologiia: Sbornik molodoi evreiskoi poezii* (Jewish Anthology: A Collection of Young Jewish Poetry). In the same year Jaffe launched a literary journal, *Sborniki Safrut*, devoted to Jewish cultural life in Russia. Between 1917 and 1918 three volumes appeared.[1] During the short period between the final days of tsarism and the formation of the new Soviet state, intellectuals in Russia used these outlets to engage in activities and form dialogues that later would seem contradictory. A close relationship between Zionists and the Russian and Russian-Jewish intelligentsia emerged at this moment.

Because Jaffe attracted a group of Russia's most important poets and writers, including Valery Bryusov, Vyacheslav Ivanov, Aleksandr Kuprin, and Maksim Gorky, these volumes have lasting importance for Russian literature. Besides the luminaries of Russian culture already mentioned, Vladimir Korolenko, Fyodor Sologub, Sergei Bulgakov, Vladislav Khodasevich, and the Lithuanian poet Yury Baltrushaitis agreed to take part. In addition, such important Jews in the Russian elite as Mikhail Gershenzon, Andrei Sobol, Leonid Pasternak, and Samuil Marshak also participated. Remarkably, such renowned figures in Jewish national life and Zionist literature as Mendele Mocher Sforim, Baal Machshoves, Vladimir Jabotinsky, Shimon An-sky, Yosef Klausner, and Hayyim Grinberg were also represented.

The cooperation of such a large group of Jews with varying degrees of Jewish identity makes it difficult to categorize these writers simply as "Jewish nationalists" or conversely "members of the Russian intelligentsia." To define these individuals accurately, one would need several categories. Framed between those who expressed an exclusive Jewish identity and others who were fully assimilated into Russian culture, the majority of Jews in the Russian and

---

[1] Although *Sborniki Safrut* was initially supposed to come out regularly, only three volumes ever appeared. The articles from volumes 1 and 3 were combined and republished in Berlin in 1922.

Jewish cultural elite probably fell between the two poles, basing their identities on varying degrees of attachment to Jewish and Russian culture. In 1917, there were still many Jews who felt that a synthetic identity, Russian-Jewish, was still possible and were intent on displaying dual loyalties.[2] Others, such as Jabotinsky, had chosen to abandon the Russian intelligentsia, adopting a Zionist identity entirely, while still others, such as Semyon Vengerov, had accepted full membership in the Russian intelligentsia, even going so far as to accept baptism in the Russian Orthodox Church.[3]

The volumes themselves drew attention because, instead of serving political goals directly, the majority of the articles were devoted to aesthetics, albeit related to Jewish themes. Jaffe permitted cultural issues broadly understood to occupy a prominent place. In addition to translations, the Russians provided original stories and poems. There were illustrations by such artists as Natan Altman and Ephraim Moses Lilien, and articles dealing with questions of Jewish poetry and the role of the national poet. An example of the modest place held by politics is the fact that, although issue 1 of *Safrut* came out only a few months after the announcement of the Balfour Declaration, only one of the fourteen articles touched on this subject directly.[4]

Russians and Jews joining together on behalf of Zionism may seem astounding given the fact that the already sharp contention over nationality politics had further intensified; 1917 was not 1905. Although the Provisional Government had legislated equality for all nationalities in one of its first laws, it had been careful not to single out Jews. The liberal Kadet Party, one of the bases of the Provisional Government, had always been afraid of seeming too pro-Jewish. The artistic intelligentsia had also become less tolerant toward the empire's national minorities over the decade. The shift was signalled by the so-called "Chirikov scandal" of 1908.[5] Questions about Russian national iden-

---

[2] I am thinking of those Jews in the Constitutional Democratic Party (Kadets)—Maksim Vinaver, Henrik Sliozberg, Vladimir Gessen—as well as the Socialists Lev Shternberg and Leon Bramson.

[3] Vengerov's mother reacted with deep sadness and regret to her son's conversion. See Pauline Wengeroff, *Rememberings: The World of a Russian-Jewish Woman in the Nineteenth Century*, ed. Bernard D. Cooperman, trans. Henny Wenkard (Potomac: University Press of Maryland, 2000), 218–26.

[4] The Balfour Declaration was made on November 2, 1917. The appendix of *Sborniki Safrut* did include some documents related to the First Zionist Congress: "Predvaritel'-noe ob"iavlenie o 1 sionistskom kongresse," "Pis'mo Gertselia k pravleniiu evreiskoi obshchiny v Miunkhene," "Spisok uchastnikov pervogo sionistskogo kongressa v Bazele," "Bazel'skaia programma," and a short article devoted to the ten-year anniversary entitled "Na prazdnike (13-go avgusta 1911 g.)" and signed by "Dreamer."

[5] The Chirikov scandal refers to a confrontation between Sholem Asch and Evgeny Chirikov over whether Russians have the right to write about Jews. See Viktor Kel'ner, "Dva intsidenta: Iz russko-evreiskikh otnoshenii v nachale XX v.," *Vestnik Evreiskogo universiteta v Moskve* 3: 10 (1995): 190–99.

tity had been raised, which halted the automatic affiliation of Jews in the Russian intelligentsia. Belonging to the Russian intelligentsia was now formulated on ideological and religious rather than purely political categories. Individuals who refused to subordinate their Jewish identities could join the secular national Jewish culture, which expressed itself in various ways and from a variety of political points of view.

The collaboration of Russians and Jews in itself was not unique. At least since the Great Reforms under Alexander II with its promise of greater rights for all subjects of the Empire, Russians and Jews had been working together in the cultural realm. Admittedly, fruitful interaction occurred in so-called Jewish journals that appeared in Russian to which non-Jews were invited to contribute. But there were not many journals and most were short-lived.[6] Moreover, the Russian contributors, while themselves capable writers, were not members of Russia's highest intellectual elite. At the same time many Jews worked for the Russian (liberal) press without drawing attention to themselves and their Jewish background.[7]

The other area of interaction, which admittedly had a high profile, was the defense of the Jews by well-known Russian writers. It became something of a tradition for leading Russian intellectuals to decry the government's anti-Jewish policies and publish apologetic texts that portrayed Jews in a positive light. The goal in almost every case was to rebut hostile accusations disseminated in the Russian press. In this context interaction between Russians and Jews was surprisingly minimal, since the Russians took upon themselves the task of speaking out on behalf of Jews.

From the point of view of the Zionists, it may seem strange that money was being earmarked for Russian-language publications, which one could argue were already peripheral to the Zionist project by 1917.[8] Certainly, one of the reasons why Jaffe sought to issue a Russian-language journal toward the end of World War I was because it was impossible to publish in Hebrew. During the war, the government prohibited the printing of materials in the Hebrew alphabet or Yiddish script. For propagandistic purposes Jaffe headed a publishing house, also entitled Safrut, which issued a number of books devoted to Zionist matters, including Theodor Herzl's *The Jewish State* and a book of essays by Ahad Ha'am, both in Russian translation. It could be argued, therefore, that in order to disseminate information, Jaffe had little choice about language.

---

[6] The periodicals were *Rassvet, Sion, Vestnik russkikh evreev, Voskhod, Rassvet* (the second *Rassvet*), *Russkii evrei, Evreiskoe obozrenie*, and *Budushchnost'*. Only *Voskhod* lasted longer than four years.

[7] G. Aronson, "Evrei v russkoi literature," 361–99.

[8] My thanks to an anonymous reader of this chapter for making this very important point.

But the question is clearly more complicated. I would argue that the Hebrew-Russian divide was not as clear-cut as Zionist propaganda, or even Jaffe's own statements in favor of Hebrew, would have it.[9] Hebrew may have been the future language of Zionism, but Russian was the language of the present. In fact, the policy of *Gegenwartsarbeit* (of working to strengthen Jewish life in the Diaspora, set in 1906 at the Helsingfors Conference) was one symptom. Still another was the fact that the Zionist Russian-language newspaper, *Evreiskaia zhizn'*—which had superceded *Rassvet*—appeared throughout the war, and even major Zionist figures, such as Vladimir Jabotinsky, Avraam Idelson, and Daniil Pasmanik, continued to write in Russian. It could very well be that there were various Zionisms with differing emphases represented by groups of Zionists who had Hebrew, Yiddish, and Russian orientations.[10] Furthermore, it is worth pondering whether Jaffe desired collaboration with the liberal and religious members of the Russian intelligentsia because he considered himself a Russian poet and looked to modern Russian culture as part of his own inheritance.[11] Jaffe's publishing work in Russian, his editing of the *Evreiskaia zhizn'*, and his own three original books of poetry written in Russian reflect a pro-Russian formation typical of some Zionists of his generation.

In light of the complicated linguistic, social, and political situations for the empire's Jews during the war and after the February Revolution, Jaffe's volumes raise important questions regarding the image of Zionism among the Silver Age Russian elite and the attitude toward Russia, the Russian language, and its literature, among prominent Zionists. In view of the fact that the official Zionist movement provided funding and that the Russians and acculturated Jews were aware of the volumes' ideological purpose to show off the Zionists' aesthetic values and cultural ambitions, I think it is a fair question to ask why Russians signed on to collaborative projects during and just after World War I and why the Zionists would want them?[12]

---

[9] Jaffe claims that *Sborniki Safrut* existed to highlight the enormous leaps in progress that Hebrew had made in Palestine. See his introduction to volume 2 of *Sborniki Safrut*.

[10] However, I do not think this is the case here. It may be useful to look at *Sborniki Safrut* as an example of what Michael Berkowitz calls a "supplemental nationality," i.e., Zionism had the function of deepening the Jewish identity of russified Jews, allowing them to "be a part of this nationality without living in the territory that served as its focus." Berkowitz, *Zionist Culture and West European Jewry before the First World War* (Chapel Hill: University of North Carolina Press, 1993), 6.

[11] For an analysis of the influence of Russian literature on two generations of modern Hebrew writers, see Bar-Yosef, "Vliianie russkoi literatury," 115–16; also Hamutal Bar-Yosef, *Magaim shel dekadens: Byalik, Berdits'evski, Brener* (Bersheva and Jerusalem: Ben Gurion University and the Bialik Institute, 1998).

[12] Such important projects as *Sborniki Safrut* and *Evreiskaia antologiia* have not escaped the attention of scholars of Russian-Jewish literature. After emigrating from Russia, Khodasevich republished his translations in a volume entitled *Iz evreiskikh poetov*

Admittedly, the first volume featured writings by Zionists. Yet non-Zionists also appeared, such as Elias Cherikover and Edward Bernstein, individuals associated with the labor movement. Similarly, several articles dealt with Diaspora Jewry in France, Austria, and the United States. On the cultural front, Jaffe included a translation by Sologub of Bialik's "Yadati, Beleil Arafel," and Khodasevich translated Saul Tchernichovsky's poem "Brit Mila." Marshak wrote an original poem, "Jerusalem," and Sobol contributed a short story. Machshoves contributed a memoir about Mendele Mocher Sforim, who had recently passed away. The third volume of *Sborniki Safrut* was similar to volume 1 in mixing poems, stories, and memoirs with political articles.[13]

The second issue of *Safrut*, however, had a different focus. It was entirely devoted to the 20th anniversary of the First Zionist Congress in Basel in 1897. Due to the narrow Zionist subject matter of this volume, no Russian intellectuals or non-Zionists took part. Rather, leading Zionists, such as Max Nordau, David Wolfssohn, Efim Chlenov, and Yosef Klausner contributed articles and reminiscences about Theodore Herzl and the First Congress.[14]

Clearly, by dropping the Russians in the second volume, Jaffe signaled the limits of ideological cooperation between Zionist and Russian intellectuals. One should not exaggerate the commitment of these Russians to Zionism. It is hard to imagine that these Russian intellectuals, with the exception of Gorky, cared a lot about Jewish nationalism or the formation of Jewish autonomous institutions, the language used in Jewish schools, or the organi-

---

(Berlin, 1923). Among the secondary literature, see Greta N. Slobin, "Heroic Poetry and Revolutionary Prophecy: Russian Symbolists Translate the Hebrew Poets," *Judaism: A Quarterly Journal of Jewish Life and Thought* 51: 4 (Fall 2002): 408–18; L. Bernhardt, "Khodasevich i sovremennaia evreiskaia poeziia" *Russian Literature*, no. 6 (1974): 21–27; R. Timenchik and Z. Kopel'man, "Viacheslav Ivanov i poeziia Kh. N. Bialika," *Novoe literaturnoe obozrenie*, no. 14 (1995): 102–15.

[13] Volume 3 featured essays on Zionism by Buber, Idelson, Hayim Greenbaum, and Bialik, translations into Russian of Bialik and Tchernichowsky, as well as original poems by Bryusov and Ivan Bunin. An-sky contributed his own rendition of a Jewish legend and Simon Dubnov published his memoirs of S. Y. Abramovich (Mendele). Since the *Sborniki Safrut* volumes are so difficult to find in the U.S., it may be helpful to know that a list of the articles appeared in V. Kel'ner and D. Eliashevich, *Literatura o evreiakh na russkom iazyke, 1890–1947* (St. Petersburg: Akademicheskii proekt, 1995), 167, 439–40.

[14] From the choice of articles and contributors in the 1922 edition, one can conclude that volumes 1 and 3 centered on cultural issues and questions on Jewry generally, whereas volume 2 of *Sborniki safrut* focused narrowly on Zionism. It is significant that, in their bibliography, *Literatura o evreiakh*, Kel'ner and Elyashevich separate volume two of *Sborniki Safrut* from volumes 1 and 3, placing the former in the category of Zionist literature and the others in general Jewish literary collections.

zation of Jewish self-governance.[15] While they likely did not concur with Pyotr Struve's chauvinist statement of 1911 on the need for a "great Russia," they were skeptical about minority rights for all the nationalities.[16] I have found no evidence that these Russian intellectuals were enthusiastic at the prospect of mass emigration to Palestine. For many Russians, emigration was a national embarrassment.[17] The intellectual confluence in this Zionist-Russian alliance inevitably reveals vast areas of disagreement.

Nonetheless, there existed a distinct overlap in the use of political symbols and literary motifs by Zionists and Russians.[18] Among commonalities, one can identify the frustration of the Jewish and liberal Russian intelligentsia with the tsarist government. A few religious thinkers, among them, Vyacheslav Ivanov and Sergei Bulgakov, were enthusiastic about Zionism's utopian strivings and espied in them an omen of the cataclysmic transformation of the world they believed was just around the corner.

After the February Revolution, the Zionists were by far the most popular political party among Jews in Russia. In local elections across the Pale of Settlement, the results showed that a combination of the general Zionists, worker Zionists, and Mizrachi (religious Zionists) had a full majority and sometimes won up to 75 percent of the electors. Moreover, in the months following the Balfour Declaration Zionists were hugely optimistic and enthusiastic about the possibilities both within Russia and in Palestine. But the light dimmed almost as quickly as it had come on.[19]

Jaffe later wrote about this period, saying:

---

[15] For more on Gorky's attitude toward Zionism, see M. Gor'kii, *Iz literaturnogo naslediia: Gor'kii i evreiskii vopros*, comp. and ed. M. Agurskii and M. Shklovskaia (Jerusalem: Hebrew University, 1986), 13–26.

[16] Pipes, *Struve*, 88–89; Susan Heuman, *Kistiakovsky: The Struggle for National and Constitutional Rights in the Last Years of Tsarism* (Cambridge: Harvard Ukrainian Research Institute, 1998), 34–35.

[17] A summary of the attitudes of the Russian intelligentsia to Zionism and emigration can be found in an article by G. I. Gordon, "Sionizm i khristiane," *Russkaia mysl'*, no. 7 (1902): 178–96.

[18] This claim makes sense when you consider Eli Lederhendler's argument that Zionism used the images and rhetoric of messianism, but members who were entirely secular led the movement and their ideology was predominantly secular state-building. See Eli Lederhendler, "Interpreting Messianic Rhetoric in the Russian Haskalah and Early Zionism, the Semantic Conundrum: When is Messianism not Messianism?" *Studies in Contemporary Jewry* 7 (1991): 14–24.

[19] Shmuel Eizenshtadt, "Le-toldot ha-tsiburyot ve ha-tarbut ha-ivrit be-rusiyah," *He-avar*, no. 15 (May 1968): 134–35.

The days of the Bolshevik putsch had arrived. Turbulent events shook Moscow; demonstrations did not stop; demobilized soldiers and deserters wandered in crowds along the city's streets and squares. Theft and robbery increased; alcohol was dragged out of cellars and people got drunk; people stood on the streets the whole day and argued until late at night, cursing each other, supporters of Kerensky with the Bolsheviks, the Bolsheviks with the anarchists and so on.[20]

In the same memoir, Jaffe tells about food shortages, the lack of heating fuel, and rapid inflation that destroyed people's entire savings. The ration cards given to Muscovites, he writes, hardly provided enough food to keep from starving.[21]

Cooperation between the Russian and Jewish intelligentsia was symbolized in the personal relationship of Leib Jaffe and Vladislav Khodasevich, the two editors of *Evreiskaia antologiia*. They met nearly every day from mid-1916 to the end of 1917, working long hours at Khodasevich's small and dilapidated basement apartment. In his memoir Jaffe describes how he became close to Khodasevich and shared all his thoughts with him. "Khodasevich listened," Jaffe writes, "understanding and sympathizing." Sometimes, Khodasevich said that he was envious, since his world, the world of Russian culture, was "heading towards its twilight."[22] Their personal affinity also found a creative outlet in translation.[23] Jaffe was enthusiastic about Khodasevich's renditions, writing, "Khodasevich penetrated the secrets of Jewish poetry with his entire being and soon made himself a resident in it.... He especially liked to translate Tchernichowsky's idylls. He was especially able to transmit their special spirit and ebullient feeling."[24]

According to Jaffe, the reason for organizing *Sborniki Safrut* was to bring quality writing about Jews to a market that was eager for serious Jewish liter-

---

[20] Quoted in Zoia Kopel'man, "Istoriia etoi knigi," in Vladislav Khodasevich, *Iz evreiskikh poetov* (St. Petersburg: Z. I. Grzhebin, 1923; repr., Moscow and Jerusalem: Gesharim, 1998), 17–18; the source for the original text is not given in this publication.

[21] Leib (Lev) Jaffe, *Ketavim, igrot, ve-yomanim* (Jerusalem: Ha-Sifriyah ha-Tsiyonit, 1964), 48–53; see also Kopel'man, "Istoriia etoi knigi," 17–18.

[22] Kopel'man, "Istoriia etoi knigi," 17.

[23] In his introduction to *Iz evreiskikh poetov*, Khodasevich writes, "I must say that the transpositions here made available were done not from originals, but from literal translations that were completed primarily by L. B. Jaffe, to whom, above all, I am indebted for many instructions and clarifications. It goes without saying that the accuracy of the translations was my constant worry. Nevertheless, translating from a word-for-word translation, I always used a Latin transcription of the Jewish text. In that way the phonic particulars of the original, such as the meter, structure of the lines, the rhythmic character, number of lines, and so on, were preserved" (99).

[24] Jaffe, *Ketavim*, 52.

ature, but was deprived because of difficult conditions. In his introduction to the first volume of *Sborniki Safrut*, Jaffe explains: "During the war years Jewish literature nearly disappeared completely. Newspapers and pamphlets replaced Jewish literature in the Russian language, literature that had been designed for readers unable to access Hebrew.... [*Sborniki*] *Safrut* is a modest attempt in part to fill this lacuna, which has become especially palpable lately and [is needed] until the time when the creation of a Jewish monthly in Russian will again be possible."[25]

Because of the sudden impoverishment of individuals and extreme increase in the price of paper caused by the revolutionary upheavals, the financing of publishing drastically changed. It has to be said that some Russian authors may have chosen to publish in *Evreiskaia antologiia* or *Sborniki Safrut* more out of desperation rather than conviction; these publications were among the few that paid honoraria at this time. Whereas in the past the price of paper had been constant and publishers could pay for expenses with capital or advance subscriptions, now all the costs had to be paid on the spot. Thus, only political parties, which had the resources of membership dues or personal donations, could afford to subsidize literary activities.[26] Several philanthropists, such as Abraham Stybel (Stybel Publishing) and Shushana Persitz (Omanut Publishing), helped the Zionists in their literary endeavors. We can get a sense of the problems facing publishers from a remark in a personal letter of September 3, 1917 from Jaffe to Gershenzon: "It is unbelievably difficult to publish books now, but we decided to go ahead. We found two printers, bought a wagon full of paper. We're in a rush because the longer we wait the more difficult it will be."[27]

There can really be no doubt about the Zionist content of the special Bialik issue of *Evreiskaia zhizn'*. Although every author used the opportunity to celebrate Bialik's talent, and acknowledge his vital role in the fight for Jewish dignity, they all noted his Zionist vision for the future. Inevitably the extensive commentary about the poet's angry voice in "Be-ir ha-haregah" (In the City of Slaughter; 1904) turned to the promise of a better world in Palestine. Sobol, for example, wrote:

> And the deeper the people's sleep, the more painful its awakening from a half-dead slumber, the more intense the poet's grief, the sharper his pain.... And then the poet is alone. But in his loneliness,

---

[25] L. Jaffe, "S.n.," *Sborniki Safrut*, no. 1 (1918): 3.

[26] See "Russia," *Encyclopedia Judaica*, ed. Cecil Roth, 16 vols. (New York: Macmillan, 1972), 14: 457.

[27] L. Jaffe to M. Gershenzon, 3 September 1917, in "Pis'ma L. Jaffa k M. Gershenzonu," ed. B. Horowitz, *Vestnik Evreiskogo universiteta v Moskve*, no. 2 (18) (1998): 218.

on the high mountain of his solitude, he sees the future more clearly, knows the future, and sets landmark after landmark for those who are below, landmarks of a new path.[28]

The works in *Evreiskaia antologiia* emphasized the cosmopolitan aspect of modern Hebrew poetry. For example, Jaffe purposely excluded Bialik's "Be-ir ha-haregah" and other works related to the sufferings of the Jewish people. For the most part, Jaffe featured poems that were exclusively non-didactic, with the "I" of the narrator in the poems standing not for the Jewish people or an abstract idea, but merely for the individual poet.[29] Among the common themes of the poems, one can name death, loss, the indifference of nature, love, youthful energy, and the joy of writing.

A characteristic poem is Bialik's "Holekhet at me'imi" (You Are Leaving Me), which depicts a man's calm resignation to the loss of love and his joy in the perception of nature. The poem, translated by Baltrushaitis, begins this way:

> You are leaving me, go then in peace...
> Let you have freedom on your way,
> And peace, wherever you may breathe.
> And me? My orphan emptiness will pass.
> And for me divine stars are brilliantly lit.
> My riches have not been fully expended,
> And the key to my happiness is not diminished...
> True, you've been taken from me, but for me
> The enormous world is now in the green of spring
> Now in gold, now in winter's white raiment...[30]

Bialik continues to describe a wonderful world full of nature's beauty in which the narrator describes his quiet joy, which allows him in the end to overcome his loss.

The universal themes in the volume amazed the critic Mikhail Gershenzon, a fully assimilated Jew who had devoted his entire life to the study of Russia's intellectual legacy, such as the Slavophiles, the Decembrists, and Aleksandr Pushkin. Ecstatic that Jewish poets could refrain from treating specifically Jewish problems, Gershenzon remarked how dissimilar this was from earlier Jewish writing, which tended to deal with sadness, oppression,

---

[28] A. Sobol', "Bialik," *Evreiskaia zhizn'*, no. 14–15 (1916): 28.

[29] It is interesting to note that Rina Lapidus describes a similar egoism among Hebrew poets. See Rina Lapidus, *Between Snow and Desert Heat: Russian Influences on Hebrew Literature, 1870–1970* (Cincinnati: Hebrew Union College Press, 2003), especially her chapter on Saul Tchernichowsky, 155–72.

[30] This is my translation from the Russian edition. Kh. Bialik, "Ty ot menia ukhodish'," in Khodasevich and Jaffe, *Evreiskaia antologiia*, 64–65.

and poverty. In his introduction Gershenzon wrote, "These young poets love, and just as the youth of all countries, they freely and loudly sing their love; the life of nature is open to them and they depict it with love. They reflect about life, humanity and God, the obsessive thought of Jewish worry does not persecute them."[31] They were free from worry, and that represented a great achievement, since the main obstacle to happiness for the Jew had always been anxiety and isolation from the rest of humanity.[32] Despite seeming to give credence to Gershenzon's attempt to de-nationalize Hebrew poetry, Jaffe resisted.[33] In his own introduction he tried to draw the reader's attention to the volume's Zionist perspective, claiming that the hero of *Evreiskaia antologiia* was the Hebrew language, which was undergoing a renaissance. Maintaining that Hebrew had never ceased to develop, Jaffe recalled that Hebrew had accompanied the Jewish people through its entire history, the destruction of political independence, experience of exile, and even its own demise as a mother tongue. The proof of its evolution, Jaffe exclaimed, was the poetry before us, the fact that Hebrew "has arrived in our day alive, mature, a ready vessel for the transmission of modern concepts and ideas." Furthermore, Jaffe recalled that in Palestine Hebrew "was being revived not only as a literary language, but also as a mother-tongue."[34]

Jaffe expressed a different position altogether from Gershenzon regarding the source of Jewish creativity. Inspiration did not originate from the liberation from Jewish life, but rather emerged from a deepening and transformation of it. The Jewish artist found his strength by embracing the Jewish national movement and identifying himself fully as a Jew. This identification paradoxically did not cut him off from European movements, but actually bound him more tightly with them. Jaffe explains:

> Under the influence of the Jewish national revival, under the influence of contact with the historical homeland of the people and the new life created there, under the influence of the enrichment of Jewish national life by means of the best elements of Western culture, Jewish poetry has become filled with a new content up to now unknown, has blossomed with new colors. In [Jewish poetry], just as

---

[31] M. Gershenzon, "Predislovie," in Khodasevich and Jaffe, *Evreiskaia antologiia*, vi.

[32] By identifying nature as the source for poets' spontaneities, Gershenzon was criticizing the Jewish experience, since, at least in Russia, Jews were primarily an urban people and a religious and national minority. It was their economic and political insecurity that produced the anxiety-ridden Jew.

[33] In his introduction to *Evreiskaia antologiia* Jaffe even writes, "The song rings out in line with the superlative, incomparable grief and higher religious ecstasy, a song common to all times and peoples, a song of grief and happiness of concrete life, about love, female beauty, nature. In this poetry universal motifs sing out with national ones" (11).

[34] V. Khodasevich and L. Jaffe, "Ot redaktsii," in *Evreiskaia antologiia*, ix–x.

poetry throughout the world, we find a reflection of problems that agitate the modern person. But one hears in this poetry clearer than anything else the delicate and complex experiences of the soul of a new Jew who is searching for liberation from a division of self, from the spiritual shackles of [living in] a foreign country, striving for wholeness and unity.[35]

If there was any ambiguity about the Zionist message in *Evreiskaia antologiia*, it became less in *Sborniki Safrut*, where Jaffe overtly declared his desire to bring awareness to Zionism. In his introduction to the first volume Jaffe wrote that *Safrut* would be "dedicated to a discussion and penetration of the fundamental problems of Jewish national thought, a clarification of questions of Jewish public life and the Zionist movement, and also an acquaintance with Jewish literature and art."[36] While Zionism is only one of the three subjects listed, Jaffe attempted to link the official Zionist program with the broader spheres of Jewish artistic creativity.

Jaffe's belief that culture should play a central role in the Zionist program reflected more than mere political goals. It characterized a whole generation of Zionists who were brought up on the ideas of Ahad Ha'am and his "cultural Zionism." Such individuals were engaged in intellectual self-perfection, were highly educated, well traveled, conversant in European languages, and sophisticated in cultural matters.[37] Yet they departed from the model of their mentor because they advanced political work to expand the physical presence of Jews in the Yishuv.[38] The careers of the writer-activists Jabotinsky and Pasmanik reflect such a synthesis.[39]

Jaffe himself was born in Grodno in 1875.[40] He studied philosophy in Heidelberg and later in Leipzig and Freiburg, and started writing verses in

---

[35] Ibid., xii.

[36] L. Jaffe, "Predislovie," *Sborniki Safrut*, no. 1 (Moscow: Safrut, 1918): 1.

[37] See Steven J. Zipperstein, *Elusive Prophet: Ahad Ha'am and the Origins of Zionism* (Berkeley: University of California Press, 1993), 147. For a lucid discussion of culture among this generation of Zionists, see ibid., 151–52.

[38] Yishuv: Jewish settlement in Palestine from 1880 to the independent Israel.

[39] For a discussion of Jabotinsky's contributions to literature, see Michael Stanislawski, *Zionism and the Fin de Siècle: Cosmopolitanism and Nationalism from Nordau to Jabotinsky* (Berkeley: University of California Press, 2001), 116–230. On A. Idelson, see Iu. Brutskus et al., eds., *Sbornik pamiati A. D. Idel'son* (Berlin, 1925).

[40] I received the bulk of my information for this portrait from L. Jaffe, *Ketavim*; and L. Jaffe and B. Jaffe, *Be-shlikhut am: Mikhtavim u-teudot le-Leib Yaffe le-yom huladeto ha-shivim, 1892–1948* (Jerusalem: ha-Sifriyah ha-Siyonit, 1968. I also used an unpublished letter from L. Jaffe to Iu. Gessen, Archive of Israel Tsinberg, Archive of the Institute for

his youth, publishing three collections of poetry in Russian.[41] Although one ungenerous critic wrote that Jaffe never missed "an opportunity in verse and prose to propagandize the Zionist solution to the Jewish question," in Jewish circles Jaffe's poetry was well regarded.[42]

In politics, Jaffe early on aligned himself squarely with the cultural Zionists. In 1900, he became an organizer of the Council of Zionist Theoretical Circles. He participated in the so-called Heidelberg Commission that formulated the program of the Democratic Fraction, and at the Fifth Congress of 1901 he defied Herzl, walking out with the Fraction's 36 other members. The group returned only after the Congress accepted most of their demands, such as the creation of modern Jewish schools in Hebrew and increased funding for publishing activities and public lectures.[43] As did the other members of the Democratic Fraction, Jaffe also opposed the so-called Uganda solution in 1903.

Later Jaffe grew closer to political Zionism. He sought and attained high positions in official Zionist institutions. For example, after being elected to the executive committee at the Helsingfors Congress of Russian Zionists in 1906, Jaffe was admitted to the Central Committee of the World Zionist Organization.

For the rest of his life he remained connected to the Zionist movement. In 1916, he moved to Moscow to edit the Zionist weekly *Evreiskaia zhizn'*, and in 1918, he moved to Vilna, where he barely survived a pogrom perpetrated by the Polish army in 1919. In 1920, he made *aliyah* to Palestine, where he was employed in various positions in the World Zionist Organization.[44] His life ended in tragedy in 1948, when he was killed by a terrorist's bomb in the courtyard of the World Zionist Organization in Jerusalem.

---

Eastern Studies, St. Petersburg, f. 86, op. 3, d. 147. For more information on Jaffe, see Benjamin Jaffe and Mordekhai Levin, *Leyb Yafeh: Bibliyografyah* (Jerusalem, 1977).

[41] Leib Jaffe, *Griadushchee: Stikhotvoreniia* (Grodno: Tip. S. Lapina, 1902); Jaffe, *Gorod Lovchen* (Moscow: I. V. Velikovskii, 1916); Jaffe, *Ogni na vysotakh: Stikhi* (Riga: Izd-vo Evreiskogo obshchestva sodeistviia iskusstvu i natsii v Latvii, 1938).

[42] M. Vishniak, *Dan' proshlomu* (New York: Izd-vo im. Chekhova, 1954), quoted in R. Timenchik, "Russko-evreiskaia literatura," *Kratkaia evreiskaia entsiklopediia*, 10 vols. (Jerusalem: Obshchestvo po issledovaniiu evreiskikh obshchin, Hebrew University, 1996), 7: 539.

[43] For more on the cultural controversy, see Shmuel Almog, *Zionism and History: The Rise of a New Jewish Consciousness*, trans. Ina Friedman (New York: St. Martin's Press, 1987), 84–100; David Vital, *Zionism: The Formative Years* (New York: Oxford University Press, 1982), 190–98; Izhak Maor, *Sionistskoe dvizhenie v Rossii*, trans. from Hebrew by O. Mints (Jerusalem: Safrit-Alia, 1977), 108–17.

[44] Jaffe was in the United States fundraising in 1943. Once he learned about the slaughter of European Jewry, he tried unsuccessfully to convince American Jewry to make a more serious and active response. See R. Medoff, "Our Leaders Cannot Be Moved": A Zionist Emissary's Reports on American Jewish Responses to the Holocaust in the Summer of 1943," *American Jewish History* 88: 1 (2000): 115–26.

Jaffe's emphasis on culture can be explained in large part by the realities of political oppression in tsarist Russia, which forced Zionists, like Russian opponents of the tsarist regime generally, to employ the tool of culture, while narrowly defined political work continued underground.[45] Culture, in the form of literary societies, book and newspaper publications, and the organization of schools, embodied the strategy of *Gegenwartsarbeit*—a concern with the welfare of Diaspora Jewry and the legal means, including parliamentary struggle, to win the ideological war among Jews in tsarist Russia.

To understand why such a large group of Russian writers forged a temporary alliance with Zionism, we have to reexamine the attitudes of the Russian intelligentsia to both Russia's Jews and Zionism. Certainly a part of the Russian intelligentsia disseminated antisemitic ideas. In addition to the conservative intelligentsia that contributed to the semiofficial newspaper *Novoe vremia*, there were members of the artistic elite who were convinced that Russia had a mystical purpose which precluded a Jewish presence. While Vasily Rozanov was at times a genuine antisemite, others, such as Andrei Bely and Kornei Chukovsky, expressed antisemitic views at one time in their careers, notably Bely's "Shtempelovennaia kul'tura" (Culture with a Label; 1909) and Chukovsky's "Evrei i russkaia kul'tura" (Jews and Russian Culture; 1908).[46]

During this period, however, another part of the intelligentsia was notably philo-Semitic. This group was made up of politically progressive writers such as Gorky, Korolenko, and Leonid Andreev. Gorky and Korolenko opened their journals, *Znanie* and *Russkoe bogatstvo*, respectively, to Jewish writers and were instrumental in cultivating a serious Jewish literature in the Russian language. Among intellectuals sympathetic to Jews one can also point to Russia's leading modernist writers, especially among the so-called "Older Symbolists," who united artistic experimentation with commitment to political justice.

As discussed above, Russian collaboration in Jewish publishing enterprises was by no means unique, beginning in the mid-19th century. However, cooperative efforts intensified in the 1890s, when Vladimir Solovyov, the

---

[45] Minister of the Interior Vyacheslav von Pleve outlawed the Zionist party in 1902, which forced it underground. It was given legal status again after 1905 but was made illegal after 1907. It was legalized only when, in 1917, the Provisional Government reversed the tsarist government's earlier banning of unfriendly political parties.

[46] See M. Bezrodnyi, "O 'iudoboiani' Andreia Belogo," *Novoe literaturnoe obozrenie* 28 (1997): 100–25; I. Andreeva, "Istoriia odnoi nevstrechi, rasskazannaia v retsenziiakh i pis'makh M. O. Gershenzon i K. I. Chukovskogo," *Literaturnoe obozrenie*, no. 11–12 (1992): 63–72; B. Horowitz, "Jewish Identity and Russian Culture: The Case of M. O. Gershenzon," *Nationalities Papers* 25: 4 (1997): 699–713. For more on antisemitism in the Russian intelligentsia, see again Kel'ner, "Dva intsidenta," 190–99.

noted Russian philosopher, collaborated with the Jewish scholar Faivel Gets. Their collaboration culminated in the 1891 publication of Gets's book *Slovo podsudimomu* (A Word to the Condemned), which included a defense of the Jews and featured letters from Lev Tolstoy, Boris Chicherin, Solovyov, and Korolenko.[47] Later in 1901, the volume *Pomoshch' evreiam, postradavshim ot neurozhaia* (Aid to Jews Who Have Suffered from Famine) appeared. Gorky, Korolenko, and Solovyov published works in it, and all the proceeds from sales were sent to Jewish famine victims in Ukraine.[48]

These cooperative efforts, however, were only the start of a growing trend that included many tangible achievements. For example, the Jewish weekly *Voskhod* was the home for several important non-Jewish writers, such as Eliza Orzeszkowa and Nikolai Gradovsky, while Vladimir Stasov and Baron David Guenzburg together completed *Evreiskii ornamentalizm* (*Ornementation des anciens manuscrits hébreaux*) in 1902.[49] In 1907, Count Ivan Tolstoy and the Jewish historian Yuly Gessen published a volume on the Jewish question, *Fakty i mysli* (Facts and Thoughts).[50]

It is clear that during this time Russian intellectuals were becoming more interested in Jewish culture and devoting some of their intellectual energies to an investigation of it. Vladimir Stasov in particular played a key role in attracting Jews and Russians to Jewish culture. A promoter of talent, Stasov urged Jewish musicians, such as Anton Rubinstein, and sculptors, such as Mark Antokolsky and Ilya Gintzburg, to use Jewish folk imagery in their work, just as Ilya Repin had done with the Russian folk.[51] In his 1872 article on the architecture of the main synagogue in St. Petersburg, Stasov encouraged the cultural interpenetration of East and West, Sephardic and Ashkenazi, Jewish and Russian, announcing that Jews were artistically productive not only in historically remote epochs but in the present as well.[52]

In terms of contributions by Russians in defense of Jews during World War I, the publication of *Shchit* (Shield) in 1915 was an event of major impor-

---

[47] F. G. [F. B. Gets], *Slovo podsudimomu: S pis'mami L. N. Tolstogo, B. N. Chicherina, V. S. Solov'eva, V. G. Korolenko* (St. Petersburg: Novosti, 1891).

[48] *Pomoshch' evreiam, postradavshim ot neurozhaia: Literaturno-khudozhestvennyi sbornik* (St. Petersburg: Tip. I. Gol'dberga, 1901).

[49] Vladimir Stasov and Baron David Guenzburg, *Ornementation des anciens manuscrits hébreaux* (Berlin: S. Calvary and Co., 1905).

[50] I. Tolstoi and Iu. Gessen, *Fakty i mysli: Evreiskii vopros v Rossii* (St. Petersburg: Obshchestvennaia pol'za, 1907).

[51] V. Stasov, ed., *M. M. Antokol'skii: Ego zhizn', tvoreniia, pis'ma, i stat'i* (St. Petersburg, 1905).

[52] V. Stasov, "Po povodu postroiki sinagogi v S.-Peterburge," *Evreiskaiai biblioteka*, no. 2 (1872): 453–73. More work needs to be done on Stasov's contribution to Jewish culture.

tance.[53] In *Shchit*, a faction of the Russian intelligentsia expressed its solidarity with the Jews, many of whom were persecuted by the Russian army during the war. The message was apparently timely, and public demand for the volume warranted a second and then a third edition. Leonid Andreev, one of the editors, expressed the views of all the participants in the introduction, where he lashed out at antisemitism.

> Who needs [antisemitism]? Whom is it good for? After all, if it exists, is supported, passionately and ceaselessly promoted by someone, then there must be a definite purpose. Clearly the Pale of Settlement, the quota on access for Jews to education, and the rest [of the liabilities] increase the sum of happiness for humanity, raise life up high, expand the limits of human potential. [But in truth] … no one needs it, it is not good for anyone; it not only does not increase the sum of happiness in the world, but causes many entirely unnecessary, senseless sufferings, tears and blood; it represses some and horribly corrupts others.[54]

*Shchit* showed that at least one part of the intelligentsia was prepared to stand up to the government in protest. The volume was particularly significant in this regard because in 1915 many public figures were insisting on a halt to criticism of the government as a means of aiding the war effort. Furthermore, it is a wonder that the volume appeared at all, since the government was strict about freedom of information and doubly so in connection with the Jews.[55]

It must be said, however, that, besides eliciting sympathy for the Jewish victim, the volume did little to show off the importance of Jewish culture. There were stories and poems by Gorky, Bunin, Sologub, Konstantin Balmont, Bryusov, and Korolenko, and even a posthumous letter by Lev Tolstoy, but there were no articles by Jews themselves. This may be explained by the custom practiced in Western Europe that philosemitic organizations not include Jewish participation so as not to give the impression that the contributors were merely following orders from Jewish masters. In fact, efforts by some in the Russian intelligentsia to battle antisemitism took institutional

---

[53] L. Andreev, M. Gor'kii, and F. Sologub, eds., *Shchit: Literaturnyi sbornik* (Moscow: T-vo tip. A. I. Mamontova 1915).

[54] L. Andreev, "Pervaia stupen'," in Andreev et al., *Shchit*, 5.

[55] The 1915 decree prohibiting the publication of material written with Hebrew letters had the result of denying news to over a million people who read only Yiddish or Hebrew. Moreover, it confirmed the growing suspicions of the Jews themselves that, although their sons were fighting and dying for Russia, the Russian government looked upon them as a potential fifth column. The decree was implemented on July 5, 1915. For more on this, see "Evreiskaia pechat'," *Novyi put'*, 26 February 1915, pp. 4–5.

form in the Russian Society for the Study of Jewish Life.[56] Apparently, no Jews were invited to join. Formed in 1915, it lasted until 1918 and counted among its members Andreev, Ivan Tolstoy, A. Kartashev, and D. Ovsianiko-Kulikovsky.[57]

Despite the participation of Solomon Pozner, a Jew who served as one of the editors of *Shchit*, the volume was not an example of Russian-Jewish cooperation. The absence of Jewish contributions necessitated a different project. Apparently Gorky had in mind such a collaborative effort, when in a private letter to Bryusov in 1915, he suggested that Bryusov organize a series of volumes that would include the story of Esther, the life of Moses, Isaiah the Prophet, and Jeremiah.[58] Gorky expressed the view that ordinary Russians would feel greater sympathy for Jews if they were familiar with Jewish culture.[59] Known for his appreciation of Jewish culture and even Zionism, Gorky especially lauded Jewish self-defense after the Kishinev Pogrom in 1903. Although Bryusov declined, Jaffe took up the idea, publishing *U rek Vavilonskikh* (By the Rivers of Babylon), a volume of translations into Russian of biblical and medieval Hebrew poetry in 1918.[60] Perhaps not entirely surprising, considering the extensive appropriation of the Old Testament in Russian culture, many of the translations used by Jaffe were by Russian poets from the first half of the 19th century.[61]

The defense of Russia's Jews was only one reason why Russian intellectuals signed on to a Zionist project. Christian messianism also drew some Russians closer to Zionism. In *Shchit* Ivanov and Bulgakov expressed the need to celebrate the return of the Jews to Zion. Bulgakov, a religious thinker who became a Russian Orthodox theologian in 1917, wrote:

> There are holy symbols and monumental ideas that force the most sacred strings of the heart to vibrate. For example, Christian Constantinople, the cross at Saint Sophia, or the liberation of the Lord's coffin from the hands of the heathens, possess this significance. The question of Palestine and the realization of great universal promises must have similar significance for both the Jewish and Christian heart (I

---

[56] For more on the society, see Gor'kii, *Iz literaturnogo naslediia*, 16.

[57] Ibid., 240.

[58] M. Gor'kii to V. Ia. Briusov, 23 February 1917, in Gor'kii, *Iz literaturnogo naslediia*, 255–56.

[59] Although there is a large literature on Gorky and the Jews, one can begin with M. Agurskii and M. Shklovskaia, "Sovremennye mysli," in Gor'kii, *Iz literaturnogo naslediia*, 5–26.

[60] L. Jaffe, ed., *U rek Vavilonskikh: Natsional'no-evreiskaia lirika v mirovoi poezii* (Moscow: Safrut, 1917).

[61] Jaffe used translations by 19th-century Russian writers such as A. Maikov, A. Pleshcheev, and P. Kozlov

underline the word *both* three times), [at a time] when the sacred roots of history are laid bare and the idea has caught fire again, and the question emerges as contemporary, close at hand and capable of resolution, if not today, then tomorrow.[62]

For his part, the poet Ivanov confirmed the view that Christians have to support the messianic yearnings of the Jews. He arrived at that conclusion by asserting that the body of Christ was divided, and once the parts were reunited, a Golden Age would reign. According to Ivanov, the body of Christ refers also to the Jews, who in their struggles for Zion also realize the mission of Christianity:

> The body of the Church for a mystic is the true one, although it is also the invisible body of Christ, and through Christ, it is the body of the tribe of Abraham. This latter body, similar to the curtain in the Jerusalem Temple, was ripped in two at the hour of the death by crucifixion. And that half which is Judaism frantically searches for unity, is weary and envies, and bitterly enraged at the other half, which for its part yearns for the unification and completeness of the mystical Israel.[63]

Maintaining that a true Christian should not only sympathize with the Jews, but must identify himself as one of them, Ivanov pleaded for the fulfillment of the Jewish prophecy as a means to complete the Christian mission.[64] Following in Vladimir Solov'ev's footsteps, Ivanov and Bulgakov promulgated Solov'ev's hope for the unification of Christianity and Judaism through the Jews' voluntary conversion.[65]

The prophetic image of Judaism provided only one point of attraction for Russian Symbolists. Just as important were what one might call "surface parallels." As did Russian Symbolists, Zionists yearned for monumental changes that would transform life and usher in a new state of politics. In a private letter to Gershenzon from July 1915, Sergei Bulgakov exclaimed,

---

[62] S. Bulgakov, "Sion," in Andreev et al., *Shchit*, 42.

[63] V. Ivanov, "K ideologii evreiskogo voprosa," in Andreev et al., *Shchit*, 85.

[64] Compare this discussion in 1915 with a later one in emigration in which Ivanov writes, "As a Christian I thought a lot about the fate of Judaism and believe that it is necessary for the Jews to be scattered throughout the entire world, but it is also necessary that at the end of time they move to Palestine. Only Zionism can become a religious movement. And your language should be Hebrew.... I worked on Bialik and I wanted the entire energy of the nation to go into the Hebrew language." From M. S. Al'tman et al., *Razgovory s Viacheslavom Ivanovym* (Moscow: INApress, 1995), 52, quoted in Khodasevich, *Iz evreiskikh poetov*, 79.

[65] V. Solov'ev, "O narodnosti i narodnykh delakh Rossii," in *Sobranie Sochinenii*, ed. E. Radlov and S. Solov'ev, 6 vols. (Brussels: Foyer Oriental Chrétien, 1965), 3: 28.

I am horrified to recall what Europe was like (and Russia too) before the war, how we could reconcile ourselves to it, how Europe could endure its own self! The image of Europe on the edge of war, it is true, remains for me more terrible than the image of war, which has ripped off all the facades and conventions. Therefore, in the very end, as you can see, I bless the ways of Providence and give unto him "myself, each other and our life."[66]

Such derision for bourgeois Europe blended easily with Zionist discontent. In "V chas resheniia" (In the Moment of Decision; 1917) Jaffe wrote: "Whatever the resolution of the war, which is obviously approaching its end, one thing is indisputable: humanity cannot return to the old order [to answer] any of the questions that the war has raised and thrown up on to the surface of life."[67] Just as did Zionists, Russian Symbolists felt the promise of utopia. But for them it was not a political utopia that was imagined, but rather the transformation of the material world into a new life of the spirit. Incidentally, many of Russia's intellectuals interpreted the Bolshevik Revolution of October 1917 not as a political takeover by the proletariat, but as the realization of a spiritual advance in the history of humanity.[68]

On their side, Zionists, especially of Jaffe's stripe and at this early time, were not as much believers in messianism as followers of a positivistic philosophy of the nation-state. Probably influenced by such thinkers as Gottfried Herder, Arthur de Gobineau, and others, Leo Pinsker and Theodore Herzl believed that nations were characterized by several qualities—language, religion, ethnicity, culture, and land. The Jews were unique and their situation particularly unfortunate because they lacked land. But Palestine could provide the land where Jews could be "regularized" and made a nation like every other.

Certainly, Zionist theorists like Ahad Ha'am felt vague sensations of mysticism and messianic longing, but they were skeptical of Bolshevism and its violence, on the one hand, and uncomfortable with religious authority, on the other.[69] In Russian Symbolism they felt closer to Nietzschean understandings

---

[66] S. Bulgakov to M. Gershenzon, 8 July 1915, in S. Bulgakov, "V ozhidanii Palestiny: 17 pisem S. N. Bulgakova k M. O. Gershenzonu i ego zhene, 1897–1925 gg.," in *Neizvestnaia Rossiia*, ed. V. A. Kozlov, 3 vols. (Moscow: Istoricheskoe nasledie, 1992), 2: 134.

[67] L. Jaffe, "V chas resheniia," in *Voina i evreiskaia problema* (Moscow: Izd-vo Moskovskogo komiteta Sion Narodnoi Fraktsii 'Tseire-Tsion, 1917), 47.

[68] For descriptions of the October Revolution as an emblem of a higher spiritual transformation, see V. Ivanov and M. Gershenzon, *Perepiska iz dvukh uglov* (St. Petersburg: Alkonost, 1921), esp. 44–46.

[69] Regarding Bialik's bostility toward the Bolsheviks and revolution, see Hamutal Bar-Yosef, "Bialik and the Russian Revolutions," *Jews in Eastern Europe* 1: 29 (Spring 1996): 25–28.

of individual self-perfection than the Christological ideas of world spiritual transfiguration.[70]

Zionism had its supporters, but it also had its Russian and Jewish detractors. A well-known 1902 article by Iosif Bikerman in the leading Populist journal, *Russkoe bogatstvo*, mocked the entire Zionist enterprise.[71] In his study Josse Goldstein describes the absolute hostility of the whole Russian intelligentsia to Zionism before 1905.[72]

At the same time, Zionism inspired acculturated Jews to reexamine their Jewish roots.[73] Intellectuals of Jewish origin such as Lev Shestov, Nikolai Minsky, and Akim Volynsky, who had earlier suppressed their Jewish identities, recognized the importance of Judaism in their backgrounds. In their youth, in the 1880s, a dual identity had not seemed possible; they had been forced to choose between Russian and Jewish culture. It was aggravation over that painful decision which motivated Simon Dubnov to refuse to be listed in a dictionary of Russian writers, despite his admittance that, by all definitions, he belonged there.[74]

Clearly Zionism's celebration of Jewish pride galvanized the identity of some Jewish members of the Russian intellectual elite. The critic Arkady Gornfeld, for example, admired the rise in self-esteem that Zionism had brought to Russia's Jews.[75] Mark Aldanov was also proud of his Jewish identity, while Khodasevich, a non-Jew, became deeply involved in translations of Hebrew poetry perhaps out of reasons of guilt—he regretted his grandfather Jacob Brafman's actions—but also perhaps because he felt a certain connection with his Jewish roots.[76] Even Mikhail Gershenzon became inspired.

---

[70] Bar-Yosef, "Vliianie russkoi literatury," 132–33.

[71] I. Bikerman, "O sionizme i po povodu sionizma," *Russkoe bogatstvo* 7 (1902): 27–69.

[72] Y. Goldstein, "Ha-tenuah ha-tsiyonit be-rusyah, 1904–1987" (Ph.D. diss., Hebrew University, 1982), 120–55.

[73] On Shestov and Judaism, see B. Horowitz, "The Tension of Athens and Jerusalem in the Philosophy of Lev Shestov," *Slavic and East European Journal* 43: 1 (Spring 1999): 156–73; and chap. 13 in this volume (232–49). On Volynsky, see Elena Grekova, "Staryi entuziast," *Pamiati A. L. Volynskogo* (Leningrad: Izd-vo Vserossiiskogo soiuza pisatelei, 1928), 47–68. There needs to be more study on the question of Zionism's role as a primary stimulus for such a resurgence of Jewish identity in late tsarist and early Soviet Russia.

[74] Khodasevich, *Iz evreiskikh poetov*, 100.

[75] "Gornfel'd, Arkadii Geogievich," in *Kratkaia evreiskaia entsiklopediia*, 8 vols. (Jerusalem: Obshchestvo po issledovaniiu evreiskikh obshchin, 1982), 178.

[76] Mark Aldanov, "Russkie evrei v 70–80-kh godakh (istoricheskii etiud)," in Frumkin, Aronson, and Gol'denveizer, *Kniga o russkom evreistve*, 44–49. Jacob Brafman played a nefarious role in inciting anti-Jewish sentiment through his infamous book *Kniga kagala* (The Book of the Kahal, 1869), in which he claimed that Jews represented a world conspiracy bent on taking control over Russia and the entire world.

Despite being thoroughly integrated into Russian society, Gershenzon experienced a positive reevaluation of his Jewish roots during the war years. Despite the fact that he was an enemy of Zionism, Gershenzon began to study Jewish history and the Old Testament, studies that culminated in his 1921 book *Kliuch very* (The Key to Faith).[77] He was deeply impressed by the expression of Jewish national feeling and could not contain his excitement about what it might mean. In an article from 1916 he writes,

> There is song in the latest sadness, and inconsolable weeping is always sonorous. There is an acute vivaciousness at the bottom of grief. [This vivaciousness] has been sung in Bialik, who for the first time since Yehuda Halevi represents the spirit of the Jewish people. It is a foreign song, an angelic-earthy song! Does it not presage the resurrection of the Jewish soul? Or is it true that only the land of Palestine can provide Judaism with a new creative myth? I do not know, but I strongly believe that the people are alive in their lethargic sleep and at the decisive moment they will awaken.[78]

Russian collaboration in Jewish culture had definite and limited parameters. As *Shchit* and earlier volumes showed, illustrious Russians were accustomed to see this activity in terms of philanthropy. Help for the Jews expressed itself in special volumes, where, as members of a superior culture, intellectuals generously and somewhat patronizingly lent their voices for the sake of the oppressed. When Jews refused the help, scandals could ensue. Solomon Pozner's refusal to publish the Russian philosopher Nikolai Berdyaev's controversial article in *Shchit*, because it was insufficiently philosemitic, caused much bad blood between Sologub and Gorky. At the same time, Machshoves's criticism of Gorky's well-meaning Society for the Study of Jewish Life and his request that the Russian leave the Jews to take care of themselves brought offense to Gorky and discomfort to Jaffe, who suppressed the polemic by refusing to publish Machshoves's second polemical response.[79] These two incidents reflect the demands for ideological suitability or what today we call "political correctness" on both sides that was a part of the defense of the Jews by the Russian intelligentsia.

Although Jaffe's volumes were somewhat different because they were organized by a Jew, it is worth noting that Russian writers participated in those

---

[77] M. O. Gershenzon, *Kliuch very* (St. Petersburg: Epokha, 1922). For his statement on Zionism, see M. Gershenzon, *Sud'by evreiskogo naroda* (St. Petersburg: Epokha, 1922). For more on Gershenzon's reevaluation of his roots, see Brian Horowitz, "Unrequited Love for Russia," *Midstream*, no. 10 (October 1996): 37–40.

[78] M. O. Gershenzon, "Narod, ispytuemyi ognem," *Evreiskaia nedelia*, no. 1 (1916): 28.

[79] Baal Machshoves, "Listki," in Gor'kii, *Iz literaturnogo naslediia*, 230–32, 235–38.

activities where cosmopolitan culture was emphasized—such as in *Evreiskaia antologiia* and volumes 1 and 3 of *Sborniki Safrut*—dropping out when the central focus shifted to the Zionist political program, such as in the second volume of *Sborniki Safrut*.

Moreover, we may ask whether there was a genuine interpenetration of cultures in these volumes. Any claim would be difficult to prove, but one may cautiously answer that a true synthesis of cultures did take place. It is significant that the Russians not only provided translations from Hebrew originals, but that in *Sborniki Safrut* Bryusov and Bunin published original poetry using Jewish motifs.[80] Furthermore, many of the poems in *Evreiskaia antologiia* were more than mere transpositions from one language to another, but were literary creations in their own right. In this sense, one can view the Russian participation in *Evreiskaia antologiia* and *Sborniki Safrut* as a departure from some earlier patterns of Russian-Jewish collaboration in which little or no synthesis of cultures could be detected. Sadly, while Russian literature had a huge influence on modern Hebrew literature, one cannot say the same about the influence of Hebrew on Russian.[81]

Although *Evreiskaia antologiia* and *Sborniki Safrut* were short-lived, the collaboration of Jews and Russians reflects a moment when the paths of the Russian intelligentsia and Zionist intellectuals temporarily crisscrossed. The volumes also belong to an integral part of Russian-Jewish literature, which, although it began only in the first quarter of the 19th century, radically expanded at the end of the 19th and beginning of the 20th centuries. Moreover, sociologically speaking, this cooperative effort points to the comfortable interaction of non-Jews and Jews at the highest intellectual levels. Regarding Zionism in a Russian idiom, the volumes reveal that in its utopian aims Russian Zionism was not some kind of anomaly in the Russian intellectual context, but rather part of a general utopian fervor that beset Russian intellectual life broadly. Instead of the isolation of Jews from the artistic avant-garde, we find an alternative history that locates Jews cooperating with Russians in the most ideological utopian and culturally dynamic period of the 20th century.

---

[80] Bryusov contributed the poem "Bibliia" and Bunin published "Blagovestie o rozhdenii Isaaka," both of which appeared in the third volume of *Safrut* (Berlin, 1921).

[81] Hamutal Bar-Yosef has made this point in several places, most notably in "Reflections on Hebrew Literature in the Russian Context," *Prooftexts* 16: 2 (1996): 127–49.

# Chapter 5

# Hail to Assimilation: Vladimir "Ze'ev" Jabotinsky's Ambivalence about Fin-de-Siècle Odessa

Vladimir Jabotinsky's novel *Piatero* (The Five; 1936) has bewildered the author's biographers. And rightly so: no matter how much one tries to read the novel through Zionist lenses it does not work. Shmuel Katz's 1,800-page political biography has only one reference to the novel, and it does not even appear in Katz's index.[1] The many encyclopedia articles on Jabotinsky give intentionally short shrift to a work that, published only four years before his death, seems at odds with the personality of its author. Jabotinsky's name has become associated with militancy and militarism. He was famous as the creator of Zionist revisionism, organized the Jewish Legion under British command during World War I, and in the 1920s, openly confronted the British government with the demand for a Jewish state on both sides of the Jordan River. As a result of Jabotinsky's extremism, he was ejected from the leadership of the official Zionist organization. In the 1930s, he started his own party, Betar, attracting many thousands of young Zionists to his program, which included the encouragement of illegal immigration to Palestine.

*Piatero*, a novel/memoir of Russia's Silver Age, points to a paradox: Jabotinsky, a Zionist devoted to the goal of Jewish separatism, was intensely attracted to universal ideas, including the unity of all people and their assimilation. The novel actually shows that borders between Jewish separatism and ultimate assimilation can be porous. In fact, the image of a political activist and apologist for military force clashes with that of the author of *Piatero*, which tells of the demise of an assimilated Jewish family in fin-de-siècle Odessa. As the talented historian Michael Stanislawski writes, "[T]he narrator as Jabotinsky (or Jabotinsky as narrator) concludes his story with a jarring ideological passivity in regard to the very essence of the real-life creed and the real-life—indeed life-and-death—battles of Vladimir, also known as 'Ze'ev' (The Wolf) Jabotinsky."[2]

Stanislawski is right when he argues that for some Zionists, and Jabotinsky in particular, the motivation for Zionism lies not in traditional Jewish life or even in Jewish national struggles, but in the universal ideals of brother-

---

[1] Samuel Katz, *Lone Wolf: A Biography of Vladimir (Ze'ev) Jabotinsky* (New York: Barricade Books, 1996).

[2] Stanislawski, *Zionism and the Fin de Siècle*, 235.

hood, equality, and utopian cravings for a better world.[3] For Jabotinsky, an important source for these ideals and cravings is Odessa circa 1905. There, among decadent intellectuals and individuals engaged in "life-creation" (*zhiznetvorchestvo*)—modeling one's life according to aesthetic principles— Jabotinsky encountered strivings for eternal beauty and individual self-realization. On the surface, these ideas seem far from collective Zionist politics and the establishment of a Jewish state, for instead of fully rejecting bold individualism and aestheticism, which contradict Jewish separatism, in the novel he expresses an attraction to them.

*Piatero* is composed of 29 chapters, which revolve around the lives and fates of the five children of the Milgrom family in the years preceding and succeeding the Revolution of 1905. The five are Marusya, Marko, Serezha, Lika, and Torik. At the novel's beginning, Marusya, the eldest, is an attractive and passionate woman who has had affairs with many men. Marko is a dreamer, absorbed by the intellectual currents of the time such as Buddhism, Nietzschian decadence, and revolutionary socialism, but is unable to form an attachment to any single philosophy. Serezha is a highly talented poet and musician, but is bereft of practical skills. Lika, anti-social and ascetic, is obsessed with the coming revolution. Torik alone is depicted as interested in Jewish culture. Significantly, he reads Heinrich Graetz's *History of the Jews* and learns Hebrew from tutors. The parents, formerly from the provinces, have made enough money to give their children a place in the intellectual jet set.

But each child has a moral flaw that leads to tragedy. Within a few years, Marusya and Marko are dead, a jealous husband maims Serezha, Lika becomes the lover of a spy in the pay of the tsar, and Torik converts to Christianity for the sake of his career. The parents, having witnessed their children's ruin, are emotionally broken. For consolation, the father turns to the Book of Job and the Jewish God.

Many readers have interpreted the novel as a castigation of assimilation. That view has some merit, because Jabotinsky shows the tragedy of an assimilated Jewish family. Alice Nakhimovsky, for example, has written, "The novel may have a message congruent with Jabotinsky's teachings—that assimilation is a form of death....."[4]

However, there is a problem with this point of view. First of all, no character serves as an ideological counterweight to assimilation. Neither the author nor any other character gives an example of what Jewish nationalism or traditional Judaism would look like. In fact, in this circle of Odessa Jews, assimilation is the unmarked characteristic; everyone is assimilated. Moreover, the narrator is not hostile to the Milgroms or repulsed by them. Rather, he is

---

[3] Ibid., 10.

[4] Alice Stone Nakhimovsky, *Russian-Jewish Literature and Identity: Jabotinsky, Babel, Grossman, Galich, Roziner, Markish* (Baltimore: Johns Hopkins University Press, 1992), 63.

full of deep and elegiac love, cares for them as though they were his own family. The narrator, one quickly realizes, is himself an assimilated Jew. He has little knowledge of or feeling for traditional Jewish life and fully shares his protagonists' modern secular interests. Thus, Jabotinsky's attitude toward assimilation is unclear. Displaying sympathy for the lofty ideal of the unity of all peoples, he also expresses the deference for Jewish separatism characteristic of a Zionist.

An examination of some formal aspects of the novel/memoir can help illuminate the fundamental paradox. Deliberately playing with the problem of fictional biography, the author invites the reader to identify the person of Jabotinsky with the narrator. For example, the narrator has the same characteristics as Jabotinsky: he is a liberal journalist famous for his witty feuilletons and is known for his pro-Jewish-nationalist views. By fusing the identities of author and narrator, Jabotinsky is patently directing the reader to interpret the text as a biographical source. Nakhimovsky insightfully argues that the novel has a broad autobiographical subtext and features Jabotinsky's own self-identity, his "emotional essence," as she calls it. The actual person, then, becomes less important than the image of Jabotinsky fashioned for the readers' perceptions.

Another crucial factor is time. Like such highly aestheticized memoirs as Vladislav Khodasevich's *Nekropol'* (Necropolis) or Osip Mandelshtam's *Egipetskaia marka* (Egyptian Stamp), *Piatero* uses two contrasting time frames. The narrator speaks in the present time, when he is writing his memoir, but evokes voices from a retrospective time in the past. As in Khodasevich's and Mandelshtam's memoirs, the split perspective allows for the intrusion of commentary and clarification, thus enabling the narrator to manipulate the readers' attitudes toward that former world. In the case of *Piatero*, Jabotinsky—the author—emphasizes his affiliation with Odessa's intellectual elite. Using a retrospective viewpoint, the narrator identifies himself with the Odessa of 1905.

> Most likely I'll never see Odessa again. It's a pity because I love it. Even as a child I felt indifference to Russia. I remember I was always gleefully nervous when I went abroad and wouldn't want to return. But Odessa is something else. Driving up to Razdel'naia, I already became agitated in an exalted way. If I were to drive up there today, my hands would probably shake. I am not indifferent just to Russia, in generally I'm not attached to any country. I was in love with Rome for a long time, but even this passed. Odessa is something else, [my love] hasn't and won't pass.[5]

Through his examination of Odessa, Jabotinsky creates a snapshot of intellectual life in the city. Debating the issues of the age—assimilation, Jewish

---

[5] V. Jabotinsky, *Piatero* (Tel Aviv: Biblioteka Aliia, 1990), 227.

identity, socialism, freedom, and revolution—the narrator supports plurality of thought. The characters often embody views not shared by the narrator. For example, the narrator agrees with arguments that exonerate the Milgroms, in spite of the fact that such arguments should be repellent to a Zionist. Surprisingly the accusation of assimilation is used not to indict, but to defend. Engaged in a tête-à-tête with a well-known lawyer, himself a fully assimilated Jew, the narrator transmits the lawyer's words:

> [O]ne cannot close one's eyes to the fact that the initial stage of mass assimilation is a difficult phenomenon. Russian culture is great and as bottomless and pure as the sea. But when you leave the shore and enter the water you have to sail the first dozen meters through disgusting slime, wood chips, watermelon rinds.... Perhaps the entire genuine content of morality, even the concept of a cultured person consists of prejudices. But in every culture these [prejudices] are one's own, original, and when one turns from one culture to another a long time must pass. The former [prejudices] fall away, but new ones have not yet been adopted; a very long time must pass, perhaps not just one or even two generations, but more.[6]

Although Marusya does not seem to have any attributes that would attract a Jewish nationalist, she is the embodiment of fin-de-siècle sexuality that Jabotinsky cannot resist. Enchanted by her grace, seductive coquetry, and positive life force, here the narrator is happy to relinquish moral judgment. For him she represents the eternal feminine, a force of spiritual salvation. The narrator confesses:

> In the whole world I never met girls better than Marusya. I cannot forget her. People have reproached me, saying that in all my incursions into belletristics inevitably she always appears, her way of being, her defiant rules of sincerity, her red hair. I cannot help myself. Glancing at her from the corner of their living room, I suddenly remembered the phrase of Enrico Ferri, I don't remember about whom, that I heard in Rome at his lecture, "che bella pianta umana," "a beautiful human flower." And at that time I still didn't know exactly how beautiful this flower really was, how strong her character was, and how all these things, wild, horrible, monstrous, and sublime would end.[7]

Although Ferri was hardly a romantic, by applying the quote to Marusya, the narrator underscores his admiration both for her spiritual and physical beauty.

---

[6] Ibid., 197–98.

[7] Enrico Ferri (1856–1929)—Italian criminologist. Ibid., 35.

The narrator and Marusya were great friends prior to her marriage and he recounts one particular night of intimate platonic communion. In those days, the narrator tells us, true spiritual love was more meaningful than mere physical contact. Marusya is portrayed as an extraordinary woman, a result not of her own achievements, but of her personification of female qualities: erotic attraction, intelligence, kindness, and artistic sensibility. Her feminine portrait coincides unmistakably with Dostoevsky's idea of the accursed woman who nevertheless can save the world.

At the novel's beginning, we see her as the hostess of one of Odessa's most popular salons; her home is open to many "passengers"—the word her family uses for visitors. Later she nearly marries a Russian sailor, but changes her mind at the last minute out of fear that her children "won't belong to her," i.e., won't be Jewish. Instead she marries Samoilo Kozodoi, a down-to-earth, unimaginative Jewish pharmacist. The two move to a provincial city near Odessa, where she gives birth to two children. There she meets her death after falling victim to a fire. Wounded, she is finished off by her pharmacist husband. This sacrifice makes a martyr out of her.

None of the other characters are as idealized as Marusya. The author inflicts on all of them cruel punishments, showing his disapproval of their behaviors. For example, Marko receives a death sentence for his purposeless idealism. He drowns when he jumps into a Petersburg canal on a foggy winter night after hearing what he thinks is a call for help. The woman he hoped to save, it turns out, was not drowning at all, but merely fighting with her boyfriend. Marko's heroic response to a false alarm reflects his frivolous, mock-heroic character.

Serezha also pays a high price for his weakness of will and desire for aristocratic ease. A husband and father enraged by Serezha's sexual liaisons with the man's wife and daughter throws acid on his face, ruining his exceptional beauty. Serezha's guilt is compounded by his extortion of money. In 1905, when it was common for Jews to steal from their rich brethren for the sake of the Revolution, Serezha extorted money from his own uncles.

Lika is also a morally reprehensible character, spying on the tsarist spy with whom she is romantically involved. We are hardly surprised to discover that years later Lika is working for Stalin in the Lubyanka Prison in Moscow.

Torik, the youngest, saddens the narrator because he decides to convert to Lutheranism. But despite this conversion, the author does not depict him as morally bankrupt. His arguments have an impeccable logic that even the narrator acknowledges. When the narrator tries to repel the attraction of assimilation with an appeal to the Bund or Zionism, Torik responds:

> The Bund and Zionism, if you reason clinically, are really the same. The Bund is a preparatory class or, let's say, a public school; it readies you for Zionism. It seems that Plekhanov said about the Bund that they're "Zionists who fear sea sickness." And Zionism is like a high

school. But the university, where everyone is unconsciously heading, is called assimilation. Gradually, without desire, joyless, for the majority it will even be disadvantageous, but still it is unavoidable and irreversible, with baptism, mixed marriages, and the full liquidation of the race. There is no other way. The Bund clings to Yiddish. They say it's the most amazing language in the world. I only know a little, but my tutors, unable to get into the university, quote the word "Boychik," i.e., simple fellow from [the Yiddish speakers in] Whitechapel [in London], and they say it is a tour de force. Elements of three languages in one little word and it sounds natural, it's an ideal amalgam. But in twenty-five years there won't be any Yiddish. And there won't be any Zion. Only one thing will remain: the desire "to be the same as other nations."[8]

Although the narrator doesn't agree with this prediction of the end of Russian Jewry, he remains silent, since Torik has "leak-proof" answers to every one of his counter-arguments. The narrator's silence again reflects the interpenetration of conflicting viewpoints in the novel.

Trying to understand the tragic ends of the five children, the narrator offers the following explanation, which is provided by the lawyer who defended Serezha's attacker. The flaws of the Milgroms are related to the Nietzschean demonism of the period, the absence of moral limits or, as the lawyer puts it, "Pochemu nel'zia?" (Why is it prohibited?). Echoing Dostoevsky's "Esli net Boga, to vse pozvoleno" (If God is dead, all is permitted), the characters question the basic foundations of morality. Why are some things considered wrong? Aren't moral limits just another kind of superstition, like religion or fear of authority, which restrain people from fully liberating themselves? For Jabotinsky, it is the lack of a moral compass among an entire generation that leads to the destruction of the Milgroms. This is the dark side of the Silver Age, but there is also a bright side.

According to the narrator, Odessa was a place where "people learned to laugh at themselves and everything in the world, even at their pains and things they love."[9] The amazing achievement of Odessa, we learn, was tolerance. Gradually one's customs disappear, one stops taking one's own sanctuaries seriously, gradually understanding the single most important secret in the world: "What is sacred to you is stupidity to your neighbor, and your neighbor is not a thief or a vagrant..."[10]

We need not be surprised at Jabotinsky's praise of tolerance and, subsequently, assimilation. In the context of Odessa in 1905, assimilation appears to the narrator as a road leading to a higher level of reality. The narrator con-

---

[8] Ibid., 224.

[9] Ibid., 228–29.

[10] Ibid., 229.

tinues, "Torik said 'disintegration.' Maybe he is right. The lawyer … spoke about decadence, but he added that epochs of decadence are sometimes the most fascinating times. Who knows? Perhaps not only fascinating, but also superior in their own way? Of course I am in the camp that struggles against disintegration, I do not want neighbors, I want all people to live on their own islands. But who knows?"[11]

That question, "Who knows?" marks Jabotinsky's internal dialogue with his Zionist convictions. In spite of the Milgroms' sad lives, the narrator acknowledges that ethnic, religious, and ideological differences served to enrich the people of Odessa. Assimilation seemed to symbolize the start of something new, beautiful, and ideal. Attracted to the dreams of universal brotherhood, the narrator announces a utopian vision.

> One thing is already a proven historical truth: one has to pass through disintegration to reach renewal. This means that disintegration is like a fog before the birth of the sun or like a pre-dawn dream. Marusya said that the most wonderful dreams are pre-dawn ones. Whose poem is this? "The prophesy of dawn is still imperceptible, emerald and cornelian, lilac and azure: the unsung words drift into my mind, perhaps, of an unborn poet, the singer of a country still not created by the creator, where invisible visions are silent like music and whose shroud for a moment, the moment before awakening, lifts up pre-dawn dreams to us." I am afraid that these verses are my own. Getting old, I quote myself more and more often. I quote (for the second time) the following: "I am a child of my time, I love all its stains, love its full poison."[12]

The last part of his speech—I am a child of my time—is entirely comprehensible, and his confession of love for the poison of his culture also makes sense. But what are we to make of the pre-dawn dreams, the reaching beyond to a better world? What is the higher stage that should emerge from assimilation?

Certainly the allusion to dreams, the use of synaesthesia—silent music—and such paradoxical language as "unborn poets" and "a country not yet created by the creator" recalls concepts of the Silver Age, with its emphasis on the intangible, ideal, and spiritual aspects of being. This last quote, a confession of sorts, serves as a perfect example of the complicated and contradictory quality of Jabotinsky's "emotional essence." For the author, assimilation appears as wonderful, dangerous, ideal, and unattainable.

Jabotinsky expresses mixed feelings toward assimilation, which is not unusual. At the start of the Zionist movement, many Jews yearned for inclusion in non-Jewish society. In fact, the failure of assimilation acted as one of the

---

[11] Ibid.
[12] Ibid.

primary causes for the creation of Zionism. The creation of a Jewish state was supposed to regularize the position of the Jews, and in the period of its infancy, Zionists dreamt of an ideal state, which might come about through cooperation with non-Jews. It is very possible that the optimism of the early Zionists was connected with the spiritual goals they encountered in their host cultures, such as those Jabotinsky encountered in Odessa.

It is difficult to identify the motivations that prompted Jabotinsky to write *Piatero*. Certainly the sale of the book was necessary for the financially strapped Jabotinsky, but that alone is not enough. It is possible that Jabotinsky sought to answer some of his critics from both among non-Zionists and the Zionist left, such as Hayim Weismann, that his revisionist Zionism was not the hateful brand of chauvinism they claimed it to be. Giving his brand of Zionism an idealistic pedigree, Jabotinsky could show that his motivations were ideal and his ends were right, even if his methods seemed extreme.

Whether one is convinced of this or not, one thing is certain: in the mirror of himself that he drew in *Piatero*, there is no separation between militant Zionism and Silver Age decadence. To end his book, Jabotinsky idealizes the world of Odessa. The author muses about kindness: "Everything that is good in the world is a kindness: the moonlight, the sea wave and the rustling of branches, the smell of flowers and music—all of this is kindness. And God, if you manage to reach him, to discuss, awaken, and reproach him for everything that he's done, and then forgive and put your head on his lap—he too is probably a kindness. But the best and brightest kindness is called 'woman'.... It was an amusing city; and laughter is also kindness. By the way there probably isn't any trace of the Odessa of my time, but there's no reason to feel sorry that I won't ever make it there. And in general my story is over."[13]

At the very end Jabotinsky alludes one last time to the Silver Age; this time to Vladimir Solovyov and his ideas of the joy and wisdom found in the feminine principle. This optimistic ending lays bare a quandary in Jabotinsky's novel—how to reconcile Marusya and the fin-de-siècle attitudes that so evidently charmed him with the Zionist ideals that she does not hold, but that the author was politically committed to realize.

---

[13] Ibid., 232.

# Conceptualizing a Nation Apart:
# Politics and Historiography

# Introduction to Part 2

This section deals with so-called "liberal nationalists," historians, and civic activists, who strove to fashion a modern Jewish nation in the prerevolutionary period and at the same time promoted the integration of Jews in Russia. Ideologically they followed the lead of Simon Dubnov, who imagined a Russia where Jews were not only tolerated, but also given equal rights—including national rights, such as the right to separate schools and cultural institutions, and the right to self-governance over internal Jewish affairs. Although not all Jewish liberals agreed with the need for a national program, they all acknowledged that only democracy and rule of law could guarantee respect for the civil rights of Jews.

Nationalist-leaning intellectuals viewed the five-million-strong Jewish population in Russia as desperately in need of modern Jewish institutions, such as secular Jewish schools, libraries, a Jewish university, and teachers' colleges. The period following the 1881–82 pogroms and the promulgation of the so-called May Laws was characterized by Jewish demands for national rights in addition to individual or civil rights. This period also coincided with the proliferation of political and economic groups that were independent of government control. Jews exploited the new opportunities for free assembly to revive national consciousness.[1]

The experience of building community cohesion in the decade previous to 1905 proved useful in developing a grass-roots approach that succeeded, as much as could be hoped, in uniting Jews of differing classes and groups. The proliferation of self-help groups that provided small loans and self-defense organizations among Jews reflected the growing consciousness that modernity did not have to mean a loss of Jewish consciousness, although it did contribute in many cases to a loss of religious faith.

As Jews opened up to the outside world, a kind of cosmopolitanism reigned in which strivings for integration and the development of Jewish self-consciousness hung together surprisingly well. Ideally, Russian Jews were supposed to succeed in the economic marketplace, speak Russian as natives, but also acquire a depth of knowledge in Jewish culture. If possible, they

---

[1] Charles E. Timberlake perceives the rise of a middle class among the professionals in the zemstvos. Timberlake, "The Zemstvo and the Development of a Russian Middle Class," *Between Tsar and People*, 164–66. Jeffrey Veidlinger, "Jewish Cultural Associations in the Aftermath of 1905," in *The Revolution of 1905 and Russia's Jews*, ed. Stefani Hoffman and Ezra Mendelsohn (Philadelphia: University of Pennsylvania Press, 2008).

should study Hebrew and Yiddish, knowledge of which would, it was hoped, instill a feeling of responsibility toward other Jews and prevent assimilation.

I try to expose the relationship between historiography and politics, or the way historical studies underpinned distinct political orientations. Since there were few professional historians and the majority involved in the writing of history were amateurs, there was a distinct tendency for historical knowledge to find application in other fields, such as law and politics. The lawyers featured in this section studied history in large part to justify better treatment of Jews. Since they often could not find more tolerance in the Russian past, they were apt to defend Jews by criticizing the disorganization and backwardness of the Russian law code and demanding reform.[2]

On another level, it makes sense that Russia's most important Jewish liberals were involved with law professionally. Besides the personal benefits of having a university education, such as the right to live outside the Pale of Settlement, Jewish lawyers dreamed of a progressive and democratic Russia that would provide protection of the rights of all its citizens. In a cruel turn of fate, after having suffered countless offenses under tsarist rule, these same individuals were not liberated by revolution, but were forced to take up arms against the Bolsheviks to defend civil liberties in general and Jewish rights in particular. By 1930, all the individuals I feature here had either died or left the Soviet Union.

Jewish liberals interest us today not only because they provide rich material for the historian, but also because their alternative—"the road not taken"—would have led, or so it seems, to a better Russia. Moreover, despite the present push of the Putin government away from a rule-of-law state, the example of the Russian liberals of a century ago has been mentioned as a useful model for Jews in contemporary Russia. In this case it is worthwhile to gauge how successful these individuals actually were in the struggle to enhance Jewish self-consciousness, gain respect for Jews, and win increased rights for the legendary "outcasts of humanity." In these essays I try to give answers to these and other questions.

---

[2] Il'ia Orshanskii, "Russkoe zakonodatel'stvo o evreiakh," *Evreiskaia biblioteka* 3–5 (1872–74).

## Chapter 6

# "Dialogue" with Heinrich Graetz, Polemic with Avram Harkavy: Simon Dubnov's Struggle for the Domination of Russian-Jewish Historiography, 1883–93

Simon Dubnov's relations with Heinrich Graetz reflect a nexus of intersecting tendencies of his life and thoughts in the key years when Dubnov was defining his mission in life. On the most surface level, Graetz's death sparked a strong emotional reaction, that of a student who finally decides to strive for intellectual independence. In his memoirs Dubnov relates:

> In my entry of the new year in 1892, I noted, "The aim of my life has become clear: the propagation of historical knowledge about Judaism and the scholarly study of Russian Jews. I had become a missionary of history as it were. To achieve this goal, I refrained from writing criticism and journalism. In those days I was fascinated with Graetz, whom I depicted in my long essay "The Historian of Judaism." The essay was written in an excited state, as you can judge from the following passionate tirades in the introduction: "With the battle cries of our time—Baron Hirsch, Argentina, the massive emigration of Russian Jews, conferences, committees in foreign lands—suddenly the terse announcement broke through the noisy choir: Graetz is dead!... In those days when the coffin holding the remains of the deceased historian traveled from Munich to Breslav, along the whole Eastern Prussian border stretched a procession that was no less sad, although this procession was not ending in a funeral. Tens of thousands of sons of the ancient Jewish wanderers were leaving their fatherland and setting off across the sea in search of bread and a quiet corner [to rest] their insulted heart.... The historian has died; history is preparing material for the future Jewish martyrs.... Won't our memory memorialize him, the one who memorialized the entire past of our people in a single magisterial literary monument?"[1]

---

[1] Dubnov, *Kniga zhizni*, 182–83.

In 1892, in that excited state, Dubnov set out on a new course that was to become decisive for his intellectual development. He decided to take the mantle from Graetz and become the most celebrated historian of the Jews in Russia. Gradually veering away from Graetz's approach to Jewish literary history toward social history, Dubnov began to question his own views of rationalism, rabbinical Judaism, and assimilation. At the same time Dubnov confronted Avram Harkavy, who was his main rival in Russia. It is my contention that not only Graetz, but Harkavy, too, was extremely influential in the formation of Dubnov's worldview. While Dubnov idealized Graetz, now a martyr, he attacked Harkavy, a living person, who had to absorb the brunt of Dubnov's polemics during the period of intense intellectual development, when he made the major transformations from book reviewer to philosopher of history and cosmopolitan thinker to Jewish nationalist.[2]

Examining Dubnov's attitudes toward these two historians, I propose as a fundamental characteristic of Dubnov's creative process the paradigm of conflict, but not conflict pure and simple or for its own sake. From conflicts with intellectual influences, Dubnov borrowed ideas that enriched his worldview. Indeed, as his memoir, *Kniga zhizni*, shows us, in the late 1870s, Dubnov entered into extended "dialogues" with Western and Jewish culture, absorbing the ideas of Ernest Renan, Jeremy Bentham, and John Stuart Mill, as well as the literary works of Aleksandr Pushkin, Mikhail Lermontov, and Ivan Turgenev. I call such interactions "dialogues." Although it is true that he did not have an actual "dialogue" with those thinkers who lived before him, he approached even these thinkers as though he were speaking with them. He actively posed questions about their ideas, modified their views, and juxtaposed them to one another, giving his ultimate evaluation.[3] In Dubnov's case, dialogue involves the calm and methodical selection of those aspects of another's thought useful for his own creative thinking.

During the vital ten-year period between the late 1880s and 1890s, Dubnov entered into a dialogue with both Harkavy and Graetz, which inspired his idea of historiography as a path to Jewish cultural revitalization. Although he sided with Graetz and bitterly mocked Harkavy, he ultimately came to adopt aspects of Harkavy's thought in his formulation of the purpose of history for the Jewish people.

---

[2] Robert Melvin Seltzer offers ambition as an important motive for Dubnov's evolution. See Seltzer, "Simon Dubnow: A Critical Biography of His Early Years" (Ph.D. diss., Columbia University, 1970), 15–90.

[3] Itamar Elbogen describes the same phenomenon this way: "Dubnov above all valued synthesis. Synthesis was one of his most beloved tasks and during the whole of his working life he tried to create a synthesis of different facts and points of view. This reflects his entire character. His aim was to create, build, and unite. He was a wrestler, an aggressive person, he always strove for justice, peace and truth." Elbogen, "Pamiati Semena Markovicha Dubnova," *Evreiskii mir* 2 (1944): 71.

In the years before he wrote his long article on Heinrich Graetz (it appeared serially in *Voskhod* from April–September 1892), Dubnov was obsessed by the idea of becoming a leading Jewish historian in Russia. In 1891, Dubnov decided, "My goal in life has become clear: the dissemination of historical knowledge about Judaism and special studies on the history of Russian Jews. I have become a missionary of history, so to speak."[4] Summarizing the accomplishments already made in historical research in Russia, Dubnov mapped out the work ahead. Of first importance, he recommended the establishment of a Jewish Historical-Ethnographic Society.[5]

In his memoir, Dubnov writes in 1882 that "I yielded too strongly to the influence of the Ukrainian sympathizer [Dmitry] Kostomarov on the one hand and our Graetz on the other."[6] And in the same year he looked to Graetz for his mission. "I was inspired by the thought that Graetz's great work in the field of the history of Eastern Jewry had been turned over to me..."[7]

In fact, it is hard to overestimate Graetz's importance in Dubnov's intellectual development. For example, even after 30 years Graetz still mattered to Dubnov. In 1910, Dubnov devoted a lecture at one of the meetings of the Jewish Historical-Ethnographic Society to the question of Graetz's contributions to historiography, and a few years later described in the introduction to a new three-volume work on modern Jewish history his "desire to repair Graetz's methodological flaws."[8] Significantly, the publication date of that book was 1914; after that, Dubnov stopped speaking about Graetz's influence. Not by chance, that point coincided with the end of one period in Dubnov's career. After the October Revolution and in emigration Dubnov devoted himself to carrying through to completion work begun earlier.

Dubnov's 1892 essay "Historiographer of Judaism: Heinrich Graetz, His Life and Works" was part objective study, part memorial tribute, and part personal confession. The various genres reflected Dubnov's goals. Identifying

---

[4] Dubnov, *Kniga zhizni*, 165.

[5] S. Dubnov, *Ob izuchenii istorii russkikh evreev i ob uchrezhdenii russko-evreiskogo istoricheskogo obshchestva* (St. Petersburg, 1891), 84.

[6] Dubnov, *Kniga zhizni*, 94.

[7] Ibid., 269.

[8] Dubnov writes, "In the 11th volume of Graetz's *History*, which went up to 1848, separate moments of cultural history were depicted with the usual mastery of this historian, but the political (the struggle for liberation) and social economic history is given short shrift." Dubnov, "Predislovie k pervomu izdaniiu," *Noveishaia istoriia evreiskogo naroda*, 3rd ed. (Berlin: Grani, 1923), x. The first edition came out in 1914.

himself with Graetz, Dubnov underscored their common task as Jewish national historians. In contrast to the historian of any European nation who received access to state archives, the Jewish historian was extremely hampered, wrote Dubnov. Unable to dream about an "unbroken chain of historical facts," he must deal with "twenty doubtful or inconclusive facts for every single substantiated one."[9] "He doesn't have any official government chronicles, but has to look for facts in the most usual and unusual places, in religious books, scientific, philosophical, or mystical writings, the authors of which 'unintentionally expunged' historical material; in folktales, legends, prayers or tombstones, and in the literature of those countries where Jews lived and where a chronicler or memoirist exploited a chance opportunity to speak about them."[10] For this reason the Jewish historian has to be simultaneously "a bricklayer, a carpenter, and an architect. He has to do all the spadework and the finishing touches. He himself has to spend a month making a brick, preparing the mortar, and building according to his own plan, and then he must appear before the public not in a black workman's apron with frayed sleeves and hands spotted with clay, but in a suit and tie, 'entirely in proper attire' and clean. Imagine, what a task!"[11] Complaining that Jewish historians do not receive state subventions and relating his own insecurity about not having a reliable source of income, Dubnov accentuates that the historian "is left with only his inner strengths and works at his own personal risk."[12]

Besides his admiration of Graetz the man, there was much that Dubnov admired in the historical.[13] Dubnov lauded Graetz's idea of treating the Maccabees as courageous fighters on behalf of a national idea. He also celebrated Graetz's new understanding of the Middle Ages, the period following the fall of Babylonia and the rise of Spain, when the Jews found themselves wandering from Asia to Europe. "It was Graetz's achievement that he understood that the Jews in the Galut, without a territory of their own and speakers of many languages, were in fact elements of a single nation."[14]

Inspired by the idea that suffering does not necessarily lead to national destruction, but rather to cohesion and revitalization, Dubnov used Aleksandr Pushkin's phrase "to ruminate and suffer" (*chtoby myslit' i stradat'*) to encapsulate Graetz's synthesis of *Geistesgeschichte* and *Leidenschaftgeschichte*; the Jews appeared melancholic, but inside they make giant steps of spiritual

[9] Dubnov, "Istoriograf evreistva," *Voskhod*, no. 8 (1892): 64.

[10] Ibid., 64.

[11] Ibid., 65.

[12] Ibid., 66.

[13] Heinrich Graetz, *Geschichte der Juden von den ältesten Zeiten bis aud die Gegenwart: Aus den Quellen neubearb*, 11 vols. (Leipzig, 1874–1902).

[14] Dubnov, "Istoriograf evreistva," *Voskhod*, no. 4 (1892): 11.

progress.[15] Lauding Graetz's distinction between external and internal history, Dubnov writes, "The external history of this period is a story about sufferings which no other people has experienced to such an extreme degree, in such a vast space. The internal history consists of the multifaceted history of literature based on theological inquiry, but open in its depths to all the scientific movements which it absorbed and assimilated. Learning and wandering, thinking and suffering, knowing and enduring—that is the task of Judaism throughout this broad period."[16]

The achievement of Judaism in overcoming its trials makes Dubnov reassess Jewish history. Instead of seeing the political weakness of the Jews as a sign of their inferiority, he concurs with Graetz's idealism. "The Jewish people in his view has the gift of spiritual superiority, such an abyss of originality and intellectual energy, such abilities, that it can serve in every way as a model for other peoples. The Jews are a unique example of a *purely spiritual nation*, which stands infinitely higher than all territorial political nations, it is free from their prejudices and petty passions."[17]

Clearly, the vision of the Jews as a spiritual people has direct consequences for Dubnov's political and social understanding of Russian Jewry. This perspective radically departed from the position Dubnov took in the years just after the pogroms of 1881–82. In his article of 1883 "What Kind of Self-Emancipation Do the Jews Need?" Dubnov responded to Leon Pinsker by arguing that the eternal political weakness of the Jews was a symbol of their failure to achieve in Russia what Jews in Western Europe had managed to accomplish: integration, prosperity, and citizenship. Instead of attributing the bad situation of Jews in Russia to the hate of non-Jews, Dubnov blamed Jewish isolation. According to the young Dubnov, the Orthodox rabbis were particularly guilty, since they condemned any compromise with secular society as a betrayal of Judaism.[18] At that time Dubnov concurred with the idea of the Jew as defined exclusively by religious affiliation and not by membership in a Jewish nation. After all, this idea had positive consequences for Western Jewry, since religious affiliation did not impede integration with one's neighbors.[19]

While accepting Graetz's conception of Jewish spiritual nationhood in 1892, Dubnov nevertheless had differences with his German teacher regard-

---

[15] Dubnov, *Kniga zhizni*, 165.

[16] Dubnov, "Istoriograf evreistva," *Voskhod*, no. 3 (1892): 67.

[17] Ibid., no. 7 (1892): 111–12.

[18] S. Dubnov, "Kakaia emansipatsiia nuzhna evreiam?" *Voskhod*, no. 5 (1883): 219–30.

[19] "A single link connects the Jews: *religious unity*. The feeling of belonging to a religious cult (by the latter is meant the totality of external rituals and habits), the idea of the chosen people, on the one side, and centuries of persecution, on the other. This is the reason why Jews remain an ethnic unit. The Jews do not have a *national* unity, but only a religious one..." (Dubnov, "Kakaia emantsipatsiia nuzhna evreiam?" 218).

ing the dominance of Orthodox Jewry and the Talmudic tradition in Jewish history. For example, refusing to share Graetz's contempt for Judaism's mystical tradition, Dubnov had an entirely different perspective on the Aggadah, that part of the Talmud based on oral sources. Instead of condemning it offhandedly as "disorganized" and "subjective," Dubnov considered that this material reflected an integral intellectual worldview. "It is not a rationalistic philosophy, like Mamonides's or [Joseph] Albo's system, but a *philosophy of feeling*—and specifically *national* feeling."[20] Criticizing Graetz for his lack of appreciation for Jewish mysticism in general and the Kabbalah in particular, Dubnov writes:

> Such a [negative] view would be reasonable from the standpoint of a strict rationalism that judges intellectual phenomena according to their absolute scientific-philosophical value. But with Graetz taking a historical-psychological view, it is simply an inconsistency. If Graetz makes a virtue of the fact that Talmudism saved the Jewish mind from stagnation and gave it strict, but nonetheless abundant nourishment, then, in addition, he should acknowledge the same virtue for Kabbalah. It saved Jewish religious feeling from ossification, and, giving nourishment to the imagination, it distracted thinking from the awful, deathly impression of reality and carried it into infinity.[21]

Graetz's indifference to Jewish mysticism angered Dubnov, since the latter considered mystical strivings a sign of the social vigor of the Jewish people and a means for personal spiritual development. Moreover, Dubnov was convinced that mysticism could be a means for revitalizing and healing Jews, lifting Judaism from the medieval stultification caused by Talmudic *pilpul* (rhetorical debating), and revitalizing the link between Judaism, its precepts and books, and the living Jewish people. Offering as an example of the revitalizing effect of mysticism, Dubnov describes Isaac Ben Judah Abrabanel, who lived in Spain in the 11th century:

> When the misery of those exiled reached its apogee and it seemed to many that the "eternal people" was reaching its end, Abrabanel extracted the balm of salvation for the suffering Jewish soul from his mobile pharmacy. He resurrected messianism. He consoled those who were suffering, he told them that salvation was at hand, that if "the tortures of messianic times" had begun, then it followed that the Messiah himself was close by. He himself, suffering more than the others, strengthened his spirit with this mystical faith. He cured both himself and others. In Abrabanel's personality there is something grandiose, the whole tragic course of Jewish history is embodied in

---

[20] Dubnov, "Istoriograf evreistva," *Voskhod*, no. 3 (1892): 68.

[21] Ibid., no. 5 (1892): 62–63.

him, and therefore his personality is immortal. His personality is extremely complex, reflecting not naked theoretical ideas, but the violent movements of the people's soul. To explicate Abrabanel means to illuminate the most mysterious corners of the people's soul, to give a sketch of historical psychology. Unfortunately we did not find such a psychological understanding in Graetz's depiction.[22]

Dubnov's intoxication with mysticism and his conviction that mysticism should be identified with the creativity of the masses is clearly visible from this passage. Valorization of mysticism must be seen in connection with Dubnov's rejection of the rationalist *pilpul* education of his youth and his contempt for the cold-headed and cold-hearted Talmudic tradition.[23] At the same time he also directed his hostility at the rationalism of the Haskalah, which began in the West, since Haskalah had contempt for feeling as an illegitimate remnant of religious faith.

But Dubnov was not hostile to rationalism pure and simple. What he apparently disliked in the Talmudic tradition was the striving for monolithic and unchallenged authority and indifference to intellectual currents in the non-Jewish world—science, politics, and literature. For example, Dubnov displays impatience with Graetz over Spinoza because Graetz repeats the accusations "unproved" centuries earlier and has no appreciation for Spinoza's metaphysics or theology. Instead of pride in Spinoza for extending Jewish creativity into modern philosophy, Graetz fears that Spinoza represents a weak link in the structure of Judaism, a potentially rebellious seed that could infect and destroy Judaism.[24]

Inevitably one can guess where Dubnov is heading with his criticism. Although not saying it directly, Dubnov made a distinction between Western and Eastern Judaism. In 1910, Dubnov makes this distinction explicit, saying that "[i]n Graetz the development of Western historical scholarship reached its highest point."[25] As opposed to Western Europe, characterized by rationality and the deadened study of Talmud, the masses of Eastern European Jewry were the locus of emotional feeling. Dubnov perceived in Hasidism, a movement based primarily on feeling, the true descendents of the medieval mys-

---

[22] Ibid., no. 7 (1892): 66.

[23] *Pilpul* refers to intellectual casuistry. About *pilpul* Dubnov writes in his memoir, "[T]he first day of the study of the tractate 'Beitsah' in the heder was the beginning of my later revolt against tradition. In any case, from the Talmudic study in the heder I acquired that deep revulsion to any kind of casuistry and intellectual sport which later saved me from many mistakes in the course of the search for religious, scholarly, and philosophical truth" (*Kniga zhizni*, 27).

[24] Dubnov, "Istoriograf evreistva," *Voskhod*, no. 5 (1892): 74–75.

[25] S. Dubnov, "O sovremennom sostoianii evreiskoi istoriografii," *Evreiskaia starina*, no. 1 (1910): 151.

tical tradition.[26] Since feeling is the source for living Judaism and Jewish nationhood, Dubnov predicted that Russia would soon become the leading cultural force in world Judaism.[27]

Here, surprisingly one can see in Dubnov's criticisms both the influence of Slavophilism and Graetz's own spiritual-national conception of Russian Jewry. The view of Russian Jews as spiritually superior by virtue of their mystical roots and the Western Jews as inferior because of their reliance on lifeless rationalism drew inspiration from parallel Slavophile ideas. The original Slavophiles predicted the demise of the West and the success of the Russians on the world stage thanks to the power of their "young" civilization.[28] Dubnov, who attacked Slavophilism for its pro-Russian chauvinism and intolerance of Jews, was nevertheless influenced by an East-West dichotomy.

At the same time, Dubnov emphasized that Russia's Jews correspond best to Graetz's paradigm of a spiritual people. Unable to assimilate due to government oppression, Russian Jews were not inactive; beneath the surface they created fully viable social units characterized by autonomous communal institutions. Moreover, their spiritual life reflected the formation of a modern nation, since their communal institutions took on those functions conventionally fulfilled by the state. For this reason, Dubnov called Russia's Jews the most historic of all the Jewish peoples and linked their spiritual resources to their great potential as a modern nation.[29]

Although it may not be discernible to the ordinary reader, Dubnov's work on Graetz was inextricably connected with Avram Harkavy. Although colliding in various ways with Harkavy, Dubnov acquainted himself with congenial ideas regarding the meaning of Diaspora, the purpose of historical research, and the value of Orthodox Judaism in Jewish history. Dubnov's polemics with Harkavy began as early as 1883, with, not by coincidence, a review of the Russian translation of volume 5 of Graetz's *History of the Jews*. Dubnov, recently hired to take Judah Leib Gordon's place as the literary review editor

---

[26] See S. Dubnov, "Vozniknovenie khasidizma: Ber iz Mezhiricha, preemnik Beshta, i prochie ucheniki Beshta (1760–1772)," *Voskhod* (1899): no. 9 (3–21); no. 10 (3–18); no. 11–12 (38–53) and (1890): no. 1 (23–42).

[27] Dubnov, *Ob izuchenii istorii russkikh evreev*, 64.

[28] See Andrzej Walicki, *The Slavophile Controversy: History of a Conservative Utopia in Nineteenth-Century Thought*, (New York: Clarendon, 1975).

[29] Dubnov, *Ob izuchenii istorii russkikh evreev*, 89–90. In his book *Isreal and the Diaspora*, Ben Zion Dinur describes Dubnov's extensive borrowing from Graetz in the creation of his own historical conception: "On the question of the relation of Jewish to world history Dubnov also, in all essentials, merely explains and slightly expands Graetz's views." Dinur, *Israel and the Diaspora* (Philadelphia: Jewish Publication Society of America, 1969), 34.

of *Voskhod*, launched an attack on Harkavy's extensive explanatory notes. But the attack was really nothing less than the first salvo in the fight over Graetz's legacy in Russia.

Dubnov attacked Harkavy for his attempt to "clean up," that is, modify Graetz's views in order to vindicate Orthodox Jewry. For example, defending Graetz's assertion that "the Talmud eclipsed the Bible" in the religious life of medieval Jews, Dubnov attacked Harkavy for claiming that the Bible was studied as much or even more than the Talmud. Dubnov writes:

> With regard to the synagogue reading of the Bible and Psalms, this does not prove at all that the Bible was studied with penetration or even that it was understood. We have the same readings today and more than likely only one in a hundred "readers" understands the simple meaning of the biblical words, let's not even speak about serious study. Everyone knows that such study was often prohibited by Orthodox Jews in the recent past and even now is considered unlawful in certain circles. The interpretation by the Talmudists of "every word, every letter in the biblical text" distorted everything that was healthy, everything sublime-poetic and philosophical in the Bible, and precisely transformed it fully into a senseless pool of words from which extremely capricious combinations were made.... Talmudists removed the soul of the Bible for their own ends in order to produce various operations over its corpse. A revival of the corpse is entirely useless for them; the corpse could slip from under their operations and expose them.... No, there can be no doubt: "the Talmud eclipsed the Bible from the people's consciousness!"[30]

Claiming that medieval Jewish Orthodox rabbis shared the same negative attitude toward the Bible as today, Dubnov nevertheless unfairly interpolated his own personal experience to prove his point. In the same review, Dubnov criticized Harkavy's contempt for the Karaites. Continuing his anti-Talmudic diatribe, Dubnov claimed that the Karaites were extremely important, since by offering a rare alternative to Talmudic Judaism, they showed that "anti-Talmudism was not a stillborn idea, but inspiring, capable of life and development."[31]

Harkavy did not calmly accept criticism from the upstart and beginning writer. In response to "What Kind of Self-Emancipation Do We Need?" Harkavy led a delegation to *Voskhod's* publisher, Alfred Landau, with the threat that either Dubnov be fired or a ban of excommunication, a *herem*, would be

---

[30] S. Dubnov, "Gretts, *Istoriia evreev, tom piatyi: Ot vremeni zakliucheniia Talmuda (500) do epokhi rastsveta evreisko-ispanskoi kul'tury (1027). Perevod s 2-go nemetskogo izdaniia, s pribavleniiami*, SPb: Izdanie Obshchestva rasprostraneniia prosveshcheniia mezhdu evreiami v Rossii, 1882," *Voskhod*, no. 4 (1883): 22.

[31] Ibid., 23.

imposed on the journal. Landau, a stodgy defender of the cause of assimilation, but an unyielding defender of academic freedom, stood up to Harkavy and refused.[32] The *herem* apparently did not work, since Dubnov kept his job and no more about it is mentioned in memoirs of the time.

Dubnov and Harkavy again locked horns in the early 1890s. It makes sense that Dubnov would go after Harkavy, since after the death of Ilya Orshansky, the best historian of Russian Jewry of his time, Harkavy was the only person in Russia who could present a challenge for the position of leader. For many reasons, Harkavy was the man to beat. He had permanent residence in St. Petersburg and access to the city's famous public library. He also had strong connections in the Petersburg office of the Society for the Promotion of Enlightenment among the Jews of Russia, being its secretary and later a member of the Steering Committee. As the only legally recognized, independent Jewish organization devoted to the goal of the education of Russia's Jews, the OPE (as the society was known) attracted the participation of some of Russia's smartest young intellectuals.

Writing in 1893 in a series of articles in *Voskhod* about the state of Russian-Jewish historiography, Dubnov was forced to admit that the Historical Commission of the Society for the Promotion of Enlightenment based in St. Petersburg held out the best hope for leading historical scholarship forward. Dubnov even counseled the members to take themselves seriously since it was likely that the commission would make up the core of a future Jewish historical-ethnographic society.[33] In his remarks, however, one inevitably detects a note of anger, since Dubnov was also frustrated that he was unable to participate in the Historical Commission because he could not get a residence permit to remain in St. Petersburg.[34] As revenge perhaps, Dubnov lashed out, hardly veiling the fact that Harkavy was the object of his anger. (Incidentally, in his memoirs Dubnov reveals that Harkavy was indeed the object of his attack.)

> There are many "priests of history" who, like the priests of the ancient heathen temples, make every effort to hide from the "laymen" "higher truths" and knowledge that have been attained by them out of fear that the people, having understood these truths, will no longer need their services and will become convinced of their leaders' spiritual weakness. This profit-oriented priestly spirit is especially hateful in such a lively field as historiography. Historiography's place is not under a nightcap, but in the forum. We recount the past for the entire people and not just for a dozen archeologists and numismatists, we

---

[32] Dubnov, *Kniga zhizni*, 434.

[33] S. Dubnov, "Istoricheskie soobshcheniia," *Voskhod*, no. 7 (1893): 9.

[34] Dubnov, *Kniga zhizni*, 146.

work for the purpose of the people's consciousness and not for our own intellectual sport.[35]

What doubly fueled Dubnov's anger was Harkavy's "rationalism," his "narrow-scholastic method from which scholarship had not yet liberated itself even in the present."[36] Dubnov hated factography and the study of history for the sake of dispassionate knowledge. In Dubnov's view, historical study existed to strengthen the Jewish nation. In contrast to an ordinary academic scholar—"a priest of history"—Dubnov viewed himself as a kind of prophet who offered the Jewish people nationhood through self-consciousness. Using the image of the prophet Ezekiel's gathering of the Jewish armies to fight the Romans and Syrians, Dubnov writes: "Dry bones, the remains of past generations are strewn in a valley. 'Will these bones come alive?'—the prophet asks. And suddenly the bones begin to come together, veins and flesh appear, they tighten up with skin, only there is no spirit in them.... And I begin to prophesy; and suddenly spirit arrives and the bones become animate and stand up, an exceeding great army. And the Lord said to me: 'Son of Man! These bones are the entire house of Israel.'" Here Dubnov interjects, bringing the story up to date: "Yes, we will soon witness and even participate in the great act of resurrection."[37]

Dubnov grounded his belief that historical knowledge led inexorably to Jewish national consciousness on empirical grounds. How can it be, he wrote, that individuals who have no religious faith, so-called *penseurs libres*, make up most of the Jewish nation's strongest supporters? Instead of religion, their loyalty is conditioned by "the general memory about our past, rich with events, our former glory, our centuries-long sufferings, and our sad wanderings. The infinite chain of monochromatic experiences that our ancestors had, which accumulated over centuries in the Jewish soul, has left a strong residue that unites us together."[38] According to Dubnov, the more one knew about one's history, the more intense one's feeling of national identity.

Of course in his desire, as Dubnov puts it, "to derive history from contemporary life," one can see an expression of the general anti-positivist tenor of the period in which he worked.[39] In Russian works of the same period, such as Nikolai Berdyaev's biography of Aleksei Khomyakov or Mikhail Gershenzon's *History of Young Russia*, the historian acknowledges a preference for subjective intuition over objective facts in the reconstruction of the

---

[35] Dubnov, "Istoricheskie soobshcheniia," 11.

[36] Dubnov, *Ob izuchenii istorii russkikh evreev*, 31.

[37] Ibid., 88.

[38] Ibid., 6.

[39] Dubnov writes, "We do not modernize history, do not draw contemporary life from it, but on the contrary, in a scholarly way we draw history from contemporary life." Dubnov, "O sovremennom sostoianii evreiskoi istoriografii," 158.

past.[40] Moreover, Russian thinkers, especially those associated with neo-Slavophilism, sought to make the past relevant to the present by depicting individuals who reveal spiritual accomplishment rather than dealing with political events alone.

Unconvinced of a link between history and national self-identity, Harkavy viewed historical research in a different political context. A man of the 1860s, Harkavy believed in gradual acculturation. Therefore, Jews did not compose a political nation, but were a people with distinct religious and ethnic origins. These origins, however, did not interfere with the Jews integrating with their Russian neighbors and becoming loyal and patriotic citizens. Harkavy's viewpoint can be explained by his age and experience. A close friend of Baron Horace Guenzburg, Harkavy had seen Jewish intercessors win many increases in rights for the Jews during the reign of Alexander II. It was in this context that he tried to prove an extensive and long-standing Khazar settlement in the Russian lands; he was confident that such evidence would stop the government from viewing the Jews as outsiders and convince the government of the Jews' loyalty.[41]

Dubnov inevitably clashed with Harkavy politically, since, impatient with the failure of Jewish intercessors, Dubnov demanded that the Jews struggle for their rights using modern pressure politics. On the historical plane, Dubnov mocked Harkavy's archeological inclinations, ridiculing his fixation on the Khazars.[42]

> After all, the heated and still unresolved debate about "the origins of Rus'" between [Mikhail] Pogodin and Kostomarov does not prevent either one of these scholars from studying later periods of Russian history, which they have enriched with their wonderful works. However interesting the "question of the Khazars" is and however much the question of ancient Jewish settlements is connected with it, we should not make the living and huge task of Jewish historiography dependent on its resolution, which really entails a single point. Otherwise we will stand in place and never do anything of value later....[43]

Disagreeing with Harkavy's conclusions about a long-standing Khazar community as based on flimsy and unconvincing evidence, Dubnov argued that a

---

[40] See especially the introduction to M. Gershenzon, *Istoriia molodoi Rossii* (Moscow: I. D. Sytin, 1908), 3–10; also Nikolai Berdiaev, *Aleksei Stepanovich Khomiakov* (Moscow: Put', 1912).

[41] A. Harkavy, *O iazyke evreev, zhivshikh v drevnee vremia na Rusi* (St. Petersburg, 1865), 1–25.

[42] Dubnov, *Ob izuchenii istorii russkikh evreev*, 30.

[43] Ibid., 31.

convincing study of Jews in Russia had to begin with the migration eastward of Polish Jews at the time of the First Crusades in 1096.[44]

Dubnov and Harkavy's disagreement about the Khazars reflected two contrasting views of Jewish wandering. While Harkavy wanted to give the Jews long-standing roots in Russia in order to show their right to legal entitlement as citizens of the Empire, Dubnov forged the idea of movable centers. In Dubnov's model, the Jewish nation traversed the globe in search of a suitable place to create its autonomous communities. The Jews' peripatetic evolution did not prohibit them from fighting for their own political interests in coalitions with other groups with similar goals.[45]

Dubnov's dialogue with Graetz did not end in 1893. Despite the passing of years, Dubnov continued to ponder the value of Graetz's methodology. In 1910, he delivered his talk on Graetz, "On the Contemporary Condition of Jewish Historiography."[46] Making a distinction between teleological and theological approaches, Dubnov regretted that Graetz had refused to challenge the Orthodox rabbis of Germany in his treatment of the biblical period. For that reason, there was more objectivity in his work on the post-biblical period.[47] But even there, in the modern period, Dubnov averred, Graetz subordinated his work to an ideological position; the history of the Jews became a history of Jewish literature. "If the Jewish people exist in the Diaspora for the fulfillment of a certain mission, for the demonstration of a certain religious-ethical teaching, then the people's literary, spiritual activity should make up the primary content of its historical life. Therefore, the history of the people becomes identified with the 'history of the book,' teaching, literature."[48] Part historian of Jewish literature and part chronicler of Jewish martyrdom, Graetz could not maintain scholarly objectivity, since the theologian and spiritualist dominated over the scholar of historical evolution.[49]

---

[44] Ibid., 40. It is not difficult to understand Dubnov's strong reaction to the idea of a Khazar kingdom, since scholars have disputed the proposition that the Khazars were truly Jewish. See "Khazars," *Encyclopedia Judaica* (Jerusalem: Kater Publishing House, 1972), 10: 948–49. Perhaps Dubnov was also contradicting Harkavy's view that the Khazars were speakers of Slavic, as opposed to Turkic, which was one of Harkavy's central ideas.

[45] See the political program of the Volkspartei, *Evreiskaia Narodnaia Partiia* (St. Petersburg: Evreiskaia Narodnaia Partiia, 1907).

[46] "O sovremennom sostoianii evreiskoi istoriografii" was delivered February 21, 1910, and appeared in *Evreiskaia starina*, no. 1 (January–March 1910): 149–58.

[47] Ibid., 153.

[48] Ibid.

[49] Ibid., 155.

Dubnov advised that students of Jewish history could learn from Graetz's mistakes. In place of a theological or teleological method, modern historians should adopt a sociological approach. Such a method would deal with the social, political, and economic forms Jews have created for themselves in their unique environments and follow this through the entire history of the Jews in their evolution. "We should resolve the problem of how the people creates its political history when it has an independent state, and its social, spiritual, and overall cultural history when in place of the absent state, an autonomous community and worldwide national-cultural union are created in the Diaspora. Autonomy in individual communities and the presence of a common union of the whole of Judaism in different countries—these are the basic generating forces of the epoch of the Diaspora."[50]

Complaining that Graetz couldn't achieve this level of objectivity, in a moment of self-admission Dubnov regrets that he too has failed. "I have to admit that at the start of my scholarly work I myself was not free from the old ways and that I would not sign my name to much of what I wrote about the philosophy of history nearly twenty years ago."[51]

Although Dubnov does not explain exactly what he means, we can presume that he acknowledged his own weakness for teleological thinking. But blindness to objectivity may be only part of the total picture. Perhaps the main difference between Dubnov's social method and his earlier approach hinges on his reevaluation of spiritual achievement. In promoting as his theoretical lynchpin the idea of hegemonic centers—centers of Jewish civilization that dominate over the others and influence their development—Dubnov emphasized the value of social structures, communal institutions, and their interrelationships. He saw the seeds for national identity in the internal autonomous economic, social, and political relations. He now stressed the value of communal institutions rather than the internal creative endeavors of a single individual.[52]

Paradoxically, Dubnov continued his debate with Harkavy in the years after their personal conflict ended. It will strike one as unexpected that Dubnov arrived at his concept of the Council of the Four Lands, one of the central ideas of his conception of Jewish life in the Diaspora, through his study of Harkavy.[53] In fact, Harkavy had come to this subject first. But whereas Harkavy studied this material precisely to prove Jewish political loyalty, Dubnov saw in the same material his own view of Jewish autonomous communities.

---

[50] Ibid., 156.

[51] Ibid., 157.

[52] Ben Zion Dinur discusses the ways late Dubnov diverges from early Dubnov in *Israel and the Diaspora*, 35. Further on Dinur strongly criticizes Dubnov's philosophy of history (38–44).

[53] See A. Harkavy, "Istoricheskie ocherki sinoda chetyrekh stran," *Voskhod*, no. 2 (1884): 1–15; no. 4 (1884): 9–27.

Interestingly, Dubnov also shifted his perspective on Orthodox Jewry. In 1893, only a year after his essay on Graetz appeared, Dubnov made his first attempt to synthesize all of Jewish history in his article "What is Jewish History?"[54] There, instead of condemnation, Dubnov credited the Talmud with crystallizing "national feeling." We recall that feeling was previously associated with mystical movements. Although admitting that the Talmud regulated life down to its finest details, Dubnov praised it for solidifying the nation during the nearly 2,000-year experience of statelessness. "Judaism, denied political sovereignty, created for itself a spiritual fatherland. It was united by the infinite variety of monochromatic religious, quotidian, and so-cial norms established by the Talmud."[55]

By viewing the Talmud in its rightful place, not in contrast to mysticism, but as part of a religious life that incorporated all the creative endeavors of the Jewish people in their long journey, Dubnov demonstrated his intellectual growth over the decade. His reevaluation of the Talmud paralleled a retrac-tion regarding Orthodox Jewry, which he no longer viewed as he had earlier, as absolutely deleterious to the people. Instead of viewing himself as a revo-lutionary *maskil* (secularist), he portrayed himself as a leader of the modern Jewish nation. But he still had to resolve the question of what value to give Orthodox Jewry, its rabbis, and books.

Since he was incapable of valorizing Orthodox Jewry in the present, he accorded it a laudable place in the past. Inventing a tripartite scheme pre-cisely to deal with the issue of how to understand the fate of modern Jewry, Dubnov created a dialectic based originally on Hegel's model: "thesis," "anti-thesis," and "synthesis." In Dubnov's view, Orthodox Judaism belonged to the period of thesis, when all Jews lived lives fully turned toward internal problems and excluded the outside world. Antithesis was the period of assim-ilation, and synthesis represented the period of modern nationalism. Ortho-dox Judaism had given the Jews strong feelings of ethnic cohesion, but reli-gion would not necessarily take a central role in the period of modern nationalism.[56]

It may bewilder or disappoint the contemporary reader to find out that the great historian Simon Dubnov competed so aggressively with his intellectual predecessors and contemporaries. But at the same time, one can understand that such competition whetted his intellectual appetite. Through a process of

---

[54] S. Dubnov, "Chto takoe evreiskaia istoriia?: Opyt kratkoi filosofskoi kharakter-istiki)," *Voskhod*, no. 10/11 (1893): 111–40 and no. 12 (1893): 78–112.

[55] Ibid., no. 12, p. 83.

[56] S. Dubnov, "Evreistvo kak dukhovno-istoricheskaia natsiia sredi politicheskikh natsii," *Voskhod*, no. 1 (1898): 34; reprinted in Dubnov, *Pis'ma o starom i novom evreistve*.

adoption and negation of others' ideas, Dubnov rose to higher levels of intellectual achievement. For example, in response to Graetz's exploration of the Frankists, Dubnov studied the mystical movements around Sabbatai Zevi, the Frankists, and Hasidism, arriving at a more holistic view of Jewish culture than Graetz's Talmudic-centered approach had permitted.[57] Furthermore, by criticizing Graetz's valorization of Jewish literary history, Dubnov articulated a more socially dynamic and holistic sociological method. Finally, in polemics with Harkavy, Dubnov revealed his conception of the meaning of historical study for national self-consciousness and defended the centrality of mobility for Diaspora Jewish history.

It is important to note that Harkavy got personal revenge for Dubnov's attacks in 1891, when Dubnov approached the Petersburg OPE for financial aid to fund his historical research and was refused. According to Dubnov, "Passing through Odessa, Harkavy himself boasted to my close friends that he had managed "to get my request thrown out...."[58] Nevertheless, Dubnov's rivalry with Harkavy calmed after 1893. Resigning himself to living in Odessa, Dubnov moved into leadership positions in the city's social and political life. He was a leader of the nationalist group that sought more Jewish content in Odessa's OPE-sponsored schools in 1902, and later he became a central figure in the Volkspartei during and after the Revolution of 1905.[59] Moreover, with the appearance of his *Letters on Old and New Judaism*, his *History of Modern Jewry*, and the establishment of the Jewish Historical-Ethnographic Society in 1908, Dubnov cleared for himself the path of intellectual leader of Russian Jewry.

Perhaps realizing that he had been too harsh to Harkavy, Dubnov wrote in his memoirs that his criticism of Harkavy's notes to the Russian translation of volume 5 of Graetz's *History* had been unfair. Moreover, Dubnov expressed pain at the time of Harkavy's death in 1920: "A. Harkavy died recently, 84 years old. He died and was buried like everyone these days; I found out about his death from an announcement in the state newspaper when it was already too late to make the procession and burial. They say that only a few people walked with his corpse to the cemetery. I would have wanted to pay my respects exactly because our relations had been unfriendly."[60]

---

[57] See Dubnov, "Sabbatai Tsevi i psevdomissionizma v XVII veke," *Voskhod*, nos. 7–10 (1882); idem, "Iakov Frank i ego sekta khristianstvuiushchikh," *Voskhod*, nos. 1–4, 9–10 (1883); idem, "Vozniknovenie khasidizma: Zhizn' i deiatel'nost' Beshta," *Voskhod*, nos. 5–10 (1888).

[58] Dubnov, *Kniga zhizni*, 172.

[59] For information on Dubnov during these years, see Sophia Dubnova-Erlikh, *The Life and Work of S. M. Dubnov: Diaspora Nationalism and Jewish History*, trans. J. Vowles, ed. J. Shandler (Bloomington: Indiana University Press, 1991), 112–60.

[60] Dubnov, *Kniga zhizni*, 424.

Admittedly, Dubnov was not an easy partner in dialogue, since he preferred to attack first, and only later settle things calmly. The dialogue with Graetz and Harkavy that seemed so dark and impassioned had a bright side, since through his conflict with rivals Dubnov developed the central ideas of his unique Diaspora thinking.

## Chapter 7

# The Society for the Promotion of Enlightenment among the Jews of Russia and the Evolution of the Petersburg Russian-Jewish Intelligentsia, 1893–1905

Established in 1863 by Baron Evzel Guenzburg and other wealthy Jewish merchants who had recently been granted the right to reside permanently in the capital, the Society for the Promotion of Enlightenment among the Jews of Russia (known as OPE, its Russian acronym) was the first—and for two decades the only—legal and nationwide institution of Russian Jewry. During its 63-year existence, OPE was a vital force on the Russian-Jewish cultural and educational landscape. Its founders (soon joined by *maskilim*, primarily from Odessa, and by sympathetic non-Jewish government officials) set as their initial goal the integration of ordinary Jews into Russian society.[1] Although the demand for expanded legal rights was never made explicit, OPE leaders believed that once Jews were educated and appeared more "like Russians," they would receive full legal rights as citizens of the Russian empire.

Over the years, OPE expanded and evolved. In 1867, a branch was established in Odessa, whose Jewish community was less wealthy than that of St. Petersburg, but at the same time more daring in its attempts to foster both religious reform and russification. (As will be seen, the two communities were often in competition.[2]) The government for many years refused to permit the organization's further expansion. Only in 1898 was a branch in Riga opened, followed by a branch in Kiev in 1903. In 1908, the restrictions were eased, and OPE was allowed to establish branches wherever at least 25 dues-paying members were to be found. At its peak, the society had 29 branches that were distributed among large cities and in far-flung places such as Tomsk, Akker-

---

[1] For a list of the OPE's early members, see "Protokol obshchikh zasedanii chlenov OPE za 1863–1865," in the OPE archive in the State Historical Archive (RGGA, St. Petersburg) f. 1532, op. 1, d. 11, l. 45; for the original charter, see RGGA f. 1532, op. 1, d. 1, ll. 3–4. See also I. M. Cherikover, *Istoriia Obshchestva dlia rasprostraneniia prosveshcheniia mezhdu evreiami v Rossii* (St. Petersburg: Obshchestvo dlia rasprostraneniia prosveshcheniia mezhdu evreiami v Rossii, 1913), 42 (hereafter *Istoriia OPE*).

[2] On the OPE in Odessa, see Peter W. Shaw, "The Odessa Jewish Community, 1855–1900: An Institutional History" (Ph.D. diss., The Hebrew University, 1988), 88–104.

man, Riga, and Samara.[3] All general meetings, however, took place in St. Petersburg, and members of the Steering Committee were all from the capital.[4]

During its first two decades, OPE subsidized the publication of books, in Russian and in Hebrew, on "useful" subjects such as general science, world history, lexicology, and grammar, and also arranged for the translation of Jewish religious works into Russian.[5] The bulk of the budget, however—some two-thirds of an average annual expenditure of 9,229 rubles in the 1860s—was allocated to Jews seeking higher education.[6] Russian-Jewish university students, totaling only 129 in 1865, were supposed to serve as models for their co-religionists; proof of what Jews could become, given propitious circumstances.[7]

The OPE's leaders, the so-called *shtadlonim* (literally "intercessors"), derived their political influence from their wealth and, more importantly, from their connections with government officials. At the same time, being dependent on the government's good will for privileges such as the right to live outside the Pale, they were limited to urging reform rather than making explicit demands. Accordingly, they publicly supported only those activities that facilitated economic improvement, leaving demands for political representation on the sidelines. Nevertheless, they were optimistic concerning the future for Russian Jews, expecting that Alexander II's early reforms would continue, perhaps even at an accelerated pace.

---

[3] Apart from the towns and cities already mentioned, OPE had branches—not all of them particularly active—in Balt, Bobruisk, Belostok, Vilna, Vitebsk, Voronezh, Homel, Dvinsk, El'ts, Elizavetgrad, Kazan, Kishinev, Kursk, Minsk, Mogilev gubernia, Moscow, Orel, Perm, Pinsk, Slutsk, Taganrog, Tomsk, and Kharkov. See the annual report *Otchet Obshchestva dlia rasprostraneniia prosveshcheniia* (St. Petersburg, 1911), 11 (hereafter *Otchet OPE 1911*).

[4] With initial membership dues of 25 rubles, the OPE was for years controlled by Russian Jewry's wealthy elite. Over time, however, the dues were lowered, first to 10 rubles and eventually to 3. Moreover, "intellectuals," including scholars, rabbis, editors, writers, and scientists, were given honorary membership and exempted from dues. "Trustees" were those who contributed at least 500 rubles a year, whereas "honored members" contributed at least 100 rubles annually. See Cherikover, *Istoriia OPE*, 45.

[5] Among those works subsidized by the OPE were Kalman Schulman's nine volume history *Divrei yemei 'olam* (1867–84); an appendix on natural science edited by Hayim Slonimsky that appeared in the Hebrew weekly *Hameliz*; and selections from the Talmud.

[6] See the appendix to Cherikover's *Istoriia OPE*, 256. On attempts to improve elementary school education for Russian Jews in the 1860s, see Steven J. Zipperstein, "Transforming the Heder: Maskilic Politics in Imperial Russia," in *Jewish History: Essays in Honor of Chimen Abramsky*, ed. A. Rapoport-Albert and S. Zipperstein (London: P. Halban, 1988), 87–110.

[7] See "Prosveshchenie evreev v Rossii," *Evreiskaia entsiklopediia*, 13: 50.

As it turned out, such optimism was misplaced. In 1867, a reform was enacted that gave select Jewish artisans the right to live outside the Pale.[8] This, however, marked the last of the tsarist reforms with regard to the Jews. Gradually, it became clear that the link between education and rights was illusory. Despite a gradual increase in the number of Jewish university students in the 1860s, followed by a surge in enrollment in the wake of the recruitment regulations of 1874 that bestowed various privileges upon students (the most important being a shortened term of compulsory military service),[9] the government refused to pursue further emancipatory measures. Blocked by government politics, the OPE found itself bereft of any purposeful ideology and it fell into a kind of paralysis. In his 1889 review of Leon Rosenthal's publication of OPE documents from the 1860s and 1870s, Simon Dubnov offered a gloomy assessment:

> Who thinks today about this institution, [recalling] that it actually still exists, who is interested in its activities, who expects its initiative or help in any major social project of any kind? The Society for Enlightenment, which not long ago stood in the center of Jewish intellectual life, has been pushed by the force of events into a far corner and itself seems to hurry there "to find peace," like an aged invalid who has outlived his life. One can assume that it no longer lives, even though it has not yet actually died... [10]

Dubnov was perhaps too pessimistic. During the 1880s, the OPE's budget and membership actually rose, albeit slowly.[11] Yet it is true that the organization

---

[8] Previously, only merchants of the first merchant guild, Jewish military veterans, and those who had received a university degree had been given the right to live outside the Pale. On legislation concerning the Jews during Alexander II's reign, see Nathans, *Beyond the Pale*, 23–44.

[9] On Jewish students in modern educational institutions during the 1860s and 1870s, see "Prosveshchenie evreev v Rossii," 13: 49–50; see also Semion Krieze, "Batei sefer yehudiim be-safah ha-rusit be-rusiah ha-tsarit" (Ph.D. diss., Hebrew University, 1994), 51–124. On tsarist discriminatory policies in the realm of Jewish education, see Solomon Pozner, *Evrei v obshchei shkole: K istorii zakonodatel'stva i pravitel'stvennoi politiki v oblasti evreiskogo voprosa* (St. Petersburg: Razum, 1914), 77–134. For most, compulsory military service was five years, but there were shorter terms for individuals who had studied in a Russian school or university. See Yehuda Slutsky, "Takanon havot ha-tsava ha-kallit 1874 ve-ha-yihudim," *He'avar* 21 (1975): 3–18, esp. 6. On the revised military regulations of 1873, see "Voennaia sluzhba v Rossii," *Evreiskaia entsiklopediia*, 5: 670–71.

[10] Kritikus [Simon Dubnov], "Itogi Obshchestva prosveshcheniia evreev: Literaturnaia letopis'," *Voskhod*, no. 10 (1891): 41.

[11] In 1889, there were 740 members, compared with 557 in 1881. OPE expenditures rose from 27,832 rubles in 1883 to 41,000 rubles in 1889. See *Obshchestvo dlia raspro-*

produced no major social initiatives during the decade, nor did its priorities change; by the late 1880s, the proportion of its budget allocated to students in institutions of higher education had even increased to slightly more than 70 percent.[12] A shift of policy occurred only in 1893, when OPE decided to significantly increase its support for Jewish elementary schools.[13] This decision represented a new agenda for the organization, which during the course of the following decade became a vibrant institution committed to a national Jewish cultural renaissance.

What led to the OPE's change of focus? Clearly the rise within the society of young members of the Russian-Jewish intelligentsia such as Leon Bramson, Shaul Ginzburg, Maksim Vinaver, Pyotr (Pinchas) Marek, Solomon Voltke, and Mikhail Kreinin played a role. Nevertheless, the older generation of leaders did not lose their prominence, and it appears that they too were fully committed to change. A sizeable percentage of the OPE's budget even after 1893 still came directly from Baron Horace Guenzburg (Evzel's son), which indicates that he approved of the society's changed character.[14] Moreover, the list of members of the St. Petersburg Steering Committee for 1902 included both older and younger figures: apart from Baron Guenzburg (the chairman), there were older leaders such as Avram Harkavy, Jacob Halpern, Lev Katsenelson, and Mikhail Kulisher, alongside younger activists such as Vinaver, Aleksandr Braudo, Baron David Guenzburg (Horace's son), and Avram Tanenbaum.[15]

---

straneniia prosveshchenia mezhdu evreiami v Rossii za piat'desiat let (kratkii istoricheskii ocherk) (hereafter: OPE za piat'desiat let) (St. Petersburg, 1913), 14.

[12] Ibid., 13.

[13] The fund for schools began with 4,000 rubles, which was dispensed only to schools in which the Russian language was taught. See "Protokol obshchikh zasedanii chlenov," RGGA f. 1532, op. 1, d. 11, l. 102–03. It is interesting to note that at this same time (1892) Guenzburg's bank went bankrupt following a rush by creditors. The Guenzburgs, however, remained wealthy; they owned gold mines in Siberia, which at about this time produced sizable profits.

[14] On Baron Guenzburg's role in the budget, see OPE za piat'desiat let, 12. Although it has been asserted that Guenzburg, occupied with business matters, left many decisions to assistants, both the memoirs of Saul Ginzburg and OPE protocols describe his continuous presence and decisive influence. See Saul Ginzburg [Ginsburg], "Di familiye Baron Gintsburg: Drey doyres shtadlones, tsadoke un haskala," in Historishe verk, by Ginzburg (New York: Shoyl Ginsburg 70-Yohriger Yubiley Komitet, 1937), 2: 143–44.

[15] See Otchet OPE za 1902 (St. Petersburg, 1903), 1. Although there appears to have been no "generation gap" between younger and more veteran members of the OPE, the two groups did differ on other matters, notably concerning the Defense Bureau (Biuro zashchity), a Jewish vigilante group that was supported by many of the younger Jews, but not by Baron Guenzburg. See Jacob Frumkin, "Iz istorii russkogo evreistva," in Frumkin, Aronson, and Gol'denweizer, Kniga o russkom evreistve, 63; in

At the 1902 meeting of the OPE's provincial representatives, veteran member Mikhail Kulisher gave the introductory presentation, declaring that "the Steering Committee should not limit itself only to subsidizing, but [should] also influence the internal structure of the school..." Moreover, "the Steering Committee usually holds to the principle that its attention should be focused primarily on provincial areas and not on the large centers of Jewish population."[16] In fact, since 1893, the OPE's budget had been undergoing a shift in this direction. Whereas in 1881 the society had allocated more than 10,000 rubles to university students and only 2,000 rubles to schools, by 1893, it provided 18,673 rubles to a total of 437 university students and nearly half that amount (9,152 rubles) to elementary schools; by 1905, elementary schools—almost all of them in the Pale—were receiving more money (some 47,000 rubles) than were students (31,310 rubles).[17] Although the sums for schools were paltry before 1900, they were multiplied many times over by grants from the Jewish Colonization Association (JCA). This organization provided the OPE with extra annual funds: 26,000 rubles in 1900, 40,000 rubles in 1902, and 56,000 rubles in 1906. The extra money allowed for a dramatic increase in subsidies: 742 rubles per school in 1902, compared with an average subsidy of 75 rubles in 1897 and 93 rubles in 1899.[18]

During this period, the OPE's organizational structure also underwent expansion and change. In St. Petersburg, several special commissions had been set up by 1905: the Commission for Strengthening the Society's Financial Condition, the Historical-Ethnographic Commission, the Library Commission, and the School Commission.[19] This last commission, in particular, had an extensive scope of activities—so much so that it was subdivided into separate departments dealing with such matters as *"heders,"* *"teachers,"* *"school curri-*

---

English translation *Russian Jewry (1860–1917)*, trans. Mirra Ginsburg (New York: T. Yoseloff, 1966).

[16] Kulisher's speech is found in *Protokol soveshchaniia komiteta obshchestva dlia rasprostraneniia prosveshcheniia mezhdu evreiami v Rossii s inogorodnymi chlenami 25–27 dekabria 1902 g.* (St. Petersburg, 1903), 4.

[17] *Otchet OPE za 1881* (St. Petersburg, 1882); *Otchet OPE za 1893* (St. Petersburg, 1894); *Otchet OPE za 1905–1906* (St. Petersburg, 1907).

[18] See I. M. Cherikover, "Obshchestvo dlia rasprostraneniia prosveshcheniia mezhdu evreiami v Rossii," in *Evreiskaia entsiklopediia*, 13: 61. Baron Guenzburg was the head of the JCA office in St. Petersburg. On the relationship between the JCA and the OPE, see Steven Rappaport, "Jewish Education and Jewish Culture in the Russian Empire, 1880–1914," (Ph.D. diss., Stanford University, 2000), 82–85, 100–02. See also Gur Alroey, "Bureaucracy, Agents, and Swindlers: The Hardships of Jewish Emigration from the Pale of Settlement in the Early 20th Century," in *Jews and the State: Dangerous Alliances and the Perils of Privilege*, ed. E. Mendelsohn, Studies in Contemporary Jewry 19 (New York: Oxford University Press, 2003), 224–29.

[19] On the St. Petersburg commissions, see "Protokoly zasedanii komiteta obshchestva 1900–1901," RGGA f. 1532, op. 1, d. 182, l. 71.

cula," and "school libraries."[20] Members of the commission met at least twice a month and hosted lectures each year for members and invited guests.

A closer examination of the St. Petersburg School Commission and the manifold contributions by Leon Bramson affords a good illustration of the OPE's evolving shift away from integrationism and toward a more "national" Jewish policy.[21] Born in 1869 in Kovno (Kaunas), Bramson was awarded a degree in law from Moscow University in 1890. He then moved to St. Petersburg, where he played an instrumental role in the OPE's School Commission and later become head of the OPE's elementary school in St. Petersburg (popularly known as the "Berman" school after its founder, Jacob Berman). In 1898, he took charge of the OPE's statistical work; the following year, he became secretary of the Jewish Colonization Association in Russia. In 1905–06, he participated in the Union for the Attainment of Equal Rights for the Jews[22] and was elected to the First State Duma from Kovno, serving as a representative of the left-leaning Trudovik party.[23] Among his other works, Bramson co-edited (with Mikhail Kulisher) the *Volume in the Service of Jewish Elementary Schools* (1896) and was a key contributor to the *Handbook of Questions Concerning Jewish Education* (1901)—both volumes subsidized by the OPE—and served as editor of the two-volume *Collection of Articles on the Economic Condition of the Jews of Russia* (1904), which was funded by the JCA.[24]

---

[20] Ibid., d. 47, l. 9.

[21] My use of the word "national" reflects the way in which Russian-Jewish liberals understood the concept: nearly identical with the idea of an autonomous area for Jewish endeavors, but referring as well to the struggle for civic rights for Jews. Liberals viewed the struggle for Jewish rights as "national" since Jews were particular victims of tsarist repression, such that the overthrow of the tsarist regime was expected to bring about the possibility of national renewal.

[22] The Union for the Attainment of Equal Rights for the Jews (Soiuz dlia dostizheniia polnopraviia evreiskogo naroda v Rossii) was a coalition of Jewish political parties (politically right of the Bund) that was established in 1905 with the aim of organizing an effective Jewish bloc in the First Duma. See Christoph Gassenschmidt, *Jewish Liberal Politics in Tsarist Russia, 1900–1914: The Modernization of Russian Jewry* (New York: New York University Press, 1995), 22; Jonathan Frankel, *Prophecy and Politics: Socialism, Nationalism, and the Russian Jews, 1862–1917* (Cambridge: Cambridge University Press, 1981), 161–65.

[23] For more on Bramson, see *Rossiiskaia evreiskaia entsiklopediia*, 4 vols. (Moscow: Epos, 1994), 1: 160–61.

[24] In Russian, these works appeared as *Sbornik v pol'zu nachal'nykh evreiskikh shkol* (St. Petersburg, 1896); *Spravochnaia kniga po voprosam obrazovaniia evreev: Posobie dlia uchitelei i uchitel'nits evreiskikh shkol i deiatelei po narodnomu obrazovaniiu* (St. Petersburg, 1901); and *Sbornik ob ekonomicheskom polozhenii evreev v Rossii* (St. Petersburg, 1904).

Bramson was an advocate of the so-called "productivization of the Jews," according to which the "Jewish problem" could be solved if Jews were to engage in productive occupations, such as manufacturing, crafts, and agriculture (as opposed to trade). The notion was of course popular among Russian *maskilim*, whom Bramson admired. He had special esteem for Nikolai Bakst, the brilliant founder of ORT, the society for manual and agricultural work among Jews; and for Menashe (Mikhail) Morgulis, the founder of Trud, an artisan school in Odessa—about whom Bramson delivered a talk in April 1912 at an OPE gathering in St. Petersburg.[25]

Bramson's own views were spelled out at length in his article "On the History of Elementary Education of the Jews in Russia," in which he delineated three historical periods: up to 1804, the beginning of the reign of Alexander I (during which there was no real organization of elementary education); from 1804–55, the reigns of Alexander I and Nicholas I (when the progress of Jewish educational development was linked to a number of government decrees); and from 1856–94, the reigns of Alexander II and Alexander III (when the Jewish population began to show support for secular education and communities began to take an active role in the organization of new Jewish schools).[26]

Leaving aside the first period as one of unfulfilled expectations, Bramson argued that the failures of the second period were derived from the paradox that the government established special Jewish schools, but its generally oppressive policy toward the Jews led to deep distrust. "Each new liability, each series of expulsions," Bramson wrote, "were factors that could not but have an influence on the fate of Jewish schools, which had not yet planted deep roots, and [these factors] significantly slowed their development."[27]

In the long run, according to Bramson, the most positive development in Russian-Jewish education was the decree of 1873 that led to the closure of many Jewish educational institutions, among them the state-supported rabbinical seminaries in Vilna (Vilnius) and Zhitomir, state-run Jewish secondary schools, and most of the schools providing basic secular education for Jews. This "reform" was designed to encourage Jews to study "in regular Russian schools and universities," although, beginning in 1887, a *numerus clausus* limited the number of Jews studying in Russian institutions of secondary and higher education.[28] Bramson argued that the closure of government-spon-

---

[25] Bramson's talk was later published as *Obshchestvenno-kul'turnaia deiatel'nost' M. G. Morgulisa* (St. Petersburg, 1912).

[26] L. Bramson, "K istorii nachal'nogo obrazovaniia evreev v Rossii," in Bramson and Kulisher, *Sbornik v pol'zu nachal'nykh evreiskikh shkol*, 280, 324.

[27] Ibid., 324.

[28] For the government's explanation of the reform, see "Izvlechenie iz ob"iasnitel'nykh svedenii k polozheniiam o evreiskikh nachal'nykh uchilishchakh i o evreiskikh uchitel'nykh institutakh," *Vestnik russkikh evreev* 20–21 (1873): 618. Members of the russified

sored schools forced Jews to become much more involved in their own education, from establishing and funding their own schools to determining the curricula of Jewish and secular studies.

The validity of Bramson's contention is reflected in the figures. By 1898–1900, there were 851 modern Jewish schools in Russia and the former kingdom of Poland (644 of them in the Pale of Settlement), with a total of 96,844 pupils. This was an increase of 355 percent in the number of schools and 354 in the number of pupils in contrast with 1880, when there had been only 187 schools and 21, 308 pupils. During the same period, there was an increase of only 33 percent in the number of Jews in the overall population, from 4,000,000 to 5,300,000.[29]

Although the OPE deserves credit for its role in facilitating the expansion of modern Jewish education, its primary contribution was not in the dispensation of subsidies: its budget was too small to allow it to maintain any single school apart from the Berman school in St. Petersburg. More important by far was the organization's educational program, which came into its own with the creation of the School Commission in 1895.[30] A year earlier, the OPE's statistical unit had prepared a lengthy questionnaire that was sent to more than 200 teachers, along with civic and religious leaders.[31] Some of the questions dealt with school buildings, teachers, curricula, textbooks, and salaries, whereas others reflected a broader focus on communities and their structure, the attitude of each community toward modern education, the relationship between government officials and the local Jewish population, and the possibility of community support. This information gleaned from responses to this questionnaire proved useful to defining the goals and strategies of the School Commission, whose activities in St. Petersburg were divided into two spheres: the creation of school materials and aid to local activists.

In the *Handbook of Questions Concerning Jewish Education*, the OPE offered sample programs for four- and five-year elementary schools, giving a breakdown of how many hours should be spent on secular (as opposed to traditional Jewish) subjects and providing advice about, among other things, text-

---

Jewish intelligentsia were pleased that, as a result of the reform, Jews would finally leave the "dark corners" of the shtetl and enter Russian educational institutions. See Il'ia Trotskii, "Evrei v russkoi shkole," in Frumkin, Aronson, and Gol'denveizer, *Kniga o russkom evreistve*, 355.

[29] See Rappaport, "Jewish Education and Jewish Culture in the Russian Empire," 52. In this fine work, Rappaport comes to his conclusion after comparing a variety of statistical sources. The information he acquired through much hard work has significantly eased my own research on the organizational history of the OPE.

[30] The first description of a "School Commission" is found in the report of the society from 1895. In earlier reports, we find language such as "activity in elementary education." See *Otchet OPE za 1895* (St. Petersburg, 1896).

[31] *Otchet OPE za 1894* (St. Petersburg, 1895), 38–40.

books, teaching methodology, and school hygiene. In addition, there were sections devoted to the organization and proper administration of professional schools for artisans and farmers. Since government restrictions at the time prevented the OPE from establishing its own schools, the OPE devoted an entire section of the Handbook to legal issues, giving not only a summary of the relevant statutes, but also providing sample petitions for opening private and community-run Jewish schools.[32] The handbook, it was stated, was the culmination of some six years of hard thinking about the needs of Jewish schools in the Pale.[33]

In St. Petersburg, a pedagogical bureau set up by Bramson facilitated contacts between schools with available teaching positions and prospective teachers. More important, the School Commission sought to organize teacher-training programs. Only in 1907 was the OPE granted permission to establish its own teacher training college in Grodno; until then, the School Commission improvised, giving grants to promising high-school graduates and creating pedagogical courses for students in Kiev, St. Petersburg, and Kovno. Because the need for teachers was so great, the OPE even offered grants to traditional Jewish teachers of religious subjects (melamdim) in order to prepare them for state examinations, although most of the melamdim never took the exams.[34] In addition, in 1900, the OPE entered into negotiations with the Prushim yeshiva in Kovno. This yeshiva was a kollel institution providing financial support for the families of the married men who studied there for three or four years; the OPE offered to provide secular courses for the yeshiva bokhrim if seminarians would consider a career in teaching.[35] At the same time, the OPE took over the Talmud Torah in Grodno, which later became, in 1907, the OPE Institute for the Training of Teachers. In this school, prospective teachers were required to give practice lessons in Russian, Yiddish, and Hebrew.[36]

---

[32] One of the first charters sent by OPE leaders to the government in the early 1860s included a provision that the organization be allowed to open its own schools. The government rejected this demand; as a result, most Jewish-run schools were privately owned and received a subsidy from the OPE. Only in 1908 was the OPE granted the right to open its own schools. See Cherikover, Istoriia OPE, 41.

[33] Spravochnaia kniga po voprosam obrazovaniia evreev, 17–20.

[34] Otchet OPE za 1894, 29–30.

[35] "Protokoly zasedanii chlenov OPE," RGGA f. 1532, op. 1, d. 214, ll. 11–16. Kollel refers to an institution of higher learning administered with community funds; bokhrim are young male students of Torah. Negotiations broke down when agreement could not be reached concerning the number of hours of secular studies to be offered, the extent of the OPE's financial contribution, and the organization's intention in making its offer. On the Prushim yeshiva, see "Yeshivot," Encyclopaedia Judaica (Jerusalem, 1972), 16: 769.

[36] "Protokoly zasedanii bibliotechnogo otdela i shkol'no-uchebnoi komissii za 1905–1906 gg.," RGGA f. 1532, op. 1, d. 493, l. 23.

Under Bramson's supervision, the position of traveling inspector was created in 1900. An OPE representative traveled through the Pale of Settlement examining OPE-subsidized and other schools (including *heders*) and making suggestions for their improvement; the aim was to provide a bridge between the central organization in St. Petersburg and the communities of the Pale.[37] In the same spirit, local teachers and Jewish leaders were invited to come to St. Petersburg for consultations in 1902, and summer courses were held for Jewish teachers in 1904 in Belaia Tserkov' in Ukraine.[38]

In defining the proper content of schools, in developing teacher training programs, and in assisting local activists in opening schools, the OPE helped bring about both the expansion and the modernization of Jewish education. While it is hard to quantify such achievements, the establishment of dozens of local organizations devoted to Jewish education beginning in 1908 (when the government allowed such activities) testifies to the OPE's influence.[39]

Many OPE initiatives expressed specific Jewish concerns beyond that of setting up Jewish-sponsored schools. The OPE's "ideal" school program (which was realized in the Berman school) devoted considerable time to traditional Jewish subjects. In the "preparatory" (first year) grade, 16 weekly hours were devoted to Jewish subjects, including Hebrew language (6 hours), Bible, translation of prayers, Jewish law, and Jewish history; in the higher grades, 13 hours a week were devoted to Jewish subjects.[40]

To be sure, the St. Petersburg branch of the OPE refrained from explicitly championing "national" goals. In 1902, when the "ideal" school program was published, the OPE in St. Petersburg simply noted, without further explanation, that it had decided to promote only those programs in which "Jewish subjects are given a comparatively large number of school hours and in which … the academic plan of the [Jewish] subjects mentioned is broader and fuller."[41] Yet other modern Jewish elementary schools—including the schools subsidized by the OPE in Odessa—devoted as little as two to five weekly hours to Jewish subjects. Dubnov, for his part, lauded the "national character"

---

[37] Among OPE traveling inspectors were such illustrious individuals as Dr. F. Lerner, Pyotr Marek, and Hayim Fialkov. A portrait of Fialkov can be found in Hirsz Abramowicz's *Profiles of a Lost World: Memoirs of East European Jewish Life before World War II*, trans. E. Z. Dobkin, ed. D. Abramowicz and J. Shandler (Detroit: Wayne State University Press, 1999), 126–31.

[38] See M. Kulisher's speech welcoming guests to the 1902 convention, published in *Protokol soveshchaniia komiteta OPE*, 4–5.

[39] One can obtain a good picture of the intense activity of Jewish society in the "chronicle" section of every issue of the *Vestnik Obshchestva Rasprostraneniia Prosveshcheniia Mezhdu Evreiami*, which began publishing in November 1910.

[40] See *Spravochnaia kniga po voprosam obrazovaniia evreev*, 121–25.

[41] Ibid., 121.

of St. Petersburg's school program in comparison with the "assimilationist" program of the Odessa OPE.[42]

What impeded the creation of a truly national program at this time was the absence of a strategy for dealing with the traditional *heder*. At the 1902 meeting with the provincial representatives held in St. Petersburg, opinions were divided on the subject. Some delegates supported OPE involvement in *heder* reform, but others were skeptical about the feasibility of undertaking such a large effort, especially given the organization's limited budget. In the end, the issue was left open, as OPE leaders (to their credit), did not wish to commit the organization to any program it could not carry out. Over the course of the decade, however, the necessity for reform became increasingly apparent, and by 1912, *heder* reform had become part of the OPE's educational program.[43]

Of course, not all the OPE's activities were successful. One failure in particular, involving the establishment of a school for artisans, illuminates the complicated attitude of the St. Petersburg School Commission toward Jews in the Pale. As noted, in 1896, the OPE took control of the Berman elementary school in St. Petersburg. Opened in 1865, this school had served mainly the children of retired soldiers and so-called city dwellers (*meshchane*) rather than the children of merchants. Bramson wanted to expand the curriculum and create a special school for artisans, with classes devoted to metalwork, woodwork, and timber-cutting for boys, and tailoring and embroidery for girls. Moreover, unhappy with the lack of space in the school, he proposed to the St. Petersburg Jewish community to build a three-story building on the site next to the main St. Petersburg synagogue, on Ofitserskaia and Bol'shaia Masterskaia Streets. In 1894, Baron Horace Guenzburg contributed 40,000 rubles to start the project.[44] By the time it was finished in 1898, the building cost between 102,000 and 108,000 rubles. Providing the bulk of the money for the project were the leading 300 Jewish families in the capital.[45]

Bramson's goal was to make the school a model for similar institutions to be established in the Pale. As noted, this school offered the OPE's "ideal" basic five-year elementary school program—but Bramson wanted more. His plan was that, following graduation, students would be invited to begin their

---

[42] Simon Dubnov, "O natsional'nom vospitanii," *Pis'ma o starom i novom evreistve*, *Voskhod*, no. 1 (January 1902): 94. Dubnov undoubtedly took the opportunity here to attack the leaders of the Odessa branch of the OPE, whom he hoped to overthrow in coming elections. Nevertheless, he sincerely admired Bramson's efforts.

[43] See the OPE-sponsored pamphlet, *Sovremennyi kheder po obsledovaniiu Obshchestva dlia rasprostraneniia prosveshcheniia v 1912* (St. Petersburg, 1912), 3–5.

[44] See "K istorii Sankt-Peterburgskikh evreiskikh uchilishch," Archive of L. M. Bramson, Central State Historical Archive of the URSR (Kiev) f. 992, op. 2, d. 5, l. 95.

[45] Ibid., l. 19.

studies at the artisan school, whose program would be four years for boys and three years for girls.[46]

By 1898, there were 457 pupils at the school, most of them studying free of charge. The five-year program was quite rigorous for the time, including courses in Hebrew, Jewish religion, biblical history, Russian language, arithmetic, Russian history, geography, natural history, penmanship, and singing. On the secondary level, matters were more complicated. Bramson was eager to encourage students from the Pale to earn a diploma from the artisan school because holders of a certificate of "skilled artisan" (*podmaster'e*) were allowed to live anywhere in Russia.[47] But why did future artisans first need to acquire a five-year general education? Who was interested in becoming an educated artisan? Certainly not the students from St. Petersburg, who were far more likely to continue in a Russian *gymnasium* or else take up better-paying employment. Artisans, after all, even skilled ones, earned meager salaries of between 32 and 36 rubles a month, and had a comparatively low social status.

Thus, it was mainly children from the Pale who wanted to attend the artisan school. This situation was problematic. For one thing, such children needed to obtain special exemptions to live in the capital, which took time and effort to arrange. In addition, they were not well prepared for the five-year general educational program that preceded the artisan program, and school trusties began to complain that they were having a negative influence on the other pupils.[48] Few of them, in any event, actually finished the elementary school program. In consequence, there were very few students in the artisan school. Even in 1906, the year of peak enrollment, it had only 80 students, compared with 390 students in the elementary school.

Although the artisan school received a 9,800-ruble subsidy from the JCA, its costs were twice that. The deficits had to be covered by the regular school, but in 1904, the school administration decided to separate the two programs. No longer subsidizing the artisan school, the regular school could become financially solvent. The artisan program, however, was forced to close after 1906.

Bramson's idea of creating educated artisans turned out to be an expensive delusion, not least because there was little use for the excellence of craft that students gained in their training. Given the enormous competition in the Pale and elsewhere, handicrafts had to be made quickly and often badly in order to bring any profit. But apart from being a chronicle of a failed experiment, the story of the St. Petersburg artisan school illuminates the condescension and resentment of the local trustees toward the "provincial" students. Such students, it was claimed, brought into the school a "foreign element" that could not but "reflect negatively on the pedagogical operation of our

---

[46] According to Bramson, this would be "three schools in one." Ibid., l. 14.

[47] Ibid.

[48] Ibid., l. 123.

schooling."[49] Furthermore, the cost of providing for students from the Pale "hardly answered the needs of the Petersburg Jewish population."[50] Clearly the trustees saw their subsidy of the provincial students as a costly and not particularly beneficial act of philanthropy.

In their defense, it should be noted that OPE members in St. Petersburg had good reason to complain about the financial burden, as their local dues were used nearly exclusively for projects in the Pale. (All projects in St. Petersburg, such as the OPE school, were funded from proceeds from fixed capital investments or from donations from the capital's elite.) The community, moreover, had been contributing increasingly large sums in order to finance OPE-expanded activities, as evidenced by the 41,000-ruble school bill for 1904. At the same time, the resentment expressed toward Jews from the Pale reveals that St. Petersburg activists viewed provincials with some prejudice. Inevitably, philanthropy toward the Jews of the Pale bred a kind of patronizing condescension among the capital's Jewish elite.

After serving for several years on the School Commission and as head of the OPE schools in St. Petersburg, Bramson resigned. "My health is significantly shaken after four and a half years of uninterrupted work in the school," he wrote in 1904, "and with a feeling of genuine regret, I am forced to inform the Commission that I no longer consider myself capable, in such an exhausted condition, of carrying out those obligations placed upon me, obligations that demand fresh energy."[51] Nonetheless, as noted, he continued to play an active role in Jewish affairs, both retaining his position as secretary of the JCA and becoming, in the following year, a major leader of the Jewish Democratic Group.[52]

Another institution that reflected changes among the OPE leadership was the Historical Ethnographic Commission. Founded in 1891, this group was the forerunner of the famous Jewish Historical Ethnographic Society, which was established in St. Petersburg in 1908.[53] Although not as multifaceted and

---

[49] Ibid.

[50] Ibid., l. 50.

[51] Ibid., l. 78.

[52] The Jewish Democratic Group (Evreiskaia demokraticheskaia gruppa), established in 1907, was a successor to the Union for the Attainment of Equal Rights for the Jews. It was politically left of Dubnov's Jewish People's Group (Evreiskaia narodnaia gruppa), especially in its commitment to social justice.

[53] Dubnov describes the significance of the OPE for the creation of the Jewish Historical Ethnographic Society in "Uchreditel'noe sobranie i publichnye zasedaniia Evreiskogo Istoriko-Etnograficheskogo Obshchestva," *Evreiskaia starina*, no. 1 (1909): 158.

dynamic as the School Commission, the activities of the Historical Ethno-graphic Commission also displayed the turn toward a more assertive sense of Jewish identity that evolved among the St. Petersburg Jewish elite from the early 1890s to 1905. As Isaiah Trunk has noted: "Experience has shown that in the life of nations the growth of national feeling is always accompanied by the development of historiography."[54]

It is generally believed that the Historical Ethnographic Commission came about following the publication of Dubnov's celebrated essay of 1888, "On the Study of the History of Russian Jews and the Establishment of a Russian-Jewish Historical Society," which inspired the members of the St. Petersburg OPE to begin meeting regularly to study Jewish history in Russia. Maksim Vinaver promulgated this view in his famous memoir "How We Studied History." The truth, however, is that the cultivation of historical study began as early as the initial formation of the OPE, whose charter in-cluded the goal of encouraging the publication of historical studies in Hebrew and Russian; as early as 1866–67, the OPE put together its *Collection of Articles on Jewish Literature and History*.[55] This collection was held up for nearly four years by the government censor, who was hostile to research on Jews in Russia.[56] In any event, the work's intended readers—Jews who were both in-terested in Jewish history and fluent in Russian—hardly existed in Russian society of the 1860s.[57]

Another not very successful early venture was the attempt to publish a history of Russia in Hebrew. Unsatisfied with previous translations, the OPE in 1869 commissioned Solomon Mandelkern, then a student at St. Petersburg University, to produce a Hebrew-language history, complete with a section on the Jews in Russia, by the following year. In the end, three volumes were published, but only in 1875, six years after the original commission.[58] For sev-

---

This article was first given as a talk at the organization's first meeting, on November 16, 1908.

[54] I. Trunk, "Istoriki russkogo evreistva," in Frumkin, Aronson, and Gol'denveizer, *Kniga o russkom evreistve*, 21.

[55] In Russian, the two-volume work was titled *Sbornik statei po evreiskoi istorii i litera-ture, izdavaemyi obshchestvom dlia rasprostraneniia prosveshcheniia mezhdu evreiami v Rossii* (St. Petersburg, 1866–67). For a good summary of the OPE's early approach to aiding historical research, see Shmuel Feiner, *Haskalah and History: The Emergence of a Modern Jewish Historical Consciousness*, trans. Chaya Naor and Sondra Silverston (Portland, OR: Littman Library of Jewish Civilization, 2002), 209–10, 243–44.

[56] See Cherikover, *Istoriia OPE*, 81–82.

[57] Letter of Lev Levanda to Isaac Zal'kind, cited in Alfred Landau, ed., "Iz perepiski L. Levandy," *Evreiskaia biblioteka*, no. 9 (1901): 56.

[58] Feiner, *Haskalah and History*, 215–16; according to Feiner, it took more than a decade for the project to come to fruition.

eral years, this experience acted as a damper on the OPE's activities in the realm of scholarly publication.

In 1880, however, Avraam (Alfred) Harkavy's request for funds to allow for the publication of historical studies was granted.[59] Born in 1835, Harkavy belonged to the early generation of OPE leaders. A former student at the government-sponsored rabbinical seminary in Vilna (which also taught secular studies), Harkavy enrolled in the Oriental studies department of St. Petersburg University in 1863 and eventually completed a doctorate there. He also taught at the university, but was forced to give up his position when he refused to convert to Christianity.[60] Later, he worked as the director of the Oriental division of the St. Petersburg Public Library and, with the establishment of the Historical Ethnographic Commission, became its head.[61]

Between 1880 and 1885, Harkavy was instrumental in publishing two volumes of documents collected by Sergei Bershadsky on the history of Lithuanian Jewry,[62] along with the fifth volume in Russian of Heinrich Graetz's *Volkstümliche Geschichte der Juden*. At the same time, Leon Rosenthal, a wealthy businessman who was one of the OPE's original members, was active in facilitating the publication of works in Hebrew. In 1885, a commission was established to compile and publish *Haasif*, a volume of articles commemorating the centenary of Moses Mendelsohn's death. Toward the end of the 1880s, Rosenthal also published the two-volume Hebrew translation of OPE documents from the 1860s and 1870s (which, as will be recalled, prompted Dubnov's critical assessment of the organization's resembling "an aged invalid").[63]

According to OPE archival records, the first proposal to create a Historical-Ethnographic Commission was made in the OPE general meeting of 1887, when Harkavy suggested establishing a body for the "collection and study of material concerning the history of the Jewish people in general and Russian Jews in particular" as a means of honoring Heinrich Grätz on the

---

[59] See *OPE za piat'desiat let*, 12. The unknown author of this work claims that Harkavy established a Historical Commission in 1881, but I have found no documents confirming this assertion.

[60] See "Avraam (Al'bert) Iakovlevich Garkavi," *Evreiskaia entsiklopediia*, 6: 180.

[61] A festschrift to honor Harkavy's work was published in 1908, *Festschrift zu ehren Dr. A. Harkavy. Aus Anlass seines am 20 November 1905 vollendeten siebzigsten Lebensjahres*, ed. David Guenzburg (St. Petersburg, 1908; repr., New York: Arno Press, 1980).

[62] Three volumes were ultimately published as *Russko-evreiskii arkhiv* (St. Petersburg, 1882, 1884, and 1908). Volumes 1 and 2 carried the same subtitle, *Dokumenty i regesty k istorii litovskikh evreev*, and volume 3 appeared with the subtitle *Dokumenty k istorii pol'skikh litovskikh evreev*.

[63] See *Otchet OPE za 1885* (St. Petersburg, 1886), 5; Leon Rosenthal, ed., *Toledot hevrat marbei haskalah beyisra'el be'erets rusiyah*, 2 vols. (St. Petersburg, 1886–90).

occasion of his 70th birthday.[64] After drawing up a more detailed proposal, Harkavy received a 150-ruble allocation for the project.[65] Four years later, in the OPE report of 1891, pedagogical, legal, and economic arguments were advanced in support of the proposed commission. "One should acknowledge that the knowledge of the past fate of one's own people and a broad acquaintance with its present, especially in that country which for thousands of years was the fatherland for a large part of Jewry, is one of the main constituent parts of a genuine education," it was noted.[66] Therefore,

> desiring to devote our weak forces to produce a scholarly literary service for Judaism, the individuals on the [attached] list ... intend to publish a "Russian Jewish annual" (or a series of separate Jewish scholarly works). In addition to Jewish history, bibliography, and the like, we envision placing a compendium of facts and information in the annual that will deal with all questions concerning the condition of the Jews in Russia[67]

Although the annual was never published, the Historical-Ethnographic Commission was officially launched in 1891. Two years later, in a talk before the general OPE membership Harkavy noted that "in all the corners of our country one cannot find a single work of scholarship, so that our two-thousand-year-old history [in Russia] lies untouched and unknown."[68] The following year, in a lecture to OPE members entitled "From the History of the Culture of Russian Jews," such scholarship was put on display, as Harkavy drew attention to the history of Jewish book publishing in Eastern Europe from the 16th century onward. Using archival material that had been uncovered by members of the Historical Ethnographic Commission, he argued against the perception among enlightened Jews that East European Jews at the time of the Khmelnytski uprising were culturally backward. In fact, Harkavy argued, both Hasidic Jews in southwest Russia and in Poland and *mitnagdim* in Lithuania had been avid book publishers; documentation had been found for no fewer than 62 publishing houses:

---

[64] *Otchet OPE za 1887* (St. Petersburg, 1888), 6.

[65] *Otchet OPE za 1888* (St. Petersburg, 1889), 7.

[66] Harkavy claimed that the Jewish community in Russia was thousands of years old, established "by Jews who migrated from the region of the Black Sea and Caucasus, where their ancestors had settled after the Assyrian and Babylonian exiles." See *Encyclopaedia Judaica*, 7: 1342. Harkavy's theory is fully expressed in his book *O iazyke evreev i o slavianskikh slovakh, vstrechaemykh u evreiskikh pisatelei* (St. Petersburg, 1865).

[67] RGGA f. 1532, op. 1, d. 35, l. 1.

[68] *Otchet OPE za 1893*, 53. Harkavy acknowledged the fine work of historians on Polish Jewry, which he said revealed even starker contrast with the lack of such work on Russian Jews.

I must add that [the compilation of] a full catalogue of Jewish books printed in our fatherland even during the most heated polemics ... have proven to be profoundly instructive for the history of the cultural development of Russian Jews in connection with other issues. Such a catalogue bears witness to the fact that even in those God-forsaken shtetls, about which we are accustomed to thinking that no one could not expect anything except darkness and fanaticism, intellectual work was carried on and books were published. [The catalogue] visually demonstrates that the Jews had spiritual interests everywhere and always, and that the need for knowledge, for understanding of the essence of Judaism and the historical fates of the Jews, did not expire in Israel.[69]

Harkavy's valorization of Russian-Jewish history may seem apologetic, but it is important to recall that most enlightened Jews were known to have profoundly negative feelings about both Hasidim and *mitnagdim*. It took courage for Harkavy (standing before a group of people who had consciously broken away from the Pale and its religious and communal shackles) to claim that the world of the shtetl had its own unique culture and that this culture belonged to modern Jews as well, and that was therefore worthy of study. It is true that others, notably Dubnov, had come to the same conclusion.[70] Nonetheless, this lecture given under OPE auspices signaled an attitude that would gain dominance in the following decade.

At least until 1881, elite, educated Jews viewed their identity in terms of acculturation in Russian society. They were generally loath to identify themselves with their poor brethren in the Pale; they preferred to view themselves as part of a multinational Russian intelligentsia. Even among the few secular scholars of Judaism, studying the distant past was preferred. Trained as rabbinic scholars, they were at home in the Talmud; modern historical methods were foreign to them. And, in any case, the documents for the study of modern Jewry were not yet available; most of them were located in the hands of individuals who did not understand their value. It was not until the 1890s that Jewish intellectuals such as Harkavy urged the study of Russia's Jewry as a means of legitimating the unique contribution of their own culture.[71]

Under Harkavy's guidance, the Historic Ethnographic Commission set itself the goal of collecting and organizing material, found in Russian books

---

[69] A. Garkavy, "Iz istorii kul'tury russkikh evreev," in Bramson and Kulisher, *Sbornik v pol'zu nachal'nykh evreiskikh shkol*, 108.

[70] An early sympathetic portrayal of Hasidism is already found in Eliezer Zweifel's book *Shalom 'al yisra'el* (Zhitomir, 1868). Dubnov's article is entitled "Vozniknovenie khasidizma: Zhizn' i deiatel'nost' Izrailia Beshta," *Voskhod* (1888): no. 5–6 (113–41); no. 7 (81–100); no. 8 (3–21); no. 9 (3–16); no. 10 (27–44).

[71] Simon Dubnov stresses this point in his long essay on Graetz, "Istoriograf evreistva," *Voskhod*, no. 8 (1892): 36–38.

and archives, on Russian Jewry. In 1893, members of the commission began work on a collection of laws and decrees relating to the Jews, which came out in three volumes between 1897 and 1903. Containing "more than 2,450 decrees and fragments from inscriptions, materials, and reports," this work was meant to "help the scholar find his way through the printed documentation."[72]

Such historical research appears to have galvanized the participants' senses of Jewish identity. Many of them belonged to the highly acculturated St. Petersburg elite. Meeting in each other's homes twice a month for more than a decade, they would read the acts and decrees that they had prepared over the previous fortnight. Vinaver describes how participants competed with each other to find antisemitic expressions in the legal documents they researched:

> One looking into the crowded room ... would be amazed at the scene before him. Ten or fifteen people would appear, each with a packet of cards, which each took out of his packet with pride, showing off the abundance of his catch. And the reading began. The unfortunates who had not succeeded in catching a single mention of the word *zhid* [in their documents] would looked depressed and confused, and would ask everyone to take them at their word that they had indeed read through the fat tome—but alas, entirely in vain.[73]

In addition to researching tsarist documents, the commission hosted between 10 and 12 lectures a year by members and invited guests. Since members were working mainly with official documents, many of the lectures reflected legal matters. For example, in 1897, Vinaver spoke about land ownership in the 15th and 16th centuries, and Vol'tke presented a paper on the condition of Jewish artisans. In 1900, Akiva Ettinger spoke about Jewish farmers in Bessarabia, while Katsenelson spoke on religion and politics in the biblical period. Some of the members—themselves lawyers—found the work of the commission helpful in their own work, especially when they attempted to improve the legal condition of the Jews in appeals to the First Department of the Administrative Senate.[74] Except for Harkavy, none of the members of the

---

[72] *Registy i nadpisi: Svod materialov dlia istorii evreev v Rossii*, 3 vols. (St. Petersburg, 1897, 1901, 1903); the latter two volumes were published by the Jewish Historical Ethnographic Society as one volume in 1908. The quote is from Trunk, "Istoriki russkogo evreistva," 21.

[73] M. Vinaver, "Kak my zanimalis' istoriei," *Evreiskaia starina*, no. 1 (1909): 41–54; reprinted in *Evrei v Rossiiskoi imperii XVIII–XIX vekov: Sbornik trudov evreiskikh istorikov*, edited by Aleksandr Lokshin (Moscow: Evreiskii universitet; Jerusalem: Gesharim Press, 1995), 70.

[74] On the relationship between the legal and historical professions among Russian Jews, see Benjamin Nathans, "Conflict, Community and the Jews of Nineteenth-

commission were trained historians. Such lack of training, however, was typical of the time; even famous scholars such as Dubnov, Gessen, and Israel Tsinberg (who were also members of the commission) did not have a university degree in history.

Not surprisingly, the Historical Ethnographic Commission gave pride of place to earlier Russian-Jewish intellectuals, creating as it were a pantheon of figures who embodied OPE's newly evolving national values. Hagiographic accounts were presented on such national Jewish cultural figures as Osip Rabinovich, Judah Leib Gordon, and Isaak Baer Levinsohn. But there were talks on less well-known figures who also embodied nationalist thinking. In one talk, for instance, Katsenelson spoke about the *maskilim* Kalman Shulman and Abraham Baer Gottlober. According to Katsenelson, these two Hebrew writers from the 1840s–80s had contributed to Russian Jewry by expressing skepticism about russification and secularization, worrying that modernized Jews were alienating the following generation from Judaism. Speaking about Gottlober—and himself—Katsenelson noted:

> More than anything else, the radical change in the education of the younger generation and the removal of the Jewish language [i.e., Hebrew] from the curriculum depressed him. And really, either we do not care a whit about Judaism or it is dear to us, and if we want to keep our children within the fold of our dear religion, then we should not neglect the cement that connects the future with the past, that is, language and literature. The short instruction book [used in Jewish schools] about the Jewish religion in Hebrew is too pitiable an instrument in the struggle against the temptations awaiting our children. Being a Jew is sometimes a difficult act—moreover, it is not an act of a single minute, but chronic, one that lasts a long time. Whoever prepares his son for this kind of heroism, must provide him with a strong shield against which all the arrows of temptation may be deflected. Such a shield can only be Jewish ethics, acquired from the living source of the nation's literature.[75]

Katsenelson's viewpoint, it appears, was the rule rather than the exception. As indicated in the records, members of the Historical Ethnographic Commission were more concerned about the loss of Jewish identity than about how to attain successful acculturation. Proposals to publish works of Jewish literature in Russian, for instance, were motivated by the argument that such works would help "restrain assimilation." Accordingly, during this

---

Century St. Petersburg," *Jahrbücher für Geschichte Osteuropas* 44: 2 (Spring 1996): 103–05. Known in Russian as the Pervyi departament pravitel'stvuiushchego senata, the First Department of the Administrative Senate was the administrative arm of the tsarist bureaucracy.

[75] *Otchet OPE za 1898* (St. Petersburg, 1899), 37–38.

period, OPE members proposed new translations into Russian of the Talmud and the Hebrew Bible, while at the same time making plans to publish a new textbook of Jewish history that would "make it easy for young Jews to become acquainted with the history of the Jews through the work of the best scholars, and also to become acquainted with the best literary monuments of ancient times."[76]

Commission meetings that had begun in private apartments in the early 1890s became livelier and more disputatious by the end of the century. Vinaver writes that

> in time we moved to our permanent home in that large, somewhat dark hall upstairs in the Jewish school. At first it was somewhat uncomfortable and empty; there were too few of us. But gradually the audience grew. A permanent contingent of listeners who filled the hall was formed, a permanent small circle came into being of individuals who constantly presented and discussed the presentations. Those who attended our meetings remember the heated argument that took place, especially when Katsenelson argued from history to defend the apolitical nature of the Jewish people and condemned to death every attempt at political resurrection, or when someone, under the pretense of "ethnography," spoke about his trip to Palestine and defended the practical potential of the Zionist program.[77]

As seen in Vinaver's account, in the years just prior to 1905, the OPE served as a multifaceted venue for discussions among Jewish intellectuals of differing orientations about such issues as Zionist politics, national identity, and the role of Yiddish in education. In this sense, the OPE was exceptional among Jewish organizations, where hostility between various factions (for instance, Bundists versus Zionists) was the rule. In fact, the OPE was a rare instance of a kind of national parliament without political power, a training ground for democratic rule and political organization. Decision-making in the OPE was democratic; the leadership was elected by the members, and important decisions were often brought before the entire membership for consultation and confirmation.[78] The OPE's legacy proved valuable in 1905–06, when the commitment to democratic principles was retained in subsequent political organizations such as the Jewish Democratic Group and Union for the

---

[76] Ibid., 22.

[77] Vinaver, "Kak my zanimalis' istoriei," 74–75.

[78] For many years, it is true, the St. Petersburg branch dominated the organization. General meetings took place in the capital city, their agendas set by the Steering Committee. On occasion, the Steering Committee refused to acknowledge demands for greater responsiveness on the part of the provincial rank and file. In time, however, there was an increase in the number of debates held at general meetings and in the number of issues brought to a floor vote.

Achievement of Equal Rights for the Jews, both of which included a number of OPE members.[79]

The OPE's general political orientation was moderate, certainly to the right of the Bund. On its Steering Committee were so-called liberals, members of the Constitutional Democratic party, such as Vinaver, Henrik Sliozberg, and Gregory Landau; General Zionists such as Pyotr Marek, Mikhail Kreinin, and Boris Brutskus; and socialists such as Bramson, Ratner, and Maksim Krol'. Despite the general orientation toward the center, moderation did not necessarily prevail in 1905. During the early months of that year, the OPE membership debated what if any position the organization should take vis-à-vis the strikes and demands for political power that were being raised by various Russian organizations. Under the influence of Vinaver and Krol' (and against the advice of Baron Horace Guenzburg), the OPE sided with the Union of Unions calling for the overthrow of the tsarist regime.[80] This spontaneous support for the revolutionary left evaporated after the October pogroms and especially after the dissolution of the First Duma, when it became clear that the tsarist government had endured.

Although the OPE in its later phases included Zionists and Diaspora nationalists in its ranks, there remained room for confirmed integrationists, such as Baron Horace Guenzburg. Nevertheless, as has been shown, a general pro-nationalist attitude took hold among many in the years before 1905. In addition to the assignment of hours for Jewish subjects in OPE-supported schools and increased interest in Jewish history, increased national feeling was expressed in a greater respect for Yiddish, which was accepted as an official language of the society in 1906 and used as a language of instruction in OPE's teacher training school in Grodno.[81] In addition, there were signs of a more positive attitude toward the *heder*, which members began to view not so much as an incorrigible and embarrassing institution, but rather as the locus of many traditional virtues.[82]

---

[79] Apart from Bramson (whose role has already been mentioned), Vinaver, Dubnov, and Sliozberg were also members of the Jewish Democratic Group and the Union for the Achievement of Equal Rights for the Jews. For more on these groups, see Gassenschmidt, *Jewish Liberal Politics in Tsarist Russia*, esp. 49–54.

[80] A copy of the proclamation accepted by OPE members and published in the newspaper *Rus'*, no. 53 (February 27, 1905) can be found in RGGA f. 1532, op. 1, d. 422, l. 32.

[81] See Il'ia Trotskii, "Samodeiatel'nost' i samopomoshch' russkogo evreistva," in Frumkin, Aronson, and Gol'denveizer, *Kniga o russkom evreistve*, 477. For a list of subjects in which applicants for the Grodno Teachers Courses had to be proficient, see "Protokol zasedaniia Komissii po narodnomu obrazovaniiu pri Komitetete Obshchestva dlia rasprostraneniia prosveshcheniia," Archive of the Vernadsky Ukrainian State Library, Near Eastern Division, f. 321, op. 3, d. 2027.

[82] Although the 1902 meeting of provincial leaders of the OPE had decided that the task of reforming the *heder* was financially and pedagogically unfeasible, many of the

Given that the OPE turned out to be a politically "unreliable," it may seem puzzling that the government nonetheless allowed it to grow and develop in an autonomous fashion. The answer lies in the way the OPE provided services for the Jewish community that the government itself ignored, such as the establishment of schools and teacher training programs, curriculum advice, and information about student hygiene and health.[83] To be sure, the government was prepared to deny the OPE any activity it deemed threatening. For example, the government refused to allow the OPE to found a theological seminary in St. Petersburg to train modern rabbis, and it interfered with the OPE's attempts to establish summer schools for Jewish teachers. Local authorities constantly harassed activists, and before 1908, as noted, the OPE often found itself stymied in its attempts to create branches in various cities.

In its work in both the Historical Ethnographic Commission and the School Commission, the OPE called for a strongly positive Jewish identity. Although it is difficult to distill a single attitude from among the many ideological orientations held by its leaders, one common position can probably be identified: A majority of OPE members appeared to repudiate the identity of "Russian Jew" (*russkii evrei*) and no longer imagined themselves, or hoped to become, members of the Russian nation. Rather, they considered themselves to be "Jews in Russia" (*evrei v Rossii*), composing an independent national group within the Russian state, similar to other ethnic minorities such as Poles, Ukrainians, and Latvians. Still committed in principle to the goal of integrating the Jews in Russia, these intellectuals now insisted on national rights in addition to individual rights, especially in the areas of school curri-

---

members complimented the institution. At the meeting Lev Katsenelson, for instance, noted that

> the substitution of all heders for correctly organized schools would demand such enormous costs that it would not be feasible for any nation. The strength of the traditional heder lies precisely in its simple arrangement and low cost.... On the other hand, the modern school, which has brought much good to the Jewish people, leaves a lot to be desired in the area of Jewish teaching. Such masters of Hebrew, which the heder produced, the modern school has so far not produced.

A full transcript of this meeting is found in RGGA f. 1532, op. 1, d. 20, l. 58; an abridged transcript was published as *Protokol soveshchaniia komiteta OPE* (see n. 16).

[83] A similar argument concerning the zemstvos and their role in Russian society can be found in Thomas Fallows, "The Zemstvo and the Bureaucracy," in *The Zemstvo in Russia: An Experiment in Local Self-Government*, ed. T. Emmons and W. Vucinich (Cambridge: Cambridge University Press, 1982), 177–241. Fallows makes a helpful distinction between the "political" and "administrative" functions of the zemstvo, which apply to any other quasi- or fully-independent social institution in tsarist Russia.

culum and programs for adult education, and the organization of museums, lectures, and cultural societies.

It is clear that the OPE's activities between 1893 and 1905 revived the stagnant organization and made it one of the most important Jewish institutions in Russia. At the same time, the OPE served as an important model for later political struggles and social organizations among Russian Jews. The creation of organizational networks, the expansion of links with representatives from the Pale, and the sharing of resources and information built up networks that proved invaluable in other contexts. Such links, for example, were very useful in the development of Jewish political parties after 1905 and in facilitating aid for Jewish refugees during World War I. Vinaver notes:

> And it seems to me, when I remember the atmosphere of that large hall, when I remember the sonorous voices of the young section heads loudly declaiming the decrees from their notes, it seemed to me that our original consideration was not mistaken, that, with this peaceful activity, we prepared ourselves for wartime.[84]

None of these activities would have taken place had there not been an explosion of energy among the St. Petersburg branch of the OPE, whose members changed the shape of their community—from one dominated by integrationist bankers and notables to a nationally oriented cultural and organizational center of pre-World War I Russian Jewry.

---

[84] Vinaver, "Kak my zanimalis' istoriei," 76.

# Chapter 8

# Henrik Sliozberg:
# A Mirror of Petersburg Jewry in Late Tsarist Days

In Russia in the second half of the 19th century there appeared a significant group of Jews who, joining the Russian intellectual elite, began together with Russians to offer a liberal political alternative to the tsarist government. Such Jews lived primarily in St. Petersburg and worked as lawyers, doctors, engineers, and journalists. Among this elite one can name Aleksandr Passover, Lev Katsenelson, Mikhail Kulisher, Jacob Halpern, Leon Bramson, Aleksandr Braudo, Oskar Gruzenberg, and Henrik Sliozberg.

Like these men, Sliozberg was comfortable both with *shtadlanut*—the intercession with the government on behalf of the Jewish people by wealthy Jewish leaders—and a democratic politics based on liberal notions of rule of law and respect for individual rights. Professionally, he served as Baron Horace Gintsburg's lawyer and was given wide latitude to fight on behalf of Jewish causes in those institutions of the government where he could be effective, such as the State Senate. At the same time Sliozberg had a leading role in Petersburg's Jewish philanthropic institutions: the Society for the Promotion of Enlightenment among the Jews of Russia (OPE) and the Society for the Promotion of Jewish Farmers and Artisans (ORT). He was one of the organizers of the Defense Bureau, "an office established to defend the rights of Jews though organized legal action," and after 1905, a leader of the Russian Constitutional Democratic Party (Kadets).[1] He also served as a leader of the Union for the Attainment of Equal Rights for Jews (1905–06) and the Jewish People's Group (1907).[2] He played central roles in the Kovno Conference of 1909 and the Rabbinical Conference of 1910. He was also active in the Jewish War Relief Committee (Evreiskii komitet pomoshchi zhertvam voiny—YEKOPO), the committee dedicated to providing relief to Jewish refugees during World War I. We know a great deal about his life and the world of Jewish St. Petersburg thanks to his three-volume memoir, *Dela minuvshikh dnei: Zapiski russkogo evreia* (Events of Past Days: Sketches of a Russian Jew), published in 1933.

His attitudes and activities embody the mindset of a Jew in late tsarist Russia who was both a Russian patriot and felt responsibility to help the Jew-

---

[1] Y. S. [Yehuda Slutzky], "Henry Sliozberg," *Encyclopedia Judaica*, 14: 1667.

[2] See Gassenschmidt, *Jewish Liberal Politics in Tsarist Russia*, 20–44.

ish masses. An undeterred patriot, Sliozberg was in love with Russia. His younger colleague, Oscar Gruzenberg, described it thus: "Why do we love Russia, how can one explain it? We love it for the way the sun shines and warms us, which is unique, the clouds flow in the sky in a different way, the rivers sing, and sand crunches under our feet.... And our consciousness gives rise to different thoughts there.... In the presence of Henrik Borisovich Slioz-berg no one dared speak badly about Russia."[3]

Despite repeated pogroms, Sliozberg had confidence in the inherent goodness of the Russian people and was convinced that Jews could find a secure haven in Russia. He believed that antisemitism was motivated solely by political interests and that it was a temporary phenomenon which would be eradicated with the end of the tsarist regime.

Sliozberg's love for his country motivated his conviction that, "despite the empirical condition of Russia, ultimately she will rid herself of autocratic and arbitrary rule and will transform herself into a democratic state based on rule of law." Therefore, Russia was a true homeland for Jews. Sliozberg explains with the help of a metaphor: "Speaking about our national self-consciousness, I allow myself to compare the attitude of Jewry toward Russia with the attitude of a passenger on a ship. Such a passenger is concerned that his own cabin should be in order, but he also understands that the fate of his cabin depends on the fate of the entire ship."[4]

Sliozberg's viewpoint reflects the tremendous optimism of that generation of Jews who came of age in the 1860s and 1870s in Russia. Educated in Russian schools and universities and offered work in the state service, this group managed to avoid the struggles of an earlier generation and the *numerus clausus* of the next. Sliozberg and his contemporaries regarded the reforms of Alexander II as a harbinger of inevitable process. The legal reform of 1864 emerged, they held, from autocracy's incontrovertible contradictions, and just as the tsar had to turn to liberal legal institutions for help in regulating society, so too the state would have to establish democratic institutions and rely on society as a partner in order to govern a modern capitalist state.[5] In other words, Russia was inevitably moving from an *ancién regime* with feudal social divisions to one without these distinctions. The role of the Jew, Sliozberg maintained, was to fight on behalf of a liberal transformation.

It is not surprising that many members of the Petersburg Jewish elite were lawyers. A diploma from a Russian university provided Jews with the right to live outside the Pale of Settlement and in Petersburg and Moscow. But that was not the only reason for the attraction to law. The 1870s were a

---

[3] O. O. Gruzenberg, *Vchera: Vospominaniia* (Paris, 1938), 160.

[4] Ibid.

[5] Ilya Orshansky famously predicted that Russia's Jews would inevitably assimilate and dissolve in the Russian mass. Orshanskii, "Sushchestvuet li evreiskii vopros," *Rassvet*, no. 2 (1879): 56–57.

euphoric time for lawyers in Russia. The legal reform provided for an independent bar association and courts of law based on the English adversarial system, giving lawyers political power that no one in Russia outside the tsar himself and his bureaucracy possessed. People at the time thought that this reform might be expanded to other areas of government, permitting in time the participation of all society in the governance of Russia.

Sliozberg's biography has barely been studied. He is mentioned only in short encyclopedia accounts, and contemporary scholars have not given him the attention he deserves.[6] The reasons are obvious enough. In Soviet Russia it was dangerous to pay attention to liberals, and even in the West scholars lost interest in Western-oriented Russians whose vision of reality departed so radically from Soviet life. Because of ideological reasons related in part to the Holocaust, in Israel there was little interest in non-Zionist Jews who defended Jewish integration in Europe. Today, Sliozberg is hardly known outside of a small circle of specialists.

Memoir accounts tend to idealize Sliozberg. Evgeny Kulisher, a leading Jewish activist in St. Petersburg, announced: "Sliozberg's name will enter history as the embodiment of an entire epoch of Russian-Jewish civic activism—an epoch represented by the struggle for the equal rights of the Jews, which is inextricably connected to the struggle for the liberation of the Russian people."[7] M. Gol'denshtein, another Petersburg lawyer, wrote, "Sliozberg was not only a leader of his people, but also their servant. And it seems to me that above all he should be proud precisely of that. It has been said that the son who helps his old father put on shoes will be blessed forever. Sliozberg will also be blessed. He should be given a monument that has no equal in greatness and beauty and memorializes the efforts of thousands and thousands and illuminates their blood and tears."[8] Gol'denshtein refers here to the thousands of court cases that Sliozberg took up on behalf of Jews during a career that spanned over 30 years.

Symbolically, Sliozberg begins his memoirs not with a description of his earliest or latest years, but with a declaration of his credo. On the first pages of his memoirs (which were begun in 1912 and finished in 1933), he immediately describes the essential principles of his Jewish identity: "Since childhood I became accustomed to regarding myself above all else as a Jew. But already at the start of my conscious life I also felt myself a son of Russia. Observing at

---

[6] The exception is Nathans, *Beyond the Pale*.

[7] E. Kulisher, "Pamiati G. B. Sliozberga," in *Evreiskii mir* (New York: Union of Russian Jews, 1944), 421.

[8] Quoted in Samuil Kucherov, "Evrei v russkoi advokature," in Frumkin, Aronson, and Gol'denveizer, *Kniga o russkom evreistve*, 234.

the end of my days my entire life and work, I must say that, having loved my people and valued them above everything else, and not only because I was born among them but also because of their lofty spirit, the ideals which shined before me and which I considered the ideals of Judaism, I have also always loved Russia."[9]

His credo emphasizes the desire to be at once a Jew by virtue of birth, intellectual conviction, and religious faith, and also a patriot of his Russian homeland. A Jew appears as a member of two worlds, Russian and Jewish. In fact, Sliozberg found solidarity with liberals who sought to check absolute autocracy with a democratically elected parliament. As a Jew, he called for Jewish integration, especially Jewish participation in Russian cultural life, while condemning conversion to Christianity. In addition, he disliked Zionism and Bundist socialism. A political conservative and realist by nature, Sliozberg unconditionally rejected all kinds of radicalism and was unimpressed with utopian plans to move world Jewry to an undeveloped backwater of the Turkish Empire.

In contrast to ideas of Jewish separatism, Sliozberg tried to show the advantages of a Russian-Jewish cultural synthesis. Born in an Orthodox Jewish family in the Belorussian shtetl of Mir, Sliozberg had an easy time acquainting himself with Russian culture, since his father moved the family to the city of Poltava when he was still an infant.[10] Although Sliozberg attended *heder*, as an adolescent he switched to a Russian *gimnaziia*. This decision was not well received by the women in his family. In his memoirs he describes their reactions: "My appearance in a student uniform caused my relatives genuine grief. My mother and grandmother broke out crying, seeing me in the dress of a heretic."[11]

In the 1860s, education provided a path to full acculturation. Jews of that time believed that the reforms of Alexander II were the beginning of bigger changes that would lead to the full equality and enfranchisement of the Jews. Sliozberg was one of a growing group of Jews whose educational achievement gave them the right to reside in the country's capital. Moreover, thanks to his experiences and contacts at St. Petersburg University, he felt fully at home in Russian intellectual circles.[12]

However, Sliozberg always maintained that his Jewish background was an advantage, especially in the field of law. For example, he claimed that it was thanks to his religious education that he won a highly prestigious gold medal (similar to a degree awarded summa cum laude) and caught the attention of Professor N. Sergeevsky, who taught civil law. "In the words of the

---

[9] Sliozberg, *Dela minuvshikh dnei*, 1: 3.

[10] When Sliozberg was less than a year old, his father moved the family to Poltava. Sliozberg studied in that city until he enrolled in St. Petersburg University.

[11] Sliozberg, *Dela minuvshikh dnei*, 1: 71.

[12] Nathans, *Beyond the Pale*, 236–38.

judge who awarded me the gold medal I espied a reference to my enthusiasm for the rabbinical commentary of 'Maharsha,' which I experienced as a ten-year-old boy."[13]

Sliozberg's attachment to Jewish tradition is reflected in his refusal to convert to Christianity as the price for acceptance in the university's graduate program and ultimately a professorial chair at the university. Instead he continued his studies in Western Europe, attending classes at universities in Leipzig, Berlin, and Lyon, hoping that circumstances would change and he would be allowed to teach law after returning to Russia. Since conversion to Christianity was still a *sine qua non*, Sliozberg was forced to give up his dream of dedicating himself to research. His decision to fight to change the legal conditions in Russia emerged from his experience of injustice. "Oppression perceived subjectively, the inability to choose a profession according to one's propensities and qualifications only because that choice was closed due to anti-Jewish laws, led to my decision to "devote myself to revealing the evils that caused this injustice."[14]

While working as a lawyer, Sliozberg managed in various ways to continue his research. He was an editor of the scholarly journal *Iuridicheskii vestnik* (Legal Messenger), and was involved in Petersburg's Society for the Study of Law. In the early years of the 20th century, he was a regular contributor to the Jewish newspaper *Voskhod*, and then *Novyi voskhod*, where he responded to questions sent in by readers regarding legal rights.

Sliozberg expressed the theoretical and historical premises for his legal work in his book *Pravovoe i ekonomicheskoe polozhenie evreev v Rossii* (The Legal and Economic Condition of Jews in Russia).[15] Published in 1907, the volume consisted of his articles that had appeared in scholarly journals as well as petitions to high government officials he had sent on behalf of his patron, Baron Horace Gintsburg.[16] Sliozberg maintained that there was a close relationship between the treatment of Jews in the 19th century and the fate of political reform generally. Connecting the attainment of equal rights for Jews with the

---

[13] Sliozberg, *Dela minuvshikh dnei*, 1: 55. Maharsha—Morenu Ha-Rav Shemu'el Adels, 16th-century Talmudic commentator in Poland (*Encyclopedia Judaica*, 6: 363–64).

[14] Sliozberg, *Dela minuvshikh dnei*, 1: 199.

[15] Sliozberg, *Pravovoe i ekonomicheskoe polozhenie evreev v Rossii*.

[16] Sliozberg writes in his introduction to *Pravovoe i ekonomicheskoe polozhenie evreev v Rossii* that the book "presents only some of the material that at various times was presented to high officials for their examination of the Jewish condition. In its entirely this material does not exhaust the subject of the so-called Jewish Question, but is capable of giving an introduction to the body of restrictions that affect Jews and contribute to their terrible material condition" (xxxi).

process of democratization occurring in the country, Sliozberg maintained that the absence of rights for Jews coincided with the government's retention of "personal" serfdom for the peasant.

> Antisemitism as it appeared in our case has its birth in the serf system. At the time [the Jewish question] was formulated, it was shaped in relation to the slavery of the serf. And if later, serfdom was repealed for the individual peasant, nevertheless in our day public serfdom has remained in effect. Slavery, which disappeared formally, left behind individual slaves for whom a denial of rights and an element of slavery are somehow necessary. And that is why from that time on dark forces have tightly held onto the Jewish question with their greedy claws, that is why reactionary forces control the Jewish Question so stubbornly. They need Jews without rights.[17]

Wanting to deny the peasant political rights, it was easiest of all to keep the Jews down and in this way show the peasant that he was not placed on the lowest rung, that there were others even lower. Supposedly, the peasants would not take issue with their status as long as Jews were treated worse. Thus, the Jew's absence of rights was part of an overall strategy by the ruling classes to deflect energy from the struggle for democracy.

Sliozberg insisted that the government was solely responsible for antisemitism. Analyzing Russian history, he came to the following conclusion. "[O]ne can properly assert that the entire reign of Nicholas I was in essence foreign to antisemitism and during that time there was no collision between the Christian population and the Jews. There was a struggle of interests, but there was no racial or religious hatred."[18] Although one might find this view surprising, Sliozberg maintained that antisemitism had no historical roots in Russia and was a modern import that served reactionary political interests.

Therefore, Sliozberg rejected the explanation that the pogroms of 1881–82 were caused by "Jewish exploitation" and revenge for the profiteering of Jewish suppliers during the Russian-Turkish War. He regarded the pogroms rather as a "preemptive reactionary action" to stop Jewish demands for rights.[19] Convinced that the source for antisemitism lay in the absence of political rights, Sliozberg refused to countenance the Zionist idea of irrational religious or ethnic hatred. On the contrary, he exonerated the peasantry, although his contemporaries, such as Simon Dubnov and Ahad Ha'am, considered the peasants irremediably antisemitic. Sliozberg's one-sided view of antisemitism is connected with the traditions of Russian *Haskalah*, with its belief in the power of reason and the conviction that hatred of Jews can be eradicated.

---

[17] Ibid., v.

[18] Ibid., xvii–xviii.

[19] Ibid., xviii.

Representing private clients and practicing on behalf of Baron Horace Gintsburg, Sliozberg witnessed the Jews' worsening economic situation in the 1880s. Despite many instances of arbitrary rule, he had seen that legal argumentation could be effective in curtailing the government's discriminatory policies. Dubnov describes Sliozberg's work this way: "For decades he ceaselessly fought by handing in petitions to the [State] Senate objecting to the arbitrary interpretation of laws by the police chiefs and other local administrators that harmed Jews. In this way 'the lawyer of Judaism' succeeded more than a few times in preventing a mass eviction of Jews and further encroachments on their rights even beyond those that were already enacted regarding where Jews could live and what professions they could practice."[20]

According to Evgeny Kulisher, "Sliozberg's primary client was the Jewish people with all their collective and individual legal needs. After Sliozberg left Russia, the Bolsheviks got his archive and in it they discovered over one hundred thousand dossiers. Civil cases composed only a small part. The countless rest consisted of pro bono cases and petitions regarding Jews: [with subjects such as] permission to open a school, prayer hall, establish a cooperative, regarding enrollment in an educational institution, and, most important, the rights to live in certain areas, conduct trade, or work as an artisan."[21]

Even Sliozberg's arch nemesis Vladimir Jabotinsky admired his work.

The task of the *shtadlan* is to cause a change in the attitude in the one who has power, encourage him personally on behalf of a given demand.... The task of a political struggle is to gather, concentrate, and bring to bear before the person with power such pressures which force his capitulation, entirely independent of whether his attitude has changed for the better or remained hostile as earlier. Sliozberg's political work belongs to the second category.... G. B. Sliozberg did not influence, but precisely struggled.[22]

Like other talented Jewish lawyers, including A. Passover, O. Gruzenberg, and M. Vinaver, Sliozberg often appeared in court. He considered public trials an effective method of fighting for national rights. In his book on the political institutions of tsarism (1933), he described the way lawyers used the opportunities given to them by the legal reform of 1864. "Before the beginning of the [20th] century arguing in court was the only available tribune for lawyers. The bar association used it in full measure, and it was nearly impossible to name a single instance until the [October] Revolution when this freedom was curtailed. The only exception was the control that belonged to the presiding judge, who acted as the policeman of the court. This freedom was

---

[20] Dubnov, *Kniga zhizni*, 2: 22.

[21] Kulisher, "Pamiati G. B. Sliozberga," 419.

[22] V. Zhabotinskii [Jabotinsky], "Vvedenie," in Sliozberg, *Dela minuvshikh dnei*, ii.

especially valuable in criminal cases which had a political character."[23] Strangely, Sliozberg forgets to mention the military trials during and after the Revolution of 1905 and similar summary executions that took place during World War I. Nevertheless, the system of adversarial trials was particularly useful during the Mendel Beilis case (1911–13), when the defense was able to use the power of public opinion, including international opinion, to win acquittal for the defendant and elicit respect for Russia's Jews.

Bringing petitions before the State Senate was another means, albeit limited and provisional, of gaining respite from harsh and unjust laws. Jabotinsky describes his own personal admiration for Sliozberg in this regard:

> He left one of the meetings of the Union for Full Rights for Jews (Soiuz evreiskogo polnopraviia), and he was not in the camp in which I was fighting. Contradicting us, he said: "I envy you, for you the Jewish question represents a dream about the future; but for me a single sentence in an edict about the wine trade—that is also a large piece of the Jewish question." H. B. Sliozberg probably did not imagine that during the night after our meeting we, his rivals, and especially the young enthusiasts of our camp, discussed his phrase for a long time. This phrase, prosaic, bureaucratic, pronounced without particular enthusiasm amazed us. It reminded us about the terrible tragedy of everyday life, about how in three lines of a bureaucratic text was often hidden a death sentence for hundreds of thousands, about the enormous idealistic value of realism.[24]

Sliozberg not only defended the Jewish masses from oppressive legislation, but by petitioning before the State Senate and arguing in court trials, he presented an "absolute moral," promulgating eternal values and principles of justice, as well as advocating the idea of a state committed wholly to rule of law.

As a liberal, Sliozberg abhorred political violence. His innate conservatism led him to find in Baron Horace Gintsburg a perfect patron and friend. In the second half of the 19th century, in the absence of democratic political institutions that gave Jews a political voice, the expression of Jewish political needs was handled in various ways, among them *shtadlanut*. Horace Gintsburg acted as an intermediary between the Jewish people and the government.

---

[23] G. Sliozberg, *Dorevoliutsionnyi stroi Rossii* (Paris, 1933), 162.

[24] V. Zhabotinskii [Jabotinsky], "Vvedenie," in Parkhomovskii, *Evrei v kul'ture russkogo zarubezh'ia*, 2: 569–70. The Union for the Attainment of Full Rights for Jews operated from 1905–06.

By the 1870s, however, *shtadlanut* had changed. Instead of back-door negotiations and promises of trading favors, Gintsburg hired Sliozberg as counsel.[25] Sliozberg presented thousands of petitions to the government on behalf of Jews throughout Russia who approached Gintsburg with their requests. Although Sliozberg knew that *shtadlanut* was deeply flawed, he felt that in the absence of an alternative, Gintsburg's money and reputation permitted him the most effective position from which to help Jews. Significantly, after 1905, when political parties were legalized, Sliozberg joined and became a leader of the Constitutional Democratic (Kadet) Party.

Nevertheless, Sliozberg idealized Gintsburg and sympathized with his deep feeling of responsibility for Russian Jewry. According to Sliozberg, Gintsburg "was occupied with Jewish issues day and night and there was no personal business, however, important, that could not be placed on the back burner as soon as the question of Jews appeared, or as he called them, 'my Jews.'"[26]

Sliozberg was proud of the baron's ability to build positive relationships with the Russian intellectual elite. Participating in the literary circle that revolved around Mikhail Stasiulevich, the editor and publisher of the main periodical of Russian liberalism of those years, *Vestnik Evropy*, Gintsburg spent time with Ivan Turgenev, Ivan Goncharov, Vladimir Stasov, Dmitry Kavelin, Vladimir Solovyov, and many others. In the 1870s, these relationships helped form Gintsburg's views and made him understand the frustration that liberal Russians also felt in tsarist Russia. [27]

Liberals politically on the center-right believed that radicals surrounded them on both sides. From the left, there were the revolutionaries, and from the right, members of Russian nationalist parties. Within Jewish society, traditional rabbis, who, so Sliozberg thought, could be a natural ally, inhabited the right. In fact, Sliozberg reached out to leading rabbis in 1910, when, as a leader of the government's rabbinical commission, he called for the establishment of a single rabbinate, instead of the dual rabbinate—the institution by

---

[25] Benjamin Nathans writes about this with much acumen. See his *Beyond the Pale*, chap. 4.

[26] G. B. Sliozberg [Henrik Sliozberg], "Baron G. O. Gintsburg i pravovoe polozhenie evreev," in *Perezhitoe*, 4 vols. (St. Petersburg, 1901–11), 2: 119. In the preface to his biography of Gintsburg, which appeared in 1933, Sliozberg writes, "I considered myself the appropriate person to compose this sketch because I have been a close associate of the unforgettable man, Horace Osipovich [Gintsburg], for more than twenty years and enjoyed his avuncular friendship. I always showed him the respect and love of a son." G. Sliozberg, *Baron G. O. Gintsburg: Ego zhizn' i deiatel'nost'* (Paris, 1933), 7.

[27] On the relationship of Stasiulevich and H. Gintsburg, see V. E. Kel'ner, *Chelovek svoego vremeni: M. M. Stasiulevich, izdatel'skoe delo, i liberal'naia oppozitsiia* (St. Petersburg: Izd-vo Rossiiskoi natsional'noi biblioteki, 1993), 181–208.

which every community had a "state" and a "spiritual" rabbi.[28] Nevertheless, he raised some ire by advocating the creation of new rabbinical seminaries, which could improve a rabbi's knowledge of secular subjects.

He also supported the political demands of religious Jewry in other venues. For example, at the Kovno Conference of 1909, which dealt with the political democratization of the Jewish community, he defined Jews as a "religious group" and protested against the special Jewish taxes (*korobochnaia sborka*), preferring to finance the needs of the community with a general tax, a *Gemeindesteuer*, since individuals who did not eat kosher meat were still Jews and were obligated to pay for communal needs.[29] He also condemned Jews who converted to Christianity for the sake of money or career and was an antagonist of radical religious reform. In the years before 1917, Sliozberg displayed sympathy for Knesset Israel and Tifereth Bochurim—organizations representing Orthodox Jewry—since they shared an emphasis on gaining political rights for Jews within Russia itself.[30]

Nevertheless, he did not hide his critical attitude toward the indifference of religious Jews to general political problems faced by all members of the Russian state. Moreover, he was not blind to some rabbis' determination to use the liberal intelligentsia for their own aims. "Spiritual rabbis, in particular, Hasidic ones under the influence of the Lubavitcher rabbi Zalman Shneur Shneerson had a political goal in their striving to retain the orthodox composition of Jewish life and customs, which in their view the government should support. Orthodoxy was engaged in a struggle, not always visible, but hidden, against the Jewish intelligentsia. It was clear that orthodoxy, condemning the liberation movement among Jews, tried to acquire the goodwill of the government."[31]

Sliozberg's views toward radicalism and Zionism were equally negative. He rejected the Bund because of the latter's emphasis on class struggle, arguing that the Bund "brings harm to Jewish trade and industry in the initial stages of their development."[32] He especially condemned the obstructionist

---

[28] G. B. Sliozberg, "Ravvinskaia komissia," *Novyi voskhod*, no. 10 (11 March 1910): 15. "State" rabbis kept official records, such as dates of birth, death, and marriage documents. These rabbis were often the object of resentment since their salaries were covered by local taxes.

[29] For more on the Kovno Conference, see Isaac Levitas, *The Jewish Community in Russia, 1844–1917* (Jerusalem: Posner, 1981), 18–21; Sliozberg, *Dela minuvshikh dnei*, 3: 259–65.

[30] See Bacon, *Politics of Tradition*.

[31] Sliozberg, *Dela minuvshikh dnei*, 3: 265.

[32] Ibid., 3: 136.

tactics of the Bund during the elections to the First State Duma, when the Bund waged a campaign for boycotting the fledging institution.[33]

At the same time Sliozberg disliked Zionism. In his own words, Zionism was a "surrogate, necessary in view of the absence of a sense of national unity on that part of Jewry which has moved far away from the traditions of the past and does not live a common spiritual life with the Jewish masses."[34] Sliozberg saw Zionism's danger in that it "placed Jews in a false position with regards to those peoples among whom they live; Zionist slogans strengthen the conviction that Jews are only temporary citizens of that state organism of which they make up a part."[35]

It is intriguing that Sliozberg would view Zionism and radicalism as equal dangers. In fact he continued to make this point even while in emigration, even after the Bolshevik takeover of Russia, when it was clear that the danger from the left was greater than that of Zionism. Certainly he remembered the conflicts between liberals and Zionists during the attempt to form a coalition of Jewish interests in the State Duma (1907–08). But that still does not explain his profound hostility, which likely had an ideological basis. Sliozberg probably could not tolerate the view that Jewish life in Diaspora was illegitimate. Such a contention contradicted his deeply felt ideals and insulted him personally.

His activity was only partially political; much of his work took place in the social institutions that characterized Petersburg Jewish life and were developed to support modern Jewish schools and the training of artisans. In 1908, Sliozberg helped create the Higher Jewish Courses in Eastern Studies in Petersburg (really a Jewish University) and together with Maksim Vinaver organized a conference about Jewish economic life (March 8–9, 1908). He also worked hard to promote Jewish economic life by taking leading posts in the Society for the Promotion of Artisans and Agricultural Work (ORT) and the Society for the Promotion of Enlightenment among the Jews of Russia (OPE).

During the period of the first two Dumas, 1905–07, Sliozberg actively participated in political life, collaborating with Russian liberals to influence Duma members to extend rights for Jews.[36] Nevertheless, Sliozberg was not entirely satisfied with the Kadet party.[37] "I did not want to be a Kadet of the Mosaic Persuasion,' which is what many of the members of the central committee [of the Union of Equal Rights] were and had to be, having joined the

---

[33] For more on the relations of the Bund toward the Kadet Party, see Frankel, *Prophesy and Politics*, 140–80; also Ezra Mendelsohn, *Class Struggle in the Pale: The Formative Years of the Jewish Workers' Movement in Tsarist Russia* (Cambridge: Cambridge University Press, 1970).

[34] Sliozberg, *Dela minuvshikh dnei*, 2: 294.

[35] Ibid., 2: 296.

[36] Gassenshmidt, *Jewish Liberal Politics*, especially chaps. 2–3.

[37] Sliozberg, *Dela minuvshikh dnei*, 3: 193.

Kadet Party and its leadership."[38] Speaking about the events of the first Russian revolution in 1905, Sliozberg emphasized that he participated more as a Jew than as a Russian liberal. He contrasted himself with Vinaver, who symbolized for Sliozberg blind faith in the unity of interests between Jews and Russians. Dubnov, however, saw this conflict differently, regarding the two figures as representing two types of Jewish leadership, old and new. Dubnov wrote, "In contrast to Vinaver's political work, Sliozberg was more a social activist or philanthropist. He presented petitions to the government, Vinaver organized opposition to this activity. Sliozberg joined up with the right wing of the Kadet Party, while Vinaver belonged to the center."[39]

Truth be told, Sliozberg never repudiated *Shtadlanut*. Sliozberg even made such personal appeals after Baron Gintsburg's death in 1909.[40] For example, in 1913, when the Kadet party drafted legislation in the Duma on the freedom of Russia's citizens, in which the Jewish question was not specifically mentioned, Sliozberg went to see Vladimir Kokovtsov, the Prime Minister, in order to ask whether the minister would use his influence to help Russian Jewry.[41] Sliozberg defended himself from accusations that he was a government collaborator by claiming that he could not wait for change to occur automatically but was obligated to help people in the here and now, even if that meant conforming to the conventions of the tsarist system and in a sense lending it legitimacy. He was convinced that anarchy had to be avoided at all costs because only centralized power could provide the ultimate defense against massive violence that would likely harm Jews and Russians both. Considering the mass murder that took place during the Russian Civil War, one cannot discount this position entirely.

Sliozberg thought that legal successes might create a bridge between the masses and the wealthy educated elite and put to an end the conflict between religious and secular Jewry. He sought unity among Russian and Jewish liberals, believing that as a minority, Jews needed the help of Russians to pressure the autocrat to make necessary political concessions. In the final analysis, such a position failed because Jewish liberals, just like Russian liberals, did not have the institutional power or popular support to change the structures

---

[38] Ibid., 3: 192–93.

[39] Dubnov, *Kniga zhizni*, 2: 22.

[40] John Klier writes about the weakening of the *Shtadlanut* after the pogroms of 1881: "Of course the Shtadlanut did not end with the events of 1881. Many obstacles interfered with the construction of a new politics. There were no permanent institutions in which it could be realized. Judaism's ideology and geography led to the lack of a concentrated political leadership. In this context, despite its weakening and failures, the politics of Shtadlanut continued." Klier, "Krug Gintsburgov i politika shtadlanuta v Imperatorskoi Rossii," *Vestnik Evreiskogo universiteta v Moskve* 3: 10 (1995): 39.

[41] Gassenschmidt, *Jewish Liberal Politics*, 118.

of governance that would have permitted the realization of a democratic state over the long term.

Sliozberg interpreted the victory of Bolshevism as a personal defeat and a tragedy for Russian Jewry. Already in emigration he wrote, "The Bolshevik regime of the time eliminated professional occupations, removing the need for that kind of work to which I dedicated decades of my public life. We were left with taking care of starving Jews and searching for money to help the victims of pogroms that had recently occurred in Ukraine."[42]

During the Russian Civil War, Sliozberg stayed in cold and hungry Petrograd and began writing his memoirs. Making reference in his title to the fictional account of Jews in Nicholas I's Russia by Grigory Bagrov, *Zapiski russkogo evreia* (Notes of a Russian Jew), he combined elements of autobiography, historical chronicles, and descriptive accounts of daily life. Writing his memoirs had a positive effect on his psychological condition. "One had to sharpen one's will sufficiently in order in such circumstances—in an unheated apartment with only meager amounts of food—to remember the past. But perhaps it is precisely recalling the past that made it possible more easily to survive the present, the result of the revolution."[43]

In emigration, Sliozberg wrote two books in addition to his memoirs, *Dorevoliutsionnyi stroi Rossii* (The Pre-Revolutionary Constitution of Russia; 1933) and *Mest' Spinozy za "Kherem"* (Spinoza's Revenge for his Excommunication; 1933). In these works Sliozberg tried to make sense of his experiences in Russia. Using various genres—memoirs, historical study, and philosophical commentary—he wanted to find an answer to very painful questions about the relations of secular and religious traditions, Jewish identity, and his own generation's political failings.

Unfortunately, we do not have a lot of information about Sliozberg's life in the emigration. He arrived in France in 1920 and became "the head of the Russian-Jewish community in Paris." In 1934, Sliozberg "appeared as a witness in the trial against the Protocols of the Elders of Zion in Berne."[44] Louis Greenberg depicts Sliozberg's activity in emigration this way: "He continued his philanthropic work, but now on behalf of Jewish and Russian intellectuals. The organization he established for this goal was called 'Jacob's Tent.' During visits to the United States he gave several lectures in various Jewish communities, speaking about the difficult condition of the Jews in Europe. Not long before his death he created an outline for a book on Jewish ethics. In his final letter to Shaul Gintsburg, the historian, he wrote, 'Let our children know the invaluable contribution Judaism has made to the history of humanity.'"[45]

---

[42] Sliozberg, *Dela minuvshikh dnei*, 1: 1.

[43] Ibid., 1: 2.

[44] *Encyclopedia Judaica*, 14: 1667.

[45] Louis Greenberg, *The Jews in Russia*, 2 vols. (New Haven: Yale University Press, 1944–51), 2: 134.

Sliozberg's life coincided with a tragic epoch for Russian Jewry. Violence against Jews broke out in 1881–82, 1902–07, and 1914–21. During much of this time the tsarist government placed drastic limitations on the number of Jews permitted to study in Russian schools and universities and worsened conditions for Jewish artisans, merchants, and workers. It was directly responsible for the excesses of the army during World War I. The change of government in October 1917 did not please Sliozberg, who reacted skeptically to the Soviets' promise to resolve once and for all the Jewish question in Russia.

As a lawyer and writer, Sliozberg left a remarkable body of works regarding the history of Russian Jewry. He was an advocate of the idea of a dual identification for Jews, uniting modernity and Orthodox Judaism, secular life and religious practice. He loved Russia deeply, without reserve, infinitely, and that love brought him great pain.

Is it possible to understand his love for Russia or should one just dismiss it as lunacy, given the discrimination that he experienced personally? Admittedly, a realist in everything else, Sliozberg was an idealist on the subject of Russia. His devotion represents a conundrum especially for today's readers who, while understanding how it could happen, remain confused about why Sliozberg linked the struggle for human dignity so closely with his own personal patriotism. His feelings of devotion to the good and beautiful in Russia and his ability to separate everything good from everything bad in Russia seem, at least to me, wishful and illusory. I understand, nonetheless, that even this unrequited love serves as a mirror of a unique consciousness that paradoxically was entirely representative of the Petersburg Jewish elite of its time.

Menashe (Mikhail) Morgulis – civic leader. From the collection of
"Petersburg Judaica" of the European University of St. Petersburg

Maxim Vinaver – lawyer and political leader. From the collection of "Petersburg Judaica" of the European University of St. Petersburg

Leon Bramson – civic leader. From the collection of "Petersburg Judaica" of the European University of St. Petersburg

א. א. הרכבי.

חברת „לבנון"    № 162

Albert (Avraham) Harkavy – historian. From the collection of
"Petersburg Judaica" of the European University of St. Petersburg

Shimon Dubnov – historian, philosopher, and literary critic.
From the collection of "Petersburg Judaica" of the
European University of St. Petersburg

Ahad Ha'am (Asher Ginzburg) – Zionist thinker. From the collection of "Petersburg Judaica" of the European University of St. Petersburg

David Gintsburg – scholar and philanthropist. From the collection of
"Petersburg Judaica" of the European University of St. Petersburg

Horace Gintsburg and Henrik Sliozberg. From the collection of
"Petersburg Judaica" of the European University of St. Petersburg

Mikhail Gershenzon – historian, literary critic, and philosopher.
From the private collection of M. A. Chegodaeva

Herman Rosenthal – librarian, writer, and civic activist.
From the photographic archive of the Slavonic Division
of the New York Public Library

Shimon Frug – poet. From the Frug family archives

Vladimir Jabotinsky – writer and Zionist.
With permission of the Jabotinsky Institute

# Chapter 9

# Integration and Its Discontents: Mikhail Morgulis and the Ideology of Jewish Integration in Russia

Mikhail Morgulis (1837–1912), a Jewish civic leader, journalist, and lawyer in Odessa, came of age in the 1860s, but lived until 1912[1] — into the period dominated by Jewish nationalism. Holding firm to a faith in Jewish integration, in the last two decades of his life Morgulis shared the fate of many 1860s Jewish intellectuals, such as Emmanuel Levin, Avram Harkavy, and Mikhail Kulisher, who as progressives in an earlier era now found themselves treated as backward conservatives in a new environment. Because his evolution took him from the ideological limelight to the periphery, Morgulis's life and works can tell us a great deal about changes in the composition of the Russian-Jewish intelligentsia, its social conditions, and intellectual trends.

Morgulis's orientation toward integration coincides with his generation's striving for a synthesis of Jewish and Russian cultures. Nevertheless, as opposed to radical Russifiers, who either predicted the end of Judaism or limited its role to that of a religion, Morgulis believed Russia's Jews had a right to independent political, cultural, and religious institutions. Because of his commitment to the self-determination of Russia's Jews, Morgulis can actually be seen as a kind of proto-nationalist. Despite the fact that in 1902 such nationalist militants as Simon Dubnov and Ahad Ha'am condemned him, there is an undeniable genetic connection between civic activism as Morgulis practiced it and the grass-roots struggle of self-help as later nationalists understood it.[2]

---

[1] I would like to thank Antony Polonsky, Marc Raeff, and Michael Beizer for their suggestions. Responsibility for any errors of fact or judgment is my own.

[2] There has not been much research on this very impressive civic activist. See principally Shaw, "Odessa Jewish Community"; M. L. Polishchuk, *Evrei Odessy i Novorossii: Sotsial'no-politicheskaia istoriia evreev Odessy i drugikh gorodov v Novorossii. 1881–1904* (Jerusalem: Gesharim; Moscow: Mosty kul'tury, 2002); Eli Lederhendler, *The Road to Modern Jewish Politics: Political Tradition and Political Reconstruction in the Jewish Community of Tsarist Russia* (New York: Oxford University Press, 1989). In these books, Morgulis figures as a social activist and leader who helps create modern philanthropic and educational institutions and as an innovative organizer of Jewish politics in the decades before 1905.

Morgulis's name is inextricably linked to Odessa, and in many ways he reflects that city's vibrant personality. Odessa was ahead of other cities in offering the Russian-Jewish intelligentsia a leading role in providing creative solutions to social problems. By the late 1860s, intellectuals rather than notables were running the Odessa branch of the Society for the Promotion of Enlightenment among the Jews of Russia (OPE).[3] At the same time these intellectuals served as advisers to the government on issues related to Jews. The power of the intelligentsia was demonstrated by the dominance of this group in Odessa's Jewish parliament, known as "The Hundred Representatives," which was established in Odessa to regulate Jewish life in the city in the early 1860s.[4] The goals of democratic-leaning intellectuals, such as Morgulis, reflect populist inclinations and trust in social modernization and secularization. For example, intellectuals in Odessa, such as Leon Pinsker, Emmanuel Soloveichik, Ilya Orshansky, and Morgulis, sought to replace traditional *heders* by creating modern schools for Jews, to transform traditional *hevrot* into democratically-run institutions of social welfare, and to educate modern rabbis to serve as community leaders.

Because Morgulis discounted radical solutions and devoted himself to gradual amelioration, there was some controversy about his legacy at the end of his life. Certainly Jewish liberals gave him a huge tribute. In 1912, the chair of the St. Petersburg Society for the Promotion of Enlightenment, Jacob Hal'pern, listed Morgulis's achievements:

> As a civic activist, Mikhail Grigor'ev [Morgulis] harmonized his deeds with his word. Without a moment's rest, he struggled to organize the public at large, train artisans, while spreading enlightenment and developing Jewish knowledge. In Odessa, the site of his constant activity, there was almost no Jewish institution which did not owe him a debt either for its birth or energetic support. Many of those institutions [which were] created in Odessa had a large influence by serving as examples for other Jewish communities.[5]

---

[3] For information about the Odessa branch of the OPE, see E. Cherikover, *Istoriia Obshchestva dlia Rasprostraneniia Prosveshcheniia mezhdu Evreiami v Rossii*; see also Zipperstein, "Transforming the Heder," 87–110.

[4] Mikhail Polishchuk writes, "In the early 1860s the Mayor got permission from the Minister of Finance for the election of a broader representative structure, 'The Hundreds,' which functioned under the control of the city's Duma. In 1863 this structure was expanded to 120 members. It had jurisdiction only over elections of representatives to the Duma or the Magistrate, the state rabbi, head of the Jewish hospital, *talmud tora*, burial society and other community institutions, but in reality it strove to take up all the community's problems" (Polishchuk, *Evrei Odessy i Novorossii*, 30).

[5] Manuscript of speech by Jacob Hal'pern on April 29, 1912, in the file: "Protokol soveshchanii i perepiski s chlenami obshchestva po organizatsii chestvovaniia 75-letiia so

Zionist leaders, however, viewed him with disdain. They saw in him a symbol of a failed Diaspora politics, a whipping boy of the *shtadlanut* system (intercession on behalf of the Jewish community before state and local authorities, lobbying; from *shtadlan* 'intercessor'), and a politician who settled for half-measures.[6] Peter Shaw explains the unlucky aspect of Morgulis's image. "Despite the undeniable contributions he rendered to Odessan Jewry, Morgulis has been all but forgotten in the historical literature. To a certain degree, Morgulis himself bears responsibility for this state of affairs by having failed to go with the tide of history, i.e., by having refused to align himself with the eventual 'winners' in the struggle for Russian Jewry—the Zionists."[7]

Since there is still not a single published article, much less a book, devoted to Morgulis, one is justified in saying that he deserves additional critical examination, especially now in the post-communist and post-Zionist political environment. In Russia, such figures are receiving a great deal of popular attention because they seem to embody ideas of democratic liberalism, which some Russians would like to rescue for use in today's political wars.[8] At the

---

dnia rozhdeniia M. G. Morgulisa," *Rossiiskii gosudarstvennyi i istoricheskii arkhiv* (Russian State Historical Archive, RGGA) f. 1532, op. 1, d. 1237.

[6] Hovevei Zion, not wanting to participate in the 50th anniversary of Morgulis's literary career, claimed that "sisyphian labours" were no cause for rejoicing. See Shaw, "Odessa Jewish Community," 58; also *Novyi voskhod*, no. 18 (1912), 18–19.

[7] Shaw, "Odessa Jewish Community," 58. Incidentally, Simon Dubnov felt some personal animus toward Morgulis for slights during his early years in Odessa. In his memoirs Dubnov writes, "A popular lawyer in Odessa, a member or chair of various societies and committees, an essential orator at meetings, Morgulis did not rise above average in all these areas. His originality was perhaps diminished by his involvement in too many things, he wanted to be a player everywhere, although he was not capable of penetrating all these affairs.... In general he acted in a proper manner, but being an opportunist himself, he could not stand people with definite convictions and consistent methods" (Dubnov, *Kniga zhizni*, 56–57).

[8] Jeffrey Veidlinger, for example, has written that "[i]ndeed, the shtetl, the metonym of Jewish life in Eastern Europe, no longer fascinates scholars as it once did. The desire to 'imagine Russian Jewry,' to use Steven Zipperstein's phrase, as a foundation myth of Ashkenazic culture, has declined. The shtetl has lost much of its mystique as the former Pale of Settlement has become more accessible to both American 'heritage tour groups' and Russian 'historical-archeological expeditions,' both of which have found that the venerated shtetls of their grandparents' stories are now little more than concrete-laden suburbs. Rather than return to a mythologized past of klezmer music, joyous weddings, and the simple values of faith and family, as reflected in the writings of Sholem Aleichem, Isaac Leyb Peretz, and other classic Yiddish writers, a new generation of scholars have instead championed the more mundane and practical values of acculturated Jewry in the capitals and their struggles to be accepted on equal terms within Russian society as a whole." Veidlinger, "From Shtetl to Society: Jews in 19th-Century Russia," *Kritika: Explorations in Russian and Eurasian History* 2: 4 (Fall 2001): 324–25.

same time, for the historian, Morgulis's life and works offer a chance to explore the emotional and spiritual sources of the Russian-Jewish intelligentsia, since Morgulis wrote extensive memoirs. These memoirs offer a bird's-eye view of an inimitable emotional and intellectual evolution and give a portrait of the mindset of his generation.

Born in 1837 in Berdichev during the reign of Nicholas I, in his childhood Morgulis attended a traditional *heder*. When he was 10, his family moved to Odessa. Describing Odessa's Jews in the 1840s, Morgulis recounts how young men eager to learn Russian congregated together. Such individuals were known as "Let the Virgils," since the best-loved and first story from their Russian textbook began with "Let the Virgils praise the Augustins [the poets praise the rulers]."[9] According to Morgulis, this epithet was inevitably used ironically, since many students never got past the first few pages. Moreover, the appellation may also have evoked laughter since Jews who were eager to acquaint themselves with Russian culture were still rare and perhaps seemed strange. We can get an impression of the skepticism regarding Russian-Jewish interaction in the 1840s from the surprise Morgulis expresses at the hospitable reception he received from the Christian director of the Zhitomir Rabbinical Seminary.[10]

The gentle school principal is contrasted with the local police chief, who chased after Jews in his carriage in order "to force them to put out a cigarette that might somehow lead to a fire." The police chief also overturned baskets of fruit and crushed them in order "to maintain the city's hygiene level," or arrested Jews for wearing skullcaps or cut their *payes*, even going as far as whipping them in front of the police station.[11] However, Morgulis took pride in the fact that at least once Odessa's Jews took revenge. During a celebration for Tsar Nicholas I, who was expected to pass through the city, the police chief tried to make his usual mischief. Instead of allowing him, a group of Jews "lifted him up with a cry of 'hurray.'" "When as usual he brought his fists into play," Morgulis writes, "K-v was met by fists in a quantity that he had never seen nor could see.... The affair ended with the police chief retreating from the field of battle and leaving his responsibilities to the city's administrator, Ts-v."[12]

Like other progressives, Morgulis was inspired by the government's attempts to change Jewish life in the late 1850s. These efforts led to feelings of

---

[9] M. Morgulis, "Iz moikh vospominaniii," *Voskhod*, no. 4 (1895): 21.

[10] Ibid., 31.

[11] Ibid., 29.

[12] Ibid.

patriotism for Russia, which, according to Morgulis, Russian Jews had previously not experienced.

> Young people rejoiced. They found a basis for their self-consciousness. Downtrodden and oppressed more by people within their own milieu than outside it, they threw themselves into the open arms of those outside Judaism. Young people felt a ground under their feet; they all started to consider themselves citizens of a homeland and they received a new fatherland. Each young man was full of optimistic hopes and prepared himself selflessly to serve the homeland, which had extended its hands so maternally to her stepchildren. All threw themselves into the study of Russian language and literature; everyone thought only about how he could quickly emulate and entirely integrate with the surrounding milieu.[13]

The government's good intentions were not just an abstraction without a human face. For the educated Jews of Russia's southwest, the importance of the image of Nikolai Pirogov cannot be overestimated. As the head of the Odessa educational district from 1856 to 1858, Pirogov encouraged the modernization of the Jews by supporting the activities of secular intellectuals. Morgulis explains how Jews of the time saw this humane official:

> Pirogov was the first who saw in the Jew not just a person, but also a useful citizen. He was the first to point out the high virtues of Jewish behavior, the first to put under his protection the Jewish youth, towards whom he felt ardent love and backed in the struggle with obscurantism. He was the first to extend not a passive, but an active hand to the education of the Jews, spreading among them a unified force in the name of enlightenment.[14]

The sense of gratefulness toward Pirogov was so great that a cult of his image took hold among educated Jews. The writer Lev Levanda, for example, advised his friends to purchase Pirogov's photograph, since "in each Jewish house a portrait of this exemplary Christian should be found."[15]

In his early teens, Morgulis enrolled in the Zhitomir Rabbinical Seminary, one of two rabbinical seminaries sponsored by the government. There, in addition to Judaica, he studied foreign languages, including German and Russian. Instead of taking a position as a government rabbi after graduation, as he was obligated to do according to the stipulations of his scholarship, Mor-

---

[13] Morgulis, "Iz moikh vospominanii," *Voskhod*, no. 2 (1895): 108.

[14] M. Morgulis, "Nikolai Ivanovich Pirogov i ego otnoshenie k evreiskomu voprosu (po povodu ego piatidesiatiletnego iubileiia)," *Voskhod*, no. 8 (1881), in *Vosprosy evreiskoi zhizni*, 521.

[15] L. Levanda to S. Zalkind, 12 May 1861, "Iz perepiski L. Levandy," *Evreiskaia biblioteka*, no. 9 (1891): 21.

gulis received special permission to study law at the University of St. Vladimir in Kiev. He indicated his proclivity for Jewish matters by choosing as his thesis the question of inheritance under Mosaic Law.[16]

Morgulis's description of his experience in the Zhitomir Rabbinical Seminary is valuable not only for a reconstruction of the genesis of his worldview, but also as a way to understand the internal workings of this seminary. Zhitomir, one of two rabbinical seminaries—the other was in Vilna—was equivalent to a Russian gymnasium in many respects; there, boys as young as eight or nine started a program of study that was complete after eight or nine years. The level of education, however low it may seem to critics, was high in comparison with what other non-nobles received at the time. In the 1850s, state serfs and privately owned peasants received little or no education at all.[17] Certainly, the seminaries did not provide the same education that children of nobles or wealthy merchants received in pensions or the famous lyceum in Tsarskoe Selo, but they are comparable to a gymnasium rather than to a Russian Orthodox seminary, where the children of so-called "white" clergy were trained, because of the number of serious courses in classical languages and history.

Although the students apparently wished to spend most of their time on general subjects, such as literature, history, and foreign languages, formally the Jewish seminaries had narrow vocational aims. Two programs were offered: one prepared teachers for government Jewish schools and the other prepared future "state" rabbis. The faculty was made up of both non-Jews, who taught secular courses, and Jewish scholars, who taught the courses on rabbinics. The directors of the schools themselves were usually Russians who often had military backgrounds.

Nevertheless, what links the Jewish and Russian Orthodox seminaries is violence. Morgulis's experience can be compared to that related in Nikolai Pomyalovsky's brutal description of a provincial Russian Orthodox seminary for boys, *Ocherki bursa* (Seminary Sketches).[18] Morgulis writes that it was not by chance that the rabbinical seminary was located across from the city penitentiary, since in the seminary one felt as though one were in prison. Family visits were extremely rare, and pupils were forbidden to leave the premises, except on holidays and rare exceptions. Furthermore, violence in the seminary was pervasive. Not only did teachers beat the students, older students viciously whipped younger ones in hazing rites. Moreover, students learned little in classes. If they were called upon to answer questions, they would use

---

[16] His thesis was published as "O davnosti vladeniia nedvizhimost'iu po talmudskomu pravu" (St. Petersburg, 1893).

[17] Ben Eklof, *Russian Peasant Schools: Officialdom, Village Culture, and Popular Pedagogy, 1861–1914* (Berkeley: University of California Press, 1986), 27.

[18] N. Pomialovskii, *Ocherki bursa* (St. Petersburg, 1860).

an ingenious method of long-distance reading that gave the impression that they had memorized their homework.[19]

What is surprising is the extent to which the students' minds were concentrated on subjects that bore little relation to the profession of rabbi. Morgulis describes how seminarians preferred dance to study. In Zhitomir, one of the non-Jewish teachers was a dance instructor, and with his help the seminarians were given proper lessons that allowed them gracefully to adorn any ball. Morgulis writes that "even the most serious young students began to shift their feet, forgetting about their position in the future and propriety in the present. Having learned to dance, the students began to set off to masquerade balls in the Zhitomir theater."[20] Alluding to the decadence and secular orientation of the seminarians, he queries, "Who would have thought that the first meeting of a rabbinical student with Jews of the gentler sex would occur not through the office of preacher, but on the ballet teacher's wooden floor?"[21]

Besides frivolity, student life in the seminary had a serious side, although it too was independent of the classes. The students set up their own organizations, which reflected their love of learning. For example, the most respected students were those who read intensely. In a garret room of one of the students, known as the "common apartment," many seminarians read for hours at a time, sharing forbidden books and holding discussions. Morgulis describes how among the students there developed a system whereby the older students mentored the younger ones. As with the Greek ideal on which the mentoring system was founded, erotic attraction accompanied the transfer of knowledge. "Love among the pupils of the common apartment was extremely developed. A great many dreamed about their lover, and usually in the twilight evenings, when there was nothing to do, longing, intimate conversations were carried on about love." Feelings were often expressed in physical ways. "The sensual partner [Morgulis calls him a 'lover,' *erotik*] squeezed the hand of his lover strongly, pressed it to his face, and from time to time kissed the face on which intense pleasure was reflected."[22]

Although we cannot entirely judge the nature of these apparently homoerotic exchanges, the relationships were associated with quests for knowledge. The students in the seminary were eager to acquire secular knowledge, to gain an understanding of science and humanistic scholarship. Proudly pointing to the experience of the seminary as enriching for Russian Jews, Morgulis ecstatically describes his own encounter: "[I met] the names of the Russian poets, [Aleksandr] Pushkin, [Vasily] Zhukovsky, and stories about their works; new disciplines—geography, history, and others; new Jewish

---

[19] Morgulis, "Iz moikh vospominanii," *Voskhod*, no. 11–12 (1895): 90.

[20] Morgulis, "Iz moikh vospominanii," *Voskhod*, no. 7 (1895): 92.

[21] Ibid., 92.

[22] Ibid., 101–02.

names covered with the laurels of particular veneration, such as [Jacob] Eichenbaum [1796–1861], [Mordechai] Suchostaver [1790–1880], Segal [Israel Ben Moses of Zamość, 1710–72], and the rabbi of Rovno. This was all so alluring that I wanted to join in the new movement and be carried away by the stormy flow of the new life that was being born."[23]

The experience in Zhitomir had an unambiguously positive effect on the minds, although perhaps not the bodies of the students, since there was never enough food. They were exposed to the classics of Western culture, especially German Romanticism, which gave them high and lofty values. The secluded environment, combined with the ceaseless message that the seminarians were going to play a central role in transforming Russia's Jews, gave them at once dreams of a better world and the drive to achieve it. Morgulis describes the self-perception of the students this way:

> Each rabbinical student was imbued with the very best ideals connected with the good of the Jewish people. Each one of us looked upon himself as a future reformer, a Mendelsohn in his own way, and therefore in the quiet of solitude one would often conceive of a plan of action which one carefully hid from his comrades. Rabbinical students were sincerely convinced that they would succeed in effecting a full revolution in the consciousness of the people and impatiently waited for the moment when they would act.[24]

Let out into the world at large, many of these students did not melt into Russian society, but struggled to achieve the goals that they had imbibed as students.[25]

Morgulis's early writings from the 1860s reflect the ardor of a young man inspired by Haskalah. According to the logic of Haskalah, the Jews were basically good and capable of reform. They were burdened, however, by bad traditions and ingrained habits. If these nefarious traditions and habits could be

---

[23] Morgulis, "Iz moikh vospominanii," no. 4 (1895): 30.

[24] Ibid.

[25] Without complete lists of students, it is impossible to determine what the vast majority did after finishing the school, but a partial reconstruction of the student body shows that the first generation of graduates included the following famous and influential Russian Jews N. I. Nakst, H. Barats, B. Bertenson, Y. Gershtein, A. Goldfaden, E. Kagan, S. Kaplan, S. Kovner, A. Landau, L. Levanda, A. Liberman, Z. Minor, M. Morgulis, A. Paperna, L. Pinsker, I. Soloveichik, and M. Veisbrod. Together with the teachers listed above these men constituted the literary, intellectual, and political elite of Russian Jewry from the 1840s to the 1870s and the creators of the new Russian-Jewish culture. Stanislawski, *Tsar Nicholas I and the Jews*, 107.

eliminated, the Jews would doubtless be integrated into Western society. Progressive Jews felt common cause with the government and were ready to help sweep away those elements of Judaism that were impeding modernization.

Like many others, Morgulis was carried away by the optimism of the time. He, too, was convinced that Alexander II's reforms marked the beginning of a new era for Jews in which everyone would soon receive equal rights. Doing his part, he criticized immutable superstitions and dogmatic traditions, but he nevertheless defended certain rituals from blanket condemnation. For Morgulis, an example of a bad institution was Hasidic Jewry and, in particular, its dynastic rabbinical leaders, the *zaddikim*.[26] *Zaddikim*, Morgulis claimed, lived extravagantly by exploiting the people. They held on to power by forming coalitions with the richest members of the community; such coalitions were unholy because "the *zaddikim* transferred the people's money into the rich men's pockets, while of course receiving protection against government officials."[27] As if presaging arguments anti-Jewish writers were to use soon enough against all Jews, Morgulis accused the *zaddikim* of forming a "state within a state." It angered him that if you "ask any Hasid where the center of the southern region lies, he will point to an insignificant town, the residence of the head *zaddik*, instead of Kiev. Such is the omnipotence of the *zaddikim*."[28]

A believer in the government's power to do good, Morgulis turned to the authorities for a solution. The way to fight, he claimed, was to put Hasidic leaders under house arrest and send them to Lithuania, where Jews do not respect Hasidism and where *zaddikim* will be incapable of spreading their influence.[29] Not surprisingly, his plan was rejected by the government, which by the 1850s had decided to take a neutral role in intra-Jewish conflicts.[30]

At the same time, Morgulis also defended Russia's Jews against unfair accusations. In response to allegations that the Jews gave false testimony in court in exchange for payment, Morgulis demonstrated that Russians also sold their testimony, serving as character witnesses for people they did not know. Lying under oath, he explained, was a job in Russia, and a lucrative one at that, providing perjurers with the extra income they needed for basic necessities. The problem lay not with faithless Jews or Russians, but with a judicial system that encouraged disrespect for law.

---

[26] M. Morgulis, "Byt' ili ne byt' Zaddikizmu v Iugo-zapadnom krae," in *Sobranie sochinenii* (Chernigov, 1869), 41.

[27] Ibid., 37–38.

[28] Ibid., 43.

[29] Ibid., 44–45.

[30] For a discussion of the influential power of the Hasidim in the 1850s, see A. Zeltser and I. Lurie, "Moses Berlin and the Lubavich Hasidim: A Landmark in the Conflict between Haskalah and Hasidim," *Shvut: Studies in Russian and East European Jewish History and Culture* 5 (21) (1997): 32–54.

Morgulis expressed strong pride in the Jewish tradition, praising its humane legal code. In "A Sketch of the Court of the Jews according to Talmudic Law," Morgulis pointed to the role of the biblical courts as a reflection of Jewry's high humanitarian values.[31] As opposed to the barbaric practices of other tribes in the ancient world, in ancient Israel an accused person was given every chance to prove his innocence. In fact, no person could be condemned on the basis of assertion alone, courts had to provide hard evidence. Similarly, judges were selected for their high probity and incorruptibility. According to Morgulis, in ancient Israel there was no profession more highly esteemed than judge. "The best reward for a judge was the respect of the people, which served as the most accurate measure of his competency. The people viewed with indifference and contempt those judges who were appointed not according to merit; such a judge was looked at as though he were a mule in a man's clothes."[32] Just like such pro-Russian reformers of the 1860s as Osip Rabinovich or Lev Levanda, Morgulis understood *Haskalah* as a balance between self-criticism and defensive pride, permitting himself the expression of deep love for the achievements of Jewish civilization.

Morgulis's attitudes changed in the 1870s. When it became clear that the promised civil equality of the Jews was not going to happen, many intellectuals began to reverse their previous boundless appreciation for the tsarist government. The indifference of the government to the pogrom of 1871 in Odessa also led people to wonder if the government might even come to be an enemy.

A believer in knowledge as a weapon for changing attitudes, in 1869 Morgulis, together with Ilya Orshansky, eagerly took control of the Odessa newspaper *Den'*. In *Den'*, Morgulis devoted himself to an extensive defense of Jewish interests, refuting claims that Jews avoided the military draft, were sympathetic to Polish rebels, or used Christian blood for ritual purposes. If *Den'* was less self-critical than Osip Rabinovich's earlier newspaper, *Rassvet* (1860–61), it was because the situation had changed. Jews needed defenders against a hostile press, a repressive government, and an unkind public.[33]

In particular, Morgulis confronted the libels of Jacob Brafman, published in *Kniga kagala* (The Book of the Kahal), a book extremely well received

---

[31] M. Morgulis, "Ocherk ugolovnogo Suda evreev po talmudskomu pravu," in *Sobranie sochinenii*, 76–102. The article first appeared in the volume *Ocherki iz istoricheskogo i iuridicheskogo byta evreev* (Kiev, 1866).

[32] Morgulis, "Ocherk ugolovnogo Suda evreev," 85.

[33] See John Klier, "The Jewish *Den'* and the Literary Mice, 1869–71," *Russian History*, no. 1 (1983): 31–49.

among Russia's leading statesmen.[34] Brafman argued that the Jews were bent on world dominance and secretly planned the takeover of Russia and enslavement of the Russian people. Although, unfortunately, few paid attention to Morgulis's objections, in a series of articles published in *Den'* in 1871, he conclusively refuted Brafman's claims.[35] Pointing out the staggering number of mistaken interpretations and grammatical errors in Brafman's book, Morgulis explained the true significance of the *kahal*.

Reconstructing the overall historical context, Morgulis pointed out that the *kahal* first appeared in the 15th century and performed an important function in early modern Europe, where the "Jews were not considered subjects of the state and had to keep up a real struggle with multifarious groups in society," such as "the local merchants and the guilds."[36] They also had to endure the arbitrary actions of the government. In this context the *kahal* actually served the government, taking account of its financial interests and overseeing the relationship between the Jews and society as a whole. According to Morgulis, Brafman entirely misunderstood the significance of the *kahal*. Instead of viewing it as an "institution of the highest power and subordinate to it," he saw it as an "organ itself of power, subordinating to itself the commands of justice and judgment."[37]

Disputing Brafman's claim that the Jews formed a state within a state, Morgulis expressed regret for the loss of the *kahal*. Many problems that the *kahal* had managed to resolve were festering from lack of attention. Aspects of the *kahal* should be reinstated, Morgulis argued, since the government was unable and unwilling to deal with the problems of internal Jewish life. In an 1879 article, "Vozmozhno-li i sleduet-li predostavit' evreiam pravo samoupravleniia obshchestvennymi delami?" (Can and Should the Jews be Given the Right of Self-Governance in their Communal Affairs?), Morgulis petitioned for the establishment of an independent Jewish communal administration. He asked why it was that, although the Jews were treated as an inde-

---

[34] Brafman's *Book of the Kahal* was published in four separate editions within a 15-year period—in 1868, 1869, 1875, and once again in 1882. This infamous book came to enjoy a tremendous popularity, especially among important tsarist bureaucrats, and its author was given a state sinecure as a "Jewish expert." For more on Brafman, see Morgulis's article "Brafman, Iakov Aleksandrovich," *Evreiskaia entsiklopediia,* 16 vols. (St. Petersburg, 1905–13), 4: 920–21.

[35] M. Morgulis, "Kagal, ego istoricheskoe proiskhozhdenie i uchrezhdeniia magdeburgskogo prava: Po povoodu [povodu] 'Knigi kagala,'" *Den'*, nos. 4, 5, 6, 11, 13, 14, 19, and 21 (1871).

[36] Morgulis, "Kagal, ego istoricheskoe proiskhozhdenie i uchrezhdeniia magdeburgskogo prava." Reprinted in *Voprosy evreiskoi zhizni: Sobranie statei* (St. Petersburg: Tipolit. A. E. Landau, 1899), 360.

[37] Morgulis, "Kagal," 387. A decade later Morgulis published another series of articles entitled "O Kagale (istoricheskii etiud)," *Russkii evrei*, nos. 46–52 (1882).

pendent estate (*soslovie*) according to tsarist law, they did not have their own institutions of self-rule.[38] Recalling that, since the abolition of the *kahals* in 1844, the task of governing the Jews had fallen on local administrations, which were indifferent, incompetent, or malicious, he insisted that it was necessary to reestablish the *kahals*, "bring them into the open," and "make the Jews responsible for their affairs and actions."[39]

While these ideas made sense from the Jews' point of view, they were highly unrealistic. At this time *Kniga kagala* enjoyed huge popularity, and many Russians were absolutely convinced that the Jews indeed comprised a "state within a state." In addition, the call for self-government, however laudable in itself, was starkly at odds with attitudes among tsarist officials, who, having legislated tumultuous reforms in social and economic life, such as liberating the serfs and establishing the zemstvo, became cautious about expanding rights for Jews beyond certain categories, such as merchants of the first guild, scholars, select artisans, and veterans of the army.[40]

Despite Morgulis's nostalgia for internal Jewish self-governance, Dubnov recalled the evils of the *kahal* in his 1890 review of Morgulis's volume of essays:

> The *kahal* really existed for the government, which only worried about the regular deposits of taxes from the Jews; it was like a useful institution, a kind of internal Jewish police, which provided social peace and security. But how huge was the cost for the Jews themselves to have this police, which behaved with a kind of cruelty that the normal police would never have done. No, it is not for us to remember fondly the old *kahal*! It was as burdensome for Judaism as any uncontrolled corporate power would be; it served as a stick in the hands of those people who had awarded its power and those under its power had to experience the charms of this cudgel of the fatherland for a long time. Let present-day Judophobes accuse us of *kehilla*-type cohesion. We will tell them that there were never two more horrible scourges than the *kehilla* in the past and Judophobia in the present![41]

The pogrom of 1871 in Odessa, which Morgulis witnessed firsthand, had a huge effect on his understanding of the Jewish problem. His memoirs give an

---

[38] M. Morgulis, "Vozmozhno-li i sleduet-li predostavit' evreiam pravo samoupravleniia obshchestvennymi delami?" in *Voprosy evreiskoi zhizni*, 464.

[39] Ibid., 479.

[40] For more on "limited emancipation," see Nathans, *Beyond the Pale*, 45–82.

[41] Kritikus [S. Dubnov], "Prezhde i teper'," *Nedel'nyi vypusk Voskhoda*, no. 1 (1890): 33.

almost minute-by-minute depiction of the development of mass violence over the course of three days. A sharp observer, he drew the conclusion that the perpetrators tended to be weak and feckless, growing in force only when they were sure the police would not resist. In the case of Odessa, the inactivity of the police was perceived as a green light.

> It is curious, above all, to note that early Monday morning opened with an attack on the house of Kaplanogol and the breaking of his windows. This house was situated on Police Square across from the main building of the Odessa Police Department, which, however, did not prevent the brawlers from carrying out their mission. It was obvious that, before setting off to burn houses, the crowd checked the pulse of the police, and, realizing their acquiescence, felt courage for the whole day. Apparently the crowd was not mistaken in its calculation. This was borne out in the fearlessness of the crowd at the homes of A. Rabinovich on Jewish Street and the banker Rafalovich on Italy Street.[42]

In Morgulis's view, "the material of the first pogrom, the first stage in the so-called 'people's anger against the Jews,' was instructive." Primarily, it revealed the fragmentation of a state divided into antagonistic elements. According to Morgulis, a pogrom poses a danger first of all to the state, but if the state doesn't see the danger, the "native" population should perceive it and do everything in its power to stop it.[43]

For both Morgulis and Ilya Orshansky, the pogrom of 1871 signaled a huge turning point, although each drew his own lessons. While Orshansky put the blame on the discriminatory laws that left Jews unprotected by the state, Morgulis saw an internal Jewish problem. But there was one area in which they agreed; both saw the need to study the history of Russian institutions in order to gain awareness of the origins of the government's maltreatment of Jews.

While Orshansky studied the Russian legal code, Morgulis devoted his energies to an in-depth investigation of the government's attempts to educate Jews, especially the construction of its school program in the 1840s.[44] He came to the conclusion that, in putting all its weight behind the construction of schools that the people did not want, the government wasted energies that could have been used more effectively. Moreover, Morgulis pointed out that while the government did build schools, it actually made no effort to change Jewish society, so that graduates of these schools and rabbinical seminaries

---

[42] M. Morgulis, "Bezporiadki 1871 goda v Odesse (Po dokumentam i lichnym vospominaniiam)," *Evreiskii mir*, no. 2–3 (1910): 2, 49.

[43] Ibid., 44.

[44] M. Morgulis, "K istorii obrazovaniia russkikh evreev," in *Voprosy evreiskoi zhizni*, 1–196; first published in *Evreiskaia biblioteka*, vols. 1–3 (1872–73).

could not find jobs.[45] And the government was not alone to blame. Jewish *maskilim* also contributed to the failure of the school initiative. Morgulis points to the ambiguous contributions of Max Lilienthal and Leon Mandelstamm, arguing in particular that Mandelstamm became wealthy by creating textbooks, anthologies of Hebrew texts in German translation. Although in subsequent studies Shaul Gintsburg disproved the claims that Mandelstamm enriched himself via textbooks, Morgulis looked askance at the *maskilim* who promoted the school program for their apparently selfish interests.[46]

From this work, Morgulis drew the lesson that the contemporary Jewish intelligentsia should refrain from forcing its program on the masses, but try instead to win their trust and create an alliance with them. The intelligentsia had to lead, but it had to adapt positions according to the real needs of the masses. For example, to win the people's support, the intelligentsia had to modify the schools, making them a place where both Jewish subjects and secular courses could be taught together.[47]

Nevertheless, not everyone agreed with Morgulis's conclusions. In the same issue of *Evreiskaia biblioteka* in which the last installment of Morgulis's study appeared, Lev Levanda disputed the view that the masses had been overly hostile to secular education.[48] Admitting that some Orthodox Jews boycotted the schools, Levanda claimed that many Jews in the 1840s understood the necessity for secular education and felt an enormous attraction to it. Levanda mentions as his example the achievements of David Lurie, schoolmaster and teacher in Minsk, whose success in combining Jewish and secular subjects in a single school broke down the resistance of wealthy Jews, who were "angered to see the children of their poorer neighbors get a better education than their own kids."[49] Levanda also claimed that Morgulis's hostile criticism of the *maskilim* was simply unfair. The mythic image of the *maskil* sacrificing himself for the sake of the community was still valid for Levanda.

In formulating his solution to the Jewish problem, Morgulis wanted to heal the divisions among Jews and between Jews and Russians. As opposed to his colleague Ilya Orshansky, who put great hopes on natural assimilation, looking to the expanding capitalist economy to generate rights for Jews that

---

[45] Ibid., 75.

[46] Morgulis, "K istorii obrazovaniia russkikh evreev," 124. Saul Ginzburg disputed this claim in an article on Leon Mandelstamm. See S. Gintsburg [Ginzburg], "Iz zapisok pervogo evreia-studenta v Rossii," in Ginzburg and Tsinberg, *Perezhitoe*, 1: 4–5.

[47] M. Morgulis, "O sovremennykh obshchestvennykh shkolakh evreev," *Voprosy evreiskoi zhizni*, 203; originally published in *Rassvet*, nos. 5–8 (1880). Previously Jewish state schools were dominated by instruction in secular subjects, while there was little or no secular study in the traditional *heder*.

[48] L. Levanda, "Po povodu stat'i M. G. Morgulisa (pis'mo k izdateliu *Evreiskoi biblioteki*)," *Evreiskaia biblioteka*, no. 3 (1873): 365–76.

[49] Ibid., 368–69.

were withheld artificially by the reactionary regime, Morgulis was anti-capitalist.[50] Attempting to bridge the rifts in classes caused by capitalism, he argued for a change in Jewish economic life, advocating so-called "productive occupations."[51] By this, he understood farming and crafts, which would take Jews away from exploitative professions into less lucrative, but morally superior activities. In addition, he believed that discriminatory laws had to cease. The masses "have to be given the chance to engage in productive work, the chance to move from those places where their hands are inactive to those where there is a pressing need for them."[52]

Morgulis's ideas were anchored in the view that the conflict of the Jews with their neighbors was not based on any inherent antipathy, but was due solely to economic tensions. "Religion and nationality only mask the true simple causes of antipathy. These causes can be found in the conditions of life, which create dissension and disagreement even among peoples (*narodnosti*) confessing the same religion."[53] According to Morgulis, Jewish infighting and antisemitism from outside could be eliminated only if one were to remove those conditions that contributed to economic and spiritual competition. Like the Russian populists, Morgulis was strongly hostile to capitalism. He was unaware of the fact that capitalism was capable of breaking down corporate identities and bringing about gradual integration.

At the same time, Morgulis was not blind to the national aspect of his economic program. Russia's Jews should no longer react to directives from without, but as a people should set their own goals. He explained his purpose in language that presaged the vocabulary of Jewish nationalism:

> We need only to come to the realization that it is necessary to get started energetically and to recall the proverb: "If I am not for me, then who is?"—a proverb born on Jewish soil obviously, since Jews in every epoch have had to think for themselves, and even in those cases where others think for them, they nevertheless have to think for themselves in order to realize those alien ideas in practice.... Let us *think* for ourselves, and not only think, but *act* too![54]

Morgulis realized some of his ideas in Trud, the trade school in Odessa, whose director he became in 1871. Under his leadership it became the largest school of its kind in Russia. For Morgulis, Trud presented an opportunity to transform Jews into productive laborers and also to show that Jews were

---

[50] M. Morgulis, *Il'ia Grigor'evich Orshanskii i ego literaturnaia deiatel'nost'* (St. Petersburg, 1901), 10.

[51] M. Morgulis, "Chto nam delat' s russkimi evreiami?" *Voprosy evreiskoi zhizni*, 294–342; originally published in *Rassvet*, nos. 3–6 (1879).

[52] Morgulis, "Chto nam delat' s russkimi evreiami?" 294.

[53] Ibid., 304.

[54] Ibid., 324.

capable of organizing their own schools. In his article of 1896 "O professional'nom obrazovanii evreev v Odesse" (On Professional Education of Jews in
Odessa), Morgulis stated that in 1891 the school received 15,000 rubles annually from the city's *korobka* taxes and in 1890 gave 212 students their diplomas.
Organized as a workshop, the school also brought in 20,081 rubles from work
orders.[55]

Similarly, in the 1880s, Morgulis counseled the expansion of modern *talmud torah* schools organized under the aegis of the Odessa branch of the OPE,
where he was a leader.[56] Despite his efforts to create institutions, Morgulis
did not repudiate hand-outs for individuals. He organized help for poor students in Odessa of clothing, books, and food.[57]

Eli Lederhendler therefore was only partially right when he wrote:

> The answer Morgulis offered was not auto-emancipation in the Zion-
> ist sense of the term which [Leon] Pinsker was to use four years later.
> But his solution was something closely akin to auto-emancipation,
> which he identified as a restoration of coordinated leadership on a
> national level, a rebuilding of political community. Only this—not
> temporary local philanthropy nor even civic equality—had any hope
> of actually changing the circumstances of Russian-Jewish life.[58]

Although Lederhendler perhaps did not realize the extent of Morgulis's attachment to philanthropy and the goal of civic equality, he was correct in
saying that Morgulis was leaning toward a modern Jewish politics. Despite
the fact that his activities tactically followed the lead of Russian populists and
their program of "small deeds," by demanding Jewish autonomy and self-
governance Morgulis was ahead of his time.

Politically, the 1880s were tumultuous years for Russia's Jewish intellectuals.
Following the pogroms of 1881–82, the Jewish intelligentsia split into rival
groups. Some saw a solution in emigration to America or Europe, others advocated colonization in Palestine, while still others were convinced that political revolution in Russia itself held the answer. In addition, the pogroms ap-

---

[55] M. Morgulis, "O professional'nom obrazovanii evreev v Odesse," *Sbornik v pol'zu
na[c]hal'nykh evreiskhikh shkol* (St. Petersburg, 1896), 389–90.

[56] V. D-v, "Iubilei 'prosveshcheniia': O dvadtsatipiatiletnei deiatel'nosti Odesskogo
Otdeleniia Obshchestva prosveshcheniia mezhdu evreiami v Rossii (1867–1892 g.),"
*Voskhod*, no. 8 (1893): 20–21.

[57] "Mikhail Grigor'evich Morgulis," *Otchet Odesskogo otdeleniia OPE za 1911* (Odessa,
1912), 4.

[58] Lederhendler, *Road to Modern Jewish Politics*, 153.

peared to have galvanized the resolve of the younger generation, who began to speak out in favor of radical solutions.[59]

In 1883, Morgulis entered into a polemic with one of these angry young intellectuals, Simon Dubnov, who in the article "Kakaia samoemansipatsiia nuzhna evreiam?" (What Kind of Self-Emancipation Do the Jews Need?), fulminated against traditional rabbis, blaming them for the stagnation of Jewish communities, which had left Jews outside Russian society and prepared ripe conditions for pogroms. Calling for immediate and radical change, Dubnov urged religious reform, full integration with the non-Jewish world, and equal rights.[60] Claiming, perhaps hyperbolically, that even Christianity was more progressive in embracing change, Dubnov was convinced that half-measures would not do; the Jewish community had to modernize—and quickly.

Although Morgulis must have found in Dubnov's despair much that he agreed with, he pounced on the young upstart for his weak sense of Jewish pride. Calling Dubnov's position "self-flagellation," Morgulis claimed that it was wrong to see the Jews' legal situation as some kind of punishment for their level of progress. It was time, he vigorously announced, for Jews to view their past with pride, since the contributions of Judaism to world culture justify such confidence:

> It seems time to stop playing with those who are interested in the Jews only in so far as they repudiate their past and are capable of becoming swallowed up by the external world. It is time to think about oneself, one's national individuality, which has a long past with historical value in the eyes of humanity. It is time to begin serious national work, strengthening within the people those universal principles which were present in the spirit of Judaism earlier, despite humanity's cruel treatment.[61]

Adamantly opposed to radical solutions, Morgulis showed his political conservatism when in 1888 he jumped at the chance to serve as a Jewish representative to the Higher Commission for the Examination of Existing Laws

---

[59] See Frankel, *Prophecy and Politics*, 49–132.

[60] S. Dubnov, "Kakaia emansipatsiia nuzhna evreiam?" *Voskhod*, no. 5 (1883): 245.

[61] M. Morgulis, "Samoosvobozhdenie i samootrechenie," *Voprosy evreiskoi zhizni* (St. Petersburg, 1889), 534–94, here 569. Incidentally, this article contained a polemic against Leon Pinsker's essay "Auto-Emancipation: Mahnruf an seine Stammgenossen" (1882). An example of Morgulis's criticism is the following: "But among the honest, genuine voices in which a relation of the echo of the voice of the people is heard, other voices also emerge. These voices, being also a result of sympathy for the people's interests, come out with a lousy hidden falseness" ("Samoosvobozhdenie i samootrechenie," 536).

Regarding Jews in the Empire, known as the Pahlen Commission.[62] Clearly Morgulis felt at home with Baron Horace Guenzburg and the other members of the Petersburg elite, such as the bankers Abraham Zak and Samuel Polia-kov. No *shtadlan* himself, Morgulis had seen the benefits of pragmatic cooper-ation with the government in his educational work in Odessa and, a realist at heart, Morgulis was willing to adopt the *shtadlan* approach of urging legal, as opposed to political, rights for Russia's Jews.

Certainly no one can doubt the sincerity of these efforts. In his memoirs, Morgulis describes:

> [T]he meetings of the Higher Commission took place almost every day during three and a half weeks and often continued until two o'clock in the morning, and sometimes longer. All this time the [Jew-ish] experts were obsessed by one common thought: how to help our people, bring to bear the whole arsenal of historical and logical argu-ments to affect the convictions of the majority.[63]

Apparently Morgulis played a key role, since he put forth the suggestion that the Jewish representatives hold separate meetings to develop an effective common political strategy. Morgulis attributes to himself the winning plan of dividing the Russian officials into moderates and reactionaries and attempt-ing to isolate the latter.[64] This strategy was crowned with success when the majority of Russian officials voted to recommend the abolition of the Pale of Settlement. Nevertheless, the recommendation was not enacted into law, since Alexander III ignored the commission's findings. Morgulis, who had placed enormous hopes on success, was stricken by the tumultuous blow that crushed his hopes for the immediate liberation of the Jews.

> Prince Kantakuzen-Speransky decided to overturn the decisions of the Pahlen Commission using the means which bureaucracies often turn to in their struggle with public opinion.... Total disappointment resulted. All our worries, written work, hopes for the liberation of the [Jewish] people from different forms of enslavement turned out to be

---

[62] "In the summer of 1888, by surprise, friends from my days at the rabbinical semi-nary came to me and brought word from St. Petersburg that Jewish experts will be invited to the Higher Commission on the Jewish Question, under the stewardship of Count Pahlen. Among these experts, I was named as the representative of New Russia." M. G. Morgulis, "Iz moikh vospominanii (vysshaia komissiia grafa Palena po evreiskomu voprosu)," *Evreiskii mir*, no. 6 (1909): 22. It is important to recall that the Pahlen Commission had been meeting from as early as 1883.

[63] Ibid., 38.

[64] Ibid., 24.

futile. The Russian legal code remained in the same chaotic condition as it was before. The legal situation of the Jews even worsened.[65]

In his research on the Pahlen Commission, Michael Aronson speaks about the paradox that a hostile government would create an advisory body with the goal of improving the legal status of Jews.[66] After all, the Pahlen Commission was established in 1883, just one year after the enactment of the discriminatory laws of May 3, 1882. Nevertheless, Jewish experts were given the chance to collect and present information before a group of Russian officials in order to influence government policy. Whether the tsar ever had any intention of following the commission's advice or merely established the deliberative body as a smokescreen to deflect attention away from its repressive policies is anyone's guess. In any case, the outcome of the commission showed once again that the Russian *shtadlanim* were unable to force demands, but had to acquiesce in whatever the government decided.

Due in large part to the forced stagnation in Jewish political life, in the 1890s Morgulis wrote less, but his articles reflected new theoretical ideas about the ultimate purpose of Jewry. In "Sushchnost' evreistva" (The Essence of Jewry, 1893), for example, Morgulis underscored the personal, religious, and moral aspects in defining what is a Jew, as opposed to Jewish politics, economic structures, or communal membership. He writes:

> [T]he commonality and breadth of the principle discovered by Judaism inheres exactly in the following: since people have discovered an image that is characterized by ideals which are out of their reach, they must strive for perfection, ceaselessly strive in order to come closer to this ideal. Further, this ideal consists of all that is hopeful: kindness, reason, beauty, justice, love, and so on. People, it turned out, are obliged to strive for the development within themselves of all these hopeful aspects of the unattainable ideal.[67]

At the same time that he was edging toward a definition of Judaism based on universal values of passivity and meditation, Morgulis also examined Jewish history to find models corresponding to his vision of the future. Not surprisingly, he rejected the ideals of the proto-Zionists and socialists, ignoring military heroes and farmers/workers from the Bible. The heroes of Morgulis's narrative were rabbis, Hillel and Akiva, who succeeded in creating

---

[65] Ibid., 41–42.

[66] M. Aronson, "The Attitudes of Russian Officials in the 1880s toward Jewish Assimilation and Emigration," *Slavic Review* 34: 1 (1975): 1–18.

[67] M. Morgulis, "Sushchnost' iudaizma," *Voskhod*, no. 1 (1893): 75–77. Interestingly, many Russian intellectuals of the time were inspired by Leo Tolstoy's ideas of non-resistance to evil and lauded a personal politics of passivity, while eschewing politics in the public sphere.

institutions that fortified Jewish resolve in unfortunate circumstances. In contrast to those who fought for a physical nation, Hillel and Rabbi Akiva built centers of Jewish knowledge, creating works of scholarship that inspired followers. Moreover, Morgulis admired above all in these figures their conception of universal religion. Instead of driving the Jews into isolation, these two rabbis led the Jewish people to greater understanding and openness to the outside world. Of Hillel, Morgulis wrote, "His entire work was directed towards a practical application of the great principles of reason, justice and morality. He always approached the old law from this angle."[68]

Although Morgulis probably misjudged Rabbi Akiva's commitment to meditation, as opposed to military prowess—after all Rabbi Akiva did support the Bar Kohba revolt and was flayed alive by the Romans—Morgulis's interpretation of Hillel and Rabbi Akiva reflected his own needs. Frightened by Jewish nationalists, he was worried that national demands would deflect Jews from their genuine interests in integration and modernization. Moreover, he was concerned that national demands would bring on the wrath of the Russian government and people. Therefore, he advised Jews to seek what he called the "universal in the particular": they should develop within themselves those humanistic ideals that also made them better Jews. In concrete terms, Morgulis called for the creation of centers of Jewish learning that would highlight the rare achievements of Jewish civilization. Just as had been the case in Germany, Morgulis was convinced that only that kind of scholarship on Jews that showed the high value that Jews place on moral and spiritual accomplishment would be effective in changing attitudes.[69] Meanwhile, hoping for emancipation in the long run, Morgulis counseled internal discipline and intellectual achievement in the present.

Nevertheless, Dubnov again wondered aloud whether Morgulis's proposal for internal self-perfection offered the best alternative for Russia's Jews. He asked, "Should the Jews strive for their internal-spiritual and quotidian self-perfection, despite their difficult external condition, or should they wait for everything from an improvement in the external conditions and right now not get started on their internal metamorphosis? That is a question of critical importance which serious Jewish social thought should answer."[70] Dubnov answered his own question negatively. Arguing against Morgulis, he wrote, "It is already high time to put an end to this ruinous disagreement and with all our might take up the task which is our sacred duty, the question of our whole life. And there are many tasks, but the common name for them is self-help in the broadest sense, in the spiritual and social-economic sense."[71]

---

[68] M. Morgulis, *Istoricheskie etiudy: Gilel', Akiba* (Odessa: Izd-vo Odesskago otdeleniia Obshchestva rasprostraneniia prosveshcheniia mezhdu evreiami v Rossii, 1898), 14.

[69] Morgulis, "O sovremennykh obshchestvennykh shkolakh evreev," 216–20.

[70] Kritikus [S. Dubnov], "Prezhde i teper'," *Voskhod*, no. 2 (1890): 20.

[71] Ibid., 25.

Admittedly, Morgulis's ideals reflected pessimistic resignation. The dreams of the 1860s had not come to fruition, but had led to increased repression. For his part Morgulis restricted himself to pragmatic and temporary solutions. He attended meetings of Hovevei Tsiyon (a Zionist movement), and when the organization received legal status 1890 as the Society for the Support of Jewish Farmers and Artisans in Syria and Palestine, Morgulis became a leader. Despite a commitment first and foremost to the health of the Jewish community in Russia, Morgulis was not hostile to colonization in Palestine. In fact he considered that "the resettlement of poor Jews in Palestine served a two-fold purpose by giving the settlers themselves a source of income and by reducing the level of competition in the Pale."[72] Shaw tells us that "[i]n the early 1890s Morgulis's Zionist career reached its apogee. In 1890, Morgulis was accorded the honor of being elected chairman of the Odessa Committee at the first meeting held after achieving legal status. Two years later he contributed an article to Ravnitsky's newly established journal *Hapardes*, taking his place alongside Mendele, Bialik, Ahad Ha'am, and other important figures in Jewish letters."[73] Nevertheless, Dubnov considered it strange that one of Odessa's leading representatives of "assimilation" was also an esteemed figure among proto-Zionists.[74]

Indeed, when Zionism became a political movement under Theodore Herzl's leadership and sought to establish a homeland for Jews, Morgulis switched from friend to enemy. Unconvinced that antisemitism was an immutable component of Western civilization, he believed instead that it was the result of the "machinations of unscrupulous politicians and the ignorance of the dark masses both of which could be combated through the spread of education."[75]

In 1901–02, Morgulis's political orientation led him into open conflict with the so-called Jewish nationalists over the curriculum of OPE schools, secular schools for Jews financed with OPE money.[76] This debate typifies Morgulis's pragmatism and commitment to integration.

Dubnov, together with the Zionists Ben-Ami and Ahad Ha'am, advocated a nationalist program, holding that the only schools that deserved funding were the ones in which at least half the classes were devoted to Jewish sub

---

[72] Shaw, "Odessa Jewish Community," 208.

[73] Ibid., 209. See M. Morgulis, "Le-shnei batei Yisrael," *Ha-pardes*, no. 1 (1892): 261–66.

[74] Dubnov, *Kniga zhizni*, 251.

[75] Shaw, "Odessa Jewish Community," 210.

[76] There were also conflicts in the spring of 1902 between the steering committee of OPE's Odessa branch and Jewish nationalists over the lack of nationalists on the steering committee.

jects and where the Hebrew language received sufficient instruction.[77] Morgulis, speaking on behalf of the OPE's governing committee, rejected these
arguments, claiming that an increase in Jewish subjects would be detri-
mental.[78] Since it was impossible to unite in one school both the nationalists'
demands for increased time for Jewish subjects and the same number of practical courses, it was the responsibility of the society to decide. The OPE leadership argued that first and foremost children had to receive proper vocational skills and knowledge of Western subjects in order to be prepared to
earn a living in Russia.[79] Jewish subjects, Morgulis counseled, could be made
up later in higher grades after students had acquired basic knowledge, especially knowledge of Russian.

Morgulis and the other members of the steering committee of the Odessa
branch of the OPE were sharply criticized in the Jewish press. Various
writers, including Boris Brutskus and Saul Gruzenberg, the editor of the
newspaper *Budushchnost'*, took the steering committee to task, calling their organization a "home for assimilators."[80] In one editorial Gruzenberg, described
the committee as men who

> with amazing candor repudiated everything that is dear to a Jewish
> heart. Hebrew was declared a dead philological subject that had out-
> lived its years, not only unnecessary for Jewish children, but ex-
> tremely burdensome, even harmful due to its complexity. Jewish his-
> tory is also not needed in school, since one should acquaint the child
> with the reality that awaits him and not with what occurred 2,000
> years ago. Only one thing is not explained, why Jewish children
> should remain Jews. Judaism is only a burden and it is not hard to
> prove with footnotes from American pedagogues that one should
> walk in tandem with one's epoch, be free from all prejudice, and not
> restrain one's career with various "Old Testament" ideas.[81]

The clash in 1902 led to a polemic between Dubnov and Morgulis. While
Dubnov had shared some of Morgulis's confidence in integration in the early
1880s, by the end of the 1890s, he had become inspired by ideas of national

---

[77] Ahad Ha'am et al., "O natsional'nom vospitanii: Zapiska, predstavlennaia v Komitet
odesskogo otdeleniia Obshchestva rasprostraneniia prosveshcheniia mezhdu evreiami," *Voskhod*, no. 1 (6 January 1902): 12.

[78] M. Morgulis, "Mnenie komiteta odesskogo otdeleniia Obshchestva rasprostraneniia
prosveshcheniia o evreiskoi narodnoi shkole," *Voskhod*, no. 16 (19 April 1902): 4–9.

[79] M. Morgulis, "Preobrazovanie evreiskikh nachal'nykh shkol," *Budushchnost'*, no. 16
(12 April 1902): 389.

[80] See B. Brutskus, "Pis'mo v redaktsiiu," *Voskhod*, no. 24 (13 June 1902): 11–13; and
*Budushchnost'*, nos. 2, 3, 5, 13, 14, 16, and 25 (1902).

[81] S. Gruzenberg, "Po povodu odesskogo sobraniia obshchestva prosveshcheniia,"
*Budushchnost'*, no. 25 (21 June 1902): 488.

autonomy. Attacking Morgulis's position that the best expression of Judaism was its adoption of universal virtues, Dubnov openly condemned Morgulis as a hopeless assimilator. An intellectual "at wits end," was how Dubnov characterized him, writing that such people "are suffering from a dualism in their worldview, in which national and assimilationist elements are mixed together."[82] This confused attitude, Dubnov wrote, can be seen in Morgulis's negative position toward a national school, a national political party, and Jewish cultural autonomy. According to Dubnov, since assimilation was a natural process for minorities, if one did not pursue a national program, one inevitably supported assimilation, since assimilation is "the direct practical result of the rejection of the national idea."[83]

In his response, Morgulis criticized Dubnov's historical model of Jewish development. Dubnov, we recall, posited a triad: thesis meant traditional Judaism; antithesis—assimilation; and synthesis—Jewish nationalism. Morgulis claimed that Dubnov had it wrong, that thesis and antithesis should be reversed. Instead of an inexorable development toward Jewish nationalism, Morgulis considered Dubnov's period of assimilation as a time of profound enrichment for the Jews.[84] Acquaintance with European culture deepened Jewish life by creating a Jew characterized by a synthesis of universal and Jewish traits.[85]

Stressing the need to stop using assimilation as a kind of pejorative epithet, Morgulis claimed that the nationalists should differentiate between positive and negative assimilation.[86] Whereas negative assimilation consisted of a total negation of one's identity, positive assimilation was a laudable goal. Assimilation represented "integration only in external forms with the dominant environment, but in spirit, in its strivings toward the creation of its own culture, [integration] meant love for the past and its historical monuments, sympathy for the people, and the illumination of various spheres of Jewish knowledge."[87] Confident that assimilation had positive consequences, Morgulis retained his belief that the future of Russian Jewry lay in a synthesis of Jewish and Russian qualities and the integration of the Jews into Russian culture.

Although the nationalists made many good points, the established Odessa leadership won the vote on OPE schools, albeit by the narrow margin of 78 to 71. Despite attempts by the nationalists to consolidate their position, even sending supporters a pamphlet about how they should behave at the

---

[82] S. Dubnov, "O rasteriavsheisia intelligentsii," *Voskhod*, no. 12 (1902): 87.

[83] Ibid., 74.

[84] M. Morgulis, "Natsionalizatsiia i assimiliatsiia," *Voskhod*, no. 5 (1902): 103.

[85] Ibid., 113.

[86] Ibid., 111.

[87] Ibid., 110–11.

key election meeting—they were told to retain party discipline and not to make catcalls—the nationalists still lost. Although Odessa was presumably a center of Jewish nationalism, an integrationist orientation still dominated many areas of community life in the city.

After the debates on schools, Morgulis retreated to the background. Although he continued his activity as a member of various committees in Odessa, he was not active on the political scene. He did not play an important role during the 1905 Revolution and did not speak out about the Jewish politics of the Duma, which, one presumes, gave him hope that Jewish interests would be at least partially defended in Russia's new political order. However, he did use the political freedoms following the 1905 Revolution to place the entire blame for the animosity between Russians and Jews on the government. He claimed that patriotic Russians and Jews had the same interests: fighting for their own liberation. He wrote about 1905:

> The people who acted in places so far from one another were not identical, but an identical spirit, an identical principle incited people against the imaginary enemies of the fatherland. The best people in Russia understood that the events of Kishinev, Gomel, and Zhitomir grew up from the same soil as Kursk, Saratov and Balashov.[88] Russia has become closer to the Jews, and the Jews have come closer to Russia. The same spirit of patriotism unites them, a patriotism that strives for the same thing, the liberation from the shackles of that partition which stands between the people and real truth.[89]

In Morgulis's view, 1905 showed that Jewish and Russian interests were the same, the struggle for freedom against the tsarist regime a common struggle.

In 1910, two years before his death, Morgulis took a new turn in his analysis of Jewish politics, praising Jewish political autonomy anew. Perhaps after seeing the failure of pro-Jewish legislation to gain support in the Duma, he had to admit that only political autonomy could assure respect for Jewish legal and political interests. Affirming nearly all of Dubnov's ideas about national autonomy in the Diaspora, Morgulis stated:

> [T]here is no disagreement that one should consider the ideal of an organization its full autonomy, i.e., complete free activity that embraces all aspects of communal life without exception and pushes [its jurisdiction] to the boundaries, the point where one begins trespassing on others' interests or government law begins. But however desir-

---

[88] Kishinev, Gomel, and Zhitomir are clearly sites of anti-Jewish violence, while Kursk, Saratov, and Balashov are places where battles occurred between revolutionaries and police forces during the Revolution of 1905.

[89] M. Morgulis, *Vopros, imenuemyi evreiskim* (St. Petersburg: Tip. Obshchestvennaia pol'za, 1906), 142–43.

able such free communal activity might be, in view of contemporary conditions one must only strive toward such autonomy, to the achievement of what is [presently] possible...[90]

According to Morgulis, such autonomy could be achieved by establishing local Jewish legislatures. Leaders would be elected by secret ballot with universal suffrage.[91] Morgulis claimed that in these community legislatures "the interests of a single group, whether interests of faith, knowledge, class, nationhood, or any other that is connected with living ideals of a group, must give way to general interests."[92] Community leaders would get their resources from the meat and candle taxes, the *korobka*, which Morgulis recalled was still collected by the government every year.

Certainly these ideas about national self-rule paralleled those put forth by Jewish liberals at the Kovno conference of 1909.[93] At that meeting, Jewish leaders such as Henrik Sliozberg and Maksim Vinaver attempted to modernize the relations between Jews and the Russian state, and revitalize communal institutions for that purpose. Although the representatives held no political power, they did offer as their most important suggestions the democratization of Jewish communal governance and the transformation of the *korobka* into an income tax.[94]

It is surprising that at a time when Russian Jews were being treated more and more as individuals by the state and were given the right, albeit abridged, to vote for representatives to a national Duma, Morgulis was suggesting a return to treating the Jews as a collective. It is difficult to distinguish if this position was forward-thinking—it was certainly nationalist—or backward-thinking, related to traditional forms of Jewish communal organizations. It was probably both. Morgulis had always been unhappy with the meat tax as it had been implemented in Russia. He did not approve of the way collective burdens were unequally distributed and he protested the forced payment of taxes without the establishment of Jewish political organizations to help decide how the money should be spent. At the same time, he lauded the rare experiments in Jewish political autonomy in Odessa, extolling the "Hundred Representatives" and the "United Committee of Communal Institutions," which existed for a short time after the disappearance of the "Hundred Representatives."[95]

---

[90] M. Morgulis, "Ob organizatsii evreiskoi obshchiny," *Evreiskaia nedelia*, no. 9 (1910): 4.

[91] Ibid., 6.

[92] Ibid., 4.

[93] See Gassenschmidt, *Jewish Liberal Politics in Tsarist Russia*, 85–92.

[94] Ibid., 90.

[95] M. Morgulis, "Ob organizatsii evreiskoi obshchiny," *Evreiskaia nedelia*, no. 8 (1910): 5.

Morgulis's proposal for an autonomous Jewish legislature reflects the porous aspect of Jewish nationalism. Despite the criticism he received from the nationalists in 1902, it is clear that at the end of his life Morgulis actually stood close to them. His desire for an independent Jewish politics, his conception of the Jew as a member of a Jewish community, and his social activism in Odessa, despite its old-fashioned aspect, reflected shared premises that Jews should have their own institutions devoted exclusively to Jewish interests.

At the same time, Morgulis refused to surrender his belief that integration enriched the Jew. Although he wavered between two poles, Morgulis probably did not believe the Jews should be considered a "nation" in their own right. They were already a people, a *narod*, and that was apparently enough for him. If Jews could retain their identity and simultaneously integrate into Russian society, if they were given full civic rights and permitted freely to occupy themselves with the Jewish religion and cultural affairs, then everything would be all right and there would be no need to fight. The political interference by the Russian state that made integration impossible forced Morgulis to promote autonomous Jewish institutions.

His firsthand experience of acculturation as a young boy, as a student in Zhitomir, and as an activist in Odessa shaped for him a core of essential ideas. Morgulis was convinced of the validity of integration, and he believed it could be combined with an unwavering respect for Jewish identity. Certainly his synthesis of Russian and Jewish traits was inspired by the experience of Europe, where Jews, in theory at least, were full citizens of their country, while being members of a religious association. Morgulis must have felt vindicated by the large number of Russian Jews who broke out of traditional communities, entered Russian schools and universities, and sought work in Russia proper. Integration was doubtlessly motivated by practical goals, but its practitioners, Jewish men and women, often wanted to satisfy more than mere economic needs, desiring to enrich themselves with European civilization.

In terms of the politics of his day, Morgulis aligned himself with the liberal elite, composed of bankers, lawyers, journalists, and other educated professionals. It makes sense that he did not belong to any political party; he was sympathetic to the *shtadlanut*, remaining faithful to the idea that the wealthy and powerful were more effective in an autocracy than dangerous radicals or powerless liberals. Despite his cooperation with wealthy notables, he was attracted to Russian Populism and its anti-capitalist attitudes which inspired him with the belief that making one's living from the land was morally superior to all other occupations. Apparently he never yielded the view that Jews should surrender those jobs considered "exploitative" and become farmers.

Toward the Zionists, Morgulis's negative attitude remained fixed. Since he disagreed with the central premise of political Zionism that the Jews were foreigners in Europe and needed a state of their own, he refused to debate Zionism's ideological merits. In a final article published in the year of his death, Morgulis concentrated on the practical failures of Zionism. He curtly noted that the vast majority of emigrants set voyage to America, while one, two, or three percent went to Palestine.[96] The Jewish masses, he argued, were voting with their feet.

Since he was deeply committed to the well-being of the Jews as a people, when he died in 1912, Morgulis was mourned by a variety of Jewish figures on various sides of the political fence. While the Zionists alone boycotted the 75th birthday celebrations that occurred just before his death, many nationalists did acknowledge his contributions. Among them was Simon Dubnov himself, who was ultimately able to admit the good that Morgulis had done. In his memoirs from the 1930s, Dubnov writes:

> During a lonely walk in the heart of the forest, I thought about my former friend and later rival, with whom the Odessa period of my life was connected. A few weeks before Morgulis's death, during the celebration of his 75th birthday, I nominated him as an honorary member at a meeting of the [Jewish] Historical Society. I wonder if this gesture of reconciliation reached my ideological rival?[97]

Even if Morgulis was not aware of Dubnov's gesture, surely we understand it. Dubnov acknowledged that over the long run Morgulis's ideas and actions came close to, if not entirely coincided with, the goals of Diaspora nationalists. Just as did other integrationists from the 1860s and 1870s, Morgulis could and did make temporary alliances with the nationalists on various issues, but he could not swallow the whole national program.

In conclusion, perhaps we might consider Morgulis's most important contribution to be his help in creating the image and identification of a modern Russian-Jewish intellectual. The term itself, "Russian-Jewish intellectual," was attached first of all to members of his generation. Moreover, Morgulis acted in the best spirit of this group, as a bridge between the Russian and Jewish cultures. He was also one of the early civic activists who struggled in the secular realm for the benefit of their co-religionists and helped modernize purely Jewish institutions, such as community *hevrot*, to deal with purely modern political problems. Of course, Morgulis was a practical civic leader, not a philosopher, but in many of these contexts there was no established script, no preordained means of acting and no ready-made solutions. The generation of *maskilim* before him had looked to the government for direction and leadership. Morgulis reflected a shift in approach, ceasing to look to the

---

[96] M. Morgulis, "Budushchnost' evreistva po Zombartu," *Novyi voskhod*, no. 16 (1912): 12.

[97] Dubnov, *Kniga zhizni*, 323.

government as an authority and reaching out to the masses with philan-thropic and educational aid. At the same time, he resembled his *maskil* fathers in counseling integration, productivization, knowledge of the state language, and a degree of religious reform. It was his ability to package these ideas in a modern way that permitted him to lead Russian Jewry in the difficult years from the Great Reforms until the rise of Jewish nationalism.

## Chapter 10

# The Portrait of a Russian-Jewish *Shtadlan*: Jacob Teitel's Social Solution

Jacob (Yakov) Teitel (1851–1939), a Jewish judge, criminal investigator, and philanthropist, justifiably deserves the attention of historians of Russian Jewry. His career serves as a mirror of changes in the legal and occupational status of Jewish professionals in late-tsarist Russia. Entering the Ministry of Justice in the 1870s, after it had become open to Jews as a result of the legal reform of 1864, he was forced to resign his position due to antisemitism in 1912. At that time he was the sole remaining Jewish judge in Russia and his presence in the ministry was an intolerable blemish for I. Shcheglovitov, the infamous Minister of Justice. In his various philanthropic activities Teitel applied the tenets of Russian Populism, while employing as a practical model the approach of the *shtadlan*, i.e., he sought individual exceptions to Jewish liabilities by means of personal intercession.[1] In his attitudes, behaviors, and life choices, Teitel's ideals reflect the goals of the 1860s and 70s—Jewish integration with Russia—which he managed to do early in his life and which he refused to surrender, despite changes in external conditions.

Teitel, however, also plays another, perhaps equally important role. With his vivid autobiography, he informs us about the development of the *shtadlan* approach, about his behind-closed-doors negotiations with the representatives of the Russian government. Such testimony is valuable because the *shtadlan* system is historically mute; few records exist about it. In fact, convention requires silence; the inner workings of behind-the-scenes negotiations are by definition secret and closed to the public. Therefore, Teitel's descriptions are precious for the historian.[2]

Teitel's biography also gives us valuable information about Jewish life in the provinces of Russia. Having spent the lion's share of his life in Samara and Saratov, Teitel describes the Jewish world in the most unlikely places. And yet in these areas, out of reach to most Jews, Teitel and others engaged in

---

[1] The *shtadlan* is associated with the court Jew who, using his position of influence and authority, made requests on behalf of the Jewish people. For a positive evaluation of the *shtadlan* in Russia, see Klier, "Krug Gintsburgov i politika shtadlanuta," 38–54.

[2] Steven Zipperstein suggested the ideas in this paragraph in a personal conversation on December 20, 1998.

Jewish philanthropy, confessional life, and administration of the local community.

Teitel came of age in the last decade of Alexander II's reign in the 1870s, when, despite the attainment of privileges for the "best among us," it had become entirely clear that the "Great Reforms" would not bring full civil rights to all of Russia's Jews. Furthermore, the pogrom in Odessa in 1871 already presaged worse times to come. In addition to a hostile government, forces of dissolution were tugging from within at the stagnant Jewish community. The old *maskilim* (reformers of the first half of the 19th century) were discredited by the failure to produce broad and deep political change, while in many instances traditional Jews were still reluctant to take a more assertive political role outside the Jewish community.[3] The 1870s saw many young people turning their backs on Jewish civic life, seeking career opportunities in Russia that entailed either conversion or at least nearly complete assimilation. A small, but not meager percentage of young Jews took advantage of the opportunity, still open, to enroll in Russian universities (by 1886, 14.4 percent of all students were Jews), thereby attaining privileges denied to the vast majority. Teitel found himself among a smaller, but nevertheless vocal group of individuals—whom we may call the Russian-Jewish intelligentsia—who, professing acculturation to Russia, retained a strong Jewish identity.

Inspired by the ideals of Populism, after graduation from Moscow University, Teitel wanted to be useful to Russia and her Jews. He therefore chose a career in the tsar's Ministry of Justice, becoming a criminal investigator in the provincial cities of Kazan and Samara, and later a judge in Saratov. During World War I, he worked in London collecting money for destitute Jewish refugees, and after the Bolshevik revolution, departed Russia, becoming the president of the Society of Russian Jews in Germany. Nevertheless, one can only partially explain his major achievements by pointing to his professional career. What is most important about Teitel is his philanthropic activity, through which he reveals his particular synthetic Russian-Jewish worldview.

Teitel rejected political solutions, preferring the philanthropy typical of the *shtadlan*. He deeply admired such wealthy and influential Petersburg oligarchs as Baron Horace Guenzburg and Leon Rosenthal, who served as intercessors to the government on behalf of the masses and provided the less fortunate with financial aid, educational opportunities, and occupational training. Spending funds from the Society for the Promotion of Enlightenment among the Jews of Russia, Teitel devoted his life to the kind of social activism which, while widespread in the 1860s and 70s, had become less

---

[3] *Maskilim* (plural), *maskil* (singular) (Hebrew for "enlightener") refer to representatives of the Haskalah or Jewish enlightenment. In Russia, *maskilim* were autodidacts who sought some secularization of Jewish life. They were active from the end of the 18th century until the rise of a modern Russian-Jewish intelligentsia in the 1860s. For more on the early *maskilim*, see Fishman, *Russia's First Modern Jews*.

prominent by 1905, when political parties emerged to replace the *shtadlonim* as the political leaders of Russian Jewry. To some degree, Teitel's rejection of party politics reflects an ingrained tension between the privileged and the masses. Many privileged Jews, certainly the oligarchs, were less likely to seek radical change and more likely to retain allegiance to non-institutional and informal approaches to easing Jewish liabilities. In fact, Teitel's philanthropic activities, which continue into the 1930s, reflect, I believe, the longevity of the *shtadlan* institution and psychology, still alive even after the death of the major *shtadlonim*. This view finds corroboration in Steven Zipperstein's assertion that "the magnates' continued impact (and undiminished control) on Jewish community life in the last decades of tsarist rule is frequently overlooked. Certain periods of crisis (e.g., 1881 or 1905) saw them marginalized temporarily by those more sympathetic to postliberal Jewish ideologies, electoral politics, and mass agitation."[4]

Since Teitel did not leave behind a large body of writings, in order to understand his origins and the development of his worldview we have to examine his life. Fortunately, he left behind a fascinating autobiography in which he offers vivid observations about his experiences, attitudes, and thoughts about himself, his career, and his activities on behalf of Russian Jewry. In many ways Teitel belongs to a category of individuals who are considered outstanding not for what they have accomplished, but for their spiritual natures, their radiant personalities.

At an evening celebrating Teitel's 75th birthday in Paris, Maksim Vinaver had this to say:

> Who is Teitel? Here in the emigration this question will appear on the lips of many people. But there on the Volga, in Samara, Simbirsk, and especially in Saratov, there was not a single person, it seems, who did not know this young elder, with his flashing eyes always moving, always absorbed in a mass of "affairs"—affairs which did not concern him personally, were not related to his legal work. "Affairs" always and inevitably meant errands for someone else—a friend or a stranger, it made no difference—errands, endless in quantity, infinitely diverse in content.[5]

The lawyer and civic leader Genrikh Sliozberg offered this testimony: "His favorite expression was that during his life he 'applied bandages' to the fissures in people's fates. And in reality all his life Teitel repaired lives that had

---

[4] Steven J. Zipperstein, "The Politics of Relief: The Transformation of Russian Jewish Communal Life During the First World War," in *The Jews and the European Crisis, 1914–21*, ed. Jonathan Frankel, Studies in Contemporary Jewry, no. 4 (New York: Oxford University Press, 1988), 26.

[5] M. Vinaver, in *Ia. L. Teitel': Iubileinyi sbornik, 1851–1931*, ed. N. L. Aronson (Paris-Berlin, 1931), 45; first published in *Poslednie novosti*, December 20, 1925.

broken apart due to material want, and with this work he not only saved
these lives, but constantly set a foundation of goodness in people's relationships, awakened hearts."[6]

Such descriptions do not point to any concrete actions taken by Teitel, but
to his general qualities. Indeed, the majority of such encomiums stay clear of
listing his deeds, emphasizing instead his traits of selflessness, generosity,
and kindness. Although these virtues may seem too minor to be of interest to
this historian, the world of Russian officialdom he inhabited contrasts sharply
with his character, causing one to wonder at the phenomenon of Teitel himself. The Jewish civic leader M. Sheftel formulates Teitel's paradoxes this way:

> And it was a dark mystery to me what forced this anarchist-
> individualist, who would not accept coercion against the individual,
> to dedicate a large part of his life to service to the state and, more-
> over, to that state institution which juxtaposes to individual will the
> organized force of state power in its most coercive and cruel form, in
> the form of judicial repression. In Russia's criminal-justice bureau-
> cracy Jacob L'vovich [Teitel] chose the position of judicial investi-
> gator, which he carried out for more than thirty years under difficult
> circumstances in the distant provinces, with its semi-serf peasant life,
> under the solicitous, hierarchical authority of zemstvo administrators,
> in an atmosphere of administrative, political arbitrariness...[7]

To this, one can add several other paradoxes. With his experience in the Ministry of Justice, he was well aware that civil rights for the vast majority of
Russia's Jewish population were stringently abrogated. Nevertheless, he rejected political solutions, although he must have known that politics could
put an end to the government's discrimination more effectively than social
activism. Furthermore, despite having been a target of antisemitism and witnessed pogroms personally, he did not blame the Russian people. While it is
not my goal to excuse these incongruities, his inextinguishable optimism
about improving the world is an essential fact of his biography.

Teitel's lineage and childhood point to the gradual secularization of the Jew-
ish community of southwestern Russia. Yakov Teitel was born in 1851, in
Chernyi Ostrov in the Praskurov District in the Jewish Pale of Settlement.
There his grandfather Jankel—note the polonized name—had rented a mill.

---

[6] G. B. Sliozberg, in *Iubileinyi sbornik*, 56; first published in *Obshchee delo*, November 26, 1921.

[7] Ibid., 132. *Zemstvo* refers to the institution of self-governance in the countryside, which was begun in 1864 and had the goal of providing social benefits to the peasantry.

Jankel was considered a "local aristocrat," since he met with Polish land-owners and gave his children a secular education. Teitel's father also had the reputation of a "free-thinker": he wore Western clothing, knew both Polish and Russian, and even wrote verses in Hebrew. His work as a duties collector on behalf of wine merchants brought him into contact with non-Jewish ideas and habits. Such taxmen, Teitel writes in his autobiography, "were considered liberals and even atheists, since they broke nearly all 613 obligatory commandments for an observant Jew."[8]

Teitel's character was fashioned by the secular education he received as a boy. While still in the *heder*, he was given Western novels by his elder sister.[9] Later he was sent to Kremenets, where he studied the Torah in Moses Mendelsohn's German translation. Since he showed promise as a student, Teitel's father was advised to send his son to the Volozhin Yeshiva and prepare him for a "brilliant career" as a rabbi. But as Teitel puts it, luck interfered and he entered a Russian gymnasium and later enrolled in St. Petersburg University.

As occurred with many Jewish students of this period, the university experience politicized his thinking. While he enjoyed the stimulation of studying law and the extracurricular activities of the time—he entertained a radical intellectual circle in his room—he was occupied with other than intellectual matters, namely the issue of how to "resolve the Jewish question." Like others, he placed his trust in Jewish integration and acculturation. In contrast to those who sought to achieve success for themselves alone, Teitel believed professional achievement should be used to facilitate the general merging of Jews into Russian life. In addition, Teitel was unforgiving toward those Jews who sought prestige and quick fame. Rather, he felt that what was needed was an influx of Jews in modest, but diverse positions in Russian society, especially in places where they had not yet penetrated in large numbers.[10] He understood clearly that official antisemitism was a real obstacle, yet he personally did not yield. He writes, "Although Jews were admitted to state service at the time, it was not something desired. At the beginning of the judicial reform, some Jews made it into the Senate Secretariat, the District Attorney's

---

[8] Ia. Teitel, *Iz moei zhizni: Za sorok let* (Paris: Ia. Povolotskii, 1925), 11.

[9] From the many incidents of his childhood, Teitel highlights his friendship with a Ukrainian boy: "In the cottage of Trokhim's parents I felt as if I was home, and I did not understand how one cannot like a person just because he is a 'goy' or a 'kike.' I owe a lot to dear Trokhim and him mother, a typical Ukrainian peasant woman" (ibid., 13). This episode, narrated with deep feeling, reflects Teitel's philosophy that prejudice is something unnatural, an excrescence on the human spirit. In addition, one can read this story as prophetic, since it anticipates Teitel's future as a Jew living happily among non-Jewish peers.

[10] Ibid., 32.

office, and a few got into the Magistracy, but almost all either left to become private attorneys or converted to Russian Orthodoxy."[11]

Antisemitism, which was growing in Russia in the 1870s, affected Teitel deeply. In particular, an accusation of ritual murder in Perm in 1875 incited Teitel to attempt to start a "Russian" newspaper. In his view Jewish newspapers had no effect on society, since only Jews read them. Rather, newspapers were needed that were "not dedicated exclusively to the Jewish question, that would properly illuminate all the aspects of Jewish life."[12] Although his negotiations with Grigory Bagrov, an editor and writer, were unsuccessful, four years later the weeklies *Russkii evrei* and *Rassvet* began appearing with a similar platform.[13]

Teitel's commitment to Populist ideals combined with the *shtadlan* approach found direct application in his attempts to defend Jews facing the arbitrary power of the state. For example, in Samara he interceded with the school authorities to secure the admission of one additional student:

> In particular the question of quotas was especially tricky. By law, in the Samara gymnasium 5 percent of the class could be Jewish. If there were 110 Christians, then 5 and 1/5 Jews would be admitted. I held discussions with the directors about this 1/2. I argued before the directors that in the following case one should act by analogy with the presumption of innocence, and even if you take the position that all Jewish children are defendants accused of a serious crime, then it follows that for 110 Christians 6 Jews should be admitted, since it was impossible to cut a Jewish boy in half, as much as one would have wanted to do so.[14]

In 1904, Teitel was transferred to Saratov. There he was invited to head the Jewish division of the Society for the Aid of the Poor. While he had been forced to work underground, organizing meetings in private homes in Samara, in Saratov the society was legal. This openness aided him in his campaign to secure entrance to the nursing school for poor Jewish women. In fact hundreds of them rushed to Saratov, since the quota restrictions were not enforced and the institute encouraged immigration, waiving the requirement of

---

[11] Ibid.

[12] Ibid., 24.

[13] "The direction of *Russkii evrei* will be forceful and straight. The editors will try to go forward as much as possible, dispassionately, by the straight path, no turns either right or left. In our evaluation of events, actions, and character traits, we will not allow a passionate distinction between us and them; we will praise acts worthy of imitation and condemn those worthy of censure without leniency or hypocrisy." *Russkii evrei* (31 August 1879): 3. Grigory Bogrov (1825–85), author and journalist, was an editor of *Russkii evrei*.

[14] Teitel, *Iz moei zhizni*, 130–31.

a residence permit. When the police objected, Teitel entreated Pyotr Stolypin, the regional governor.[15] Surprisingly, Stolypin, not known for his pro-Jewish attitudes, agreed. "He stopped such expulsions and advised the administration of the school to present the bylaws for approval in which a paragraph was included that Jewish girls would be admitted into the school regardless of quotas and that, having been admitted, they received the right to live in Saratov. Poor, exhausted girls came to Saratov with a strong desire to study, to be useful to society, but, of course, without any money."[16]

Teitel's influence with Stolypin proved useful during the short, stormy pogrom that occurred in Saratov on the evening of October 18–19, 1905. Once it had begun, Teitel hurried to Stolypin, who was not in the city and only returned three days later. Once back, Stolypin used his authority to stop any further anti-Jewish disturbances.[17] Later, Teitel discussed the causes of the pogroms with Stolypin who argued that the pogroms in Saratov made no sense since "among Saratov's Jews, there were no money-lenders, shopkeepers, and exploiters and no antagonism between Christians and Jews had been detected."[18]

In light of his preference for social activism, Sheftel is correct when he describes Teitel as a "typical Russian intellectual-social activist of the Zemstvo-Populist type."[19] Like the zemstvo officials, representatives of Legal Populism, Teitel also desired to improve Russia by working within established institutions. We can perhaps explain his allegiance to tsarist rule by acknowledging his middle-class status and the traditional Jewish attitude of loyalty toward the recognized ruler, which incidentally was a position also shared by the *shtadlonim*.

Part of the key to his success as an intercessor must have been his exceptional congeniality. To have influence, he instinctually understood that one has to have friendly, informal relations with a wide variety of individuals. Teitel became famous for the parties he held at his home at which archconservatives and ardent radicals were invited. Among Teitel's frequent guests were Vladimir Ulyanov (Lenin), Maksim Gorky, Nikolai Garin-Mikhailovsky, and Aleksei Alekseevich Bibikov, a friend of Lev Tolstoy.[20] Other guests included

---

[15] Pyotr Arkadevich Stolypin (1862–1911), governor of Saratov province (*gubernia*) from 1903 to 1906.

[16] Teitel, *Iz moei zhizni*, 171.

[17] Ibid., 183.

[18] Ibid.

[19] Ibid., 131.

[20] Maksim Gorky, pseudonym for Arkady Mikhailovich Peshkov (1868–1936), major Russian/Soviet writer; Nikolai Garin-Mikhailovsky (1852–1906), Russian novelist.

P. P. Rumyantsev, later the editor of *Vestnik zhizni* in Petersburg, and Mark Elizarov and Aleksandr Shlikhter, later commissars in the Soviet government.[21] Teitel describes these parties: "At our parties, or as people called them jokingly, 'assemblies,' there were between 150 and 200 people; we put them on often on the slightest pretext. Since the apartment was small, the beds and living-room furniture were carried out, we didn't even spare the flowerpots; tables and chairs from other houses were brought in. The doors to the corridor were often left open, since people stood everywhere."[22]

Teitel's defense of Russia's Jews through personal intercession may strike us as old-fashioned, as indeed it was. By 1904, in the capitals of Russia and in the Pale of Settlement Jews were organizing political parties and pressure groups, while in provincial Russia power was still organized around the governor.[23] In fact, the governor was similar to a local monarch. Teitel describes this omnipotence: "It is funny to talk about legality. Governors regarded the interference of the Directorate of Public Prosecutions as a drop in the prestige of their power. All other departments, even the most, so to say, independent, such as the Department of Justice and the military, had to adapt themselves to the views and opinions of the governor. A person, having been assigned to the District Attorney's Office, was sent on the road with the instructions of the Minister of Justice: 'Get along with the administration, i.e., the governor.'"[24] In this context, personal intercession was the only available means for a successful defense of the Jews.

Teitel's view of the Jewish religion was rather unexceptional. While he obeyed the most important rituals, Judaism was apparently a private affair, and it occupied only a very small part of his autobiography. Far more important is his sense of Jewish identity, which he conceived primarily in terms of ethnicity. From childhood in the Pale, Teitel had a strong sense of Jewish difference, and, moreover, like many educated Jews, antisemitism only strengthened his feelings of Jewish identity. When offered opportunities to convert for career advancement, Teitel refused, famously remarking, "My Judaism is not for sale!"[25] At the same time, Teitel's identity was very different from concepts such as "Russian of the Mosaic persuasion" or Judah Gordon's injunction "Be a Jew in the home and a man in the street." Teitel considered the Jews more than merely a religious designation, seeing them as a nationality, although not a nation. At the same time, he purposely did not hide his identity in public, emphasizing that his Jewish background made him a better

---

[21] Mark Elizarov (1862–1919), Communist Party leader; Aleksandr Shlikhter (1868–1940), Communist Party leader and member of the Ukrainian Politburo.

[22] Ibid., 44–45.

[23] Teitel's political life in Saratov was very different from the experience of the capitals. See Gassenschmidt, *Jewish Liberal Politics in Tsarist Russia*, 12–46.

[24] Teitel, *Iz moei zhizni*, 111.

[25] Ibid., 47.

judge and better citizen. He believed that all citizens in the multinational Russian state should be entitled to full rights and subject to duties as individuals, rather than as members of any corporate or national body, although in the oppressed situation Jews found themselves in, he felt that powerful Jewish leaders were obligated to aid their co-religionists.

Teitel's position on individual rights, however, stems less from any legal-ethical convictions than from a kind of religious mysticism that insists on individual moral incorruptibility and preternatural innocence. Given his career in the legal profession, it is surprising that, while he admired the ethical foundations of Judaism, he was more enamored of an idea of spiritual redemption that is reminiscent of Dostoevsky. "It was precisely my work as a judge that fortified my faith in man and sharpened my strength in the struggle for an improvement in his position. The long experience of many decades told me that there are no souls entirely extinguished. God's spark keeps warm at the base of the most ignorant, most criminal soul and can ignite as a bright fire if you blow on it with attention and love."[26] This view of the individual as morally redeemable and himself as the catalyst for this redemption explains Teitel's optimism about humanity, despite the evils he had witnessed. It also explains why he forgives the Russian people for antisemitism. "I continue to assert: the recent sad events [the pogroms of 1905] in which the Russian people revealed such beastly inclinations, nevertheless, cannot shake my conviction that racial and national hatred is alien to the simple people."[27] Like many other Russophile Jews, Teitel blamed antisemitism exclusively on Nicholas II's government.

Teitel himself encountered antisemitism in his work, and his progress through the ranks of the ministry was obstructed. As he himself describes it, "The district court elected me as a member of its board several times, but each time I was rejected by the Ministry of Justice which did not find it possible to assign me, a Jew, as a member of the court."[28] In this atmosphere of intolerance, Teitel's Jewish status invited rebuke. In 1911, the ministry, under the leadership of Shcheglovitov, who, incidentally, built the legal case against Mendel Beilis, let Teitel know he could no longer remain a judge.[29] Since the ministry had stopped hiring Jews in the 1880s, by 1910 there were only two Jews left: Ia. M. Galperin and Teitel.[30] Since Galperin occupied an adminis-

---

[26] Aronson, *Ia. L. Teitel: Iubileinyi sbornik*, 39.

[27] Teitel, *Iz moei zhizni*, 176.

[28] Ibid., 47.

[29] I. G. Shcheglovitov (1861–1918), member of the tsarist government and minister of justice (1906–15). In 1913 Mendel Beilis was acquitted of the charge of ritual murder in a famous trial in Kiev.

[30] In his autobiography, Teitel mentions an article that appeared in Prince Meshchersky's journal *Grazhdanin*, in which it was asserted that in a Christian state it was unac-

trative post, Teitel was actually the sole Jewish judge in all of Russia. The very existence of a Jewish judge intensely irritated many highly placed individuals. The lawyer O. O. Gruzenberg explains, "The head prosecutor often mentioned him in bitter eclogues to the ministry. There it had the expected effect: even without them Shcheglovitov felt awkward before the Unions of the Russian People, Michael Archangel, the Two-Headed Eagle, and other [antisemitic groups], that he allowed in his department such a pathological phenomenon as an unbaptized Jewish judge."[31]

In order to encourage Teitel to quit, Shcheglovitov offered him a final promotion to *deistvitel'nyi statskii sovetnik*, which was equivalent to a general's rank in the military. Shcheglovitov could be generous since, in truth, he had no complaints about Teitel's work: "'Now is no time to have a Jewish judge. I will do everything for you.... I repeat,' he said, 'neither I, nor the Ministry of Justice have anything against you personally.'"[32] Teitel writes in his autobiography that he was sad to leave, since he had gotten used to his unique status: "I didn't want to give up the title of the 'only Jewish judge in Russia.'"[33]

The October Revolution did not change Teitel's views in the slightest. In 1921 he immigrated to Germany, where he was immediately offered the directorship of the Union of Russian Jews in Germany. In 1923, he organized the philanthropic society Friends of Children (Druz'ia detei). This organization reflected Teitel's broad goals, since it addressed both the child's physical health and spiritual needs. According to witnesses, he wanted to "overcome the lack of spiritual discipline and the cruelty of children who had come into difficult circumstances during the twilight of humanitarian ideas and the diminution of love for the other."[34] In addition, in the Russian section of Berlin, a children's home was build in honor of J. L. Teitel. Teitel also organized the Women's Committee of the Union of Russian Jews in Germany and was instrumental in arranging summer retreats for needy children. Under his initiative, a commission of rabbis made a financial appeal to Germany's Jewish population, an appeal that inspired the organization of a state-sponsored

---

ceptable that a Jew could carry out a criminal investigation of a Russian Orthodox man (ibid., 191).

[31] O. O. Gruzenberg, "Pamiati Iakova L'vovicha Teitelia" in *Ocherki i rechi* (New York, 1944), 164. There were two fascist organizations with the same name, "Union of the Russian People," and both were established in 1906. The various right-wing organizations mentioned here composed in part the antisemitic group known as the "Black Hundreds."

[32] Teitel, *Iz moei zhizni*, 201.

[33] Ibid., 205.

[34] Ibid., 33.

commission devoted to aiding Russian-Jewish refugees under the directorship of Dr. Alfred Klee.

How then can we make sense of Teitel in the context of Russian-Jewish
political leadership? Certainly it is difficult to understand his intellectual immutability in this period of momentous events and fluctuating attitudes.
Indeed, his autobiography does not contain much reflection on the pogroms
of 1881–82, 1903, the political aspects of the 1905 revolution, or work of the
four Dumas. Perhaps the distance of the provinces from the center partially
explains this neglect, but it is also clear that he was occupied by other, more
concrete and pressing concerns where he was located. Another explanation
might be that the *shtadlan* method was useless in moments of explosive antisemitism, just as it was ineffectual in a parliamentary system. Since the *shtadlan* method depended on government cooperation, it could not produce results in any situation in which the government was powerless, e.g., during the
pogroms and the struggles of political parties.

In terms of the ethical questions that Teitel's actions generate, a historian
of our day might have difficulty explaining his blanket exoneration of the
Russian people for antisemitism and may wonder at his preference for social
activism above politics, since it was clear that the solutions to the "Jewish
problem" could only come through political change. And yet, instead of criticizing Teitel, based upon the hindsight of knowing how it all turned out, it is
possible to praise him as a really luminous person, dedicated and courageous,
who stood steadfastly for a positive goal and on the way helped a lot of
people.

At the foundation of Teitel's life we find a core of principles that motivate
his actions. Influenced by his Jewish background, his bourgeois class, and
Russian social and spiritual ideals, Teitel believed in the primacy of the individual before society and the perfectibility of every person. Having acquired
these eternal values, the events and experiences of a transitory reality could
not shake loose these fixed beliefs. In fact, neither the repression of the tsarist
regime, nor the crimes of the Bolsheviks undermined his positive conception
of the Russian people.

In his attitudes and methods, Teitel was clearly influenced by Russian
Populism. Interestingly, Jewish association with the Populist movement often
resulted in greater Jewish national consciousness, since the idealization of the
Russian peasant reminded Jewish intellectuals of their own people, the Jewish
masses, who were in similarly difficult circumstances and in need of attention. A telling example is Shimon An-sky, who had served as the personal
secretary of the Populist leader Pyotr Lavrov for over a decade.[35] In addition,

---

[35] Shimon An-sky (1863–1921) was a Jewish author of stories in Russian and Yiddish,
most famously *The Dybbuk*, an expert on Jewish folklore, and a political activist. He
organized the Jewish Ethnographic Expedition bearing the name of Horace Guenzburg (1912–14).

the elder of Jewish socialism, Aaron Liebermann, had his first experiences in the Populist movement.[36]

Although he was detached from the political movements of the first decades of the 20th century, remaining distant from the Bund, Zionism, and Jewish party politics, Teitel's policy of small deeds remained alive because it was effective. It was effective, at least in its own terms, precisely because it did not question the class structure of Jewish life or create conflict with Russia's rulers. For the philanthropists themselves, activism offered the successful few the means of bridging the divide between their Russian careers and Jewish identities, since they were able to put their elite positions to good use.

Although social activism came under strong criticism by the leaders of Jewish political parties, one can argue that Teitel not only provided temporary aid to individuals, but shone as a model of moral conduct for all. Perhaps this feature composes Teitel's most enduring contribution, since while many individuals were bent by the storm of political and social change, Teitel remained faithful to ideals of inherent value and humanity, ideals he had acquired in his youth and applied throughout his life.

---

[36] Aaron Liebermann (1845–80) was an important Jewish radical and editor of the Socialist monthly in Hebrew *Ha-Emet* (1877).

# Jews in the Russian Elite

# Introduction to Part 3

This section deals with Russian Jews who became prominent contributing figures in Russian culture itself, such as Lev Shestov (Shvartsman), the Russian-Jewish philosopher; Mikhail Osipovich Gershenzon, the noted historian and literary critic; and Aron Shteinberg, the philosopher and cultural observer. These individuals were far more deeply integrated into mainstream Russian culture than were the figures in the first two sections. Nevertheless, their Jewish backgrounds influenced how Russian colleagues perceived them and how they ultimately came to view themselves. Using a comparative approach, I juxtapose these figures with Russian colleagues with whom they had close personal and professional relations: Nikolai Berdyaev, Pyotr Struve, Vasily Rozanov, Sergei Bulgakov, and others.

Many centuries ago, Russian theologians feared the so-called "Judaizers," who were supposedly perverting Russians with the Jewish religion. One hears an echo of this intolerant past in modern accusations that the presence of Jews perverts Russian culture. Vasily Rozanov directly named Gershenzon as a particular danger because of his extraordinary talent.[1] In fact, one could lump Rozanov together with Fyodor Dostoevsky, Konstantin Pobedonostsev, Tsar Nicholas II, Father Pavel Florensky, and even Aleksandr Solzhenitsyn and Igor Shafarevich as individuals who felt Jews had a negative influence on Russian life.

In truth, Shestov, Gershenzon, Shteinberg, and many others raised a challenge to Russian culture: Why couldn't a Jewish person, a native speaker of Russian, who considered Russia his homeland, study the poet Pushkin, the Decembrists, Lev Tolstoy, or Dostoevsky, and come up with a new interpretation of Russian literature? Could a Jew stand at the head of Russian culture? At the same time, what do these questions and answers tell us about Russian society and its attitudes toward its Jewish members?

The articles in this section also raise the question: Why have Jews been so attracted to Russian culture? Although a better answer emerges from the essays themselves, I only note here that Russian culture was a world culture. Beyond its political message of resistance to government repression and defense of the little man, it embodied the values of spiritual profundity and individual perfection, inspiring the most talented individuals in the country. It is a sad fact that, while Russian culture beckoned to all suitors, not all were accepted. Just as in other parts of Europe, the Jewish question became linked

---

[1] Rozanov, "Levitan i Gershenzon," 78–81.

to issues of national culture. Some Russian nationalists jealously harbored a desire for a monopoly over the Russian cultural heritage. Jews and other outsiders were seen as interlopers at best, a dangerous fifth column at worst. Although this topic deserves an entire monograph to elucidate, suffice it to say that, as the contest over the ownership of Russian literature intensified, Jews did not retreat. Lauded for brilliant contributions, Jews were also targets of multifarious personal and professional accusations.

At the same time, one cannot help observing that Jews had an uncanny ability to engage with Russian culture, participate in its debates, employ its formal devices and vocabulary, and become inspired by its values. The contributions of its Jewish members changed Russian thought, added to it, and influenced its development. Without romanticizing Russian-Jewish cooperation as "a wonderful coincidence"—the words of Vladimir Solovyov—or demonizing it as a "confrontation," one can conclude that the problems, intellectual, social, economic, political, and artistic, brought to the forefront by the meeting of these two peoples, are interesting to the highest degree.

## Chapter 11

# A Jewish-Christian Rift in 20th-Century Russian Philosophy: N. A. Berdyaev and M. O. Gershenzon

> My philosophy has always been a philosophy of conflict.[1]
>
> —Nikolai Berdyaev about himself

> The erudite "Kulturtreger" several times showed me the power of the elemental forces living within him...[2]
>
> —Andrei Bely about Mikhail Gershenzon

The Bolshevik Revolution of October 1917 found the two friends, religious philosopher Nikolai Berdyaev and historian and philosopher Mikhail Gershenzon, on different sides of the conflict. Berdyaev's vehement opposition to the revolution ostensibly caused him to break off relations with the sympathizer Gershenzon. In 1952, Gershenzon's daughter, Natalia Mikhailovna Gershenzon-Chegodaeva, wrote in her memoirs that her father's friendship with Berdyaev "ended badly. During the days of the October Revolution, when my dad was completely aflame, passionately awaiting and welcoming the new, they suddenly severed relations, disagreeing over political convictions. Several painful letters remain which reflect the break."[3]

The abrupt end to the relationship between two of Russia's most creative thinkers of the 20th century is usually attributed to their differences of opinion about the October Revolution. In fact, however, politics at the time of the Revolution were only a catalyst for the break; the real cause of their estrangement lay in their irresolvable philosophical debates and the emotional conflicts arising from their Christian and Jewish backgrounds. They clashed philosophically because Berdyaev favored an idiosyncratic Christian philosophy, while Gershenzon adhered to a pantheistic religion of the "cosmos." Their personal dispute, which revolved around antisemitism, arose because of Berdyaev's exclusive attachment to Christianity. These differences are evident in

---

[1] Nikolai Berdiaev, *Samopoznanie: Opyt filosofskoi avtobiografii* (Paris: YMCA Press, 1949), 110.

[2] Andrei Belyi, *Mezhdu dvukh revoliutsii* (Leningrad: Izd-vo pisatelei o Leningrade, 1934), 286.

[3] N. M. Gershenzon-Chegodaeva, *Pervye shagi zhiznennogo puti (vospominaniia docheri Mikhaila Gershenzona)* (Moscow: Zakharov, 2000), 27.

their respective attitudes toward the Russian intelligentsia, Slavophilism, World War I, and the October Revolution.

Although scholars have shed light on the life and work of Nikolai Berdyaev, less is known about Gershenzon.[4] Mikhail Osipovich Gershenzon was born of Jewish parents in 1869 in Kishinev in the Pale of Settlement. Although he excelled at Moscow University, winning a gold medal for his work on ancient Greek history, Gershenzon was prevented from pursuing an academic career due to his status as a Jew.[5] Working as a translator, journalist, and editor to earn his keep, Gershenzon finally achieved fame with his critical articles and monographs about Russian literature and culture.

Gershenzon's multifaceted oeuvre, which ranges from scholarship on Russian thinkers of the 19th century to critical works on contemporary Russian literature and Pushkin, earned him the acclaim of critics and fellow writers.[6] Vasily Rozanov proclaimed him "Russia's best historian," while N. Kotlyarevsky helped Gershenzon to win the Academy of Science's Akhmatovsky award for the best historical work of 1909. In addition, readers called him the "Russian Carlyle" and praised Gershenzon as a "master" of Russian prose. For Gershenzon, popularity was essential because he lived most of his life without a secure income, depending on the sale of his books and articles for his livelihood.

Gershenzon was also an active observer of Russia's political life. He edited and contributed to *Vekhi* (Landmarks), the 1909 collection of essays criticizing the Russian revolutionary intelligentsia, and coauthored the famous *Perepiska iz dvukh uglov* (Correspondence from Two Corners) with the poet Vyacheslav Ivanov. Despite strong ideological differences with the Soviet regime, Gershenzon held important offices in the literary bureaucracy. He was the first president of the Moscow Union of Writers, and from 1922–25 served as the head of the Literary Section of the Soviet Academy of Sciences. He died in Moscow from heart failure in 1925.

Several descriptions of the close friendship between Berdyaev and Gershenzon are available from such firsthand witnesses as Fyodor Stepun, Evgenia Gertsyk, Andrei Bely, Natalia Baranova-Shestova, and Natalia Gershenzon-Chegodaeva, Gershenzon's daughter. The latter remembered Berdyaev as a constant visitor:

---

[4] Since this article was written, two books about Gershenzon have appeared: Brian Horowitz, *A. S. Pushkin in the Silver Age: M. O. Gershenzon-Pushkinist* (Evanston, IL: Northwestern University Press, 1997); and Vera Proskurina, *Techenie Gol'fstrema: Mikhail Gershenzon: Ego zhizn' i mif* (St. Petersburg: Aleteiia, 1998).

[5] "'Afinskaia politiia' Aristotelia i 'Zhizneopisaniia' Plutarkha" (1893).

[6] Among his chief works are *The History of Young Russia* (1907); *P. Ia. Chaadaev: Life and Thought* (1908); *Historical Sketches* (1910); *The Images of the Past* (1912); *Griboedov's Moscow* (1914); and *Pushkin's Wisdom* (1919).

In 1914–15 my parents were very close with Berdyaev and not only with him, but also with his wife, the beautiful and dignified woman (sort of a poet) Lidia Yudifovna, and her sister Evgenia Yudifovna.... The Berdyaevs lived on St. Vasil'evskii Street and at one time interaction between our houses was frequent. They did domestic errands for each other. And our cabinet with the glass doors covered with colored paper depicting fantastic little lions remains as a memory of the Berdyaevs. My parents somehow bought it from the Berdyaevs especially for us, for our books and toys.[7]

Although Berdyaev and Gershenzon began their friendship in 1909 while collaborating on *Landmarks,* their circle of friends and set of interests had been drawing them together earlier.[8] They befriended the same individuals (Semyon Frank, Sergei Bulgakov, Vyacheslav Ivanov, and Pyotr Struve) and wrote for the same journals *(Voprosy filosofii i psikhologii, Russkaia mysl',* and *Nauchnoe slovo).* Just as many other Russian *intelligenty* in the early 20th century had done, Berdyaev and Gershenzon turned away from the 19th-century preoccupations with the political struggle against the autocracy and with the well-being of the peasants, embracing philosophical idealism and the search for personal metaphysics. Concretely, Berdyaev and Gershenzon were affected by Friedrich Nietzsche and the metaphysical interpretation of his teachings as a guide to the spiritual realization of the individual. In addition, Dostoevsky, Vladimir Solovyov, and Lev Tolstoy influenced them intellectually and emotionally. These native sources helped Berdyaev and Gershenzon discover their roles as secular religious thinkers and create their own perspectives on the difficult social, political, and religious questions facing Russia.

The first decade of the 20th century was a transitional period for Berdyaev. He followed the same trajectory as Frank, Bulgakov, and Struve, leaving the camp of Critical Marxism and heading toward philosophical idealism. In 1902, Berdyaev contributed an article to *Problems of Idealism,* a volume that served as a *profession de foi* of the idealists, and during this period he attacked the philosophical premises of his old idols, Legal Marxism and neo-Kantianism.[9] In essays published five years later in *Sub specie aeternitatis,* Berdyaev ex-

---

[7] Gershenzon-Chegodaeva, *Pervye shagi,* 26.

[8] *Landmarks* was Gershenzon's idea, and since he was the editor of the volume, all the contributors had reason to correspond with him. For more information about Gershenzon and the origin of *Landmarks,* see Vera Proskurina, "Tvorcheskoe samosoznanie Mikhaila Gershenzona," *Literaturnoe obozrenie,* no. 8 (1990): 93–96.

[9] *Problems of Idealism* was a volume of essays in which several of Russia's most important Legal Marxist thinkers declared their intellectual conversion to an idealist philosophy. *Problemy idealizma: Sbornik statei* (Moscow: Izd. Moskovskogo psikhologicheskogo obshchestva, 1903) appeared under the editorship of P. I. Novgorodtsev and included articles by S. N. Bulgakov, Prince E. N. Trubetskoy, P. G., N. A. Berdyaev, S. L. Frank, S. A. Askoldov, S. N. Trubetskoy, P. I. Novgorodtsev, B. A. Kistyakovsky, A. S. Lappo-Danilevsky, S. F. Oldenburg, and D. E. Zhukovsky.

posed the anti-individualist content of Marxist thinking and the deceptive epistemology of neo-Kantianism. He claimed that Kantian idealism proclaimed certainties it could not defend. Berdaev was coming to realize... could not be attained by philosophy but only by religion which treated man not as an isolated brain but as a full person living in the world.

Berdaev's practical work also reflects his transition to idealism. From 1904–1905 he served as editor of *Voprosy zhizni*, the journal associated with the Symbolist movement, and soon after he served on the editorial board of a journal, *Put'*, devoted to the study of philosophy and religion. He was also involved in the establishment of the Moscow Psychological Society and the Moscow Religious-Philosophical Society. These practical affairs attest to Berdyaev's organization skills and his broad association with a large variety of different individuals and intellectual movements.

In contrast, Gershenzon arrived at an anti-positivist perspective in relative isolation. His idealist philosophy seems to have been formed from various sources: study of anti-positivist methods in pedagogy, German romantic literature, Slavophiles, and Symbolist poetry.[10] Particularly with Russian Symbolism, Gershenzon discovered his ideal of an egoistic individual who used his spiritual strength to transform reality.[11] While he admired powerful individuals, he claimed that spiritual accomplishments were more valuable than achievements in society. His unwavering faith in the primary value of the individual as an anarchistic destroyer of society's encrusted values aligned him intellectually with Symbolists such as Andrei Bely, Vyacheslav Ivanov, Fyodor Sologub, and Dmitry Merezhkovsky. Meanwhile, his conviction that real freedom could only be achieved in the spirit aligned him with religious philosophers such as Shestov, Sergei Bulgakov, and Vladimir Ern.[12]

In addition to initiating his friendship with Berdyaev, *Landmarks* was a breakthrough for Gershenzon because it brought him into close contact with the leading philosophers of the day. In its structure and neo-religious perspective, this volume of essays by seven non-Marxist thinkers was conditioned by its predecessor, *Problems of Idealism*.[13] But *Landmarks* was a very different endeavor. It was not merely a manifesto of the Neo-Idealist movement,

---

[10] Gershenzon was impressed with the anti-positivist ideas in German pedogogy. For example, see his "Mysli dvukh filosofov o shkole," *Voprosy filosofii i psikhologii*, no. 6 (1902): 794–825; and "Iskusstvo v shkole," *Vestnik vospitaniia*, no. 2 (1899): 51–75. Gershenzon wrote about German Romanticism in his "Ocherk razvitiia nemetskoi khudozhestvennoi literatury v XIX veke," *Russkaia mysl'*, no. 3 (1903): 1–13.

[11] Gershenzon's most declarative statement of his philosophy of this period is his review of N. Nevedomsky's book in *Nauchnoe slovo*, no. 9 (1904): 137–40.

[12] For more about Gershenzon's friends, see my article "M. O. Gershenzon and the Perception of a Leader in Russia's Silver-Age Culture," *Wiener Slawistischer Almanach* 29 (1992): 45–73.

[13] All the contributors to *Landmarks* except A. S. Izgoev and Gershenzon had participated in *Problems of Idealism*.

as was *Problems of Idealism*; more importantly, it was a critique of the ideological mainsprings of the intelligentsia in the aftermath of the unsuccessful 1905 Revolution. Thus it carried a discreet political message. *Landmarks* not only disparaged the mentality of the revolutionaries, it expressed the common sentiment of an entire group of thinkers who had resolutely turned away from revolution. According to the editor Gershenzon, writing in his introduction, the contributors expressed their shared belief in the superiority of the spiritual or "internal" life over its political or "external" facade and the need for each individual to perfect himself before taking up the task of perfecting society.

Since the contributors were calling for comprehensive changes in the intelligentsia's basic orientation, *Landmarks* elicited an enormous storm of criticism.[14] The strong response was uplifting for the contributors, since it convinced them that there was a potentially large interest in religious ideas. More importantly for the contributors themselves, however, *Landmarks* set a tone of sibling comradery, but it also created emotional and intellectual expectations from those new friendships that could not be fulfilled. In the case of Gershenzon and Berdyaev, *Landmarks* gave the deceptive impression of a unity that did not really exist.

Although once *Landmarks* appeared in print there was an immediate falling out among the contributors (B. Kistyakovsky and A. Izgoev repudiated Gershenzon's introduction because they advocated external changes, such as legal reform), Berdyaev was ideologically closest to Gershenzon and did not take issue with the introduction. Regardless of other points of dispute with Gershenzon, he could unconditionally agree that political change had to take a back seat to the transformation of the individual. As a solution to the political problems of tsarist injustice and leftist intransigence, Berdyaev emphasized the efficacy of education in the development of moral individuals who would take the lead in improving society. In tandem, Gershenzon professed his belief that society could be reformed only through the spiritual perfection of its individual members. For both thinkers, the reform of political institutions was to follow and serve the internal growth of individuals.

Despite their agreement on the primacy of the spiritual sphere of human life, Berdyaev had significant differences with Gershenzon. In fact, Berdyaev had a completely opposite view of the intelligentsia and its role in Russia's future. While Berdyaev merely wanted to change the intelligentsia's values, leaving its basic structure intact, Gershenzon envisioned all change to occur through individuals. Thus, he did not consider the intelligentsia of any positive importance.

In his *Landmarks* article, "Tvorcheskoe samosoznanie" (Creative Self-Consciousness), Gershenzon claims that the 1905 Revolution failed because of an

---

[14] For a bibliography of the Russian reception of *Landmarks* in 1909, see the index in the fifth edition, *Vekhi* (Moscow: Tipo-litografiia I. N. Kushnerov, 1910).

unfortunate severing of "consciousness" and "will" in each individual member of the intelligentsia. Such severing was caused by the negligence of the individual's personal life. For far too long the individual *intelligent* had subordinated personal goals to those of the collective, becoming a "cripple," physically, mentally, and politically unhealthy. In order to rectify the situation, Gershenzon advised a return to individual interests.

In contrast to what we would usually consider "individual interests," Gershenzon suggests that these are spiritual endeavors. Spirituality here means the dictate of the cosmos that people follow their individual "wills." Will, in contrast to reason, is that absolutely personal *(lichnoe)* part of the individual, the spirit, which perceives the natural union or "holism" *(tsel'nost')* between a person and the universe. Gershenzon explains that will, not "suprapersonal" reason, should rule the individual because it is connected with an individual's real feeling and thus is the "inner motor of his whole life." Unlike the "pure-cerebral" idea, which is "essentially dead," will is an "idea-feeling" or an "idea-passion."[15] According to Gershenzon, the individual must avoid rational thinking because being is organically grounded in spirituality, which is manifested by the pantheistic feeling that the individual is part and parcel of the universe.

Gershenzon's counsel for a return to personal life, to an internal spirituality achieved through the union of the individual with the cosmic whole, implicitly demands the complete elimination of the intelligentsia. The individual would not congregate for the purpose of changing the world or reforming the state; rather, an individual's radicalism is the transformation of his own psyche. Himself a loner, Gershenzon was not confident about the value of groups and his own personal experience had shown that only individuals treated other individuals without prejudice or discrimination.

Compared with Gershenzon's maximalist individualism, Berdyaev comes across as a moderate in *Landmarks*. His goal is not the ultimate destruction of the intelligentsia, but a sensible reform of its priorities. Admiring the intelligentsia's traditional search for truth and justice, he takes issue with its strategy. Finding its constant subordination of moral absolutes to the relative exigencies of day-to-day politics wrong and destructive, he concludes that the intelligentsia should seek its purpose in eternal truths: God, religion, and philosophy. In his *Landmarks* article, "Philosophical Truth and the Truth of the Intelligentsia," Berdyaev writes that even today "the young people in our intelligentsia cannot recognize the independent significance of science, philosophy, education, universities," and subordinate them "to the interests of politics, the parties, tendencies, and circles."[16]

---

[15] M. O. Gershenzon, "Tvorcheskoe samosoznanie," *Vekhi*, 2nd ed. (Moscow: Tip. V. M. Sablina, 1909), 77–78.

[16] Nikolai Berdiaev, "Filosofskaia istina i intelligentskaia pravda," in *Vekhi*, 2nd ed. (Moscow: Tip. V. M. Sablina, 1909), 3.

Despite these flaws, Berdyaev did not regard the intelligentsia as a use-less and dangerous association. On the contrary, he ascribed a great potential to it. The intelligentsia's venerable history as the embodiment in Russia of the eternal values of education and social progress shows its virtuous high regard for philosophy and the values of absolute truth. Although its basic attitude to-ward changing the world should remain the same, it must modify its con-sciousness toward religion. "All the historical and psychological facts say that the Russian intelligentsia can move to a new consciousness only on the basis of a synthesis of knowledge and faith," he argued. That synthesis should be one that "positively satisfies the intelligentsia's valuable need for an organic union of theory and practice, and 'truth-absolute' and 'truth-justice.'"[17]

Although before the appearance of *Landmarks* Berdyaev and Gershenzon struggled against logical positivism and rationalism in the defense of relig-ious feeling, by 1910 their thinking had radically diverged, as Berdyaev shifted markedly toward Christianity. Earlier, Berdyaev had been non-ecumenical and religious in a broad manner. Making no distinction between religion and metaphysics, he had lauded any honest attempt to penetrate the spiritual mysteries and religious purpose of life. In this respect, his attitude toward religion paralleled that of the other major secular religious thinkers of Russia of the time: Merezhkovsky, Bulgakov, Ivanov, Rozanov, and Shestov. In *Sub specie aeternitatis*, for example, Berdyaev supported such non-Christian spiritual ideas as "Mystical Anarchism," Dmitry Merezhkovsky's idiosyn-cratic "Religion of the Third Testament," and the sociological theories of F. Lassale and R. Avenarius.

By 1910, however, Berdyaev turned from his non-ecumenicalism and be-gan arguing for a social reconstruction of society on specifically Christian principles. Only Christianity, he now believed, could give an ultimate signifi-cance to man's past, present, and future and determine the unique role of every individual in history. In this way, Berdiaev trod the same evolutionary path to Christianity that the other former Legal Marxists, Sergei Bulgakov and Semyon Frank, traversed. Like them, Berdyaev found in idealism only a way station on the road to Christianity.

Berdyaev first offered his ideas on Christian freedom and election and the purpose of Christian communal life in *The Intelligentsia's Spiritual Crisis* (1910). Although the Christian views he expressed in this work were not strongly felt in his contribution to *Landmarks*, both works contain Berdyaev's conviction that the issues of politics and religion must be addressed together. In *The Intelligentsia's Spiritual Crisis*, Berdyaev claims that Christianity had been wrong to reject politics. Christians, he claims, must use the inherent freedom

---

[17] Ibid., 21.

given by God in an active way to free humanity from the unfreedom of nature and human institutions. Humanity must participate as God's son in the voluntary construction of an anarchistic, Christian theocracy—a political-religious utopia. This vision of a theocratic world allowed Berdyaev to uphold the tsarist state as a temporary good, even though overcoming the state was his ultimate goal. "The state is not the final goal of social development, this aim lies in the free power of God and in anarchy, but only through the state and its power is this aim achieved. One should conditionally sanction the state in order to overcome it absolutely."[18]

In *The Philosophy of Freedom* (1911), Berdyaev offers an epistemological basis for Christianity, arguing that at base every philosophy is founded on an unprovable premise, that is, faith, but only one philosophy is founded on freedom. Since every philosophy is inevitably subjective, Christianity is no less "rational" than Kant's idealism or Hume's empiricism. In fact, Berdyaev claims that Christianity is more rational because it treats the whole human being in the world with individual religious feelings and religious knowledge. Rationalism and empiricism deal merely with rationally verifiable matter. Thus, they wrongly give no consideration at all to the part of the human being that cannot be verified, i.e., the individual's religious feeling.

Christianity, according to Berdyaev, is the only philosophy that provides humanity with freedom. Through resurrection of the body, the Christian is freed from the material world and is no longer a slave to bodily destruction. This lifts humanity's vision from the world of the body to the world of the spirit. Moreover, in Berdyaev's view this freedom is not and cannot be coercive, it must be chosen voluntarily. For this reason, God brought his son to earth in the form of a pauper, so that man would not be tempted by material gain. The idea of freedom takes precedence even over the idea of perfection because, as he confesses in his autobiography, "it is impossible to accept obligatory, enforced perfection."[19]

Perfection, for Berdyaev, is humanity's fulfillment of Christ's promise to return to earth at the end of time. Since history is the road that must be traveled to arrive at the end, Christianity posits human history as a story of divine purpose. In Christ is the secret of humanity's freedom, the secret of the beginning and end of history and the secret of resurrection. In *The Philosophy of Freedom*, Berdyaev explains:

> At the center of the tragedy stands the divine Man-Christ. The historical movement of the tragedy goes to and from Him. Christ is the absolute center of the cosmos, and He became embodied as a man and appeared on the earth. Therefore humanity acquired a cosmic significance, in Him the soul of the world returned to God.... Christianity is

---

[18] Nikolai Berdiaev, *Dukhovnyi krizis intelligentsii: Stat'i po obshchestvennoi i religioznoi psikhologii, 1907–1909* (St. Petersburg: Obshchestvennaia pol'za, 1910), 7.

[19] Berdiaev, *Samopoznanie*, 61–62.

not even faith in the immortality of the soul, in its natural transformation, but faith in resurrection, which must be conquered universally,
prepared historically, must be a task of the entire cosmos.[20]

Human history—the evolution from the beginning of the world to its
return to God—is a specifically Christian task in which all must participate.
From this claim, one can understand Berdyaev's belief that the Jews' renun-
ciation of Christ was historically incorrect and that they must join the religion
of Christ in order to participate in the divine plan: "That Christ turned the
history of the world upside-down is a fact which the whole world is forced to
accept; not only the Christian world, but also the world foreign to Christ and
antagonistic to Him."[21]

Berdyaev's increasing attachment to Christianity underlay the conflict
that erupted between him and Gershenzon, for that attachment suffused Berdyaev's views on many other issues, over some of which he and Gershenzon
clashed vigorously. Take, for example, their attitudes toward Slavophilism.
Few Russians understood the importance of Slavophilism in the early 20th
century, especially since it was regarded as politically retrograde. Berdyaev
and Gershenzon agreed on the importance of Slavophile thought, in its own
right and for its application to contemporary philosophical problems. But
they approached the Slavophiles from different sources and therefore emphasized different aspects of the teaching. Berdyaev, like Frank and Bulgakov,
came upon the Slavophiles from an examination of Vladimir Solovyov and
found in them eloquent spokesmen for Russian Orthodoxy. In contrast, Gershenzon discovered the Slavophiles from his historical studies of such
Westernizers as Herzen, Ogaryov, and Chaadaev, and he juxtaposed the two
groups. Gershenzon interpreted the Slavophiles as spokesmen of a universal
spiritual psychology. Needless to say, he was isolated in his viewpoint.

In *Historical Sketches* (1910), Gershenzon explored the biographies and
philosophies of Ivan Kireevsky, Yury Samarin, and Nikolai Gogol in order to
shed light on three aspects of Slavophile thought. And by binding them together he hoped to show that Slavophilism was a united, whole philosophical
system. In addition, he wanted to reveal the main differences between the
Slavophile and Westernizer philosophies and demonstrate why Slavophile
thought was superior. And, finally, as he admitted when responding to Pyotr
Struve's criticisms of *Historical Sketches*, Gershenzon wrote the book because
he

> wanted to tell how the (philosophical) break came about, how one of
> the doctrines presented here, the rationalist, was completely mastered
> by the huge majority of society, and the other, religious, was distorted

---

[20] Nikolai Berdiaev, *Filosofiia svobody* (Moscow: Izd-vo "Pravda," 1989), 141.

[21] Ibid., 160. In several places Berdiaev condemns the Jews. For example, in *The Philosophy of Freedom* he repeats the charge against the Jews of mistaken obstinance.

already in its infancy and with time became more and more distorted; how they struggled at first, how their struggle became more complicated, and finally, what were the profound consequences for the individual and society due to the domination of the former and the neglect and distortion of the latter.[22]

According to Gershenzon, the victory of the Westernizers was a tragedy for Russia because their reliance on rationalism and intellectual sources for humanity's happiness contradicts man's true religious nature. The Slavophiles' universal philosophy better corresponds to human psychological needs and thus would have served Russia better.

Berdyaev, who was working on the Slavophiles at this time, held a mixed opinion of *Historical Sketches*. In 1912, when working on a book about the theologian Aleksei Stepanovich Khomyakov, he was able to write, "I highly value Gershenzon's works." He thought Gershenzon was "very sensitive to the religious motivation of the Slavophiles and their psychological features" and regarded him as one of "the first to see in Slavophilism an example of Russian national self-consciousness and not just one movement among others."[23] At the same time, however, he vehemently disapproved of Gershenzon's idiosyncratic and unfounded interpretation of the Slavophiles as teachers of a universal spirituality whose importance lies primarily outside the context of Russian Orthodox religious life. As early as 1910 he complained, "Gershenzon gives an individualistic interpretation of the essence of Slavophilism and in this lies his one-sidedness."[24]

What irritated Berdyaev most of all was the intentional exclusion from *Historical Sketches* of Khomyakov, whom Gershenzon believed a mere imitator of Kireevsky. This, in Berdyaev's eyes, was a fundamental flaw in Gershenzon's understanding of Slavophilism, for Berdyaev regarded Khomyakov as the central figure of the Slavophile group. "Khomyakov was above all a Russian Orthodox theologian, a Christian thinker, a cavalier of the Russian Orthodox Church," Berdyaev wrote in 1912. "Gershenzon clearly does not like Khomyakov and ignores him to the same extent to which he loves Kireevsky to a passion. This attitude toward Khomyakov prevents Gershenzon's evaluation of Slavophilism in its entirety, destroys historical perspective."[25]

Gershenzon believed he had good reason for ignoring Khomyakov. Unlike Berdyaev, he did not want to investigate or construct a Russian Orthodox theology or even examine the religious content of Slavophilism; rather, he sought to extract from Slavophilism a historical, universal spirituality, "to

---

[22] M. O. Gershenzon, "Otvet P. B. Struve," *Russkaia mysl'*, no. 2 (1910): 176–77.

[23] Berdiaev, *Aleksei Stepanovich Khomiakov*, 23. Aleksandr Pypin (1833–1904) was a positivist historian of Russian literature.

[24] Nikolai Berdiaev, review of *Istoricheskie zapiski* by M. O. Gershenzon, *Moskovskii ezhenedel'nik*, no. 9 (1910): 46–48.

[25] Berdiaev, *Aleksei Stepanovich Khomiakov*, 23.

husk the authentic core, the eternal religious truth, to cleanse it of its Slavophile skin which had strongly grown onto it, and clearly to explain it as simply as possible."[26] But Berdyaev regarded Gershenzon's attempt to univer-
salize the Slavophiles as methodologically dubious and historically
unacceptable:

> He takes from Slavophilism merely that which is dear to him, clearly
> perceives in Slavophilism merely that which is visible from the posi-
> tion on which he stands. One can cleanse Slavophilism of the rotten
> idealism of the backward forms of life, of assigning an absolute sig-
> nificance to the reigning form of government, but it is impossible to
> cleanse Slavophilism of the universal truth of Christianity.[27]

The vehemence of Berdyaev's criticisms is understandable, given the special interest he had in the theological significance of Slavophilism and his
focus on Khomyakov, who is manifestly a Russian Orthodox thinker. But
there is a sense in which they are overstated. Berdyaev's objection to Gershenzon's separation of Slavophilism and Russian Orthodoxy seems a bit unfair
when one considers that even Berdyaev admitted the scholar's right to remove from Slavophilism the ugly remnants of contemporary ideological and
political institutions. As a reinterpretation of Slavophilism for its time, Gershenzon's work is a valid and significant contribution to the literature. But if
Gershenzon's task is, as he himself defined it, "historical" in nature—the objective investigation of the ideas in the historical context they were created—
then Gershenzon cannot be excused in completely purifying Slavophilism of
its Russian Orthodox elements, and Berdyaev's criticisms, while one-sided in
favor of a Russian Orthodox interpretation, are justified.

The disagreement over the Slavophiles recalls the essential differences in
their thinking: the pointedly Russian Orthodox focus of Berdyaev's thinking
and Gershenzon's idea of religion as a general human urge or psychological
necessity. Of course, their disparate philosophical backgrounds and interests
help to explain their attitudes toward Slavophilism. Despite the influence of
his freethinking Voltarian father, Berdyaev was brought up a member of the
Russian Orthodox Church, and his works proclaim the preeminence of Christianity as the sole religion of salvation. In contrast, Gershenzon tried to find a
personal religion of the cosmos to replace his Judaism, which he believed was
tainted by the provincialism and backwardness of the Pale of Settlement.

In this way, while Berdyaev interpreted the Slavophiles as intellectual cat-
alysts for his own return to Russian Orthodoxy, Gershenzon used the Slavophiles as timeless spokesmen of a nondenominational spirituality, one which
satisfies the individual's psychological needs for religion without forcing
membership in any religious institution. This latter requirement was espe-

---

[26] Gershenzon, "Otvet P. B. Struve," 177.

[27] Berdiaev, review of *Istoricheskie zapiski*, 47–48.

cially important for Gershenzon because he had strong personal reasons for not wanting to renounce Judaism.[28] With pogroms and expulsions of Jews from the capitals fairly ordinary events in Russia at that time, Gershenzon's knowledge that Berdyaev's aggressively Christian argumentation could justify antisemitic activity probably exacerbated the ideological conflict. Although Gershenzon was not a practicing Jew and was completely assimilated to Russian culture, he was sensitive to ideologies that promulgated racial or religious superiority or incited anti-Jewish feelings.

The outbreak of World War I obscured Berdyaev's and Gershenzon's different religious perspectives and brought the two into temporary agreement. Both objected to the slaughter and destruction and viewed the war as a reproach: bourgeois society had revealed a hidden propensity for self-annihilation; people were tired of the old world and yearned for change. Berdyaev hoped that the war would usher in a new, religious world. The war was "providential and unavoidable," he wrote to Gershenzon in 1914, "and I believe that we and the whole world will emerge from it reborn. The genuine world can only be reached through war. The bourgeois world isn't worth a thing; it was a lie. Now my whole soul desires Russia's victory over the Germans."[29] Gershenzon revealed much the same beliefs in a 1915 article, "The Second Year of War":

> It turns out first of all that nobody thinks about personal property, not only us, but even the greedy Germans: blossoming, rich industry, wonderfully established trading contacts, comfort, and loveliness— let them get ruined and disappear, they are not worth a cent! Who could have expected such scorn for the things of this world from a European? Or in the depth of his soul did he really not cherish them before the war as well, as it would seem; that is, he pretended to cherish them, but not in the absolute, but with a certain hidden reservation to himself, that this is only until a better thing comes along, and so that nothing else pushed itself in meanwhile?[30]

---

[28] Gershenzon refused to become baptized because of loyalty to his parents and in order to preserve his dignity. He promised his mother he would never convert and he often had to show her his passport to prove to her that he had not done so. In addition, Gershenzon felt that he would lower his dignity if he accepted Christianity for the sake of economic opportunity, since he did not believe in Christ. See the chapter devoted to Gershenzon's Jewish roots in my "M. O. Gershenzon and the Intellectual Life of Russia's Silver Age" (Ph.D. diss., University of California, Berkeley, 1993), 463–521.

[29] Berdiaev to Gershenzon, 22 July 1914, Gershenzon Papers, Rossiiskaia gosudarstvennaia biblioteka (RGB) f. 746, op. 28, d. 31.

[30] M. O. Gershenzon, "Vtoroi god voiny," *Birzhevye-vedomosti,* 28 June 1915.

As the war progressed, their positions gradually diverged. Under the influence of events, Berdyaev developed his ideas concerning the essence and purpose of the nation, viewing the forces of imperialism and messianism with utopian hopefulness. In articles of this period Berdyaev expressed a new optimism. The war, he asserted, had contributed to the positive, dialectical process of preserving the self-identity of each separate nation, while secretly encouraging the unity of all nations. As he put it, in 1916, the contemporary history of humanity was undergoing a "dual process,"

> a process of universalism and a process of individualization, unification into large bodies and dissolution into smaller bodies. Nationalism is the beginning of individualization, imperialism—the beginning of universalism. At the same time that nationalism is inclined to isolation, imperialism desires an exit into the world expanse. These beginnings are of differing quality, but do not exclude each other, they coexist.[31]

At his highest point of delusion here, Berdyaev announced that, "through struggle and discord, imperialism all the same promotes the unification of humanity."[32]

Berdyaev's optimism during the war appears to be connected with his idea of "creativity," a concept he culled from Nietzsche but then transformed and applied to Christianity. In *The Meaning of Creativity*, published in 1916, although written a few years earlier, Berdyaev promoted creativity as the means for the realization of the Christian purpose and each individual's spiritual perfection. The goal of the relationship between humanity and God, Berdyaev claims, is the fusion of humanity and God in bringing about the principle eschatological purpose of Christianity: eternal life beyond the confines of history. In describing this relationship, Berdyaev writes, "God's final mystery is the birth of man in God. And this mystery is a unique mystery. For man not only needs God, but God also needs man. In this is Christ's mystery, the mystery of the God-man."[33]

In this philosophy, Jesus Christ plays the most significant role, since he is the model of the creative individual who successfully accomplished what each person is intended to do: he joined with God and creatively moved humanity closer to its goal—the end of history, perfection beyond historical time. The secret of Christ and his instruction for man was his exercise of free will—his free acceptance of the crucifixion. His freedom is the life of the spirit and not of the body, the surpassing of this life and the revelation of eternal

---

[31] Nikolai Berdiaev, "Ob imperializme" (1916), in *Sud'ba Rossii* (Moscow: Sovetskii pisatel', 1990), 108.

[32] Ibid., 108.

[33] Nikolai Berdiaev, *Smysl tvorchestva* (Moscow, 1916; repr., Paris: YMCA, 1985), 48–49.

life. In a letter to Gershenzon from June 1915 Berdyaev writes, "Christianity is above all a revelation of freedom in the spirit."

> The suffering and torture of life, the horror of death enters inside and becomes experienced as a free Golgotha and not as an imposed and enforced necessity. Christ defeated death because he experienced it not as an external, enforced fact of the natural order, but as an internal moment of life itself, as the free acceptance of the crucifixion.[34]

In Berdyaev's conception, the crucifixion exemplifies creativity. It stands for man's control of his own destiny for the sake of the realization of the eschatological aim of Christianity. In this sense, man no longer has to accept life as he finds it, but must work to change its course. Creativity, man's "overcoming of himself" in a monumental act of self-becoming, permits humanity the freedom to direct history.

Berdyaev's early optimism about the war can thus be explained by his philosophical ideas of the time. The same self-becoming that Berdyaev knew philosophically, he probably thought he espied mystically in the depths of the violent armed conflict. He was convinced that current events corresponded to the imagined course of Christian teleology. Beneath the overt destruction of material life Berdyaev saw free, creative individuals eagerly transforming the world. Christians, Germans, and Russians would join together in overcoming the body (was war not a rejection of the body?) and fulfill the imperative of realizing the Christian eschatology. Berdyaev, who had often fallen prisoner to his own esoteric concepts, did not fully notice the cleft between his ideas and reality. Only in 1917 did he understand the full scope of his mistake; at that time he renounced the war, strongly fearing that a communist seizure of power was about to take place.

In contrast to Berdyaev, Gershenzon rejected institutional religion, relying on cosmic thinking in formulating his own solution to the war. Gershenzon suggested that individuals who employ "will" and not "reason" would reject the war, since war was caused by rationalism. Rationalism had prop - agated an epistemology based on the individual's adherence to supraindividual reason, and this epistemology was not new but had merely found its most authentic expression in war. In contrast to the world founded on reason, Gershenzon dreamed of a new world which he hoped could be engendered through the "triple image of perfection": the perfect image of the self, the perfect image of society, and the perfect image of oneself in society.

In his 1918 treatise *The Triple Image of Perfection*, Gershenzon claimed that for humanity to reaffirm its own existence, it has learned to utilize other beings for its own ends; it has discovered and perfected an epistemology based on the division and reduction of things. The rationale is that complete individuals provide no utility; only by breaking them up into pieces can one use

---

[34] Berdiaev to Gershenzon, 7 June 1915, Gershenzon Papers, RGB f. 746, op. 28, d. 31.

them. Gershenzon used a tree as an example: useless while alive and whole, when cut down and broken into pieces it could be used to a variety of ends or fashioned into innumerable things. So it was with other beings which humanity once saw as complete individuals, but no longer. Now it sees in them only faceless members of a class, group, or race from which can be exacted utility. Gershenzon explains:

> Man creates his things in this way. He creates them all from their innate bodies. But each innate body is individual; taken in the living wholeness of its individual qualities, it is useless for man. In order to gain possession of it, one must first of all rip it out from the powerful unity of nature, and this means to kill its personality, that is, to cut down or rip out a tree; a corpse is made: man's first victory.[35]

The problem, however, is that by affirming one's individuality, a person destroys the image of perfection within.

There is only one way of overcoming the illness of rational thinking, and that is the realization of one's image of perfection. In this case, the individual returns to the original state of "holism" in which is perceived the unity of the whole of being and one's perfect place in the universe. According to Gershenzon, through love the individual's warped perception of the world can be corrected. In *The Triple Image of Perfection* he writes, "The image of perfection of he who loves is excited to action: either he realizes himself through the loved one, or at least he actively reaffirms himself through guarding the loved one; he who is loved, only through the affirmation of the loved one, is he taught to know in himself his image of perfection."[36]

Gershenzon is speaking of spiritual love, not erotic love; love in which the person perceives the other as a complete individual and an end in itself, not as a means toward an end. This "holistic" perception heals the spiritual wounds caused by the person's former way of thinking. Through the perception of the other as a whole, you yourself become whole as well.

In Gershenzon's view a "holistic" worldview would solve all the intractable problems caused by rationalism and its epistemology of "divide and conquer." It must be added that Gershenzon rarely, if ever, dealt with the real issues of an actual commonwealth. He seems to have believed that if all individuals possessed a holistic consciousness, the problems of society and even conflicts between countries would resolve themselves. Although such a personalist morality reflects the influence of Tolstoyan ethics, such abstract thinking was highly detached given the critical political situation at the time.

Incidentally, their differences concerning the war refer to their original divisions in *Landmarks:* just as before, so too in 1914, Berdyaev entrusted

---

[35] M. O. Gershenzon, *Troistvennyi obraz sovershenstva* (Moscow: Kn-vo M. i S. Sabashnikovykh, 1918), 6.

[36] Ibid., 28.

man's fate to organized institutions, in this case the church, while Gershenzon placed his faith solely in secular individuals detached from any organized groups. In addition, while Berdyaev put his faith in Christianity as the vehicle of salvation, Gershenzon placed his hope in a pantheistic personal religion.

The final catalyst for the break in Berdyaev's and Gershenzon's already tense relationship was a disagreement over political affiliation in September 1917. Perhaps this disagreement would not have severed their relationship in normal times, but the political radicalism of the moment demanded that each individual choose between two and only two camps: for or against the Bolsheviks. In his final letter to Gershenzon, written September 29, Berdyaev attacked him for his apparent allegiance to Bolshevism. Like the other contributors to *Landmarks*, Berdyaev felt Gershenzon had made a large ideological shift to the left, becoming in his eyes a political enemy:

> Have you finally really forgotten that you were one of the important initiators of *Landmarks*, that the most critical article against the revolutionary intelligentsia belongs to you, and you expressed disgust at its sincere cast of mind. This obligates you. How could it be, that at the moment of the revolution, when the former forces have been unchained and those same ideas and feelings which you mercilessly criticized have been thrown to the dark masses, when the enormous spiritual values have been exposed to danger, you have lost all your spiritual baggage, swim with the current and use street language foreign to you? And you began to cry out the words about "the bourgeois," "counter-revolution," "without annexation and indemnity," and so forth, although these words are empty and filled with a terrible lie. It is painful to watch. It is awful that the best writers in Russia have shown so little spiritual independence and have not found their own words at this most difficult minute of all history.[37]

Responding to Berdyaev the next day, in a letter that would be his last to his former collaborator, Gershenzon explains the essential difference between the two camps and the reasons he chose to support the revolution:

> I believe that the best people in Russia have separated into two parties: the party of the heart and the party of the idea, ideology; the first feel pain for the living person, for those in need and burdened, the other, and you among them, feel no less pain for the values—statehood, holism, and the might of Russia. People of the heart also have

---

[37] Berdiaev to M. O. Gershenzon, 29 September 1917, Gershenzon Papers, RGB f. 746, op. 28, d. 31.

their ideology—internationalism and so on; and one against the other two ideologies have risen, one for the happiness and freedom of the individual person, the other for the preservation of supra-personal values. On the one and the other side are the best, the most spiritual and honest people of Russia. Mercenary, morally empty people have attached themselves to both groups: to Lenin—those who are greedy, seeking to rip for themselves a piece of "happiness," to Struve and you—those who are awaiting the "happiness," which has already been won to return, the industrialists and landowners. The workers and the peasants pillage Russia in the name of the individual, Riabushinsky and P. N. Lvov destroy it in the name of national values! I repeat: the heart and psychology have their own ideology and for that you should respect them.[38]

Gershenzon was torn. Although he identified with the "humiliated, tortured people, in whom the feeling of the human pride, honor, and dignity of the individual had so violently appeared," Gershenzon also knew "the importance and beauty of values, their necessity and not only in their own right, but … also for each individual person." Despite Gershenzon's confession of ambivalence, however, it is a fact that the old intelligentsia was surprised by what they regarded as Gershenzon's outward change. In 1918, when Petr Struve was inviting the contributors to *Landmarks* to participate in the publication of *From the Depth,* he pointedly excluded Gershenzon, "who had become politically foreign to us," as unsuitable for a volume in which the contributors "were going to give a principled foundation for their negation of Bolshevism."[39] But Gershenzon thought Berdyaev and the others were "terribly mistaken" in their judgment about his stance. In his final letter to Berdyaev he had plaintively pointed out that "during the whole period of the revolution I have not written one newspaper article. And I have not written because my feeling is contradictory, because at one and the same time I rejoice and I am horrified."[40]

In light of his confessed inability to decide between the warring groups, is it certain that Gershenzon had become a sympathizer of Bolshevism? The case is at least more complex that Berdyaev believed. Gershenzon did not want to choose between the cultural values of "statehood" (*gosudarstvennost'*) and the "concrete individual now living," understanding the importance of both. The dispute, he wrote to Berdyaev, was "natural and beneficial," and he believed that after "the individual and the values fight once again as they have many times before," they would reach a "temporary *modus vivendi* on which they

---

[38] Gershenzon to Berdiaev, 30 September 1917, Gershenzon Papers, located at Maria Andreevna Chegodaeva's apartment, Moscow.

[39] S. L. Frank, *Biografiia P. B. Struve* (New York: Izd-vo im. Chekhova, 1956), 120.

[40] Gershenzon to Berdiaev, 30 September 1917.

will calm down for a moment and then splendidly blossom until a new confrontation." But Gershenzon had no desire to embrace one side or lend his voice in such a way that would aggravate tensions: "Russia's situation is so terrible that one side has got somehow to cede to the other and find a compromise."[41]

Clearly, Gershenzon and Berdyaev had their own distinct perceptions of the political landscape in September 1917. Berdyaev perceived the choice as one between liberalism and radicalism even before the Bolshevik Revolution. He thereby excluded the Socialist Revolutionaries as a realistic force. Gershenzon still thought the center would hold and a compromise could be found. In this case, Berdiaev was more perceptive, foreseeing that the middle would fold and the two political extremes would be left to fight for ultimate dominance.

As the whirl of events engulfed Berdyaev, he no longer remained optimistic about the course of history. In the face of Russia's fall, the inevitable defeat by Germany and the impending victory of Bolshevism, he could not remain patient. The image of Berdyaev in 1917 is that of a headstrong fighter, an uncompromising conservative. An unpublished letter from Shestov to Gershenzon, written on August 19, 1917, supports this picture. He described Berdyaev as "drowned in politics. From morning till night at meetings. He is extremely indisposed to all leftists."[42]

Berdyaev was indeed active politically with former tsarist generals and conservative intellectuals. In 1917, he contributed to and sat on the editorial board of the political journal *Narodopravstvo*, which devoted itself mainly to the war with Germany and which supported the Provisional Government's call for "war until a victorious end."[43] Because this journal carried the mildly antisemitic articles of a certain Boris Kremnev, a pseudonym, it was thought, for the journal's editor, Georgy Chulkov, Gershenzon felt Berdyaev was guilty by association, even though his own articles were not antisemitic.[44]

Judging from his later articles, one should acknowledge that Berdyaev was not a bigot. More likely, the crisis of 1917 prompted him to behave in less than absolutely justifiable ways, swallowing a dose of antisemitism larger than he would have accepted to keep a united front with conservatives.[45] In

---

[41] Ibid.

[42] L. Shestov to Gershenzon, 19 August 1917, Gershenzon Papers, RGB f. 746, op. 44, d. 13.

[43] *Narodopravstvo* appeared irregularly from early 1917 until the middle of 1918, when the Bolsheviks forced it to close.

[44] Gershenzon to Maria Borisovna Gershenzon, 2 October 1917, Gershenzon Papers, Chegodaeva apartment.

[45] Berdyaev's negative attitude toward the Jews was not racially motivated, but grounded in Christian theology. He thought that Christianity had universal historical significance and thus all people had to become Christians. Berdyaev therefore thought the Jews should convert. He did not think Christians should force conversion upon the

*Self-Knowledge,* Berdyaev acknowledged the errors he committed during this period and recalled them with a mixture of regret and shame. "I had a heavy impression when the rout of the Russian army from the front began," he wrote in 1949. "Surely, the traditional feelings burst within me, connected with the fact that I belong to a military family and my ancestors were illustrious generals. For some time I suffered a great deal and was even ready to join with the generals of the old army; all this, generally speaking, is completely alien to me."[46]

Berdyaev's refusal to compromise over the issue of the revolution effectively ended whatever chances remained for him and Gershenzon to reconcile their differences and misunderstandings. For Berdyaev, the revolution was not simply a political matter: It was also a "straight-forward religious question" because the atheistic Bolsheviks intended to create a Russia, guided by the philosophy of dialectical materialism, in which the church would be suppressed.[47] Berdyaev had always spoken out against atheism as one of the temptations of material life and as the main opponent of Christianity. In contrast, for Gershenzon the revolution promised to redress old injustices, end racial discrimination against Jews and perhaps even create a society without the former harmful institutions of culture.[48]

A look back over Berdyaev and Gershenzon's relationship shows that the disagreements over individual ideas actually point to a more general clash caused by differences in philosophy and personal temperaments. While Berdyaev based his views on his Nietzschean conception of Christianity, Gershenzon held steady to his ecumenical, cosmic spirituality. Moreover, Berdyaev's attachment to Christianity conflicted with Gershenzon's metaphysical beliefs and offended his Jewish sensibilities while Gershenzon's pantheism ran counter to Berdyaev's vision of Russian and world history.

The epilogue to this relationship is not very long. Although they were fated to meet many more times, Gershenzon and Berdyaev never renewed their friendship.[49] Gershenzon encapsulates his relationship to Berdyaev in the post-revolutionary era in a 1922 letter to Lev Shestov:

---

Jews, however, and he spoke out for tolerance. See his "Khristianstvo i antisemitizm," *Put'*, nos. 5–6 (1938): 3–18.

[46] Berdiaev, *Samopoznanie*, 263–64.

[47] Berdiaev to Gershenzon, 29 September 1917, Gershenzon Papers, RGB f. 746, op. 28, d. 31.

[48] For the source of Gershenzon's anti-cultural perspective, see his side of the "Corner-to-Corner Correspondence" ("Perepiska iz dvukh uglov"), written with Viacheslav Ivanov, in *Russian Intellectual History: An Anthology*, ed. Marc Raeff (New York: Harcourt, Brace and World, 1966), 373–401. It should be noted that Gershenzon quickly recovered from his infatuation with Bolshevism and was already its sharp critic following the breakup of the Constituent Assembly in January 1918.

[49] In an unpublished article, "Stranitsy proshlogo" (1990), about the relationship between Gershenzon and Berdyaev, Gershenzon's granddaughter Maria Andreevna

The Berdyaevs live the same way they used to, and not too badly. Both women work and earn a lot. He writes a great deal—in these years he has written, it seems, five large books; and just as before on Tuesdays they have "Church come-alongs," as I called them, with lectures on mystical, Church, and national themes. I exchange a few words with him when I see him, but only.[50]

On Berdyaev's side, one finds a touching reminiscence accompanied by regret and self-criticism. Berdyaev writes in *Samopoznanie:* "I broke off my relationship with my old friends V. Ivanov and M. Gershenzon because I saw in their behavior accommodation and cooperation. I think now that I was not completely right, especially toward M. Gershenzon. The Soviet structure at that time was still not completely worked out and organized, it was impossible yet to call it totalitarian, and in it there were many contradictions."[51]

Gershenzon was right about one thing; after the Revolution their thinking was almost completely at odds. While Berdyaev moved further in the direction of his existentialist Christianity, Gershenzon held tenaciously to his ideas of cosmic harmony. Philosophy, which had played such a great role in solidifying their friendship, played a no less important role in destroying it. Their mutual interests in Russian history, Slavophilism, and idealistic metaphysics could not hide the fundamental differences in their thinking. In the end, they let their relationship disintegrate rather than try to repair the chasm between them.

Chegodaeva writes: "According to the testimony of my mother, N. M. Gershenzon-Chegodaeva, the former closeness between Gershenzon and Berdyaev was never reestablished." In this article Chegodaeva argues that the break between Gershenzon and Berdyaev was caused primarily by Berdyaev's antisemitism at the time of the Revolution.

[50] M. O. Gershenzon to Lev Shestov, 23 April 1922, published in *Minuvshee*, no. 6 (1985): 255.

[51] Berdiaev, *Samopoznanie*, 269.

## Chapter 12

# Mikhail Gershenzon: A Jew in the Russian Elite

It was striking for his contemporaries that Gershenzon, a Jew, celebrated Russian national culture with his enthusiastic essays on Russian intellectual history. Indeed, Gershenzon was so well known as a sympathizer of conservative Russian culture that many referred to him as a "Slavophile." Indeed, an anecdote runs that N. A. Khomyakov, the prominent Octobrist and first president of the Third Duma, remarked that "[t]here is only one Slavophile left in Russia, and he is a Jew"—having in mind Gershenzon. In a letter to Pyotr Struve, Gershenzon heatedly denied the charge: "What kind of Slavophile am I, as you know, I'm a Jew."[1]

In truth, the charge, "Jewish Slavophile," does not do justice to Gershenzon's attitudes toward his Jewish past and culture in Russia, nor does it accurately describe his attitude toward Russian culture. In fact, it was not Slavophilism that Gershenzon expounded, nor was he antisemitic. Rather, he believed in a pantheistic religion of the universe, which he called "cosmic unity." This belief, in association with Gershenzon's own negative childhood experiences, colored his relations to Judaism. While he never converted to Russian Orthodoxy or rejected his background, he was also not a practicing Jew. In his many writings he did not reveal a belief in the Jewish God. Moreover, in two monographs, *Kliuch very* (1921) and *Sud'by evreiskogo naroda* (1922), Gershenzon treated the Jews and their religion critically. He chastised the Jews for their separatism, their supposed refusal to follow the cosmic imperative that all individuals, nations, and states unite together. This cosmic idea held that everything in the universe composed a unity that should not be harmed.

Gershenzon had a mixed attitude toward his Jewish roots. He criticized his past because it had caused him much personal suffering, and yet he never completely condemned it, for he knew the significance of his origins for his spiritual enlightenment and professional achievements. Unable to absolutely negate his Jewish identity and unable to absolutely affirm it, Gershenzon remained ambivalent.

---

[1] Gershenzon, "Otvet P. B. Struve," 175.

Born in 1869 to Jewish parents, Mikhail Gershenzon became one of Russia's greatest historians. Often referred to as the "Russian Carlyle," Gershenzon wrote more than 250 works, including 12 books, on Russian literary and intellectual history. Best known among them are *Petr Chaadev* (1908), *Istoricheskie zapiski* (1910), the celebrated *Perepiska iz dvukh uglov* (1921), which he co-authored with the poet Vyacheslav Ivanov, and *Vekhi*, the sensational collection criticizing the revolutionary intelligentsia (1909), which he edited, and to which he contributed a passionate article. Gershenzon was also the first president of the Moscow Writer's Union after the Revolution of 1917 and head of the literary section of the Soviet Academy of Arts from 1922 to 1925.

Looking at such achievements from the perspective of his origins, we can gauge his enormous success. His father was an unsuccessful businessman, whose failures led to bitter quarrels between his parents. In an attempt to escape the misery of the Pale, Gershenzon senior fled to Argentina, where he barely survived as a poor haberdasher. Unsuccessful there too, he perished on the return trip to Russia. Although little is known about his mother, Gershenzon did speak out about his childhood in the Pale, expressing his feelings in a letter from 1894 to his brother: "Terrible city, terrible life! From here it appears to me as a heavy nightmare which miserably depresses people; embraced as if by a dream, as if by despair, the people move like ghosts, and obeying only instinct, they execute the needs of life. I shudder at even the memory of it."[2] Recalling his youth, Gershenzon later remarked that he was "born into darkness." Gershenzon hated Kishinev, and he asserted that his horrible childhood had left deep wounds on his consciousness.[3]

Early on, Gershenzon set his hopes on a university education, but with only a silver medal from his high school, the *numerus clausus* stood in his way. His parents sent him to Berlin to study engineering. Although he successfully managed to finish the two-year course, he spent his time attending lectures on history at Berlin University. He returned home with the dream of studying history in Petersburg or Moscow.[4] In 1891, he was, surprisingly, accepted to Moscow University's Philological-Historical Faculty. Legend has it that he was accepted despite the Jewish quota thanks to a chance accident: out of the many thousands of university-age Jews, he was the only one who dared to apply to the Historical Faculty.[5] After all, a degree in the humanities could

---

[2] M. Gershenzon to A. Gershenzon, 23 October 1892, Archive of M. O. Gershenzon, Russian National Library, Moscow (Rukopisnoe otdelenie Rossiiskoi natsional'noi biblioteki [the old Lenin Library]), f. 746, op. 18, d. 1.

[3] For more on Gershenzon's childhood, see Natalia Gershenzon-Chegodaeva's letter published in O. Deschartes's introduction to *Perepiska iz dvukh uglov*, in *Sobranie sochinenii*, by Viacheslav Ivanov, ed. D. V. Ivanov and O. Deshart (Brussels: Foyer Oriental Chrétien, 1971), 3: 809–10.

[4] Horowitz, "Gershenzon and the Intellectual Life of Russia's Silver Age," 26.

[5] Vladislav Khodasevich, *Nekropol': Vospominaniia* (Paris: YMCA-Press, 1976), 147.

lead only to a university position and consequently to conversion to Christianity. The truth was that Ivan Delyanov, the minister of education at the time, accepted him as an exception to the quota. But his father didn't believe in the miracle and, sure that his son had already converted, cut off financial help. For poor Mikhail Osipovich, a student's life in Moscow was difficult, although generous Jews contributed money so that he could buy a proper uniform with a sword, although the best they could find was a uniform several sizes too large.[6]

Gershenzon quickly discovered the precarious life of a Jew in Moscow. In an ironic twist of fate, he arrived in 1891, at nearly the same time that the Russian government evicted some 20 Jews for supposedly residing in the city illegally. The evictions during the holiday of Passover were especially brutal owing to the unusually cold weather and the cruelty of the police, who engaged in nighttime arrests.

Gershenzon rose out of poverty thanks to diligence and talent, but the way was tough. Although his thesis, "Aristotle's Athenian Constitution and Plutarch's Lives," won him a gold medal and his mentor, Pavel Vinogradov, wanted to keep his prize student at the university, Gershenzon refused the offer. He considered it base to convert to Christianity solely for material gain. During the next few years he supported himself, his mother, and his brother, a medical student in Odessa, on earnings from translations. His situation improved in the mid-1890s, when the brothers Sabashnikov, Russian owners of a major publishing house, offered him a "private" stipend.[7] He was to use the money to continue his research in history with no strings attached. In the last years of the 19th century, Gershenzon turned away from Greek history to Russian intellectual history. His first book, *Istoriia molodoi Rossii*, appeared in 1908.

Despite formidable obstacles, Gershenzon achieved great fame and a modicum of financial success through writing. A master of portraiture, Gershenzon depicted Russia's greatest heroes, its legendary thinkers and writers, orienting his works toward the needs of a modern bourgeois reader influenced by decadent aesthetics and non-institutional religion rather than by politics or ethics. Thus, Gershenzon's pen transformed Pyotr Chaadaev, Ivan Kireevsky, Aleksandr Pushkin, and Ivan Turgenev from the anti-tsarist rebels or detached lyric poets of the previous generation into visionaries of a transcendent world and zealous seekers of spiritual purpose. More significantly, Gershenzon simultaneously apotheosized his heroes as carriers of Russia's national virtues. After all, his heroes were fashioned as humane, liberal, and creative builders of a harmonious world. In short, Gershenzon created an

---

[6] Ibid.

[7] M. O. Gershenzon to A. O. Gershenzon, 31 October 1892, Archive of M. O. Gershenzon, Russian National Library, Moscow, f. 746, op. 18, d. 22.

idealized representation of how Russians imagined and wanted to imagine themselves.

Gershenzon interpreted the Decembrists, for example, as spiritually "complete" (*tsel'nye*) personalities who harmoniously balanced consciousness and will. He considered their personalities so complete that they lacked any internal challenge, directing all their energies to the outside world. Gershenzon writes, "The Decembrist type is above all a person internally entirely whole, and with a clear, complete, defined psychological temperament. There is nothing he can accomplish internally and therefore he entirely faces toward the outside."[8] As opposed to the "external" Decembrists, the Slavophiles, Gershenzon claimed, revealed a desire for internal unity. In *Istoricheskie zapiski* Gershenzon writes about Ivan Kireevsky: "To become aware of his sensual 'I' and recognize it as the sole living and fully empowered organ of his person meant to concentrate all his thoughts of happiness, fulfillment, higher duty on one single aim: to organize his 'I,' transform the chaos of his feelings into a composite whole. Above all, this task was calling for attention. It appeared to Kireevsky early and did not leave him his entire life."[9]

Gershenzon depicted Chaadaev as a Christian mystic who sought the unity of the churches and, by extension, of all mankind. Even in the tragic life-story of the Jesuit Ivan Pecherin, who, having converted to Catholicism, lived his entire adult life in seclusion, Gershenzon saw a search for individual perfection and utopian harmony. In his biography of Pecherin Gershenzon notes, "Pecherin, withdrawing from life, remained as he was before. A Roman robe preserved in him the utopian idealism of the 1830s. He encased himself in Catholicism and became whole, but became whole as though fossilized. In this act was his unhappiness and also his beauty because humanity knows nothing more beautiful than the dream to which he devoted himself."[10] The dream to which Gershenzon refers is the vision of the inherent perfection within each individual and the unbroken unity throughout the universe.

Gershenzon's biographies of Russian intellectuals had more than merely professional significance. In Russian thinkers he found his ideal "holistic" individual (*tsel'naia lichnost'*) who did not suffer from a fragmented self. In contrast to his own biography, he depicted these men as having had an extraordinarily happy childhood surrounded by parental affection and concern, and as having effortlessly imbibed the aristocratic virtues of good manners, self-esteem, wit, and independence. It is worth contemplating his attraction to these Russians: Did they not possess the qualities that had eluded Gershenzon himself and that he had had to work so hard to attain?

It must be said, however, that Gershenzon distorted the historical facts about his heroes in order to make them serve as the embodiment of his ideal.

---

[8] Gershenzon, *Istoriia molodoi Rossii*, 5.

[9] M. O. Gershenzon, *Istoricheskie zapiski*, 2nd ed. (Berlin: Gelikon, 1923), 24.

[10] M. O. Gershenzon, *Zhizn' V. S. Pecherina* (Moscow: Put', 1910), 184.

As many critics of the time noticed, the Decembrists were more political revolutionaries than exemplars of spiritual wholeness, Chaadaev was more a social critic than a Christian mystic, and the Slavophiles were more closely linked specifically with Russian Orthodoxy and than with the creation of a psychological and universal religion. Gershenzon's religious interpretations of the Decembrists and Chaadaev made him an opponent of Russian Marxists like Georgy Plekhanov, while his universalistic and psychological readings of the Slavophiles brought him into sharp conflict with Russian thinkers such as Nikolai Berdyaev and Georges Florovsky. The latter, for example, thought that Gershenzon suppressed the clearly nationalistic, Russian Orthodox essence of Slavophile thought. What Gershenzon did not realize, then, is that his interpretations of the perfect individual in Russian culture did not accurately correspond to the real biographies of his heroes. His heroes represented the embodiment of an instinctual, internal desire to live in unity with the all-being to a much smaller degree than Gershenzon would have it. In his particular shortsightedness, however, Gershenzon revealed his own ideological preconceptions.

Although there was nothing in his historical portraits that revealed Gershenzon's Jewish background, Russian nationalists such as Vasily Rozanov were enraged. It was a curse, Rozanov wrote in 1910, that "in the future, our children will read Gershenzon, a Jew, when they want to learn about Chaadaev, Kireevsky, or even how to write sweet Russian prose."[11] Truth be told, Gershenzon's interpretations do not do justice to the Russian Christian dimension of Russian culture; in Gershenzon's readings Christianity as a spiritual motivating force is surprisingly absent. In fact, Gershenzon admired the Russian intelligentsia for its tolerance of members of other nationalities, although he agreed during the so-called Chirikov Affair of 1908 that non-Russians were aliens in Russian culture. The affair was played out in numerous newspaper articles in which the Jews were condemned as outsiders and imitators rather than true artists, and it was alleged that their work perverted the Russian spirit.[12]

On the question of Jews and their participation in Russian culture, Gershenzon corresponded with fellow Jewish intellectuals the Pushkinist Nikolai Lerner and critic Arkady Gornfeld. In letters to, among others, Gornfeld, Gershenzon denied any desire to contribute to Russian culture. Rather, he stressed the universal nature of his task, writing, "My whole work in the field

---

[11] Rozanov, "Levitan i Gershenzon," 78.

[12] For more on antisemitism in the Russian intelligentsia, see Kel'ner, "Dva intsidenta." On Chukovsky (Nikolai Vasilievich Kornichukov), see also Andreeva, "Istoriia odnoi nevstrechi"; Horowitz, "Jewish Identity and Russian Culture."

of Russian literature has as its subject eternal, universal themes.... My writings in the field of the history of Russian literature and social thinking ... [are] not work on a 'foreign subject'. I feel myself a man and a Jew and I do all this *sub specie humanitatis*; but it is true that I love something in Russia, love it very strongly and tenderly."[13] While such a confession reflected prevailing values, it is far from convincing. As a writer who wrote in Russian and published in Russia's leading journals on the subject of Russian history, Gershenzon could hardly pretend to be an outsider. Although this debate did not dissuade Gershenzon from continuing his research on the Russian intelligentsia, it did have the effect of stimulating his interest in Jewish issues, which intensified during and after World War I.

In many of his numerous writings about Jewish culture, Gershenzon was critical. This can be explained by the fact that while in Russian culture Gershenzon located heroes who embody the striving for universal completeness, in Jewish culture Gershenzon found intractable traditions and insoluble contradictions, which, according to him, inhibited the creation of spiritually complete individuals.

For example, in his 1916 study of Hayim Nahman Bialik Gershenzon wrote that Bialik could have been one of those spiritual geniuses had Judaism not held him back. Bialik, like any poet, should fly above worldly problems and perfect his art exclusively.[14] Unfortunately he cannot, Gershenzon asserted, because Judaism gives him, as it gives to all its members, worldly burdens and eternal sadness. The real problem for the Jewish intellectual is that Jews are fragmented by birth, unable to be "worry-free":

> The worst consequence of the two-thousand-year-old persecution is our painful genetic disease, the plague poisoning the souls of our children still in the wombs of their mother. This is the woeful agitation of the Jew, his organic incapacity to be without worries. Darkness rules in families. Even where there is already no place for fear and prosaic worries, souls, poisoned by the past, are incapable of flowering. Unmotivated agitation, unidentified melancholy, at times morose, at times sweetly sad, squeezes the heart and does not allow it to open freely.[15]

---

[13] M. Gershenzon to A. Gornfel'd, 20 January 1910, Archive of A. Gornfel'd, Central Archive of Literature and Art (Tsentral'nyi arkhiv literatury I iskusstv, TsGALI), f. 155, op. 1, ed. khr. 269, l. 2.

[14] Gershenzon was personally acquainted with Bialik. In a letter to his brother on April 23, 1917, he describes their meeting, "Yesterday night [Leib] Jaffe brought Bialik over; Jaffe's wife also came along. They stayed around three hours. I will tell you, I have seen many illustrious people, but never has such a great one as Bialik sat at our table. Marusya [Gershenzon's wife] says that from this material a Kant or Shakespeare could come" (Gershenzon, *Pis'ma*, 184).

[15] Gershenzon, "Iarmo i genii," 15.

The problem with Jewish life, he generalized, was the transference from generation to generation of pain and anxiety, an inability to relax. Ingrained habits and restrictive emotions interfere with the individual's free development. Moreover, the lack of freedom does not only pertain to the past or even the present, but continues into the future. And more importantly, such evils affect not just the simple folk, but artists as well. Gershenzon expressed himself poetically: "[T]he curse is that the dark clouds conceal the sun to the children of the sun who so rarely are born among us and do not let them fly up to it."[16]

Interestingly, Gershenzon's criticisms of the effect of Jewish life on the modern artist are surprisingly close in content and style to his complaints about his youth. Jewish life is dark, blocked from the sun, and repressive. The recurrence here of imagery used in works written two decades earlier points to a powerful psychological antipathy toward his Jewish roots.

Nonetheless, Gershenzon became deeply interested in the rich Jewish cultural life that was taking place during World War I. The Zionist newspaper *Evreiskaia zhizn'* was published in Moscow, and Gershenzon established a friendship with the editor, Leib (Lev) Jaffe. Jaffe introduced Gershenzon to Bialik and attempted to pull him into the Jewish life of the city, even inviting him to seder dinner at the home of Rabbi Jacob Maze, the head rabbi of Moscow. Jaffe later invited Gershenzon to participate in the first issue of *Sborniki Safrut*, a Zionist literary almanac, and to write the introduction to *Evreiskaia antologiia: Sbornik molodoi evreiskoi poezii* (1918). Perhaps as a result of exposure to these personal and intellectual circles, or perhaps as a result of the questions about the future that Zionists were raising, Gershenzon became more and more interested in Jewish subjects.

Gershenzon's research culminated in two books, *Kliuch very* (1921) and *Sud'by evreiskogo naroda* (1922), in which he criticized both the Jews of the ancient world and modern Zionists. In *Kliuch very*, for example, he reexamined Jewish history from the perspective of his cosmic philosophy of absolute unity. Isolating those moments in the Bible when the Jews disobeyed God and showed their preference for personal freedom as opposed to an assigned role in God's providential plan, Gershenzon noted that the Jews' natural yearning for freedom made it difficult for them to follow the providential force. According to the writer, this force, known as "God," "providence," or "fate," actually represented a cosmic imperative that would secure the total unity of all with all. Therefore, the ancient Jews were wrong to struggle against it.

Although we might expect that Gershenzon would side with freedom and the will of the individual, since his Russian historical heroes seem to em-

---

[16] Ibid.

body the desire for individual perfection, Gershenzon does the opposite.[17] Using a strange philosophical jargon that characterizes many of his works in the 1920s, Gershenzon explains the ideal unity between individual, nation, and country:

> Repudiating personal interest and freedom for the sake of one's neighbor or nation, a person fulfills his worldly duty, that is, lives cosmically correct. Here two difficulties are overcome immediately. The nation, as an organ of world will, is infallible, its will is truth; but of course it is only the pure will of the nation, linked to its essence. This pure will is lodged in every member of the nation and ... it is separate from the empirical will of the nation, which appears as the sum of all the individual wills.[18]

Gershenzon contends that besides the apparent or "empirical" will of the nation or the individual, there is another will, the cosmic will, which demands the sacrifice of one's ego and the subordination of personal will to that of the group. Gershenzon views the Jewish people as representative of empirical will, the wrong kind of will. For this reason, the history of the Jewish people is instructive only in a negative sense.

In *Sud'by evreiskogo naroda*, Gershenzon condemned Zionism from a similar position. He argued that the desire for political and territorial unity is nothing other than the ideology of European nationalism and that since nationalism is the ideological basis for Jewish oppression in Europe, it should be rejected.[19] Insisting that the Jews have no need for an independent state, since they already live as a united nation, Gershenzon claimed that their unity is internal and spiritual, although not external or political. Gershenzon writes, "Just as a river is a composite whole in the eternal shifting of its waters, so the individual is solitary and whole in the ceaseless renewal of his bodily composition and spiritual movements, and each people is a single organism in history, a single face and single fate."[20]

In Gershenzon's view, the Jewish people, like a river or an individual's body, are distinct, unique, and independent, while ceaselessly mutating. In fact, the Jews cannot cease to be a nation even if they were to try. The unity of the Jews can be seen in their amazing survival for thousands of years in the Diaspora. Despite the attempt by Jews to preserve their ethnic differences, Gershenzon recognized that the cosmic imperative was leading to the dissolution of the Jews into other nations. Since assimilation is inevitable, Zionists

---

[17] Gershenzon, *Kliuch very*, 103.

[18] Ibid., 101–02.

[19] M. O. Gershenzon, *Sud'by evreiskogo naroda* (St. Petersburg: Epokha, 1922), 29.

[20] Ibid., 19.

should not interfere in the natural evolution of history, which Gershenzon identifies again with God's providential plan.

The foundation for Gershenzon's thinking about the nation runs like this: in contrast to the individual, the nation has its origins in pre-history and is locked in its historical path and cannot diverge from it. Creativity and free will belong not to the nation, but to the individual who has the power to change his life. Since Zionists believe the nation can chose its own destiny, Gershenzon disagrees with them in principle.

> Not the nation, as Zionism claims, but the individual is genuine and real in history, because only the individual is essential and to it alone is offered a certain degree of freedom of choice. The national principle acts automatically and does not develop by itself. The individual develops and only in him, nourished by holistic development, does the nation become stronger and more pure. The national element is only one of inherent qualities and one should forget about the idea that it is separate, although it exists and will exist forever. ... We should try to be strong, free individuals full of spirit, then our nationalism, which is unconscious in each of us will be of a high quality.[21]

Instead of furthering the natural harmony in the universe by concentrating on the perfection of the individual, the Zionists want to disrupt it by trying to change the destiny of the nation and therefore trespassing into God's realm.

In both these books we can isolate a single argument: the ancient Jews and the Zionists go against the cosmic imperative. Nevertheless, it is worth asking: Why is it the case that free will exists for the individual, but is denied to the nation? Why does not the exercise of individual will also trespass into God's domain? Moreover, Gershenzon never tested the basic premise of his thought. Why is absolute unity necessarily better than ethnic, religious, or linguistic difference? And why are all people necessarily driven to unity? Gershenzon did not explain this axiom, but accepted it on faith. As he wrote to Pyotr Struve in 1910, regardless of whether or not one likes it, there exists a force uniting everyone. This is an empirical fact, like the laws of physics.[22]

In the debate on Zionism, Gershenzon's is an idiosyncratic voice, says Walter Lacqueur in his 1972 book *A History of Zionism*. According to Lacqueur, there are three types of anti-Zionist arguments: the assimilationist, the Orthodox-religious, and the left-wing revolutionary. Interestingly, Gershenzon's position does not fit neatly into any of the three categories.[23]

---

[21] Ibid., 21.

[22] Gershenzon, "Otvet P. B. Struve," 175. Gershenzon explained his idiosyncratic philosophical views in greater length in works written after the Bolshevik Revolution such as *Troistvennyi obraz sovershenstva* (1918) and *Perepiska iz dvukh uglov*.

[23] Laqueur overstates Gershenzon's sympathy for Zionism and incorrectly defines his view of the destiny of the Jewish people. Laqueur writes, "One of the most interesting

Joining Gershenzon to anti-Zionist Orthodox Jews, Laqueur argued that, like
them, Gershenzon believed there was a purpose to Jewish suffering which
transcended human understanding.[24]

It is easy to show that Gershenzon came from a divergent perspective
than anti-Zionist Orthodox rabbis. Despite his apparent acceptance of the idea
that the Jews have a historical mission, Gershenzon did not think of the Jews
as a messianic people. Seeing no tragedy in the striving for universalism, his
ultimate hope, Gershenzon left it unclear how assimilation permits Jews nevertheless to remain Jewish. In his belief in total unity, Gershenzon seems
closer to the views of the right-wing Hegelians or Friedrich Schelling than to
those of Jewish rabbis.[25]

In fact, it can be claimed that Gershenzon's idea of nationality corresponds in structure to the mystical Slavophile notion of *sobornost'*, in which the
church allows for the absolute freedom of the individual and simultaneously
the ultimate freedom of the community. This "Christian" world-conception of
voluntary unification, however, is essentially hostile to traditional Judaism.
Needless to say, Orthodox Jews would never agree to the disappearance of
the Jewish people and their ultimate dissolution into a universal oneness.

During the same years in which he criticized Judaism, Gershenzon was involved with reevaluating his Jewish roots as the source of his creative inspiration. Although he criticized Judaism because its ideas and practices did not
permit the creation of a spiritually healthy and creatively productive individ-

---

spokesmen of spiritual anti-Zionism was Mikhail Gershenzon, a Russian émigré to
Western Europe [*sic*] who developed a highly personal, mystical philosophy of history
concerning the destiny of the Jewish people. He was not an enemy of Zionism; on the
contrary, Zionism touched him; it had, he wrote, a great psychological beauty. But it
was based on the nation-state as the only norm of human existence, a false nineteenth-
century European concept." Walter Laqueur, *A History of Zionism* (London: Trinity
Press, 1970), 401–02.

[24] Ibid., 402.

[25] Gershenzon's view of the Jews' chosen status is a difficult issue. It is clear that many
critics attributed to him such a view. In the *Jüdaisches Lexikon* (1931), for instance, Isaak
Markon writes, "[S]etzt sich Gershenzon vor allem mit dem Zionismus auseinander,
den er als Verrat an der Idee der Auserwähltheit bezeichnet. In der Assimilation sieht
Gershenzon keine zufällige Erscheinung, sondern den sinnvollen Abschluß der jüd-
ischen Geschichte." Markon, *Jüdisches Lexikon* (Berlin: Jüdischer Verlag, 1931), 2: 1042.
The confusion I think comes from Gershenzon's inconsistent use of the concept, "chosen nation." For Gershenzon it seems as though there can be more than one single
chosen nation. Rather, all nations are equally "chosen." Although the Jews are special
because they are united in their identity not by land and language, as are other nations, but by spiritual concerns, they are not, according to Gershenzon, a messianic
nation.

ual, he began to understand that the case was more complex. Time and again he wavered on making a blanket condemnation, realizing that there were positive aspects of Jewish culture that had previously escaped his attention.

For example, in his introduction to *Evreiskaia antologiia*, Gershenzon described a new type of Jewish artist, who was the opposite of the anxiety-ridden, despairing melancholic that he depicted in 1916.[26] Now he wrote: "These young poets love, and just like the youth of all countries, they freely and loudly sing their love. The life of nature is open to them and they depict it with love. They reflect about life, humanity, and God, the obsessive idea of Jewish worry does not persecute them."[27] Gershenzon lauded the universal themes in the volume and reacted ecstatically to the absence of specifically Jewish problems.

While I will speculate later about why, between 1916 and 1918, Gershenzon changed his mind about the harmful effects of Jewish life; it is a fact that at this time he began to reevaluate his Jewish roots. His appreciation of Jewish life is displayed most clearly in his "Solntse nad mgloi" (1923). Gershenzon's new attitude is manifested in his relation to the painter, Rembrandt van Rijn. Making a distinction between the sun and darkness, which in Gershenzon's personal lexicon stands for self-perfection versus human misery, Gershenzon compares his own experience as a writer to that of the Dutch painter, who, he claims, lived his whole life in darkness. As we recall, "darkness" is the key word that Gershenzon consistently used to describe life in the Pale of Settlement. About Rembrandt, he writes, "I was already an adult when I saw Rembrandt's paintings for the first time. He immediately put a spell on me, and since then I looked for him everywhere and could not get enough of him. In art no one, not even Pushkin, had such a strong effect on me; no single person from among the people I knew was so close to me."[28]

Pointing to the many artists and writers who lived in the "light," in health, prosperity, and happiness, Gershenzon paradoxically values more highly those artists who lived in darkness, misery, and pain. Despite his frequent glorification of the sun, which he links with the concepts of spiritual completeness and perfection, Gershenzon reveals a significant and unambiguous sympathy with darkness:

> Like a full river clearly reflecting the sky and sun during the day and the stars at night and ceaselessly carrying its waters to the sea—this is how life should be. Maybe Aeschylus and Pericles lived this way; Goethe in his youth lived this way. Should one be envious of them? They were healthy their whole life, Rembrandt was his whole life

---

[26] M. O. Gershenzon, "Predislovie," in *Evreiskaia antologiia: Sbornik molodoi evreiskoi poezii* (Moscow, 1918). Citations are to the 3rd edition (Berlin: D. Zal'tsman, 1922).

[27] Ibid., 7.

[28] M. O. Gershenzon, "Solntse nad mgloi," in *Zapiski mechtatelei* 6 (1922): 100.

spiritually sick; and all the same, if at the moment, when I emerged, defining my fate they offered me as a choice that one or other—I, as I am today, it would be very difficult [to answer].[29]

If we allow ourselves to consider for a moment that Rembrandt might have represented Gershenzon himself—both became artists, both lived in poverty and difficulty, and Rembrandt's technique of chiaroscuro perfectly depicts Gershenzon's idea of light penetrating the darkness—we can grasp Gershenzon's positive idea that darkness, too, provides a way toward beauty, creativity, and spiritual revelation. From his own experience, Gershenzon understood that darkness indeed leads to light; from his origins in Kishinev, Gershenzon had risen to become a first-class artist. Logically, he could not negate the darkness in favor of the sun, imperfect life in favor of eternal perfection, since by doing so he would negate himself, the child of darkness and the writer who realized the importance of the sun. In Judaism there was suffering and pain, but there was also the positive stimulus for self-perfection and intellectual curiosity.

Gershenzon's change of heart with regard to his Jewish roots was so complete that he even located a hero in contemporary Jewish culture comparable with his Russian idols. Gersh-Leib, an authentic Jew from the Pale, is a poor pretzel seller. Paradoxically, Gersh-Leib is described neither as extremely intelligent nor physically attractive. Gershenzon describes him this way:

> He seems to me now in the twilight as a thick knot of darkness. He looked at least fifty or more. Short, his spine bent from worries, dressed in a worn-out discolored caftan and wearing a cap of the same color, with a dark face, dirty gray hair growing on it, a long nose, tearful eyes, swollen eyelids, and dry lips, he was inattentive to everything and eternally silent. That is how he was. Was he your brother, young Goethe? Yours Nansen, at the hour when you sailed north? He came from a nondescript Polish shtetl.[30]

Despite his external ugliness and browbeaten appearance, Gersh-Leib is the salt of the earth. Gershenzon praises him for his ability to toil, for his honesty and sense of justice. The story that Gershenzon uses to illustrate Gersh-Leib's superior qualities runs like this: Gersh-Leib earned his living in the neighborhood selling pretzels and little cakes. One day a richer Jew turns to Gersh-Leib for a loan of 25 rubles so that he can open up a grocery. Although the sum is everything Gersh-Leib has, and he has been saving to buy a cow, he agrees to lend the money. The man's business fails, and the money is lost. No effort is made to return Gersh-Leib his money. Such open betrayal and

---

[29] Ibid., 100.

[30] Ibid., 102.

dishonesty causes Gersh-Leib to stand up for himself and demand repayment. This is the scene that has impressed itself on Gershenzon's memory:

> In my memory his ruddy and strained face stands so clearly before me that I feel as if I hear his words. "I ask you Jews, where is justice? I have been living abroad three years, far from my wife and children, without a roof like a dog. My feet are breaking, I can barely sit, and every day I walk ten versts to make thirty kopeks. Someone takes my twenty-five rubles? What will God say? At home I have a widowed daughter with three children and an unmarried daughter whom I have to marry off. We've lost everything, lost our cow, and we used to live on dairy products the entire week, except the Sabbath. Then I set off in the direction away from home; I thought God will help me, I'll marry off my daughter and buy a cow. Who wants to die abroad? Suddenly a man comes to whom I have done no evil and takes my twenty-five rubles. Really, am I asking for your money? Give me my money and I will not have anything against you.'[31]

Gershenzon interjects, "The thick knot of darkness brilliantly alighted and shined. I suffered deeply for him."[32]

Gershenzon admires Gersh-Leib because he revealed his soul, pride, and dignity to the world. In a word, from darkness he brilliantly reached the light. This perhaps explains why Gershenzon can compare a pretzel seller to luminaries such as Goethe and the Norwegian explorer Fridtjof Nansen. By displaying the transcendental perfection of the human spirit, Gersh-Leib can justifiably serve as an example of Gershenzon's ideal man, although he did not create any work of art or achieve extraordinary glory. Such a positive evaluation of a man who "lived" in an exemplary and "holistic" way should not surprise us, since the criterion of "ideal living" or "living in the spirit" has always been of primary value in Gershenzon's evaluation of individuals.

Despite the incongruities between Gershenzon's own biography and the facts about Gersh-Leib, one is left with the impression that Gershenzon felt communality with the old Jew. In fact both had the same name and both had traversed a common path.

> He was so dark and cold, why is the recollection of him inextricable from me, as if he were my own brother? In all those years in our city he did not become close with anyone. He walked along the sidewalk where the children played, walked sullenly, not seeing them, entered into the court, and by many doors beautiful oleanders in green bowls blossomed with bright rose flowers. He did not see them and did not smell their almond scent. He knew the sun only from the reflections

---

[31] Ibid., 106–07.

[32] Ibid.

of the streams of water, which fell from above, and the stormy currents on the streets. In my personal life there is no memory so sympathetic as the memory of him and two or three like him.[33]

Gershenzon obviously used the image of Gersh-Leib as a projection of his own self. Gershenzon too left his origins to wander in foreign parts, he was also alienated and alone, and he ceaselessly toiled to overcome his poverty. Most important of all, he also knew himself a man of darkness who had risen up toward the sun.

This image of the Pale of Settlement embodied in Gersh-Leib sharply contradicts Gershenzon's earlier presentations, making one wonder what was responsible for the shift. Could it be that, far in time and distance from Kishinev, he began to romanticize Jewish life, as did a number of secular Jews such as Isaac Leib Peretz, Martin Buber, and Shimon An-sky? Or was there another reason? Could it also be that, having supported the Bolsheviks in 1917 and watched them subsequently trample on his dreams of justice, equality, and freedom, Gershenzon found it necessary to reevaluate his entire worldview? Certainly bitter experience in the present taught him that things were not as they seemed. Darkness and light were not always opposites, the Bolsheviks had turned Russia into a dictatorship, and Jewish life was not an absolute evil. As the example of Gersh-Leib shows, the image of holistic perfection that he found in his Russian heroes was also present in the simple Jews of the Pale. Nevertheless, we should remember that much of his positive treatment of Judaism and Jewish life comes from a retrospective viewpoint, full of nostalgia and pathos, albeit genuine. However, we should also remember that these images were published in 1923, the year after Gershenzon published his very negative *Sud'by evreiskogo naroda*.

It is interesting to note that Gershenzon was not alone among Russian intellectuals of Jewish background, who revealed closer ties to Jewish culture in the early days of Communism. I am thinking of Akim Volynsky, Eduard Bagritsky, and even Osip Mandelshtam. While these writers did not experience a religious "return" to Judaism, they began to use Jewish themes in their works and embraced the self-image of a Russian-Jewish intellectual. The reason for this may have something to do with the fact that after 1917 they found themselves without a positive identity. Not desiring to be seen as a recalcitrant bourgeois and unable to transform themselves into proletarian apologists, they were searching for new identities. Jewish identity was one among the various masks and social profiles that these writers tried on.

What emerges most vividly regarding Gershenzon's attitude toward Judaism are contradictions and vacillations. Although on so many points Jewish culture seemed to embody antithetical principles—it contradicted his idea of a cosmic spirituality, it suppressed individual freedom, and its history re-

---

[33] Ibid.

vealed a destructive, egoistic principle—Judaism held Gershenzon in fascination. The powerful myth of self-preservation, the potential of its artists, and the aesthetic imagery of *shtetl* Jews captivated him. Drowning in contradictions, ultimately he could not formulate a single principle for evaluating his Jewish background.

His paradoxical attitude is understandable in the context of his personal experience and intellectual development. When he left his origins, he automatically negated the religion and the idea of the Jews as the messianic people. This belief, however, was replaced with something equally profound. Through his study of the Slavophiles, he fell upon a religion of the cosmos, a universal spiritual ideal, which he believed had been realized by the heroes of his adopted culture. In his native Judaism he found no such ideal. Under the pressure of truly catastrophic events—revolution, starvation, and tragic disappointment—he came to understand that his own successes were based on his Jewish origins, although so too were his sufferings. Although he did not sever his ties to the Jewish people, he did not love the religion or seek its spiritual revitalization. Therefore, it is not surprising that we perceive contradictory opinions in his statements. In essence he was torn. He hated his past, but it was his, and he was loyal to it. In the end, Gershenzon, like so many secular Jews of his time, rejected the Jewish religion, but never his origins.

## Chapter 13

# The Tension of Athens and Jerusalem in the Philosophy of Lev Shestov

The reaction to *Afiny i Ierusalim* (1938), Lev Shestov's final book, on which he worked for at least ten years, is reflected by Bernard Martin, who observed in his introduction to Shestov's philosophy: "The essays and aphorisms of *Afiny i Ierusalim* represent, in many respects, the culmination of Shestov's entire lifetime of intellectual inquiry and spiritual striving, and they bring together the diverse strands appearing in his earlier writings."[1] Although *Afiny i Ierusalim* supposedly sums up Shestov's entire worldview, it is worth noting that before it was published Shestov never employed the images of these two cities to describe his philosophy. At first glance, it would appear that Shestov arbitrarily chose the title, since the book does not deal with the ancient Jews or the Greeks exclusively, but concentrates equally on modern and early philosophy. Although his main aim was to promote his idiosyncratic existentialist viewpoint, which emerged from distinctly modern sources, Shestov did not force his thought into the binary opposition that the title implies. How, then, could Shestov use Athens and Jerusalem to characterize his final, cumulative

---

[1] Bernard Martin, comp., *Great Twentieth-Century Jewish Philosophers: Shestov, Rosenzweig, Buber, with Selections from Their Writings* (New York: Macmillan, 1970), 5–6. The history of the writing of *Afiny i Ierusalim* has been thoroughly detailed by A. Akhutin and E. Patkosh in their notes to Shestov's *Sochineniia v 2-kh tomakh*, ed. A. Akhutin (Moscow: Nauka, 1993), 2: 461–65. The book first appeared in French in 1938, published as *Athenes et Jerusalem (essai de philosophie religieuse)*. A German translation by H. Rouff also appeared in 1938. In 1966, the book appeared in English as *Athens and Jerusalem*, translated by Bernard Martin from the French edition. Three parts of the book have appeared in Italian: *Parmenide Incatenato* (1944); *Ye sapere e la Liberta* (1943); *Concupiscentia Irresistibilis (della filosofia medioevale)* (1946). For more on the publication of translations, see Nathalie Baranoff [Baranova-Shestova], *Zhizn' L'va Shestova: Po perepiske i vospominaniiam sovremennikov*, 2 vols. (Paris: La Presse Libre, 1983), 2: 218–28. A Russian version of *Afiny i Ierusalim* did appear in 1952 published by YMCA Press in an edition of 1,000 copies. This volume most likely did not have a large impact in Russia, since the number of copies was so small and among those that did reach that destination, it is likely that most were placed in the special holdings of major research libraries to which readers could not gain easy access. The renewed interest in Shestov during the post-glasnost' period was sparked by the two-volume edition of Shestov's writings, which appeared in 1993.

work without either misrepresenting his philosophy or the significance of these two ancient cities?

In his very first works, Shestov sketched out a paradigm in which logic was questioned from the standpoint of religious existentialism. He criticized the reliance on logic characteristic of Logical Positivism, examples of which he found in Western and Russian literature. Later he characterized Greek philosophy as an original progenitor of contemporary Positivism. He began using the Jewish theme consistently rather late in his career, in emigration, employing images from the Old Testament to illustrate his positive conception of religious faith. In this paper I trace the evolution of Shestov's thought, showing how he arrived in the final instance at the dichotomy of Athens and Jerusalem. To carry out this task, we need to examine his philosophical development in relation to changes in the Russian intellectual life of his time.

Shestov's path from his home in Kiev (then in Russia, now the capital of Ukraine) to the heights of Athens and Jerusalem was indirect. As did many intellectuals of his time, Shestov arrived at religious philosophy through an interest in radical politics. The scion of a wealthy Kievian merchant well versed in Jewish culture and associated with the Zionist movement, Shestov was acquainted with both the Jewish tradition and Russian European culture. But, as he recounts, he "forgot" his Jewish education, and early in life he chose assimilation to Russian culture as the keystone of his intellectual development.

It is often said about Shestov that his insights were formed from his own existential experience, which, however, he never revealed to the public. According to Evgenia Gertsyk, his close friend, this revelation occurred in 1895 when he suffered a nervous breakdown.[2] However, during this same period, while in Rome, Shestov met a young non-Jewish Russian woman, Anna Eleazarovna Berezovskaya, who was traveling with friends, and quickly married her. Since his parents wanted him to marry a Jew, Shestov tried to hide from his parents his marriage and even for some time the existence of his two daughters, Tatiana and Natalia.

The first part of Shestov's career shows him traversing a common road from political radicalism to religious metaphysics.[3] He was expelled from the law school at Moscow University for participation in student protests. The dissertation he later wrote in order to earn his degree in law from Kiev Uni-

---

[2] Evgeniia Gertsyk, *Vospominaniia: N. Berdiaev, L. Shestov, S. Bulgakov, V. Ivanov, M. Voloshin, A. Gertsyk* (Paris: YMCA Press, 1973), 106.

[3] Still a child, he became involved in revolutionary politics and at age 12 was kidnapped by terrorists from the People's Will party who demanded a large ransom. Shestov's father refused to pay, and after six months the boy was released. There is good reason to believe that Shestov himself organized the crime, since he later refrained from speaking about it, calling it an "unfortunate prank." See Baranoff, *Zhizn' L'va Shestova*, 1: 10–11.

versity shows his interests at the time; it is entitled "Fabrichnoe zakonoda-tel'stvo v Rossii" (Factory Legislation in Russia; 1889).[4] The subject of the con-dition of the working class ties Shestov closely to the Legal Marxists, who also attempted to expose the deep injustices inherent in Russian society through detailed studies of various aspects of its economy.

Although politics soon lost its appeal for Shestov, he did not turn to Juda-ism for spiritual satisfaction, but devoted himself to the study of religious phi-losophy, at which he arrived through his reading of literary Modernism. Like Dmitry Merezhkovsky, Zinaida Gippius, Vyacheslav Ivanov, and Vasily Ro-zanov, Shestov discovered the realm of the spirit through the literature of Western Decadence. Unlike the leading populist critics of the day, who subor-dinated aesthetic concerns to social goals, Shestov held that the goal of poli-tics, collective liberation, was impossible since the individual knows only his own unique experience. Furthermore, personal tragedy, formerly considered the result of a bad society for which political solutions should be sought, was for Shestov the sole source for acute self-knowledge. In the first decade of his career, Shestov attempted to save the individual from the stranglehold of logic, articulating a "philosophy of tragedy," and treating the problems of "despair" and "amor fati" in the works of Shakespeare, Tolstoy, Dostoevsky, and Nietzsche.

In his first book, *Shekspir i ego kritik Brandes* (Shakespeare and His Critic Brandes; 1898), Shestov already reveals prominent features of his writing ap-proach and existential views. Using the Danish critic Georg Brandes as an intellectual opponent, Shestov reviles Brandes's view that Shakespeare articu-lates "abstract values" in his plays: pessimism, despair, joy, and love.[5] In con-trast, Shestov claims that Shakespeare portrays individuals engaged in inimit-able, actual life dramas that have no precursor and no formula for their resolution. Brutus, King Lear, and Hamlet confront situations that are beyond rational solution; the knowledge of the ages has nothing useful to offer heroes who are subject to personal pain, which no wisdom can mollify. They gain only experience, a singular, unique, inimitable knowledge of themselves.

In criticizing logic, intellectual habits, and preconceived patterns of think-ing, Shestov uses the "tragedies" of Shakespeare's characters as negative ex-amples. Hamlet is ruined not only by circumstance but also by the need to un-derstand with logic the horrible crime that he must avenge. Brutus suffers from his respect for abstract concepts of loyalty and justice, ignoring his real

---

[4] Later Shestov gave the title as "Polozhenie rabochego klassa v Rossii," but Shestov's daughter, Natalia Baranova-Shestova, believes the first title is the true one (Baranoff, *Zhizn' L'va Shestova*, 7–8).

[5] Georg Brandes (1842–1927), Danish literary critic, was the author of *Critiques and Portraits* (1870) and *Main Currents in Nineteenth-Century Literature* (6 vols., 1872–90; English trans., 1901–05). His book *William Shakespeare* (1895–96; English trans., 1898), inspired Shestov to write his own monograph in response.

calling, the imperative for action and awareness of his own desires. King Lear experiences the ultimate ignominy because of his adherence to abstract conceptions; expecting to be feted as king, he is treated as a powerless man, and his conceptions of himself and the world are cruelly undercut.

Just as do Shakespeare's characters and Shakespeare himself, the reader should not seek systems for understanding, but should become aware of the contingency of all being. He must defy logic, convention, and habit, accepting freedom and life if he wants to draw any message from the dramas. Shestov writes, "The drive for a system kills free creativity, placing strict boundaries prepared in advance. Entering the world of the human spirit in order to subjugate it to laws applicable to the exterior world means to receive everything beforehand and voluntarily to surrender the right to see."[6] By dividing the external world and the interior soul, Shestov posits an autonomous realm for the spirit, refuting the Positivist chain of dependence. In this division Shestov presages a fundamental dichotomy in his work: criticism of positivistic logic as opposed to the superior realm of religious faith.

In *Shekspir i ego kritik Brandes* Shestov presents an initial formulation of his existentialism. Incapable of answering people's real spiritual needs, the world "as a concept" leaves individuals spiritually diminished and can even destroy them. According to Shestov, Shakespeare's pessimism was not a "theoretical question to which one devotes hours of leisure, but a question of his very existence."[7] Shestov explains Shakespeare's quandary: "The poet felt that it is impossible to live, not having become reconciled with life. In the meantime Lear, Hamlet, and Othello exist, people exist who, because of chance, because of their birth or external circumstances, have become products of unhappiness or, what is more terrible, initiators of others' unhappiness, criminals; for as long as a blind force rules people, defines their fate, our life is merely a 'fable, told by a fool.'"[8] For Shestov, Shakespeare is exemplary not just because he knew the world was "out of joint," but because he refused to be silent. Literature, Shestov believes, communicates to us these cries of despair and melancholy, and it is wrong to pretend otherwise.

In his next two works, *Dobro v uchenii Gr. Tolstogo i Nitshe: Filosofiia i propoved'* (The Good in the Teaching of Count Tolstoy and Nietzsche; 1900) and *Dostoevskii i Nitshe: Filosofiia tragedii* (Dostoevsky and Nietzsche: A Philosophy of Tragedy; 1902), Shestov builds upon the existential realizations he discovered in Shakespeare. Using Friedrich Nietzsche as an intellectual companion to understand these authors, Shestov articulates his "philosophy of tragedy," holding that universal truth, truth valid for all people at all times, is a deceptive posture since, while appearing to satisfy and give meaning to the

---

[6] L. Shestov, *Shekspir i ego kritik Brandes* (St. Petersburg: Tip. A. M. Mendelevicha, 1898), 3.

[7] Ibid., 280.

[8] Ibid.

individual, it cannot account for or justify personal pain, injustice, or death.[9] The realization that evil is omnipresent and logic only a facade will inevitably cause a "crisis" of consciousness.

In his study of Tolstoy, Shestov discovered that the devotion to the universal values of virtue, benevolence, and justice contradicted another Tolstoy, who sang of the "darkness" and "evil of humanity." Although he tried not to, in works such as "The Kreuzer Sonata," "The Death of Ivan Ilych," and *Anna Karenina*, Tolstoy describes his doubts that "life in the good" is the solution to the elimination of evil. What if the good doesn't win out? What can one do and how should one live?

According to Shestov, Tolstoy faced this problem when he approached the poor residents of the Lapin building, where, despite all his help, he was forced to conclude that the poor would always be poor and that their numbers would even grow, despite the well-meaning intervention of Count Tolstoy.[10] To stave off the terrible despair of knowing that neither he nor anyone else could improve the condition of humanity, the great realist threw himself into an ethical battle against the conventions of society. He began to propagate his religious ideas, engage in farming, and wear peasant clothing.

But at the same time that he was fighting for the good, Tolstoy also suffered indecision. The fight against evil, he realized, inevitably leads one to resemble evil.[11] According to Shestov, Tolstoy realized that "one has to choose between the role of a 'moral' critic, who stands against the entire world, all of life, and love for one's own fate, for necessity, i.e., love for life, just as it is in reality, just as it will always be."[12] Faced with this paradox, Tolstoy decided against life, choosing the moral high road, the fight against evil, even at the cost of "turning life into evil." Shestov writes,

> "The Good is God," Tolstoy says to his disciples—that is merely what everyone says, what the best educated crowd says ... the crowd which he himself attacks. Meanwhile all of life becomes transformed into evil, and Count Tolstoy does not care. He does not even ask himself (more correctly, does not want his disciples to ask), how it can be that God does not rule in the world, how is it that millions live without God? He gets comfort from the fact that he rose up to the highest level of moral development![13]

---

[9] For more on Nietzsche's role in the period, see Bernice Glatzer Rosenthal, ed., *Nietzsche in Russia* (Princeton, NJ: Princeton University Press, 1986).

[10] L. Shestov, *Dobro v uchenii Gr. Tolstogo i Nitshe: Filosofiia i propoved'* (St. Petersburg: Tip. M. M. Stasiulevicha, 1900), 28.

[11] Ibid., 110.

[12] Ibid., 111.

[13] Ibid., 114–15.

Similarly, Shestov describes how Dostoevsky tried to offer humanity moral absolutes, such as the benevolent good, brotherly love, and universal happiness, although in profound moments of darkness and pain he realized this shroud of optimism could not hold. In *Dostoevskii i Nitshe* Shestov describes Dostoevsky's thoughts after his return from exile: "'I cannot, cannot pretend anymore, I cannot live the lie of ideas, but I have no other truth; let what be will be...'"[14] According to Shestov, Dostoevsky could not contain his fury caused by his prison experiences, revealing to the world all the horrors of life. His message was that there is only one truth: unabashed "egoism." The genuine Dostoevsky is best found in the confessions of the underground man, who exclaims: "Is the world to go to pot, or am I to go without my tea? I say that the world can go to pot, so long as I can always get my tea."[15]

Shestov believes that Dostoevsky became frightened of his negative critique of humanity and therefore tried as much as he could to repress this revelation. He wrote the major novels, in which he espouses a philosophy of brotherly love within the context of Russian Orthodoxy, merely to crush forever the horrible individual pain he felt in prison and after he returned to St. Petersburg.

With these two books, Shestov articulates an opposition between knowledge and experience, viewing the choices his authors made. While Tolstoy sided with the ethical good, Dostoevsky advocated suppressing egoism. Thus, one can either flee from real problems into knowledge, or embrace evil. Shestov identifies with the latter, believing that siding with evil, whatever the personal cost, is the first step to overcoming it. Shestov states, "In the laws of nature, science, Positivism, and idealism there is a pledge for unhappiness, in the horrors of life is a pledge for the future."[16]

During the writing of *Apofeoz bespochvennosti: Opyt adogmaticheskogo myshleniia* (1905), Shestov shifted the object of his analysis from the biography of an author to the harmful effects of positivistic philosophy. While the early plan of the book had been similar to that of his previous works—to show the metaphysical self-deceptions of a single writer (in this case Ivan Turgenev)—Shestov discarded most of that literary material to express his own ideas about epistemology, logic, life, and freedom. He also experimented with new narrative approaches in an attempt to give his ideas about non-logical thinking a corresponding expressive form. Instead of linear prose, he composed the work in large part with fragments and aphorisms that, he claimed, reflect his ideas of contingency, chance, and freedom.

The locus of his positive ideas is God, a God for whom "anything is possible." Showing God's power over the laws of nature and laws of logic, Shestov

---

[14] L. Shestov, *Dostoevskii i Nitshe: Filosofiia tragedii* (St. Petersburg: Tip. M. M. Stasiulevicha, 1903), 53.

[15] Ibid., 51.

[16] Ibid., 229.

declares that rational knowledge deconstructs when seen from the perspective of faith: "I am forced again to repeat that anything can occur from anything, that 'A' can be unequal to 'A' and that, consequently, for its validation logic is indebted to the empirically observable law of the comparative immutability of things existing outside us. Allow for the possibility of supernatural interference and logic loses the general necessity of its conclusions and its indisputability which so attracts the mind."[17] In the light of a transcendent being involved with our fate, logic, or inexorable and unbendable rules, cannot be defended, and thus another way of thinking must take its place.

For Shestov, that way is philosophy. But not philosophy as it has been practiced in the West for the last 3,000 years, i.e., as an attempt to provide universal and immutable laws for phenomena. Rather, Shestov claims the conventional linkage of logic and philosophy was an original error that must be corrected. He writes, "Philosophy should not have anything in common with logic; philosophy is an art, striving to break through the logical chain of inferences and leading a person to the boundless sea of fantasy, the fantastic, where everything is equally possible and impossible."[18] For Shestov, philosophy is not meant to comfort but to irritate people. It is for the "audacious," for those who are prepared to confront the impossible, unthinkable and miraculous. Philosophy's "task is to teach people to live in uncertainty, teach those who more than anything else are afraid of uncertainty and hide from it behind various dogmas."[19]

According to Shestov, the main dogma behind which people usually find consolation is Logical Positivism. Logical Positivism has a hold because it "frightens" and "subdues the individual" with its deterministic truths about what can be known. It says that only what is certain, immutable, and eternal is true. But according to Shestov, "logic in the blink of the eye carries us to far distant conclusions and predictions, reality cannot keep up with it."[20] By keeping its distance from reality, logic keeps reality at bay, just like "a disfigured woman who is still just as beautiful to us, as if nothing happened at all."[21] With logic, the horrors of life are expunged and life, or rather the semblance of life, becomes ordered, peaceful, and predictable.

Although Shestov was an uncompromising enemy of Logical Positivism, it was not reason per se that drew his anger. Rather, philosophy, at least as he conceived of it, employed a richer understanding of reason than the one that Logical Positivism accepted. This other kind of reason included the under-

---

[17] L. Shestov, *Apofeoz bespochvennosti: Opyt adogmaticheskogo myshleniia* (St. Petersburg: Obshchestvennaia pol'za, 1905; repr., Leningrad: Izd-vo Leningradskogo universiteta, 1991), 109.

[18] Ibid., 59.

[19] Ibid., 52.

[20] Ibid., 110.

[21] Ibid.

standing of such phenomena as the search for personal meaning, confronting one's mortality, and contemplating a living deity.

Although *Apofeoz bespochvennosti* is representative of Shestov's philosophy at the time of the 1905 Revolution, in it Shestov repeats the basic oppositions of logic versus life and abstract thought versus faith in the impossible. Looking at his positive concept of faith, we can make the following observations: Faith is based on the inner feeling of the individual and therefore personalistic, non-institutional, and detached from collective religious experience. Furthermore, although Shestov invoked the existence of a "living God" for whom everything is possible, he was silent about his particular features, especially saying nothing about God and various creeds or about institutional religion.[22]

Shestov's brand of existentialism enjoyed enormous popularity in the early years of the 20th century, when the leading intellectuals were involved in "God-seeking."[23] In fact, during those years Shestov's early books were instrumental in bringing Russia's youth to religion. There were Shestov societies, and teenagers wishing to taunt their parents would threaten to read Shestov and indulge in debauchery (*razvratnichat'*) if their demands were not met.[24] Religion in this case was synonymous with spiritual feeling and was primarily non-ecclesiastic and ecumenical. *The Varieties of Religious Experience* by William James was especially in vogue in Russia since it valorized spiritual feeling above institutional religious affiliation.[25]

However, between 1906 and 1914 Russia's most important philosophers gradually began moving toward a greater concern with issues of Christianity. Instead of validating any act or feeling which satisfies the individual's "metaphysical needs," these philosophers began to narrow their definition and exclusively consider Russian Orthodoxy and the Russian Church the sole acceptable religious credo and institution. In 1912, Nikolai Berdiaev finished his biography of the Slavophile theologian Aleksei Khomyakov, Sergei Bulgakov published his theological treatise *Dva grada* (? vols., 1911), and Semyon Frank

---

[22] In agreement with a suggestion by a reviewer of this article, I would like to note that the idea of God has its own intricate history in Shestov's philosophy and that the subject is too complex to be treated exhaustively here.

[23] For a good summary of the intellectual currents during the fin-de-siècle period, see G. Florovskii, *Puti russkogo bogosloviia*, 4th ed. (Paris: YMCA-Press, 1988), 452–99.

[24] A. Bakhrakh, *Po pamiati, po zapisiam: Literaturnye portrety* (Paris: Press libre, 1980), 163.

[25] The Russian translation appeared as *Mnogoobrazie religioznogo opyta*, trans. Varvara Malakhieva-Mironich (Moscow, 1910).

turned to an examination of Christian *sobornost'* (unity).[26] Among such religious thinkers, a consensus grew that the problems of Russian society could be solved by applying to social life the principles of Russian Orthodox Christian theology. As his colleagues coalesced around a common problem concerning the meaning of Christ, the role of the Russian Orthodox Church, and the importance of Christianity for daily life, Shestov came to be seen as a "solitary," detached philosopher.[27]

Shestov's isolation can be explained not only by his penchant for paradoxes, for examining the irrational and emotional side of human life, but also by his tepid participation in the dominant questions of Russian religious thought at this time. As a non-practicing Jew, his attitudes toward traditional and institutional sources of religion were complicated. He could not in good conscience embrace Russian Orthodox Christianity, since doing so would be an open betrayal of Judaism, and historically the Russian Orthodox clergy was known for its religious intolerance and even antisemitism. Nevertheless, the search for religious origins and traditions, which influenced his Russian Orthodox colleagues, appears to have increasingly agitated Shestov, and other Russian-Jewish thinkers, such as Akim Volynsky, Mikhail Gershenzon, Yuly Aikhenval'd, and Arkady Gorn'feld.[28] For them, as for Shestov, the reevaluation of Judaism in the construction of their identity and use in their works was neither simple nor immediate. In fact, Shestov's rediscovery of Judaism came later. In the first two decades of his creative work he remained faithful to his religious individualism; the need for tradition was satisfied by an expansion of his negative critique of Logical Positivism into the domain of the history of philosophy.

In his book *Sola Fide*, written in Switzerland between 1911 and 1914, Shestov took up the task of investigating ancient Greece and the medieval scholastics. He describes his task this way: "Whoever wants people to listen to him, whoever wants to leave behind a noticeable trace in history, must

---

[26] Semen Frank's writings at this time are collected in *Filosofiia i zhizn': Etiudy i nabroski po filosofii kul'tury* (St. Petersburg, 1910) and *Predmet znaniia: Ob osnovakh i predelakh otvlechennogo znaniia* (Petrograd, 1915).

[27] This view of Shestov, already established in his own day, has been repeated recently by A. B. Akhutin in his 1993 introduction to a new collection of Shestov's works. His essay is entitled "The Solitary Thinker." See Shestov, *Sochineniia*, 1: 3–14.

[28] Gershenzon became more conscious of his Jewish roots as he aged. For more on this subject, see my Ph.D. dissertation, "M. O. Gershenzon and the Intellectual Life of Russia's Silver Age," 466–521. For information on Akim Volynsky's attitude toward Judaism, see P. Medvedev, *Pamiati A. L. Volynskogo* (Leningrad, 1928). There is as yet little secondary scholarship on the life and career of Arkady Gorn'feld, although his work on the *Jewish Encyclopedia* (1906–13) and his articles on literature for Jewish periodicals evince a strong commitment to a Jewish identity.

complete a study of the Greeks."[29] Shestov decried, with few exceptions, ancient Greek thought's relentless influence on Western religious thought in general and on Christian scholastics in particular. The influence of Greek thought on religious inquiries in the Middle Ages is particularly lamentable, since the Greek legacy demanded that faith be substantiated by logic, while throughout the Middle Ages, philosophy had become the handmaiden of logic and not the other way around, as is usually thought. He saw the dominance of logic as leading ultimately to atheism, the substitution of knowledge for faith.

Just as in his earlier studies, in *Sola Fide* Shestov exposed the flaws of logic. For him Greek philosophy is founded on a basic contradiction: The Greeks consider as truth only that which is absolute, unchanging, and mental, yet such truth cannot give concrete knowledge of the world, but only disembodied, abstract knowledge. Examining the attempt to propose an abstract law to fit all circumstances, Shestov summarizes the life of Socrates: "During the course of several decades Socrates went to squares, bazaars, and other public places and convinced people of one thing only: there is nothing arbitrary in the world, an eternal, immutable law capable of defending itself stands over all living things, and not only people, but also over the gods."[30]

Even Aristotle, celebrated for his advocacy of the concrete and distinct, is sundered by contradictions. Shestov exclaims, "Aristotle wants to think that individual things compose the single reality. But he does not want to depart from Socrates and Plato. He claims that sensual perception cannot be a source of knowledge, that knowledge is directed not at what is mutable and transitory, but at what is eternal and immutable; that the object of knowledge cannot be the personal and individual, i.e., the only thing which is real according to him, but only the general, i.e., what really does not exist according to his teaching."[31] Aristotle's desire for permanent, absolute, and immutable truth led him to suppress changeability and bequeath to humanity a commitment to systems and categories.

While Shestov ostensibly attacked the Greeks because he disagreed with their rationality, his aversion to them might also be rooted in their resemblance to the hated Logical Positivism of his own time. In fact, he attributed to Greece the fundamental qualities of Positivism: the apotheosis of logic and reliance on abstract reason alone. This observation seems especially compelling when one notes how Shestov reduces Greek philosophy to a single element, the dominance of abstract logic.

In Shestov's criticism of Greek reason, however, we again note the influence of Nietzsche, especially *The Birth of Tragedy*. There one finds a similar

---

[29] L. Shestov, *Sola Fide—Tol'ko veroiu: Grecheskaia i srednevekovaia filosofiia. Liuter i tserkov'* (Paris: YMCA-Press, 1966).

[30] Ibid., 47.

[31] Ibid., 40.

dichotomy of logic and religion, individuality and the collective, determinism and freedom. Shestov follows Nietzsche in laying the blame on Socrates and the domination of logic for the lack of creativity in philosophy. But Shestov departs from Nietzsche in several ways. In particular, Shestov rejects those aspects that inspired Nietzsche—the chorus in the Greek tragedy and the elements from Greek culture outside the classical tradition, namely Dionysian cults and the power of music. Cults were unacceptable to Shestov, since he rejected collective solutions to humanity's religious yearning. Furthermore, he rejected Nietzsche's "Myth of Eternal Return," considering it merely a juvenile escape from the dead-end of Greek logic.[32] In Nietzsche, then, Shestov selected a few suitable weapons for his war against logic, but surprisingly he resisted those others which were characteristic of Symbolist thought—music, collective irrationality, and eternal return—although he had been close to Symbolism in his early years.

In fact, criticism of classical Greece was unusual for Russian writers of Shestov's time, where a new respect for the ancient world pervaded a variety of cultural domains. In philosophy, Vladimir Solovyov valorized Socrates and Plato, borrowing from them for his ideas about love, predestination, and the source of knowledge. Vyacheslav Ivanov propagated the importance of tragedy and myth, while Innokenty Annensky wrote tragedies and poetry borrowing forms from classical Greek models. Furthermore, Russia's own religious attachment to the Byzantine tradition made Greece a locus of positive opinion, in spite of the fact that the Slavs eschewed the classical texts at least until the 17th century. Several important Russian writers, among them Fyodor Dostoevsky and Konstantin Leontyev, considered Russian Orthodoxy morally superior to Catholicism and saw the source for Orthodoxy's purity in its Byzantine origins.[33] Therefore, Shestov's criticisms of Greek thought were not widely shared or particularly appreciated.

Shestov's work was disrupted by the outbreak of World War I. In Switzerland he made efforts to return to his family in Russia and managed to relocate to Moscow in 1915. There he enjoyed the company of a close group of friends. In 1916, Evgenia Gertsyk gave this portrait of Shestov in her memoirs: "He is fifty years old. It seems to me that for the first time in his life he is happy, at ease, partakes of the peaceful pleasures of ideas, friendship, fame..."[34] In

---

[32] L. Shestov, *Afiny i Ierusalim*, in *Sochineniia v 2 tomakh*, ed. A. Akhutin (Moscow: Nauka, 1993), 1: 463.

[33] Florovsky expressed deep admiration for the Greek meditation pursued by the monks on Mount Athos, while Georgy Fedotov, for instance, considered the cultural treasures of Byzantium a vital progenitor of Russian religious life.

[34] Gertsyk, *Vospominaniia*, 112.

1917, however, he was devastated by the news that his son had been killed at the front.[35] Then the February Revolution occurred, and seven months later the Bolshevik putsch took place. Rumors circulated that Shestov was a Bolshevik supporter, but in fact the opposite was true. As with many intellectuals, Shestov was conscious of the injustices of the old order and understood the necessity for change, but deplored the violence of the Reds and the overwhelming craven egoism of the Whites.[36] He was especially horrified by the pogroms that took place in the Ukraine in 1919. Although he refrained from publicizing his opinions, in private letters he spoke of the "horrors of Bolshevism" and expressed confidence that the Russian people would be strong enough to "withstand" even this disruption and in time would "reestablish order and justice."[37] In 1919, Shestov left starving Moscow, going to Kiev where he was offered a teaching position. He only managed to stay one year before circumstances again forced his emigration.

The life of post-war Paris was in many ways a tragedy for Shestov, bringing new and unpleasant challenges. Perhaps the most central were the loss of wealth, prestige, and readership. No longer young, Shestov had to rebuild his life from scratch with neither the income from his father's store nor domestic servants. France in the 1920s was not extremely hospitable to émigrés, since the country was slow in repairing its economy. The difficult conditions adversely affected Shestov's livelihood, and instead of devoting himself to new writing exclusively, his first years in exile were spent in an active struggle for survival: gaining a permanent teaching assignment (he taught one course a year at the Sorbonne), having his earlier works translated into European languages, and selling those texts which he had written but not published during the war and revolutionary period.

His main intellectual task in these years was to locate a historical precedent for his ideas and to anchor his philosophy in a concrete religious tradition. At this time, Shestov discovered the ancient Jews and came to consider them as vivid illustrations of his idiosyncratic idea of religious faith. His admiration of images from the Old Testament may have made his philosophy more intelligible to a non-Russian audience, but it is equally possible that his use of Jewish history and biblical imagery reflects a reassessment of the importance of Judaism in his personal and professional life.

---

[35] His name was Sergei Shestov, the offspring of a relationship Shestov had had with a peasant woman in his youth. Information about him is scarce; see Gertsyk, *Vospominaniia*, 112–13.

[36] Shestov's anti-Bolshevik views were expressed in his book *Chto takoe russkii bol'shevizm*, which was destroyed by Evgeny Lundberg and which Shestov was later glad was not circulated. For more information on this, see M. Gershenzon, "Pis'ma k L'vu Shestovu," published by A. d'Amelia and V. Alloia, *Minuvshee* 6 (1988): 251.

[37] L. Shestov to F. I. Lovskaia in Baranova-Shestova, in Baranoff, *Zhizn' L'va Shestova*, 1: 156–57.

The significant role Judaism would come to play in his thinking is hinted at in a letter to his sister written in 1925 in response to her invitation that he lecture in Palestine. "It is difficult to tell you how glad I am to have the chance to visit Palestine and how grateful I am to you for all your efforts. I am even beginning to think that my trip will have a more serious meaning than it seemed to me earlier. But it is too early to speak about this—we will figure it out when I arrive."[38] Although it is impossible to know to what precisely Shestov is alluding, his desire to visit Palestine reveals a growing interest in Jewish matters.

His friend Aron Shteinberg describes a major transformation in Shestov's attitude toward his Jewish roots, but he puts the moment of conversion earlier, just before World War I.[39] In his memoirs Shteinberg puts the motivation for his "transformation" on antisemitism, claiming that "already from the time of the Kiev Beilis trial [1911–13], something occurred in Lev Isaakievich's [Shestov's] consciousness which forced him to glance back into his own 'Beginnings and Ends' and view himself as the continuation of Jerusalem's spiritual genealogy."[40]

The idea that Shestov's thought was strongly influenced by Judaism has its advocates in Berdyaev, Ivanov-Razumnik, Olga Forsh, and Evgenia Gertsyk.[41] In recent years, Vladimir Paperny has considered the importance of

---

[38] L. Shestov to E. I. Mandel'berg, 8 October 1925, in Baranoff, *Zhizn' L'va Shestova*, 1: 324. Shestov did not actually succeed in visiting Palestine until 1938.

[39] Aron Shteinberg was an eyewitness of events in late Imperial Russia and in the Russian emigration. He wrote memoirs about the major Symbolist writers and philosophers of the time, which were published as *Druz'ia moikh rannikh let: 1911–28*, ed. Georges Michel Nivat (Paris: Sintaksis, 1991), 217–65.

[40] Ibid., 237. "Beginnings and Ends" is a reference to Shestov's book, *Nachala i kontsy* (St. Petersburg: Tip. M. M. Stasiulevicha, 1908). The trial of the Jew Mendel Beilis, accused of killing a Russian Orthodox boy for ritual purposes, was a cause *célébre*, akin to the Dreyfus trial in France. After spending almost two years in prison, Beilis was acquitted by a jury and released.

[41] Ibid., 237. In his article "Lev Shestov i russkaia kul'tura," Vladimir Papernyi writes, "Many commentators ... have considered Shestov's philosophy in its entirety as an embodiment of some kind of Jewish skepticism, hostile to culture in general and to Russian culture in particular. Not having any objective basis (after all Shestov was not a skeptic and Judaism is not involved here), this viewpoint is nevertheless not entirely without sense, since it points to a pertinent issue. An entirely different explanation of the character of Shestov's 'Jewish element' was offered by N. A. Berdyaev, who knew Shestov well and understood him.... Berdyaev considered Shestov's way of thinking as a whole and his religious concept in particular as an appearance of 'Old-Testament Judaism.' Shestov did not profess the God-become-man, Christ; did not profess the idea of the presence within God of a human principle—the Logos; his religious consciousness did not know grace; and therefore he remained in the place where humanity was before the announcement of the 'Good News,' in the world of the Old Testa-

Judaism for Shestov, writing that "Shestov remains a mind in the spirit of the Midrash, in principle free from any kind of obligation and coercion ... having in the very structure of his personality the traits of a mentality characteristic of a traditional Jewish intellectual ethos, in spite of his extreme legalism."[42]

Similarly, Judith Deutsch Kornblatt regards Shestov's Jewish character as stemming from his knowledge of the Kabbalah. While locating an allusion to the Kabbalah in Shestov's interpretation of the exile from the Garden of Eden, she sees his philosophical endeavor as based on the metaphor of exile, a frequent position of the Jew in the modern world.[43]

Lacking direct evidence, we cannot know exactly what motivated Shestov's renewed appreciation of Jewish matters, but in the ancient Jews he certainly discovered a theoretical counterweight to, as well as a weapon for, his criticism of logic. For instance, in *The Power of the Keys: Potestas Clavium* (1923), between endless criticisms of rational thought, one finds passages that compare the futility of Greece with the living culture of the ancient Jews:

> How could it have happened that *lumen naturale*, which in the course of centuries was cultivated in the countries with Hellenistic education, suddenly appeared under the jurisdiction and disposal of ignorant Galilean carpenters and fishermen? The Greeks were convinced that reason not only can prove to them the existence of God, not only explain absolutely everything, but can also provide the very best that humanity can dream of. And they would have to agree to admit that *ratio naturalis*, which was inherent to them in the highest degree,

---

ment, i.e., in the stage preceding Christianity, the stage of a universal religious process." Papernyi, "Lev Shestov i russkaia kul'tura," in *Evrei v kul'ture russkogo zarubezh'ia: Sbornik statei, publikatsii, memuarov, i esse,* vyp. 2, ed. Mikhail Parkhomovskii (Jerusalem: n.p., 1993), 131.

[42] Ibid., 137. "The Midrash is the designation of a particular genre of rabbinic literature constituting an anthology and compilation of homilies, consisting of both biblical exegesis" and "commentary on those parts of the Bible which include narrative, history, ethical maxims, and the reproofs and consolations of the prophets." *Encyclopedia Judaica* (Jerusalem. Keter, 1972), 11: 1507. If one were to strike out the words "Bible" and "prophets" and substitute "philosophical texts" and "philosophers," perhaps Shestov's work would resemble a "Midrash" of philosophy—a hodgepodge of commentary, observations, questions, paradoxes, and thoughts.

[43] Kornblatt writes, "Shestov's interpretation of the biblical legend is entirely untraditional and not one scholar has so far revealed its source, although one can be satisfied with the observation that the philosopher knew the Kabbalistic tradition.... In this tradition 'the Fall' ontologically and historically precedes the story of paradise and is connected not with the exile of man from it, but with the exile of one of God's hypostates, Shekhinah, from the world." I. Kornblatt [Judith Deutsch Kornblatt], "Vechnyi zhid: Lev Shestov i russkaia religioznaia mysl'," in *Russkaia literatura XX veka: Issledovaniia amerikanskikh uchenykh,* ed. Sharlotta Rozental' [Charlotte Rosenthal] et al. (St. Petersburg: Petro-Rif, 1993), 51.

should bow before the Jewish *ratio supernaturalis*—"In the beginning was the word!"—that it did not belong to the Greeks, but to the Jews! And when the ignorant Jew cried from the abyss *(clamabat ex profundis)*, God answered him, but when the educated Greek reasoned, his philosophy led nowhere![44]

In Shestov's competition between the Jews and Greeks, the Jews are the clear winners. Despite their "ignorance," God hears their cry, while Greek philosophy leads "nowhere." Although the basic dichotomy of logic versus faith stays unchanged, Shestov points to the Jews as symbols of a positive relation between humanity and the deity. Nevertheless, as far as I can tell, Shestov had neither become a partisan advocate of Judaism, nor did he feel a personal link with the Jewish people. Rather it seems that he ceded to the ancient Jews concepts that were already fixed in his thought. That explains how, while speaking of the Jews, Shestov can include an allusion to Christ and the early Christians. He does not show preference for one religion over another, Judaism over Christianity. Rather, it is religion versus logic that is at issue. The Jews provided Shestov with a concrete historical precedent for his entirely modern ideas.

The attribution of existential faith to the ancient Jews finds its ultimate realization in *Afiny i Ierusalim*. In that work, Shestov reiterates all his main concerns: that religion and positivist philosophy are antithetical, that philosophy seeks logical proof, while religion depends solely on an individual's personal faith. As Shestov explains in the book's preface, "'Athens and Jerusalem,' 'religious philosophy'—these are almost equivalent expressions, overlapping each other and, nevertheless, equally mysterious, and exasperating contemporary thought by their internal contradiction. Would it not be more correct to pose the dilemma: Athens or Jerusalem, religion or philosophy."[45]

According to Shestov, the choice is between the God of the philosophers and the God of Abraham, Isaac, and Jacob, between "knowledge" and "the horrors of life." According to philosophy, the supernatural events that occur in the Bible could never have occurred. "The history of humanity, or rather, all the horrors of the history of humanity, according to the word of the Highest One, 'are annulled,' stop existing, are transformed into apparitions and mirages: Peter did not deny, David did not kill, Adam did not taste of the forbidden fruit, no one ever poisoned Socrates."[46] But miracles did occur in the Bible. In particular, the biblical heroes Abraham and Job exemplify Shes-

---

[44] L. Shestov, *Vlast' kliuchei: Potestas Clavium* (Berlin: Skythen Verlag, 1923), 24.

[45] Shestov, *Afiny i Ierusalim*, 317.

[46] Ibid., 334.

tov's ideal. Abraham, hearing and obeying God, offered his son Isaac for sacrifice, and through his faith, gained back his son. Job, too, in spite of having lost all his worldly possessions, continued to believe and was rewarded with a new family and fortune. Shestov portrays these individuals as spiritual heroes, emphasizing their boundless faith in God and their rejection of necessity as a limit to human experience.

From the Bible, Shestov also features the myth of the Fall. In reading the story of the exile from the Garden of Eden, Shestov emphasizes less God's punishment or the snake's temptation than Adam and Eve's choice: They could choose God who gives immortality and freedom, although under the single condition—"do not eat of the tree of knowledge"—or they could defy God. The purpose of this psychological emphasis is clear; the Fall should not be read as a story with an irreversible ending, but interpreted as a repeating parable about existential choice in the present. Eden is potentially accessible to each individual who must make his own decision in favor of God or in favor of reason. Thus, what would appear at first a symbol of human transgression is transformed into a timeless crossroad for renewing faith.

It is remarkable that at the same time Shestov began his investigations of the biblical Jews, other secular thinkers of Russian-Jewish backgrounds also returned to the subject. In the early 1920s, Shestov's friend Gershenzon wrote two monographs in which he uses the ancient Jews to illuminate his "cosmic philosophy." Moreover, in his 1923 collection of aphorisms "Solntse nad mgloi" ("The Sun Above the Darkness"), Gershenzon also reversed his negative attitude toward his own Jewish roots, viewing them as unambiguously positive.[47] A similar conversion occurred in the 1920s with the Russian-Jewish critic Akim Volynsky, who had always shown a preference for European culture, but who after the Revolution began to defend the superiority of Judaism in relation to Christianity.[48]

While the majority of Russian philosophers in exile sought to anchor their identity and philosophy in Orthodox Christianity, the close similarities between Gershenzon, Volynsky, and Shestov are unmistakable.[49] Although all three were entirely assimilated and had built their intellectual careers on non-

---

[47] The two monographs are *Sud'by evreiskogo naroda* (Moscow: Epokha, 1922) and *Kliuch very* (St. Petersburg: Epokha, 1922). "Solntse nad mgloi" can be found in *Zapiski mechtatelei*, no. 5 (1923): 90–107.

[48] See A. Volynskii, "Razryv s khristianstvom," *Zhizn'iskusstva*, no. 31 (1923): 5–14.

[49] Among Shestov's Russian friends in the emigration, the majority devoted themselves to the study of the Russian Orthodox Church. Berdyaev opened an Orthodox Christian Academy, while Lev Karsavin, Florovsky, and Sergei Bulgakov became ordained Orthodox priests and Frank and Il'in became theologically inclined thinkers. It is possible that the psychological motivations explaining their changes—the need to hold on to a Russian self-identity and the desire to possess a living tradition—had a parallel in Shestov's psyche, urging him to take up the theme of the Jews.

Jewish subjects, in the 1920s they sought to underscore the parallels between their ideas and the Jewish intellectual tradition to which they now claimed to belong. Although the ideological currents of Zionism and Jewish nationalism probably played a role in the change, another important source is perhaps the Bolshevik revolution, which overturned all the former values of European humanism. Left outside the values of the new world of Communism, it is possible that these intellectuals returned to the foundation of their Jewish identity, which long had been lying dormant.

While the heroes and stories of the Bible captivated Shestov, it is clear that the actual religion left him less enthusiastic. He did not reflect on the laws and the rituals of Judaism, the institution of the rabbinate and ignored the history of the Jewish people and the problem of "chosenness." In short, he accepted only those aspects consistent with his teaching—the miracles of the Bible and the individual images of stubborn allegiance to God.

While Shestov esteems the ancient Jews for believing in the impossible, they are not the sole embodiment of faith in human history. Shestov also presents select Christians—St. Paul, Tertullian, Augustine, the young Luther, Loyola, and Pascal—all come forth to defend faith.[50] In fact he devoted a major portion of *Sola Fide* to illuminating Luther's doctrine of justification by faith alone. He wrote a long article on Pascal entitled "The Night of Gethsemane," and in many of his works he employed the first-century theologian Tertullian as his mouthpiece.[51] His positive treatment of Christian theologians is revealing, since it exposes his lack of any exclusive preference for Judaism. Shestov's motives are perhaps understandable. By accepting both Judaism and Christianity, he maintained allegiance to the religion of his birth, yet was simultaneously free to employ Christianity's spiritual wealth.

For Shestov, the ancient Jews find their place primarily juxtaposed between Athens and Jerusalem, the struggle of faith against rational logic. In this core dichotomy, however, we confront the fundamental paradox of his use of the Jews: If revelation has its origins in the Judaic tradition, why did Shestov occupy himself with it less often than with the rational tradition stemming from ancient Greece? The absence of a clear answer to this question exposes the uncertain and incomplete nature of Shestov's relation to Judaism.

Part of the answer to this paradox can be found in the nature of his writing. It appears that Shestov could not accept revelation without struggle, and therefore he took up the fight against logic. Through engaging in philosophical inquiries, Shestov hoped to subvert philosophy, returning humanity its freedom. Yet in using his anti-philosophy to fight against logical philosophy,

---

[50] For the sake of illustration, in the abridged edition of Shestov's works, *Sochineniia* (1993), the index shows that Martin Luther is mentioned 49 times, Tertullian—22 times, and Augustine—54 times.

[51] See "Gefsimanskaia noch' (filosofiia Paskalia)," *Sovremennye zapiski*, no. 19 (March–June 1924), and no. 20 (July–September 1924); republished in *Sochineniia*, 2: 278–324.

Shestov fell into a paradox. Like Dostoevsky and Tolstoy earlier, Shestov apparently became a victim of his own "philosophy of tragedy." In attempting to overturn logic, his arguments inevitably turned negative, and the battle with positivism, to a marked degree, came to precede and define faith.

Looking back now, we can see that the basic elements of *Afiny i Ierusalim* were present in the early period of Shestov's literary career: the opposition of knowledge versus experience and logical philosophy versus a free search for personal values. From the start, he already had close at hand the opposition of logic and faith, an opposition gradually developing toward Athens and Jerusalem. By the end of his career he was able to frame his ideas in bold new terms by using the image of Athens and Jerusalem, thereby emphasizing the ancient origins and eternal character of the dichotomy of reason and faith.

**Chapter 14**

# Bringing Tidings to the Jews:
# Aron Shteinberg, Dostoevsky's Disciple

The subject "Dostoevsky and the Jews" can be conceived in the broadest way as touching on antisemitism in Russia from the middle of the 19th to the first quarter of the 20th centuries. For the most part, the question has been formulated as a conundrum: How could Jewish readers, such as Avram Kovner, Leonid Tsypkin, Leonid Grossman, Grigory Fridlender, and Pavel Kogan admire Dostoevsky the way they did? Were they self-hating Jews? Did they embrace Dostoevsky in order to gain acceptance in Russian culture? Surveying such Jewish admirers, certainly we need not forget the many Jews who criticized Dostoevsky's antisemitism. Arkady Gornfeld symbolizes them, writing in the *Evreiskaia entsiklopediia* from before World War I:[1]

> From the very beginning of "The Diary [of a Writer]" (*The Citizen*, 1873), at every convenient moment Dostoevsky pointed to the nefarious role of the Jews, first economic, then political and ideological. No serious evidence or original ideas are brought forth in his accusations; this is banal antisemitism, which undoubtedly attracts the reader with the extreme pathos of certitude that characterizes Dostoevsky's publicistic writings. Dostoevsky's antisemitism is especially terrible because it affects one's emotions and not one's mind.[1]

These two poles of adoration and antipathy are well enough known. I would like to outline yet a third category designating those who neither valorized Dostoevsky's attitudes on Russian national culture nor denigrated them, but nonetheless looked to Dostoevsky as an inspiration in the construction of their own specifically Jewish perspectives on contemporary problems. For example, Dostoevsky haunted the Hebrew writer and Zionist Yosef Brenner, who translated him into Hebrew and for whom Dostoevsky defined the best in literary style. One can also look to Lev Shestov, Albert Camus, Martin Buber, or Emmanuel Levinas as other examples.

Aron Shteinberg (1891–1975), Russian-Jewish thinker, émigré, and civic leader, provides a striking example of a writer who was strongly influenced

---

[1] *Evreiskaia entsiklopediia*, s.v. "Dostoevskii, Feodor Mikhailovich" (by A. Gornfel'd), 7: 311.

in his understanding of Judaism by none other than Dostoevsky. Shteinberg employed his ideas to formulate definitions of Jewish national unity, religious epiphany, and the meaning of history.

An original member of the Free Philosophical Society, Volfil, which he organized with Andrei Bely and Ivanov-Razumnik in the days after the Bolshevik Revolution, Shteinberg became an important figure in Petersburg in the short spell between 1917 and 1922. Born in Daugavpils (Dvinsk), in what is present-day Latvia, in a religious family, Shteinberg was educated in a traditional Jewish *heder* and then Russian schools. Like many Jews of the time, the *numerus clausus* forced him to earn his university degree in Western Europe. He graduated from the University of Heidelberg with a Ph.D. in Philosophy at the age of 22. In 1912, soon after returning to Russia, he began writing articles on philosophy for the venerable thick journal *Russkaia mysl'*. Like others of his generation, he watched his world shatter under Bolshevik rule; he fled Soviet Russia in 1922.

In Berlin, Shteinberg involved himself in Jewish life. Spending the interwar years translating the work of Simon Dubnov, the Russian-Jewish historian, into German, Shteinberg also served as an editor of the English-language *Jewish Encyclopedia* and wrote numerous articles on Jewish theology and history. Making London his home, he became a leader of the World Jewish Congress, ultimately becoming its representative to UNESCO. During his life he published three books on Dostoevsky: *Sistema svobody Dostoevskogo* (1923); a play, *Dostoevskii v Londone: Povest' v chetyrekh aktakh* (1932); and a work of literary criticism in English simply entitled *Dostoievsky* (1960).

In order to make sense of Shteinberg's own philosophical oeuvre, one has to realize that he was a final representative, almost an epigone, of Russia's Silver Age, preserving its values and intellectual premises into the 1920s and beyond. Like other fin-de-siècle humanists, Shteinberg showed an indifference to disciplinary boundaries, refraining from making distinctions between philosophy, creative literature, and criticism, viewing all intellectual endeavors as an exploration of man's spiritual dimension or metaphysics. Like many others of his generation, his fascination with art was accompanied by a lack of interest in practical politics: Shteinberg personally experienced Russia's short experiment with democracy and turn to Communism, and the destabilization of democracy in post-World War I Germany and the rise of totalitarianism there.

To get an impression of Shteinberg's perspective on Dostoevsky, I turn to *Sistema svobody F. M. Dostoevskogo*, which is based on two lectures that Shteinberg gave under the auspices of Volfil in 1922. According to Shteinberg, Dostoevsky is an epistemologist, a unique thinker, who connected the dimension of eternity and pure spirit with the ontological reality of a concrete individual.

In fact, Dostoevsky linked the abstract and the particular through the idea of all-unity, which serves as a bridge between such realms. "How should one tackle this problem, to approach working it out? What does it mean to 'systematize Dostoevsky' in Rozanov's expression? Where are the objective criteria for such treatment? In order to answer these questions, one has to be aware of the central logical and ontological purpose of the whole system, the metaphysical cell out of which the whole organism develops: this cell is the idea. 'That is why philosophers say that the essence of things cannot be perceived in the world' (XII, 381). Kant's philosophy does not contradict Zosima's philosophy; both of them are Platonists, as is Dostoevsky."[2]

According to Shteinberg, Dostoevsky believes in a world of ideas in which the idea itself has its own ontological existence, an ideal form, but also exists in Kantian terms as a category of human reason. The definition of this nexus of abstract and concrete he calls "the system of freedom."

Though it seems paradoxical to say, Shteinberg holds that Dostoevsky's own philosophy can be fully identified with Russia so that Dostoevsky can be seen as a mirror of the depths of Russia. "Russian and Dostoevsky, Dostoevsky and Russia—like a question and an answer, like an answer and a question. Dostoevsky can only be measured with Russia and Russia with Dostoevsky. To understand Dostoevsky is the same as understanding Russia; understanding Russia is the same as experiencing it through Dostoevsky's mind. In his system of freedom the Russian intellectual orientation appeared for the first time as a concrete individual entity, as born of the human spirit, and therefore at one with human spirit."[3]

Dostoevsky symbolizes an epistemology of otherworldliness and idealism that is not fully explicated, but is left a mystery. Shteinberg maintains that the absolute metaphysical system is not accessible to the human mind. In another place he identifies "logic" and the "teaching of the logos" as one.[4] He speaks of a system of systems, comparing Dostoevsky to a conductor of an orchestra who turns his back on the audience and leads the voices of mankind.[5] In this embodiment, Dostoevsky represents all-unity, all-possibilities, all-thought, and all-experience.

Attributing the ideas of Kant and Plato to Dostoevsky may try one's patience at times, especially when Shteinberg ascribes to the characters from the novels, Stavrogin, Myshkin, Alesha, and Kirillov, the role of emblems of abstract ideas. While much of his discussion has little to offer a person who wants to elucidate Dostoevsky's texts as literature, one can note that Shteinberg's philosophical readings gloss over the problem of antisemitism. His

---

[2] A. Shteinberg, *Sistema svobody F. M. Dostoevskogo* (Berlin: Skify, 1923; repr., Paris: YMCA-Press, 1980), 30.

[3] Ibid., 10.

[4] Ibid., 32.

[5] Ibid., 35.

comparisons of Dostoevsky to Plato and Kant preclude any extensive treatment of Dostoevsky the man.

Thus, it may come as a surprise that Shteinberg does not ignore expressions of antisemitism among his contemporaries. In fact, as a young man he personally confronted Russia's leading writers, discussing Jewish issues with Bryusov, Bely, Rozanov, Shestov, Gorky, and others. A collection of his memoirs was published posthumously in 1991 as *Druz'ia moikh rannikh let* (1911–28) by Sintaksis in Paris, with an introduction by George Niva.

For example, during the Mendel Beilis trial Shteinberg phoned Vasily Rozanov, asking to meet. Arriving at the writer's home, Shteinberg only gradually realized that he had been invited to dinner with the whole family. Nevertheless, the soirée turned bad when Rozanov screamed out that he believed in ritual murder. In response, Shteinberg left after attempting to explain that Jews have an aversion to blood and cannot eat meat from which blood has not been drained. Later, however, he formulated a better explanation that he entered into his memoirs:

> Vasily Vasil'evich have you ever heard about such a movement as Zionism? In Petersburg their weekly journal, *Sionistskii rassvet*, comes out. Take a look at it and you will see that it is full of criticism of Judaism in the Diaspora. You say that Jews need the murder of Christian boys in order to unite themselves in the Diaspora, but Zionists say that they need to revive their holy land with its capital in Jerusalem and that for as long as it is not revived, Jews are threatened with danger.[6]

While prepared to do battle with Rozanov and Aleksandr Blok, paradoxically, Shteinberg was indulgent toward Dostoevsky. In his article "Dostoevsky i evrei" (1928), Shteinberg argues that by equating the great writer's antisemitism with the common species, the critics have misunderstood. Shteinberg notes:

> Could it be that the presence of the "ordinary" amidst the "extraordinary" is less original and mysterious than anything acknowledged as out of the ordinary? Or was Dostoevsky not such a thoroughly "distinctive" genius, as he sometimes referred to himself, whose imprint must lie on all aspects of his life without exception? Does not the very banality of Dostoevsky's attitude towards the Jews indicate some insurmountable feature in the fate of the Jewish people, something portentous in its most significant historical encounters and confrontations?[7]

---

[6] Shteinberg, *Druz'ia moikh rannikh let*, 167–68.

[7] A. Shteinberg, *History as Experience: Aspects of Historical Thought — Universal and Jewish. Selected Essays and Studies* (New York: Ktav, 1983), 247.

Despite using a tone that raises the reader's expectations of some kind of new and final explanation for Dostoevsky's anti-Semitism, Shteinberg repeats the conventional argument that as a prophetic thinker Dostoevsky despised Jews because they occupied the messianic role that he wanted for the Russians.[8]

Shteinberg's attitude toward Dostoevsky has two dimensions. Shteinberg attempted to defend Dostoevsky against accusations of antisemitism, while co-opting him to formulate his own philosophy and especially those aspects that pivot around Judaism. In a lecture written for the London P.E.N. Club, and published in 1944, "The Jewish Scale of Values," Shteinberg expresses a dichotomy of good and evil that everyone will recognize as Dostoevskian.

> For there is yet another alternative, apart from holiness, to the point of moral indifference, namely-unholiness, and it is, I believe, essential for the Jewish scale of values, that it points not only upwards to the highest possible degree of human achievement in the service and emulation of the divine Spirit, but also the bottomless abyss of human depravity and wickedness.

I think that you will agree that Father Zosima or Prince Myshkin could have uttered these words. The image of a vertical line between good and evil, from the top to the depths, and the individual who stands before a moral choice, reverberates with Dostoevskian cosmology.

I also hear Dostoevskian overtones in Shteinberg's attack on historical thought, which he identifies with Ernst Dilthei or R. G. Collingwood, i.e., the idea that all of man's values are relative in nature and subject to change because they are inextricably connected to the constraints of historical experience. Shteinberg leaps up in defense of timeless idealism, writing:

> Can it be reversed? It appears that to this end it would first be necessary to reestablish the principle that man's mind is commensurable with the idea of the absolute. With the reaffirmation of the relationship between the individual human being and the absolute, a limit would be set both to the dependence of man on the ever-changing conditions of historical life and to the senseless ambition of fellowmen arbitrarily to determine the meaning of personal existence. In consequence, philosophy of history would lose its disproportionate influence, and the unhealthy excess of the general interest in historical findings (which, incidentally, can never be final) would disappear. A regenerated idealistic tradition would help to restore to Historical

---

[8] Ibid., 258–59.

Man that humbleness of mind without which there can be no genuine step forward along the road to freedom.[9]

Those words were written in 1958, after the Holocaust, and perhaps in response to it. But if one envisions a Hitler as the villain of choice to the phrase—"senseless ambition to determine the meaning of personal existence,"—one can also imagine Raskolnikov. Here Shteinberg's struggle parallels Dostoevsky's. We find the same dualities of relativism versus eternal truth, historical time versus redemptive time, while the desire to see man as linked to the supra-human or divine tugs at the sleeve of both men.

Another example of Dostoevsky's influence is Shteinberg's conception that Judaism developed by absorbing other cultures. This perspective has parallels with Dostoevsky's "Pushkin Speech" of 1880. Shteinberg writes, "[J]ewish religious thinkers very early felt free to seek in the holy text meanings to satisfy their own spiritual needs, and to interpret them in accordance with reason. It was this attitude which enabled the orthodox [Jewish] seeker after knowledge to accept, in principle, the influence of foreign metaphysical fundamentals—whether formulated by the Greek Plato, the Arabian ibn Roshd or the German Kant—and so to assimilate them so that they eventually became an organic part of the Jewish outlook on life."[10] Just as Russia was the most European because it alone was capable of absorbing and reflecting every culture, so too Judaism became enriched through absorbing the best of Greek, Arabic, and European thought.

While there is nothing obviously un-Jewish in Shteinberg's views, they are not entirely mainstream either. In particular, the idea of morality as depicted especially as a vertical ladder with evil at the bottom and goodness at the top seems more likely to come from Christianity.

Of course the claim is undeniable that Shteinberg perceived Dostoevsky through the lens of Vladimir Solovyov and not only his. By the time that Shteinberg arrived at his Dostoevsky-neo-Platonist, Fyodor Mikhailovich had been subjected to a number of metamorphoses: Merezhkovsky's Dostoevsky, Viacheslav Ivanov's, Shestov's, and of course Nietzsche's. To them, he added his own Dostoevsky, who in a sense was philosemitic, since Dostoevsky taught Shteinberg how to think about the Jewish religion, the absolute as a concept and the means of spiritual redemption.

One is left nevertheless wondering how Shteinberg could be blind to the fact that Dostoevsky, a public figure capable of commanding huge audiences and known for his moral strivings, could indict the Jews for collective felonies. While it would be impossible to gauge the effect of Dostoevsky's writings, one can presume that they hurt real people, and that they contributed to the development of a callous attitude toward Jews in his own time and after.

---

[9] Ibid., 116.

[10] Ibid., 185.

If Shteinberg deals with the problem of suffering caused by Dostoevsky at all, it is in his drama of 1932, *Dostoevskii v Londone*, in which he depicts the writer's self-mutilation. In the first two acts, Dostoevsky finds himself in the company of the socialist luminaries of the mid-19th century, Herzen and Ferdinand Lasalle, accompanied by Natalia, Herzen's wife, and Dostoevsky's own mistress, Polina Suslova. Ultimately, Dostoevsky has a fit of madness, insults Lassalle, who refuses to fight Dostoevsky in a duel because he does not consider Dostoevsky a real gentleman, although Lassalle himself is a Jew. In the last two acts, Dostoevsky is in a grimy tavern, where he comes to the aid of a girl whose boyfriend has been thrown out and who is forced to sing for the guests. In the face of his effort to do good by defending the girl, however, it turns out that she is the owner's daughter. Moreover, everyone tells the writer to get out and go back to Russia. Dostoevsky suffers a great deal from both incidents. Like Leonid Tsypkin, who turns Dostoevsky into a Jew in order to have him experience the pain inflicted by discrimination—this time on him a Russian émigré—this Dostoevsky too is shown as the "other," demeaned, oppressed, and humiliated. I cannot tell whether this drama was written in some way to exonerate Dostoevsky; nonetheless, the pitiful writer is contrasted with the wealthy and easy-going socialists and also the self-satisfied English factory workers.

Despite the fact that many Jews condemn Dostoevsky for his anti-Jewish expressions, a number of major Jewish writers have appropriated Dostoevsky for the enrichment of Jewish thought. Aron Shteinberg is just one. In fact, a small monograph on that subject could be written that would include Yosef Brenner, Buber, Levinas, Shestov, and, of course, Shteinberg too.

# Chapter 15

## Sticking it to the Tsar: Jacob Schiff, Herman Rosenthal, and the American Fight against Tsarist Persecution of Jews

After the Kishinev pogrom occurred on April 6–8, 1903, the Russian government tried to manage the international reaction by pretending that nothing serious had happened.[1] The Minister of the Interior, Vyacheslav Plehve, apparently succeeded in convincing the U.S. Ambassador of his point of view. In New York, by contrast, the cover-up attempt infuriated Herman Rosenthal, a leading American intellectual and head of the Slavonic Division of the New York Public Library. He expressed his displeasure to Jacob Schiff, the banker and well-known defender of American-Jewish interests:

> You have always taken a deep interest in matters which concern humanity at large, and you have by word and deed extended your sympathy to the helpless Jews of Russia in the time of need. And at this time, when the whole world is horror-struck at a great crime against humanity, I wish to call your attention to some facts bearing directly on the recent massacres of the Jews in Kishinev.
>
> I was an eye witness of the anti-Jewish riots in South Russia in 1881, and I knew from evidence historically authenticated that those riots were inspired by Russian officials guided by the Minister of the Interior, Count Ignatyev; none the less I hesitated to express my suspicions as to the real cause of the deplorable events in Kishinev, although I had intimation of it from private communications received from Russia. I wanted to see the columns of the Russian press which, to put it mildly, is very conservative in reporting or commenting on events that are apt to reflect on the Russian government. Now, with these very conservative statements of the Russian Jewish and non-Jewish press at hand, and the unvarnished facts staring one in the face, one cannot help crying out in anguish at such unpardonable offense against justice and humanity.
>
> On reading of Secretary Hay's instructions to our Ambassador to Russia to inquire at the foreign office about the events in Kishinev I had hoped that he would at least inform our government as to the

---

[1] A fine study of the pogrom can be found in Edward H. Judge, *Easter in Kishinev: Anatomy of a Pogrom* (New York: New York University Press, 1992).

true state of affairs. I was sadly disappointed when I read the reply
given him by the foreign office "that the situation was well controlled, and that there was no need of supplies for which funds were
being collected in the United States." This was dated May 9th, and if
Mr. McCormick had taken the trouble to look over the newspapers
*Novosti, Novoe Vremia, Sankt-Peterburgskie Vedomosti,* published in St.
Petersburg on the 29th, 30th, and 31st of April, he could not help
seeing the list of names of the 41 Jews killed and the appeal for help
issued by the Mayor of Kishinev, Mr. K. Schmidt, and by the Wom-
en's Committee of the Red Cross Society; as well as the list of contributors, Jewish and non-Jewish, published in *Voskhod* and *Budushchnost'.* These appeals were issued with the sanction of the Governor of
Bessarabia, for no appeal in Russia may be issued without the sanction of the government. It seems hardly possible that Mr. McCormick
should have allowed himself to be misled so easily by the officials of
the foreign office, when the very air is full of the echoes of a great
calamity. The effect of the catastrophe was felt on the stock exchange
and prices dropped when the government officials' reports of the
massacres were published; as may be seen in *Promyshlennyi Mir* (The
Industrial World) of April 29th.[2]

With Schiff's encouragement, Rosenthal published documents regarding
Kishinev in English translation in the *American Hebrew,* a weekly published in
New York.[3]

Schiff was equally indignant and quickly gathered money and aid for the
victims of the pogrom.[4] Simultaneously Schiff took an instrumental role in
preparing a petition that was sent by the B'nai B'rith organization to President Theodore Roosevelt for further forwarding to Tsar Nicholas II.[5] Couched
in "respectful language," it "called upon the tsar to prevent future pogroms
and proclaim religious liberty for all his subjects."[6] Twelve thousand individuals signed it, including many prominent politicians, civic leaders, and members of the business elite. At Roosevelt's request it was sent to Petersburg,
where, nonetheless, the Russian government refused to accept it. Although
the petition did not lead to any concrete action, it indicated nonetheless that

---

[2] H. Rosenthal to J. Schiff, May 19, 1903, located in the H. Rosenthal Archive. For an
analysis of the Russian press, see Judge, *Easter in Kishinev,* 76–84.

[3] *The American Hebrew: The National Weekly of Jewish Affairs* started appearing in 1879.

[4] Schiff was aided in his efforts by Oscar Straus and Cyrus L. Sulzberger. Cyrus Adler,
*Jacob H. Schiff, His Life and Letters,* 2 vols. (New York: Doubleday, Doran And Company, Inc., 1929), 2: 160.

[5] On B'nai B'rith, see Hasia R. Diner, *The Jews of the United States, 1654 to 2000* (Berkeley: University of California Press, 2004), 191.

[6] Judge, *Easter in Kishinev,* 90.

many Americans, and especially the American-Jewish elite, were prepared to use the arm of the U.S. government to protest injustices committed against Jews abroad.

In the coming years, with Jacob Schiff's help, Rosenthal would publicize the evils of the Russian government, inciting indignation against tsarist policies.[7] At the same time, Schiff strove to injure Russia by impeding her ability to float loans on the international investment markets.[8] Both these activities worked in tandem and had two main aims: by revealing the evils of the tsarist government, Rosenthal and Schiff justified the U.S.'s open immigration policy. At the same time they blunted antisemitic attacks against new immigrants by focusing attention on the immigrants' sufferings in their home country. During the first decade of the 20th century, on-going debates took place regarding support for immigration, the qualities of the immigrants, and tolerance for different religions, ethnicities, and races within America itself.[9]

But there was still another reason for their sensitivity to tsarist policy. Both Schiff and Rosenthal felt an evil was taking place and that it was the responsibility of those capable of stopping it to do so. According to Naomi Cohen, Schiff's hostility to the Russian government "developed over time into an all-consuming passion and was prompted by motives far deeper than any wish to be freed of responsibilities for victims or immigrants." Cohen maintains, "The banker repeatedly drew analogies between the Russian situation and the biblical story of the Jews in Egypt; subconsciously, he doubtless saw himself as another Moses."[10]

By bringing attention to Kishinev, Schiff and Rosenthal portrayed themselves not just as Jews who cared about their brethren abroad, but also as self-confident Americans entitled to demand better treatment for them. This attitude points to the promises of the progressive era in American life, when immigrants, imbued with the promises of the American dream, began to feel confident that their citizenship in the republic was beyond question and that patriotic duty motivated them to demand that U.S. foreign policy be formulated according to the same moral principles that guided governance of the republic itself.[11]

---

[7] It is worth noting that in the 1890s Schiff encouraged other writers to publicize the injustices of the tsarist regime. See Adler, *Jacob H. Schiff, His Life and Letters*, 2: 115.

[8] Ibid., 2: 123.

[9] Diner, *The Jews of the United States*, 173–74.

[10] Naomi W. Cohen, *Jacob H. Schiff: A Study in American Jewish Leadership* (Hanover, NH: University Press of New England / Brandeis University Press, 1999), 124.

[11] Naomi W. Cohen, "The Ethnic Catalyst: The Impact of the East European Immigration on the American Jewish Establishment," in *The Legacy of Jewish Migration: 1881 and Its Impact*, ed. David Berger (New York: Brooklyn College Press, 1983), 134.

Both these men were part of the German-Jewish elite of the pre-World War I era.[12] Schiff was the leading Jewish *parnas* or notable of his day. He saw his mission in using his huge wealth and influence to help the Jewish masses, but viewed himself as superior to his charges by virtue of his German cultural heritage. Indeed, an essential aspect of the *parnas* is his engagement behind the scenes, in private. Schiff gave money and asked his friends to do the same on behalf of Jewish hospitals, schools, and programs to train artisans.[13] As a traditional philanthropist, he provided grants to individuals of talent and those in destitution. He became seen as the main Jewish leader in New York City and perhaps the entire country. Appointed by the city's mayor to a number of civic positions and called to arbitrate among employers and workers, he was summoned to Congress and met with the president many times.[14]

At the same time, by the first decade of the 20th century, Schiff understood the limits of the individual philanthropist, however well meaning and wealthy. He played an important role in developing the B'nai B'rith organization in 1896 and was instrumental in organizing the American Jewish Committee in 1906, which had as its goal to speak as one powerful voice in defense of Jews harmed by antisemitism. At a time of intense democratization of all aspects of life in America, it made pragmatic sense for Schiff to subsume some of his activity in collective organizations, where his goals could have greater leverage by representing larger numbers of people.

One might view Rosenthal as Schiff's disciple. In business and philanthropy Schiff did indeed employ a number of men who played essential roles in executing projects and dealing with details. However, Rosenthal was not Schiff's underling but an initiator of projects in his own right; it was only coincidence that his political agenda paralleled Schiff's own. To be sure, in his career as a leader of Jewish agricultural colonies in the United States, Rosenthal had made himself useful to notables, but he also understood the power of public opinion in a democracy. His use of print media to influence government policy reflects a break from traditional *shtadlanut*.

In the case of both these men, their deaths coincided with the end of an epoch. Both Schiff and Rosenthal died during or soon after World War I. In some ways the world in which they acted no longer existed, while in other ways their goals came to fruition in the next era.

The story of the collaboration of these two men deserves attention because it has been omitted from the historical record. For example, not one of the books on Jacob Schiff contains a reference to Herman Rosenthal.[15] Moreover, despite Rosenthal's numerous achievements, only his engagement with

---

[12] Cohen, *Jacob H. Schiff*, 41.

[13] Adler, *Jacob H. Schiff, His Life and Letters*, 1: 369–92.

[14] Ibid., 111–14.

[15] Schiff is not mentioned in Adler's *Jacob H. Schiff, His Life and Letters* nor in Naomi Cohen's biography.

Jewish agricultural colonies has received scholarly attention.[16] Although Schiff's views on Russia and Zionism have received treatment in other places, nonetheless, Rosenthal's contributions deserve proper illumination. Rosenthal's knowledge of conditions in Russia and his effective activity as a writer attracted Schiff, who lent help, enabling Rosenthal to publish two books and many articles critical of the tsarist government. The collaboration of these two individuals reflects important issues regarding American-Jewish identity, Jewish leadership, and American-Russian relations.

Jacob Schiff came to the United States from Frankfurt as a young man in the 1870s and single-handedly expanded the banking and investment firm Kuhn & Loeb, making it the second largest in the country, surpassed only by J. P. Morgan. In addition to his business and philanthropic concerns, Schiff was deeply worried that massive Jewish immigration from Russia would spark a rise in antisemitism. This led him to support attempts to settle Jews more evenly throughout the country, such as the Galveston project.[17] Convinced that Jews were leaving Russia as the result of oppression, Schiff committed himself to act to modify the tsarist government's behavior. Concretely, having refused to provide loans to Russia, he had also worked hard to convince the banking community in the United States to refrain from lending money. But he promised to remove his block if the tsarist government would end its anti-Jewish discrimination.

Herman Rosenthal was born in Friedrichstadt, Courland (present-day Latvia) to a well-to-do Jewish family. Educated in a secular school, in his youth Rosenthal left for Kiev, where he worked as a bookbinder.[18] In the 1870s, he helped establish and then edit the liberal newspaper *Zaria*. This paper reflected the views of a growing bourgeoisie, which hoped to transform the autocratic government into a liberal democracy through the participation of civil society. As government and social antisemitism heated up in Russia, Rosenthal became interested in post-liberal solutions, such as the Am-Olam [Jewish agriculture] movement.[19]

---

[16] See the article "Herman Rosenthal (1843–1917)," *Encyclopedia Judaica* (New York: Ktar, 1972), 14: 293.

[17] Cohen, *Jacob H. Schiff*, 121–22.

[18] For a biography of Rosenthal, see "Rosenthal, Herman," *The Jewish Encyclopedia: A Descriptive Record of the History, Religion, Literature, and Customs of the Jewish People from the Earliest Times to the Present Day* (New York and London: Funk and Wagnals Co., 1905), 10: 479–80.

[19] A. Menes, "Di 'Am Olam' Bavegung," in *Geshikhte fun der Yidisher Arbeter Bavegung in di Fareynikte Shtatn*, ed. Elias Cherikover (New York: YIVO, 1943–45), 2: 223–27.

By the middle of 1881, he arrived in the United States, hoping to create a Jewish agricultural colony in Sicily, Louisiana.[20] After that endeavor failed, Rosenthal held a number of positions, including head statistician for the Edison Corporation, director for the reception of new immigrants at Ellis Island, and head of the Slavonic Division of the New York Public Library, Astor Branch. Although Rosenthal had his origins in the Russian Empire, nonetheless he did not fit the definition of backward or pious Jew, being a native speaker of German whose cultural pretensions made him the antithesis of the shtetl Jew. He was an accomplished poet and scholar, a civic leader accustomed to interaction with the wealthy and powerful.

The personal archive of Herman Rosenthal, located in the Rare Books Division of the New York Public Library (5th Avenue and 42nd Street), holds 23 letters from Jacob Schiff, written between 1889 and 1912.[21] The letters deal with two main themes: in the 1890s, Rosenthal looked to Schiff for assistance in locating suitable employment, while a decade later Rosenthal wanted help in publicizing the oppressive policies of the Russian government. Finally, in a single isolated letter from 1904, Schiff explicates the reasons for his negative attitude toward Zionism. The two men remained friends until Rosenthal's death in 1917.

They may have met initially during the organization of the Woodbine Jewish Agricultural Colony, which lasted from 1891 to 1893. While Schiff was a patron, contributing his own money and administering the funds of the Jewish Colonization Association, Rosenthal was employed to choose the members of the colony. In addition, Rosenthal was also on the payroll of the Jewish Colonization Association for his work as the editor of the Yiddish newspaper *Der Yiddishe Fermer* (The Jewish Farmer).[22] After Woodbine's failure, Rosenthal was out of work and apparently turned to Schiff for help. Although Schiff refused to write—he claimed that if he started to recommend individuals to government officials there would be no end to it and his word would lose its luster—Rosenthal was directed to James Hill, a railroad executive and one of Schiff's friends. Rosenthal wrote him on July 13, 1893:

> Acting on the advice of Mr. Schiff, permit me to ask you, whether you would still extend me your influence in securing a U. S. Consulship in

---

[20] Uri D. Herscher, *Jewish Agricultural Utopias in America, 1880–1910* (Detroit: Wayne State University Press, 1981), 32.

[21] I would like to acknowledge my gratitude to Edward Kasinec, the present-day Director of the Slavonic Division of the New York Public Library, for drawing my attention to these resources.

[22] The first issue came out in November 1891 and cost two cents. The editorial offices were located at 205 Henry Street in New York City, the offices of the Baron De Hirsch Committee. Translations of the *Jewish Farmer* can be found in Uri Herscher's article, "Herman Rosenthal—The Jewish Farmer," *Mikha'el: Me'asef le-toldot ha-Yehudim be-tefutsot*, no. 3 (1975): 59–87.

Japan or China, as you yourself kindly suggested to me during my last stay at St. Paul. At that time I had some doubts as to my fitness for such a position, but after studying up the matter I have consulted Mr. Schiff and some other friends, who are thorough acquainted with the duties of a U. S. consul and who also know my abilities, and I am now convinced, that I could fill the position and be of some service in our commercial relations in the far East.[23]

Although Jacob Seligman, one of Schiff's business partners, wrote to President William McKinley directly, Rosenthal was not assigned to an overseas post, despite the fact that only a few years before he had traveled throughout Asia to gauge the potential for American investments in railroads.[24]

Although Schiff was likely aware of and perhaps even helped bring about Rosenthal's appointment as head of the newly created Slavonic Division, the two did not have any extended interaction until 1903, when Rosenthal contacted Schiff about the Kishinev pogrom.[25] In a letter to President Roosevelt in support of the above-mentioned petition regarding Kishinev, Schiff repeated Rosenthal's arguments that such a message should not be regarded as unlawful interference in the internal affairs of a sovereign country because the legal liabilities and violence against Jews were driving massive numbers to America's shores.[26] Because it had to take responsibility and pay the expense of integrating the arrivals, the American government was entitled to examine the causes of massive immigration. Rosenthal for his part was not satisfied with such pragmatic considerations, arguing for a moral response and intervention, coming into conflict with the international norms of the time.

---

[23] In a July 11, 1898 letter Schiff writes, "I have your letter of the 8th inst., and should indeed be very glad to be of advantage to you in the way you desire, had I not, once for all, had to establish the rule, not to write letters in behalf of anyone to the President or members of the administration. These requests, as you can imagine, come to me so frequently and sometimes from such intimate friends, that, but for this rule which I have made, I should be compelled to write letters of endorsement almost daily, and the expression of my good opinion about anyone would thus, in itself, become of little value."

[24] Herman Rosenthal, *Report on Japan, Corea and China* (St. Paul, 1893).

[25] Information about Rosenthal's activity in the Public Library can be gleaned from Robert H. Davis, "Slavic and Baltic Library Resources at the New York Public Library," *Canadian-American Slavic Studies* 29: 1–2 (Spring–Summer 1995): 9; and Edward Kasinec and Robert H. Davis, Jr., "Afterword: Collecting Slavica at the New York Public Library," in *Russia Engages the World, 1453–1825*, ed. C. H. Whittaker (Cambridge, MA: Harvard University Press, 2003), 167.

[26] Adler, *Jacob H. Schiff, His Life and Letters*, 2: 147–48.

Mere respect for international usage is not a sufficient excuse for enlightened nations to shrink from a duty which is clearly theirs. Considerations of far greater moment and of great concern to the world at
large, should impel them to utter a stern warning in the name of
Righteousness.... To Christian civilization of our day, after all the
striving and struggling for better things, for Justice and Truth above
all things, is it to stand idly by and see a great crime scarcely paralleled since the darkest days of the Inquisition committed without a
word of protest? Is it not the duty of the United States, which of all
countries has ever stood for what is noblest and best in all mankind to
do all that can be done in the matter?[27]

Rosenthal was ahead of his time in giving greater weight to moral rectitude
than security or economic advantage in affairs between sovereign states. In
addition to lofty and abstract aims, nonetheless both men also had down-to-
earth concerns. Trying to shame the tsarist government into treating its Jews
better, both men wanted to shore up public support for unlimited immigration from Russia, support that at times flagged under an increase in antisemitism and economic and political pressures.[28]

Rosenthal took the initiative to punish the Russian government in the
court of public opinion. Undertaking to translate from German Hugo Ganz's
The Land of Riddles (Russia of Today), which appeared with Harper and Brothers in 1904, Rosenthal hoped to turn Americans against the Russian government. In this book Ganz, an Austrian journalist of liberal bent, described a
recent visit to Russia, relating first-hand what he saw there. He spoke of the
intense police control over society, the excesses of an uncontrolled bureaucracy, the tsar's personal paranoia, and the use of the Jews as scapegoats for
the government's administrative failures. Transmitting the frustration of ordinary Russians, peasants, lawyers, intellectuals, students, and socialists, Ganz
concluded that the full blame for ruining Russia fell on its government.

This was a message that fully coincided with Rosenthal's views and
suited Schiff in his position to side with Japan in its conflict with Russia in
1904.[29] According to Schiff, good people everywhere should support the Japanese in their defensive war against the aggressor, Russia.[30] Rosenthal's preface to his English translation underscores the political context. It is important
to remember that Japan was not the American favorite during the Russo-

---

[27] H. Rosenthal to J. Schiff, 19 May 1903, Herman Rosenthal Archive, Rare Books Division, New York Public Library.

[28] Oscar Handlin, "American Views of the Jew at the Opening of the Twentieth Century," in Anti-Semitism in America, ed. Jeffrey S. Gurock, 2 vols. (New York: Routledge,
1998), 1: 187–92.

[29] Cohen, Jacob H. Schiff, 34.

[30] Ibid., 35.

Japanese War, since the public felt threatened by the dangers of the "yellow peril," an Asia rising in power and influence.[31] According to Rosenthal, the public should reverse its views of Russia, since she does not act like a European nation. "Were not the reputation of the author and the standard of his informants alike absolutely above suspicion, it would seem incredible that such conditions as those depicted could exist in the twentieth century in a country claiming a place among civilized nations. Indeed, whereas Japan has incontestably proved that she is emerging from the darkness of centuries, Russia is content to remain in a state of semi-barbarism which might be looked for in the Middle Ages."[32]

Schiff expressed his contentment with the book in a letter to Rosenthal from November 23, 1904:

> Just as I was leaving New York last week I received, through your courtesy, *The Land of Riddles*, translated by you, and which I have now completed reading. The translation is equal to the original; and I am surprised that you could do such perfect work in the short time which you had to accomplish this. I am greatly indebted to you, and I hope that the book will find a large sale so that the American public may still better become acquainted with the strange and revolting system by which Russia is governed.
>
> With all the terrible havoc which the War has wrought, I hope— and feel assured—that the end of such conditions as are pictured in *The Land of Riddles* is near, because it cannot be but that the eyes of the Russian people must have become open to the fact that-for all the suffering which the Country is now undergoing, their Autocratic Government is alone responsible.[33]

During the year of 1905, Schiff encouraged Rosenthal to publish translations from the Russian press.[34] Schiff and Rosenthal apparently rejoiced at the tsar's concessions in October that permitted the creation of a representative Duma. However, after the unlawful dispersal of the first Duma, which many in Russia and the U.S. considered a coup d'état, Rosenthal translated and published Prince Serge Dmitrievich Urussov's *Memoirs of a Russian Governor*, which appeared in 1908.[35] Schiff's role in the genesis and distribution of the volume is beyond doubt, as a letter from the publisher, G. P. Putnam's Sons,

---

[31] Diner, *Jews of the United States*, 178–79.

[32] H. Rosenthal, "Preface," in Hugo Ganz, *The Land of Riddles (Russia of To-Day)* (New York and London: Harper and Brothers, 1904), v.

[33] J. Schiff to H. Rosenthal, 23 November 1904, Herman Rosenthal Archive, Rare Books Division, New York Public Library.

[34] J. Schiff to H. Rosenthal, 8 January 1906, Herman Rosenthal Archive, Rare Books Division, New York Public Library.

[35] S. Urussov, *Memoirs of a Russian Governor* (London: Harper and Brothers, 1908).

makes clear: "We should be prepared to supply to the order of Mr. Schiff, or of the Jewish Publication Society, an edition of five thousand copies, either in cloth or in sheets, this edition to be printed specifically for such order, and to be delivered intact at the time the book was published. We should expect to print, at the same time, a supply of not less than one thousand copies for the use of the general public."[36]

In *Memoirs of a Russian Governor* Prince Urussov describes his appointment as the Russian governor to Bessarabia in the days after the Kishinev riots. His job was to calm the public and to ensure that no further disorders occurred. Although Urussov was mildly critical of the government, Rosenthal probably did not choose the book for that reason. Rather, he admired Urussov's positive and unprejudiced attitude toward the Jews of Bessarabia.

The book starts with Urussov calling into question the basic premise of the Kishinev riots. "It was asserted with much pleasure, even in Government circles, that the Jews themselves were to blame for the riots—they had been the attacking party, and, meeting the resistance of the people, suffered defeat because of Russian bravery and their own cowardice. However, I had read the actual facts in the case, and realized that this was an exaggerated interpretation."[37]

It had long been a staple of tsarist government propaganda that the Jews were behind the revolutionary movement. Noting that the police were nervous about the formation of a Jewish militia, Urussov drew his own conclusions.

> On the whole, the Israel of Kishinev was not warlike. I gained the conviction that among our Jews the inclination towards a peaceful, bourgeois life and an indifference to the more ideal side of politics may be stronger than among the other races in Russia. At least, the Jewish revolutionaries of Kishinev, in the poorer strata of the population, were almost entirely from among the very immature. A young married man, as soon as he acquired about fifty rubles, went over to law and order, and all his energy was directed towards finding means for the support of his family. I therefore came to the conclusion that the Kishinev police were too much frightened by the prevalent belief of the prominent role played by the Jews in the revolutionary movement of Russia, and hence exaggerated the importance of the power and organization of the local Jews.[38]

One cannot doubt that Urussov's admiration for Jewish farming colonies sponsored by the Jewish Colonization Association warmed Rosenthal's heart.

---

[36] Letter from G. P. Putnam's Sons to H. Rosenthal, 10 July 1907, Herman Rosenthal Archives, Rare Books Division, New York Public Library.

[37] Urussov, *Memoirs of a Russian Governor*, 8.

[38] Ibid., 53.

"A very interesting sight was presented by the Jews, mostly young people, by whose labor exclusively the ground was tilled, the plants nurtured, and the fruit preserved. There were no frightened, haggard faces to be seen; no dried-up, diseased forms; no timid, uncertain movement. The brown, red-cheeked arms, I saw in the J.C. A. reminded me of the Jewish narratives of the strong field laborers whom the Bible contrasts with the wild men living in tents."[39]

Prince Urussov, a member of the Constitutional Democratic Party (Kadets), served for Rosenthal as a model that he wished more Russians would emulate. Not prejudiced, open-minded, a lover of freedom, Urussov represented exactly the kind of leader whose policies in defense of equal rights for all the ethnic minorities of the empire might lead to an age of peace and prosperity. In contrast with autocratic power in the hands of one individual, the Kadets valorized rule of law and supported representative government based on universal suffrage.[40]

One may presume that these books were read by American political leaders and interested laymen and that they had an effect.[41] In fact, the hostility of the American public became embarrassing for France and Britain, and later for the U.S., when, entering World War I against Germany, the allies tried to justify themselves as defenders of freedom and democracy, despite their alliance with an undemocratic Russian state.[42]

While in agreement about how to relate to Russia, Schiff and Rosenthal were at odds over Zionism. Although Schiff expressed his views in numerous places, Rosenthal's position can only be sketched out because we lack direct documentary evidence. We do know that Rosenthal sympathized with the goals of Zionism and that he attended the World Zionist Congress in 1905 as a representative from the United States.[43] Although we do not have Rosenthal's original letter to Schiff, the latter's expansive response allows us to reconstruct aspects of their debate.

> I owe you also yet a reply to what you have written me about Zionism. The talk I have had with Mr. Zangwill has only the more strengthened my conviction that Zionism is not only impracticable,

[39] Ibid., 118. J.C.A. stands for the Jewish Colonization Association, which gave money to Jewish farming communities in the Russian Empire.

[40] Terence Emmons, "Russia's Banquet Campaign," *California Slavic Studies* 10 (1977): 45–86.

[41] Gerald Sorin, *A Time for Building: The Third Migration, 1880–1920* (Baltimore: Johns Hopkins University Press, 1992), 35.

[42] Peter Gatrell, *Russia's First World War: A Social and Economic History* (Harlow, UK: Pearson/Longman, 2005), 83.

[43] Invitations located in the Herman Rosenthal Archive.

but that in time it is bound to work great harm, inasmuch as in its down-going it is certain to work their greatest disappointment to the masses, who now adhere to it and set their hope in it.

Experience has amply taught us that colonization is a failure, and this refers, not only to the Jews, but to colonization in general, though in the case of the former, not a single instance can be shown where a success has been made of colonization. Only where people leave their former homes and emigrate into new regions, with the knowledge that they must overcome hardship and difficulties, looking almost insurmountable, convinced that they must surmount these difficulties or perish—as was the case when the Puritans came to our own Country—a new Nation can successfully be founded. You ought to know that the Jew, as he exists today, is not made to do this, neither in Palestine nor in East Africa; and if he is to go only to be kept there by the wealth of others, the attempt is doomed to failure from the start. But, for arguments sake, let us assume that large number of our people could be transplanted to East Africa and were willing to remain there. What would have been gained except a refuge for a limited number? This would certainly not be the Nation you and your friends are dreaming of. If Palestine, how many could it hold; and even if half of the Jews of the world would and could settle there, would that be a Nation which would secure the respect of the other world powers and which could assure protection and respect for those of the Jewish people, who remain content to live among the other Nations of the earth? Would this Nation you and your friends are dreaming of not rather become a weakling, certain to become, before long, the football of dissensions and passions from within and machinations from without, rather humiliating both its own citizens and those of its race who have remained amongst the Nations of the world?

I do not deny that Zionism has had the tendency to cement a small portion of our people and bring back some who were about to be lost, but this, I feel has only been the case because of the belief on the part of the bulk of Zionists in the dreams of Herzl and other leaders, that Palestine could be secured who have promised what they must have well known could not be obtained. Take this belief away and permit the masses to understand the hollowness of political Zionism and I fear little will remain of the Zionism which has brought so many shades of members of our race under one hood. President Lincoln's saying that "You can fool some of the people all the time and all the people some time, but, you cannot fool all the people all the time" becomes, I regret to say, eminently true in the case of Zionism.

I think I told you last summer that I felt like writing a public letter, setting forth my own views on the question of Zionism, but, I have not done so and shall, in all likelihood, not do so, because I fear the havoc and disappointment which will result when the honest and trusting masses becomes disabused, and I do not wish to do aught to hasten this. Perhaps it will be better to permit the movement to fizzle out gradually, and to let time apply the cure which will after a while be much needed. But, you will ask me where is the remedy for the unfortunate conditions which exist today, and how is the veil to be lifted under which so many of the members of our race are, at this time, almost suffocating? To this I answer—the solution of the Jewish question is to be worked out to a great extent in Russia itself, and in the United States. In Russia, where, before long, our long much suffering co-religionists are certain to be accorded humane treatment and obtain civil rights, and where they will not only then become happy subjects, but will alike become a source of blessing to their native country; in the United States, where there is amply room and unlimited opportunities for two or three millions of our race, and where the Public School and just and equal laws will rapidly make all of them the best citizens in this great Republic, and where their influence is certain to become a help to their brethren-race all over the world.[44]

While it takes some patience to unpack Schiff's arguments, one cannot deny the consistency of his thought. Just as do the Zionists, Schiff acknowledged the oppression of world Jewry, but asserted that Zionism was not the answer because it could not produce the kind of state that its supporters would hope for. Even if land in Palestine were secured, he maintained, only a limited number of Jews would go, so that the country would be subject to divisions within and machinations from without and hardly reflect its original ideals. At the same time Schiff expressed doubt that the Zionists would ever succeed in attaining a state. Therefore, while admiring Zionism's power to instill pride among Jews, he expected that they would once again fall away once they realized that the movement could not make good on its promise. The solution to the Jewish problem, he argued, must lie in a combination of changes within Russia itself and immigration to the United States, where two or three million can become "the best citizens" and "where their influence is certain to become a help to their brethren-race all over the world."

In contrast to Schiff's skepticism about colonization—a turnabout from an earlier pro-colonization position—Rosenthal was a believer. While admittedly

---

[44] J. Schiff to Rosenthal, 23 November 1904, Herman Rosenthal Archive, Rare Books Division, New York Public Library. Zangwill is Israel Zangwill, Jewish-English writer and sympathizer of the Zionist project; East Africa refers to the so-called Uganda proposal raised at the Fifth Zionist Congress. Great Britain offered the Zionists a piece of land in East Africa on which to create a Jewish settlement. Nordau called it a "Nacht-asyl," a refuge for the night.

he was, like many others, uncertain about whether Zionism would succeed in creating a state, he admired the way the movement inspired Jews to feel part of a cultural renewal. It should be noted that Rosenthal avidly fostered the revival of Hebrew as a spoken language and in 1895, he founded "Ohole Shem," a New York based group committed to promoting Hebrew language and Jewish culture in the United States.[45] One who views the minutes of the first meeting will quickly note the names of leading Hebraists, rabbis, and cultural Zionists.[46] Rosenthal was the organizer of several ventures in Hebrew. For example, he edited the journal *ha-Modia la Hodashim* (The News Messenger; 1902), which came out three times, and a single voluminous tome of poetry, criticism, and essays entitled *Yalkut ma'aravi* (Collection from the West; 1904). From the fact that he was invited to the Zionist Congress as a representative and in his efforts to propagate Jewish culture in Hebrew, one can presume that Rosenthal belonged to the Ahad Ha'am faction of cultural Zionists, who believed that cultural creation in the diaspora contributed to the transformation of the Jewish people.[47]

In the years after the appearance of Urussov's memoirs, Rosenthal published several articles on Russia.[48] At times Jacob Schiff provided some help in placing them in journals, at other times Rosenthal succeeded on his own.[49] Nevertheless, their shared disdain for the tsarist regime did not let up. Their common attitudes solidified the relationship that by 1908 had acquired a personal aspect; they became friends. The last letters in Rosenthal's archive

---

[45] *Constitution and By-Laws of the Ohole Shem Association* (New York: Baron Press, 1895).

[46] Ibid., 10.

[47] Zipperstein, *Elusive Prophet*, 112.

[48] "A Phase of the Russian Spy System" and "The Martyrdom of the Jew;" the former appeared in the *Review of Reviews* in 1911 and the latter was published in *The Outlook* in 1911.

[49] For example, Schiff writes in a letter of September 28, 1910:

Dear Mr. Rosenthal:

I have again a manuscript of Russian-Jewish conditions which appear to me attractive and suitable for magazine publication.

If you care to look into this and give me your opinion as to its availability, I shall be pleased to submit it to you, in which case I will send you the manuscript and, after you have looked it over, we can have a personal talk about it.

Hoping you are very well, I am, with kind regards,

Very very truly

Jacob H. Schiff

(Herman Rosenthal Archive, Rare Books Division, New York Public Library)

include invitations from Schiff to come visit at specific times in order to "have time to devote to you exclusively."[50]

The relationship of Schiff and Rosenthal provides a glimpse onto two important New York Jews obsessed with Russia's Jewish policy. Both Schiff and Rosenthal thought that the norms of humanism, democracy, and rule of law dictated that they side with internationalism in foreign affairs. Their position makes sense when one considers that interventionists supported progress in general, expansion of U.S. power in the world (manifest destiny), development of industry, and open immigration. They opposed isolationists who wanted to close the doors to immigrants, viewing America as rooted exclusively in the values and economy of the countryside.[51]

In many ways these two men reflected their times and their deaths represented the end of an era. Schiff and Rosenthal believed in the role of the notable and philanthropist who followed the imperative of noblesse oblige, but who was alien to the rough-and-tumble aspect of democratic politics. In this way Rosenthal can be seen as a gentleman's liege, a much needed assistant of the wealthy and powerful. Meanwhile Schiff, the uptown gentleman, was an unrepentant elitist, having little patience to negotiate or build consensus for his projects. He preferred rather to pay for them himself and execute them unilaterally.

Nonetheless, even before World War I, this elite was already fighting a rear-guard battle against democratization in New York's Jewish community and the growing power of the downtown masses. The conflict between these two groups can be viewed in the struggle between the two main Jewish defense organizations in America, the uptown-oriented American Jewish Committee and the downtown American Jewish Congress.[52]

The 1920s brought a change of Jewish leadership. Beyond the often-cited conflict between German and Russian Jews, which gave rise to new Jewish democratic leaders from Eastern Europe, the elite was also changing. Many of them were already native born and educated in American institutions of higher learning. Just as important, Jews started to gain access to power by working within the government rather than from without. The examples of Oscar Strauss, Secretary of the Treasury, and Louis Brandeis, Supreme Court Justice, are illustrative.

Moreover, the conditions that permitted Schiff and Rosenthal to struggle against the Russian government were fast evaporating. The isolationist mood was taking hold and increased antisemitism and fear of revolutionaries led to

---

[50] See Schiff's letter of December 18, 1912, Herman Rosenthal Archive, Rare Books Division, New York Public Library.

[51] Richard Hofstadter, *The Age of Reform: From Bryan to F.D.R.* (New York: Alfred A. Knopf, 1955), 213–69.

[52] Henry L. Feingold, *A Time for Searching: Entering the Mainstream 1920–1945* (Baltimore: Johns Hopkins University Press, 1992), 158.

the Immigration Acts of 1921 and then 1924, ending the liberal immigration policy of the United States. A few years earlier, however, the election of Woodrow Wilson on a morally-based internationalist plank reflected the victory of the Schiff-Rosenthal orientation. In contrast to the history of the country as a whole in which the moral imperative in foreign policy has fluctuated, in Jewish-American politics, the moral element has stayed constant. In addition, American Jews have never relinquished their right to make known their positions on foreign affairs. This Jewish outspokenness on foreign policy, I contend, is the legacy of such individuals as Schiff and Rosenthal.

# Selected Bibliography

## Archival Sources

*Russian State Historical Archive, St. Petersburg (Rossiiskii gosudarstvennyi istoricheskii arkhiv, RGIA)*

fond 1532     Society for the Promotion of Enlightenment among the Jews of Russia

fond 1565     Central Committee of the Society for the Attainment of Full Rights for the Jewish People in Russia

*Library of the Institute of Oriental Studies, St. Petersburg Branch (Institut vostokovedenii, Sankt-Peterburgskii filial)*

fond 86       Israel Tsinberg

*Archival Division of the Russian National Library (Rukopisnyi otdel, Rossiiskaia gosudarstvennaia biblioteka)*

fond 1532     Mikhail Gershenzon

*Central State Historical Archive of Ukraine, Kiev (Tsentral'nyi derzhavnyi istorychnyi arkhiv Ukrainy, Kyiv))*

fond 992      Leon Bramson

*Ukrainian State Library (Vernadskii), Kiev (Natsional'na biblioteka Ukrainy imeni V. I. Vernads'kogo)*

fond 321      Society for the Promotion of Enlightenment among the Jews of Russia

*Rare Books Division, New York Public Library*

Herman Rosenthal Archive

## Newspapers

*Budushchnost'*
*Delo pomoshchi*
*Den'*
*Der Fraynd*
*Evreiskaia biblioteka*
*Evreiskii mir*
*Evreiskaia nedelia*
*Evreiskaia shkola*
*Evreiskaia starina*
*Evreiskaia tribuna*
*Evreiskaia zhizn'*
*Ha-Meliz*
*Novyi voskhod*
*Rassvet* (1860–61)
*Rassvet* (1879–83)

*Rassvet* (1914–17)
*Rech'*
*Russkaia mysl'*
*Russkii evrei*
*Russkoe bogatstvo*
*Safrut*
*Tsion*
*Ha-Tsfira*
*Vestnik Evreiskoi Obshchiny*
*Vestnik Evropy*
*Vestnik Obshchestva dlia rasprostrane niia prosveshcheniia mezhdu evreiami v Rossii*
*Vestnik russkikh evreev*
*Voskhod*
*Zhurnal Ministerstva narodnogo prosveshcheniia*

## Printed Sources

Abramowicz, Hirsz. *Profiles of a Lost World: Memoirs of East European Jewish Life before World War II.* Translated by E. Z. Dobkin. Edited by D. Abramowicz and J. Shandler. Detroit: Wayne State University Press, 1999.

Adler, Cyrus. *Jacob H. Schiff, His Life and Letters.* 2 vols. New York: Doubleday, Doran and Company, Inc., 1929.

Aldanov, Mark. "Russkie evrei v 70–80-kh godakh (istoricheskii etiud)." In Frumkin, Aronson, and Gol'denveizer, *Kniga o russkom evreistve*, 48–53.

Almog, Shmuel. *Zionism and History: The Rise of a New Jewish Consciousness.* Translated by Ina Friedman. New York: St. Martin's Press, 1987.

Alroey, Gur. "Bureaucracy, Agents, and Swindlers: The Hardships of Jewish Emigration from the Pale of Settlement in the Early 20th Century." In *Jews and the State: Dangerous Alliances and the Perils of Privilege*, edited by E. Mendelsohn, 214–34. Studies in Contemporary Jewry 19. New York: Oxford University Press, 2003.

Al'tman, M. S. et al. *Razgovory s Viacheslavom Ivanovym.* Moscow: INApress, 1995.

Andreev, L., M. Gor'kii, and F. Sologub, eds. *Shchit: Literaturnyi sbornik.* Moscow: T-vo tip. A. I. Mamontova, 1915.

Andreeva, I. "Istoriia odnoi nevstrechi, rasskazannaia v retsenziiakh i pis'makh M. O. Gershenzon i K. I. Chukovskogo." *Literaturnoe obozrenie*, no. 11–12 (1992): 63–72.

An-skii, S. *Chto takoe anarkhizm?* St. Petersburg: Zhivoe slovo, 1907.

————. *Der iddisher khurbn fun Poyln, Galitsye un Bukovine fun togbuch 1914–17.* In *Gazamlte shriftn*, by Ansky, vols 4–6. Vilna, 1920–25.

————. "Evreiskoe narodnoe tvorchestvo." In Ginzburg and Tsinberg, *Perezhitoe*, 1: 276–310.

————. "Iz legend o mstislavskom dele." In Ginzburg and Tsinberg, *Perezhitoe*, 2: 248–57.

————. "Iz narodnykh legend o 'Goleme.'" *Novyi voskhod*, no. 4 (1910).

————. *Iz putevykh zapisok.* St. Petersburg, 1910.

————. *Narod i kniga: Opyt kharakteristiki narodnogo chitatelia.* Moscow: Universal'noe knigoizdatel'stvo, 1914.

————. "Narod i voina." In An-skii, *Narod i kniga*, 203–19.

————. *Sobranie sochinenii.* 5 vols. St. Petersburg: Prosveshchenie, 1911–13.

————. "'Uroki strashnykh vekov' (Po povodu stat'i S. M. Dubnova 'Uroki strashnykh dnei')." *Voskhod*, nos. 8–11, 13 (1906).

————, comp. and ed. *Vsiudu zhizn'.* St. Petersburg: Razum, 1909.

Aronson, G. "Evrei v russkoi literature, kritike, zhurnalistike i obshchestvennoi zhizni." In Frumkin, Aronson, and Gol'denveizer, *Kniga o russkom evreistve*, 365–403.

Aronson, Michael I. "The Attitudes of Russian Officials in the 1880s toward Jewish Assimilation and Emigration." *Slavic Review* 34: 1 (1975): 1–18.

B. I. "S. Frug." In *Leksikon fun der nayer yidisher literatur*, 8 vols., ed. Niger and Shatzky, 7: 448–57. New York: Congress for Jewish Culture, 1956.

Bacon, Gershon C. *The Politics of Tradition: Agudat Yisrael in Poland, 1916–1939.* Jerusalem: Magnes Press, Hebrew University, 1996.

Bakhrakh, A. *Po pamiati, po zapisiam: Literaturnye portrety.* Paris: Press libre, 1980.

Baranoff [Baranova-Shestova], Nathalie. *Zhizn' L'va Shestova: Po perepiske i vospominaniiam sovremennikov.* 2 vols. Paris: La Press Libre, 1983.

Bartal, Yisrael. *The Jews of Eastern Europe, 1772–1881.* Translated by Chaya Naor. Philadelphia: University of Pennsylvania Press, 2005.

————. "The *Porets* and the *Arendar*: The Depiction of Poles in Jewish Literature." *Polish Review* 32: 4 (1987): 352–69.

Bar-Yosef, Hamutal. "Bialik and the Russian Revolutions." *Jews in Eastern Europe* 1: 29 (Spring 1996): 5–31.

————. *Maga'im shel dekadens: Byalik, Berdits'evski, Brener.* Bersheva and Jerusalem: Ben Gurion University and the Bialik Institute, 1997.

————. "Reflections on Hebrew Literature in the Russian Context." *Prooftexts* 16: 2 (1996): 127–49.

————. "Vliianie russkoi literatury na stanovlenie i razvitie novoi literatury na ivrite." *Vestnik evreiskogo universiteta v Moskve* 2: 15 (1997): 114–36.

Belyi, Andrei. *Mezhdu dvukh revoliutsii.* Leningrad: Izd-vo pisatelei o Leningrade, 1934.

Ben-Ami. "Frug (Vospominaniia)." *Rassvet*, no. 10–11 (20 September 1917): 15–16.

Berdiaev, Nikolai. *Aleksei Stepanovich Khomiakov*. Moscow: Put', 1912.

―――. *Dukhovnyi krizis intelligentsii: Stat'i po obshchestvennoi i religioznoi psikhologii, 1907–1909*. St. Petersburg: Obshchestvennaia pol'za, 1910.

―――. *Filosofiia svobody*. Moscow: Izd-vo "Pravda," 1989.

―――. "Filosofskaia istina i intelligentskaia pravda." In Berdiaev et al., *Vekhi*, 1–22.

―――. "Khristianstvo i antisemitizm." *Put'*, nos. 5–6 (1938): 3–18.

―――. "Natsionalizm i imperializm." In *Sud'ba Rossii*, by Berdiaev. Moscow: Izd-vo G. A. Lemana i S. I. Sakharova, 1918. Reprinted in *Sud'ba Rossii*, 107–13. Moscow: Sovetskii pisatel', 1990.

―――. *Samopoznanie: Opyt filosofskoi avtobiografii*. Paris: YMCA Press, 1949.

―――. *Smysl tvorchestva*. Moscow, 1916. Reprint, Paris: YMCA, 1985.

Berdiaev, N. et al., eds. *Vekhi: Sbornik statei o russkoi intelligentsii*. Moscow: Tip. V. N. Sablina, 1909.

Berkowitz, Michael. *Zionist Culture and West European Jewry before the First World War*. Chapel Hill: University of North Carolina Press, 1993.

Bernhardt, L. "Khodasevich i sovremennaia evreiskaia poeziia." *Russian Literature*, no. 6 (1974): 21–27.

Bershadskii, S. *Russko-evreiskii arkhiv*. St. Petersburg, 1882, 1884, and 1908.

Bezrodnyi, M. "O 'iudoboiani' Andreia Belogo." *Novoe literaturnoe obozrenie* 28 (1997): 100–25.

Bialik, Kh. "Ty ot menia ukhodish'," in Khodasevich and Jaffe, *Evreiskaia antologiia*, 64–65.

Bialyi, G. A. "Vstupitel'naia stat'ia." In *Polnoe sobranie sochinenii S. Ia. Nadsona*, vi–viii. Leningrad: Sovetskii pisatel', 1962, vi–viii.

Bikerman, I. "O sionizme i po povodu sionizma." *Russkoe bogatstvo* 7 (1902): 27–69.

Bramson, L. "K istorii nachal'nogo obrazovaniia evreev v Rossii." In Bramson and Kulisher, *Sbornik v pol'zu nachal'nykh evreiskikh shkol*, 279–354.

―――. *Obshchestvenno-kul'turnaia deiatel'nost' M. G. Morgulisa*. St. Petersburg, 1912.

―――. "Ob"edinenie russko-evreiskoi intelligentsii." In *Aleksandr Isaevich Braudo, 1864–1924: Ocherki i vospominaniia*, edited by Bramson, 7–22. Paris: Maison du livre etranger, 1937.

Bramson, L., ed. *Sbornik ob ekonomicheskom polozhenii evreev v Rossii*. 2 vols. St. Petersburg, 1904.

Bramson, L., and Mikhail Kulisher, eds. *Sbornik v pol'zu nachal'nykh evreiskikh shkol*. St. Petersburg: Obshchestvo dlia rasprostraneniia prosveshcheniia mezhdu evreiami v Rossii, 1896.

Breimann, S. "Ha-mifneh bamahshava haziburit hayehudit bereshit shnot hashmonim." *Shivat Zion* 2–3 (1952–53): 180–84.

Breinin, Reuven. "Vorrede." In *Ale Shriften*, by S. Frug, 1: iii–xiii. New York: Hebrew Publishing Co., 1910.

Brutskus, B. "Pis'mo v redaktsiiu." *Voskhod*, no. 24 (13 June 1902): 11–13; and *Budushchnost'* 2, 3, 5, 13, 14, 16, 25 (1902).

Brutskus, B. et al., eds. *Sbornik pamiati A. D. Idel'son*. Berlin, 1925.

Budnitskii, O. V., ed. *Evrei i russkaia revoliutsiia: Materialy i issledovaniia*. Moscow: Izd-vo "Gesharim," 1999.

Bulgakov, S. "V ozhidanii Palestiny: 17 pisem S. N. Bulgakova k M. O. Gershenzonu i ego zhene, 1897–1925 gg." In *Neizvestnaia Rossiia*, edited by V. A. Kozlov, 2: 134. Moscow: Istoricheskoe nasledie, 1992.

Cherikover, I. M. *Istoriia Obshchestva dlia rasprostraneniia prosveshcheniia mezhdu evreiami v Rossii*. St. Petersburg: Obshchestvo dlia rasprostraneniia prosveshcheniia mezhdu evreiami v Rossii, 1913.

———. "Obshchestvo dlia rasprostraneniia prosveshcheniia mezhdu evreiami v Rossii." In Katzenelson, *Evreiskaia entsiklopediia*, 13: 61.

Chernov, V. M., and Viktor Shulman. *Yidishe tuer in der Partay Sotsyalistn Revolutsyonern: Biografisshe eseyen*. New York: Grigori Gershuni Brentsh, Arbeter Ring, 1948.

Cohen, Israel. *Vilna*. Philadelphia: Jewish Publication Society of America, 1943.

Cohen, Naomi W. "The Ethnic Catalyst: The Impact of the East European Immigration on the American Jewish Establishment." In *The Legacy of Jewish Migration: 1881 and Its Impact*, edited by David Berger, 131–48. New York: Brooklyn College Press, 1983.

———. *Jacob H. Schiff: A Study in American Jewish Leadership*. Hanover, NH: University Press of New England/Brandeis University Press, 1999.

*Constitution and By-Laws of the Ohole Shem Association*. New York: Baron Press, 1895.

D-v, V. "Iubilei 'prosveshcheniia': O dvadtsatipiatiletnei deiatel'nosti Odesskogo Otdeleniia Obshchestva prosveshcheniia mezhdu evreiami v Rossii (1867–1892 g.)," *Voskhod*, no. 8 (1893): 20–21.

Davidowicz, Lucy S., ed. *The Golden Tradition: Jewish Life and Thought in Eastern Europe*. New York: Schocken Books, 1967.

Davis, Robert H. "Slavic and Baltic Library Resources at the New York Public Library." *Canadian-American Slavic Studies* 29: 1–2 (Spring–Summer 1995): 1–174.

Dekel-Chen, Jonathan L. *Farming the Red Land: Jewish Agricultural Colonization and Local Soviet Power, 1924–1941*. New Haven: Yale University Press, 2005.

Deschartes, O. Introduction to *Perepiska iz dvukh uglov*, in Viacheslav Ivanov, *Sobranie sochinenii*, 4 vols., edited by D. V. Ivanov and O. Deshart, 3: 809–10. Brussels: Foyer Oriental Chrétien, 1971.

Diner, Hasia R. *The Jews of the United States, 1654 to 2000*. Berkeley: University of California Press, 2004.

Dinur, Ben Zion. *Israel and the Diaspora*. Philadelphia: Jewish Publication Society of America, 1969.

Dohrn, Verena. "The Rabbinical Schools as Institutions of Socialization in Tsarist Russia, 1847–1873." *Polin: Studies in Polish Jewry* 14 (2001): 83–104.

——. "Das Ribbinerseminar in Wilna (1840–73): Geschichte der ersten staatlichen höheren Schule für Juden in Russischen Reich." *Jahrbücher für Osteuropäische Geschichte* 45 (1997): 379–400.

Dubnov, Simon. "Chto takoe evreiskaia istoriia?: Opyt kratkoi filosofskoi kharakteristiki." *Voskhod* 10/11–12 (1893).

——. *Evrei v Rossi i zapadnoi Evrope v epokhu antisemitskoi reaktsii*. Moscow-Leningrad: L. D. Frenkel', 1923.

——. "Iakov Frank i ego sekta khristianstvuiushchikh," *Voskhod*, nos. 1–4, 9–10 (1883).

——. "Istoricheskie soobshcheniia," *Voskhod*, no. 7 (1893): 9.

——. "Istoriograf evreistva: Geinrikh Grets, ego zhizn' i trudy." *Voskhod*, nos. 3–9 (1892).

——. "Kakaia emansipatsiia nuzhna evreiam?" *Voskhod*, nos. 5–6 (1883).

——. *Kniga zhizni: Vospominaniia i razmyshleniia. Materialy dlia istorii moego vremeni*. 3 vols. Riga, 1934–35 (vols. 1–2) and New York, 1957 (vol. 3). Reprint, St. Petersburg: Peterburgskoe vostokovedenie, 1998.

——. *Noveishaia istoriia evreiskogo naroda*. 3rd ed. Berlin: Grani, 1923.

——. *Ob izuchenii istorii russkikh evreev i ob uchrezhdenii russkogo-evreiskogo istoricheskogo obshchestva*. St. Petersburg, 1891.

——. "O natsional'nom vospitanii," *Pis'ma o starom i novom evreistve*, *Voskhod*, no. 1 (January 1902): 69–115.

——. "O rasteriavsheisia intelligentsii." *Voskhod*, no. 12 (1902): 61–93.

——. "O sovremennom sostoianii evreiskoi istoriografii." *Evreiskaia starina*, no. 1 (1910): 149–59.

——. *Pis'ma o starom i novom evreistve*. St. Petersburg: Obshchestvennaia pol'za, 1907.

——. "Sabbatai Tsevi i psevdomissionizma v XVII veke." *Voskhod*, nos. 7–10 (1882).

——. "Uchreditel'noe sobranie i publichnye zasedaniia Evreiskogo Istoriko-Etnograficheskogo Obshchestva." *Evreiskaia starina*, no. 1 (1909): 158.

——. "Uroki strashnykh dnei." *Voskhod* [ezhenedel'nyi], no. 47–48 (1905): 47–50.

——. "Vospominaniia o S. M. Fruge." *Evreiskaia starina*, no. 4 (1916): 441–64.

——· "Vozniknovenie khasidizma: Ber iz Mezhiricha, preemnik Beshta, i prochie ucheniki Beshta (1760–1772)," *Voskhod* (1899): no. 9 (3–21); no. 10 (3–18); no. 11–12 (38–53) and (1890): no. 1 (23–42).

——. "Vozniknovenie khasidizma: Zhizn' i deiatel'nost' Beshta." *Voskhod*, nos. 5–10 (1888).

Dubnova-Erlikh, Sophia. *The Life and Work of S. M. Dubnov: Diaspora Nationalism and Jewish History.* Translated by J. Vowles. Edited by J. Shandler. Bloomington: Indiana University Press, 1991.

Eizenshtadt, Shmuel. "Le-toldot ha-tsiburyot ve ha-tarbut ha-ivrit berusiyah." *He-avar,* no. 15 (May 1968): 132–62.

Eklof, Ben. *Russian Peasant Schools: Officialdom, Village Culture, and Popular Pedagogy, 1861–1914.* Berkeley: University of California Press, 1986.

Elbogen, Itamar. "Pamiati Semena Markovicha Dubnova." *Evreiskii mir* 2 (1944): 74–76.

Emmons, Terence. "Russia's Banquet Campaign." *California Slavic Studies* 10 (1977): 45–86.

Ettinger, R. N. *Roza Nikolaevna Ettinger.* Jerusalem, 1980.

*Evreiskaia entsiklopediia: Svod znanii o evreistve i ego kul'ture v proshlom i nastoiashchem.* 16 vols. St. Petersburg: Obshchestvo dlia nauchnykh evreiskikh izdanii, 1906–13.

*Evreiskaia Narodnaia Partiia.* St. Petersburg: Evreiskaia Narodnaia Partiia, 1907.

Fallows, Thomas. "The Zemstvo and the Bureaucracy." In *The Zemstvo in Russia: An Experiment in Local Self-Government,* edited by T. Emmons and W. Vucinich, 177–241. Cambridge: Cambridge University Press, 1982.

Feiner, Shmuel. *Haskalah and History: The Emergence of a Modern Jewish Historical Consciousness.* Translated by Chaya Naor and Sondra Silverston. Portland, OR: Littman Library of Jewish Civilization, 2002.

Feingold, Henry L. *A Time for Searching: Entering the Mainstream 1920–1945.* Baltimore: The Johns Hopkins University Press, 1992.

F. G. [F. B. Gets], *Slovo podsudimomu: S pis'mami L. N. Tolstogo, B. N. Chicherina, V. S. Solov'eva, V. G. Korolenko.* St. Petersburg: Novosti, 1891.

Fishman, David E. *The Rise of Modern Yiddish Culture.* Pittsburgh: University of Pittsburgh Press, 2005.

————. *Russia's First Modern Jews: The Jews of Shklov.* New York: New York University Press, 1995.

Florovskii, G. *Puti russkogo bogosloviia.* 4th edition. Paris: YMCA-Press, 1988.

Frank, S. L. *Biografiia P. B. Struve.* New York: Izd-vo im. Chekhova, 1956.

————. *Filosofiia i zhizn': Etiudy i nabroski po filosofii kul'tury.* St. Petersburg, 1910.

————. *Predmet znaniia: Ob osnovakh i predelakh otvlechennogo znaniia.* Petrograd, 1915.

Frankel, Jonathan. *Prophecy and Politics: Socialism, Nationalism, and the Russian Jews, 1862–1917.* Cambridge: Cambridge University Press, 1981.

————. "'Youth in Revolt': An-sky's 'In Shtrom' and the Instant Fictionalization of 1905." *The Worlds of S. An-sky: A Russian Jewish Intellectual at the Turn of the Century.* Stanford, CA: Stanford University Press, 2006, 137–63.

Frug, Shimon. *Polnoe sobranie sochinenii.* 6 vols. St. Petersburg: Izdanie zhurnala "Evreiskaia zhizn'," [1900?].

Frumkin, Jacob. "Iz istorii russkogo evreistva (vospominaniia, materialy, dokumenty)." In Frumkin, Aronson, and Gol'denveizer, *Kniga o russkom evreistve*, 54–114.

———. *Russian Jewry (1860–1917)*. Translated by Mirra Ginsburg. New York: T. Yoseloff, 1966.

Frumkin, Jacob, Gregor Aronson, and A. A. Gol'denveizer, eds. *Kniga o russkom evreistve: Ot 1869-kh godov do revoliutsii 1917 g. Sbornik statei.* New York: Soiuz russkikh evreev, 1960.

Garkavy, A. "Iz istorii kul'tury russkikh evreev." In Bramson and Kulisher, *Sbornik v pol'zu nachal'nykh evreiskikh shkol*, 99–108.

Garkavy [Harkavy], V. O. *O iazyke evreev i o slavianskikh slovakh, vstrechennykh u evreiskikh pisatelei.* St. Petersburg, 1896.

———. *Otryvki vospominanii.* St. Petersburg: Tip. I. Fleitmana, 1913.

Gassenschmidt, Christoph. *Jewish Liberal Politics in Tsarist Russia, 1900–1914: The Modernization of Russian Jewry.* New York: New York University Press, 1995.

Gatrell, Peter. *Russia's First World War: A Social and Economic History.* Harlow, UK: Pearson/Longman, 2005.

Geifman, Anna. *Thou Shalt Kill: Revolutionary Terrorism in Russia, 1894–1917.* Princeton, NJ: Princeton University Press, 1993.

Gershenzon, M. O. "Corner-to-Corner Correspondence." In *Russian Intellectual History: An Anthology*, edited by Marc Raeff, 373–401. New York: Harcourt, Brace and World, 1966.

———. "Iskusstvo v shkole." *Vestnik vospitaniia*, no. 2 (1899): 51–75.

———. *Istoricheskie zapiski.* 2nd ed. Berlin: Gelikon, 1923.

———. *Istoriia molodoi Rossii.* Moscow: I. D. Sytin, 1908.

———. *Kliuch very.* St. Petersburg: Epokha, 1922.

———. "Mysli dvukh filosofov o shkole," *Voprosy filosofii i psikhologii*, no. 6 (1902): 794–825.

———. "Narod, ispytuemyi ognem." *Evreiskaia nedelia*, no. 1 (1916): 28–32.

———. "Ocherk razvitiia nemetskoi khudozhestvennoi literatury v XIX veke." *Russkaia mysl'*, no. 3 (1903): 1–13.

———. "Otvet P. B. Struve." *Russkaia mysl'*, no. 2 (1910): 176–79.

———. "Pis'ma k L'vu Shestovu." Edited and annotated by A. d'Amelia and V. Alloia. *Minuvshee* 6 (1985): 237–312.

———. "Solntse nad mgloi. Aforizmy." *Zapiski mechtatelei.* Vol. 5, Petrograd: Alkonost, 1922, 90–125.

———. *Sud'by evreiskogo naroda.* St. Petersburg: Epokha, 1922.

———. *Troistvennyi obraz sovershenstva.* Moscow: Kn-vo M. i S. Sabashnikovykh, 1918.

———, ed. *Vekhi.* 2nd ed. Moscow, 1909.

———· "Vtoroi god voiny." *Birzhevye-vedomosti*, 28 June 1915.

———. *Zhizn' V. S. Pecherina.* Moscow: Put', 1910.

Gershenzon- Chegodaeva, N. M. *Pervye shagi zhiznennogo puti (vospominaniia docheri Mikhaila Gershenzona)*. Moscow: Zakharov, 2000.

Gertsyk, Evgeniia. *Vospominaniia: N. Berdiaev, L. Shestov, S. Bulgakov, V. Ivanov, M. Voloshin, A. Gertsyk*. Paris: YMCA-Press, 1973.

Gessen, Iu. *Istoriia evreiskogo naroda v Rossii*. 2 vols. (Petrograd: Tip. L. Ia. Ganzburga, 1916), 2: 156–201.

————. "Lev Osipovich Levanda." *Evreiskaia entsiklopediia*, 10: 59–63.

————. "Ravvinskie uchilishcha v Rossii." *Evreiskaia entsiklopediia*, 13: 258–63.

————. "Smena obshchestvennykh techenii." Pt. 2: "Pervyi russko-evreiskii organ." In Ginzburg and Tsinberg, *Perezhitoe*, 3: 1–59.

Gets, F. B. *Slovo podsudimomu: S pis'mami L. N. Tolstogo, B. N. Chicherina, V. S. Solov'eva, V. G. Korolenko*. St. Petersburg: Novosti, 1891.

Ginzburg [Ginsburg], S. M. "Di familiye Baron Gintsburg: Drey doyres shtadlones, tsadoke un haskala." In *Historishe verk*, by Ginzburg, 2: 117–59. New York: Shoyl Ginsburg 70-Yohriger Yubiley Komitet, 1937.

————. "Iz zapisok pervogo evreia-studenta v Rossii." In Ginzburg and Tsinberg, *Perezhitoe*, 1: 3–50.

————. *Minuvshee: Istoricheskie ocherki, stat'i i kharakteristiki*. Petrograd, 1923.

Ginzburg, Saul, and Tsinberg, Israel, eds. *Perezhitoe: Sbornik, posviashchennyi obshchestvennoi i kul'turnoi istorii evreev v Rossii*. 4 vols. St. Petersburg: Brokgauz-Efron, 1908–1913.

Gol'dberg, B. A. *L. O. Levanda kak publitsist (po sluchaiu sorokoletniago iubileia vozniknoveniia russko-evreiskoi pechati)*. Vilna: Tip. D. i Kh. Ialovtser, 1900.

Goldstein, Y. "Ha-tenuah ha-tsiyonit be-rusyah, 1904–1987." Ph.D. diss., Hebrew University, 1982.

Gordon, G. I. "Sionizm i khristiane." *Russkaia mysl'*, no. 7 (1902): 178–96.

Gor'kii, Maksim. *Iz literaturnogo naslediia: Gor'kii i evreiskii vopros*. Compiled and edited by M. Agurskii and M. Shklovskaia. Jerusalem: Hebrew University and the Center for the Study of Eastern European Jewry, 1986.

"Gornfel'd, Arkadii Geogievich." *Kratkaia evreiskaia entsiklopediia*. 10 vols. Jerusalem: Obshchestvo po issledovaniiu evreiskikh obshchin, 1982, 2: 178.

Graetz, Heinrich. *Geschichte der Juden von den ältesten Zeiten bis aud die Gegenwart: Aus den Quellen neubearb*. 11 vols. Leipzig, 1874–1902.

Greenberg, Louis. *The Jews in Russia*. 2 vols. New Haven: Yale University Press, 1944–51.

Grekova, Elena. "Staryi entuziast." In *Pamiati A. L. Volynskogo*, 47–68. Leningrad: Izd-vo Vserossiiskogo soiuza pisatelei, 1928.

Gruzenberg, O. O. "Pamiati Iakova L'vovicha Teitelia." In *Ocherki i rechi*, 163–68. New York, 1944.

————. "Po povodu odesskogo sobraniia obshchestva prosveshcheniia." *Budushchnost'*, no. 25 (21 June 1902): 488.

————. *Vchera: Vospominaniia*. Paris, 1938.

Guenzburg, David, ed. *Festschrift zu ehren Dr. A. Harkavy: Aus Anlass seines am 20 November 1905 vollendeten siebzigsten Lebensjahres.* St. Petersburg, 1908. Reprint, New York: Arno Press, 1980.

Handlin, Oscar. "American Views of the Jew at the Opening of the Twentieth Century." In *Anti-Semitism in America*, vol. 6 of *American Jewish History*, edited by Jeffrey S. Gurock, 1: 187–208. 2 vols. New York: Routledge, 1998.

Harkavy [Garkavi], A. "Istoricheskie ocherki sinoda chetyrekh stran." *Voskhod* no. 2 (1884): 1–15 and no. 4 (1884): 9–27.

———. *O iazyke evreev, zhivshikh v drevnee vremia na Rusi.* St. Petersburg, 1865.

———, ed. *Sbornik statei po evreiskoi istorii i literature.* St. Petersburg: Obshchestvo dlia rasprostraneniia prosveshcheniia mezhdu evreiami v Rossii, 1866–67.

Herscher, Uri. "Herman Rosenthal—The Jewish Farmer." *Mikha'el: me'asef le-toldot ha-Yehudim be-tefutsot* 3 (1975): 59–87.

———. *Jewish Agricultural Utopias in America, 1880–1910.* Detroit: Wayne State University Press, 1981.

Heuman, Susan. *Kistiakovsky: The Struggle for National and Constitutional Rights in the Last Years of Tsarism.* Cambridge: Harvard Ukrainian Research Institute, 1998.

Hofstadter, Richard. *The Age of Reform: From Bryan to F.D.R.* New York: Alfred A. Knopf, 1955.

Horowitz, Brian. *A. S. Pushkin in the Silver Age: M. O. Gershenzon-Pushkinist.* Evanston, IL: Northwestern University Press, 1997.

———. "Jewish Identity and Russian Culture: The Case of M. O. Gershenzon." *Nationalities Papers* 25: 4 (1997): 699–713.

———. "M. O. Gershenzon and the Intellectual Life of Russia's Silver Age." Ph.D. diss., University of California, Berkeley, 1993.

———. "M. O. Gershenzon and the Perception of a Leader in Russia's Silver-Age Culture. *Wiener Slawistischer Almanach* 29 (1992): 45–73.

———. "The Society for the Promotion of Enlightenment among the Jews of Russia, 1893–1905 and the Development of the Petersburg Russian-Jewish Intelligentsia." In Mendelsohn, *Jews and the State*, 195–213.

———. "The Tension of Athens and Jerusalem in the Philosophy of Lev Shestov." *Slavic and East European Journal* 43: 1 (Spring 1999): 156–73.

———. "Unity and Disunity in *Landmarks*: The Rivalry between Petr Struve and Mikhail Gershenzon." *Studies in East European Thought* 51: 1 (March 1999): 61–78.

———. "Unrequited Love for Russia." *Midstream*, no. 10 (October 1996): 37–40.

Ivanov, V. "K ideologii evreiskogo voprosa." In Andreev et al., *Shchit*, 84–86.

Ivanov, V., and M. Gershenzon. *Perepiska iz dvukh uglov.* St. Petersburg: Alkonost, 1921.

"Izvlechenie iz ob"iasnitel'nykh svedenii k polozheniiam o evreiskikh nachal'nykh uchilishchakh i o evreiskikh uchitel'nykh institutakh." *Vestnik russkikh evreev* 20–21 (1873): 617–21.

Jabotinsky, V. *Piatero*. Tel Aviv: Biblioteka Aliia, 1990.

———. "Vvedenie." In *Evrei v kul'ture russkogo zarubezh'ia: Sbornik statei, publikatsii, memuarov, i esse*, edited by Mikhail Parkhomovskii, 5: 566–77. Jerusalem: n.p., 1992–96.

Jaffe, Benjamin, and Mordekhai Levin. *Leyb Yafeh: Bibliyografyah*. Jerusalem, 1977.

Jaffe, L., and B. Jaffe. *Be-shlikhut am: Mikhtavim u-teudot le-Leib Yaffe le-yom huladeto ha-shivim, 1892–1948*. Jerusalem: ha-Sifriyah ha-Siyonit, 1968.

Jaffe, Leib (Lev). *Gorod Lovchen*. Moscow: I. V. Velikovskii, 1916.

———. *Griadushchee: Stikhotvoreniia*. Grodno: Tip. S. Lapina, 1902.

———. *Ketavim, igrot, ve-yomanim*. Jerusalem: ha-Sifriyah ha-Tsiyonit, 1964.

———. *Ogni na vysotakh: Stikhi*. Riga: Izd-vo Evreiskogo obshchestva sodeistviia iskusstvu i natsii v Latvii, 1938.

———. "Pis'ma L. Jaffa k M. Gershenzonu." Edited by B. Horowitz. *Vestnik Evreiskogo universiteta v Moskve* 2 (18) (1998): 210–25.

———, ed. *Sborniki Safrut*. 3 vols. (1917–21).

———. "S. G. Frug." *Evreiskaia zhizn'*, no. 39–40 (25 September 1916): 11–12.

———, ed. *U rek Vavilonskikh: Natsional'no-evreiskaia lirika v mirovoi poezii*. Moscow: Safrut, 1917.

———. "V chas resheniia." In *Voina i evreiskaia problema*, 47–51. Moscow: Izd-vo Moskovskogo komiteta Sion Narodnoi Fraktsii 'Tseire-Tsion, 1917.

Jaffe, Leib, and Vladislav Khodasevich, eds. *Evreiskaia antologiia: Sbornik molodoi evreiskoi poezii*. 3rd ed. Berlin: D. Zal'tsman, 1922.

James, William. *Mnogoobrazie religioznogo opyta*. Translated by Varvara Malakhieva-Mironich. Moscow, 1910.

Judge, Edward H. *Easter in Kishnev: Anatomy of a Pogrom*. New York: New York University Press, 1992.

Kasinec, Edward, and Robert H. Davis, Jr. "Collecting Slavica at the New York Public Library." In *Russia Engages the World, 1453–1825*, edited by C. H. Whittaker, 162–86. Cambridge, MA: Harvard University Press, 2003.

Katz, Samuel. *Lone Wolf: A Biography of Vladimir (Ze'ev) Jabotinsky*. New York: Barricade Books, 1996.

Katzenelson, J., ed. *Evreiskaia entsiklopediia: Svod znanii o evreistve v proshlom i nastoiashchem*. 16 vols. St. Petersburg: Brokgauz and Efron, 1907–13.

Kel'ner, Viktor. *Chelovek svoego vremeni: M. M. Stasiulevich, izdatel'skoe delo, i liberal'naia oppozitsiia*. St. Petersburg: Izd-vo Rossiiskoi natsional'noi biblioteki, 1993.

———. "Dva intsidenta: Iz russko-evreiskikh otnoshenii v nachale XX v." *Vestnik Evreiskogo universiteta v Moskve* 3: 10 (1995): 190–99.

Kel'ner, Viktor, and D. Eliashevich. *Literatura o evreiakh na russkom iazyke, 1890–1947*. St. Petersburg: Akademicheskii proekt, 1995.

Khodasevich, Vladislav. *Iz evreiskikh poetov*. Berlin, 1923.

—————. *Nekropol': Vospominaniia*. Paris: YMCA-Press, 1976.

Klier, John. *Imperial Russia's Jewish Question, 1855–1881*. Cambridge: Cambridge University Press, 2005.

—————. "The Jew as Russifier: Lev Levanda's *Hot Times*." *Jewish Culture and History* 4: 1 (2001): 31–52.

—————. "The Jewish *Den'* and the Literary Mice, 1869–71." *Russian History*, no. 1 (1983): 31–49.

—————. "Krug Gintsburgov i politika shtadlanuta v Imperatorskoi Rossii." *Vestnik Evreiskogo universiteta v Moskve* 3: 10 (1995): 38–55.

—————. "The Polish Revolt of 1863 and the Birth of Russification: Bad for the Jews?" *Polin*, no. 1 (1986): 91–106.

Kopel'man, Zoia. "Istoriia etoi knigi." In *Iz evreiskikh poetov*, by Vladislav Khodasevich, 13–97. St. Petersburg: Z. I. Grzhebin, 1923. Reprint, Moscow and Jerusalem: Gesharim, 1998.

—————. "Sionidy—palomnichestvo dushi (k dinamike zhanra)." *Vestnik Evreiskogo universiteta v Moskve* 6: 24 (2001): 131–44.

Kornblatt, I. [Judith Deutsch Kornblatt]. "Vechnyi zhid: Lev Shestov i russkaia religioznaia mysl'." In *Russkaia literatura XX veka: Issledovaniia amerikanskikh uchenykh*, edited by Sharlotta Rozental' [Charlotte Rosenthal] et al., 46–57. St. Petersburg: Petro-Rif, 1993, 46–57.***

Krieze, Semion. "Batei sefer yehudiim be-safah ha-rusit ba-rusiah ha-tsarit." Ph.D. diss., Hebrew University, 1994.

Krutikov, Mikhail. *Yiddish Fiction and the Crisis of Modernity, 1905–1914*. Stanford, CA: Stanford University Press, 2000.

Kucherov, Samuil. "Evrei v russkoi advokature." In Frumkin, Aronson, and Gol'denveizer, *Kniga o russkom evreistve*, 404–41.

Kulisher, E. "Pamiati G. B. Sliozberga." *Evreiskii mir*. New York: Union o Russian Jews, 1944, 425–27.

Landau, Alfred, ed., "Iz perepiski L. Levandy." *Evreiskaia biblioteka*, no. 9 (1901): 1–64.

Lapidus, Rina. *Between Snow and Desert Heat: Russian Influences on Hebrew Literature, 1870–1970*. Cincinnati: Hebrew Union College Press, 2003.

Laqueur, Walter. *A History of Zionism*. London: Trinity Press, 1970.

Lazarev, M. "Zadachi i znachenie russko-evreiskoi belletristiki." *Voskhod*, no. 5 (1885): 28–42; and no. 6 (1885): 24–42.

Lederhendler, Eli. "Interpreting Messianic Rhetoric in the Russian Haskalah and Early Zionism, the Semantic Conundrum: When is Messianism not Messianism?" *Studies in Contemporary Jewry* 7 (1991): 14–33.

—————. *The Road to Modern Jewish Politics: Political Tradition and Political Reconstruction in the Jewish Community of Tsarist Russia*. New York: Oxford University Press, 1989.

Lersky, Jerzy J. *Historical Dictionary of Poland, 966–1945*. Westport, CT: Greenwood Press, 1996.

Levanda, L. O. "Avraam Iezofovich: Istoricheskaia povest' pervoi poloviny XVI-go veka." *Voskhod*, nos. 1–2 (1887).

————. *Delo bakaleinykh tovarov: Kartiny evreiskogo byta v dvukh chastiakh. Rassvet* 10–12 (1860–61).

————. "Fel'eton." *Rassvet*, no. 52 (1882).

————. *Gnev i milost' magnata: Byl' XVIII stoletiia.* Odessa: Odesskie novosti, 1912.

————. *Goriachee vremia: Roman iz poslednego pol'skogo vosstaniia.* St. Petersburg: Tip. A. E. Landau, 1875.

————. "Pis'mo iz provintsii." *Russkii evrei*, no. 3 (15 January 1882): 5–6.

————. "Po povodu stat'i M. G. Morgulisa (pis'mo k izdateliu *Evreiskoi biblioteki)." Evreiskaia biblioteka*, no. 3 (1873): 365–76.

————. [L. L.] "Privislianskaia khronika." *Russkii evrei*, no. 48 (1881): 1906–09.

————. "Russko-evreiskoe religioznoe obrazovanie." *Russkii evrei*, no. 11 (1880).

————. "Sud'by evreev v pol'skoi Rechi Pospolitoi (istoricheskii ocherk)." *Voskhod*, nos. 9–12 (1886).

————. "Sushchnost' tak nazyvaemogo 'palestinskogo' dvizheniia (pis'mo k izdateliam)." In *Palestina: Sbornik statei i svedenii o evreiskikh poseleniiakh v sviatoi zemle,* 5–19. St. Petersburg: Tip. Lebedeva, 1884.

————. "Tri pokoleniia (iz romana 'Eli Makower' G[ospo]zhy Elizy Orzheshkovoi)." *Russkii evrei*, no. 1 (1880): 32–34.

Levin, Mordekhai. *Leyb Yafeh: Bibliyografyah.* Jerusalem, 1977.

Levitas, Isaac. *The Jewish Community in Russia, 1844–1917.* Jerusalem: Posner, 1981.

Machshoves, Baal. "Otvet Maksimu Gor'komu." In Gor'kii, *Iz literaturnogo naslediia,* 235–38.

————. "Stat'ia iz 'Listkov.'" In Gor'kii, *Iz literaturnogo naslediia,* 230–32.

Malamud, Lisa Beth. "Longing for Zion in the Poetry of Judah Halevi." Honors thesis, Tulane University, 1988.

Maor, Izhak. *Sionistskoe dvizhenie v Rossii.* Translated from Hebrew by O. Mints. Jerusalem: Safrit-Alia, 1977.

Markish, Shimon. "A propos de l'histoire et de la methodologie de l'etude de la litterature juive d'expression russe." *Cahiers du monde russe et sovietique.* 36: 2 (April–June 1985): 139–53.

————. "Stoit li perechityvat' L'va Levandy? Stat'ia pervaia: Posy." *Vestnik Evreiskogo universiteta v Moskve* 3: 10 (1995): 90–104.

Markon, Isaak. *Jüdisches Lexikon* (Berlin: Jüdischer Verlag, 1931), 2: 1042.

Martin, Bernard, comp. *Great Twentieth-Century Jewish Philosophers: Shestov, Rosenzweig, Buber, with Selections from Their Writings.* New York: Macmillan, 1970.

Medoff, R. "Our Leaders Cannot Be Moved: A Zionist Emissary's Reports on American Jewish Responses to the Holocaust in the Summer of 1943." *American Jewish History* 88: 1 (2000): 115–26.

Medvedev, P. *Pamiati A. L. Volynskogo.* Leningrad, 1928.

Mendelsohn, Ezra. *Class Struggle in the Pale: The Formative Years of the Jewish Workers' Movement in Tsarist Russia.* Cambridge: Cambridge University Press, 1970.

————, ed. *Jews and the State: Dangerous Alliances and the Perils of Privilege.* Studies in Contemporary Jewry 19. New York: Oxford University Press, 2003.

Menes, A. "Di 'Am Olam' Bevegung." In *Geshikhte fun der Yidisher Arbeter Bavegung in di Fareynikte Shtatn,* edited by Elias Tcherikower, 2: 203–28. New York: YIVO, 1943–45.

Miron, D. "Introduction." *Songs from Bialik: Selected Poems of Hayim Nahman Bialik,* by Bialik, edited and translated by Atar Hadari, xvii–xxxvii. Syracuse, NY: Syracuse University Press, 2000.

Mirsky, D. S. *A History of Russian Literature.* Edited by F. J. Whitfield. New York: Knopf, 1960.

Morgulis, M. "Bezporiadki 1871 goda v Odesse (Po dokumentam i lichnym vospominaniiam)." *Evreiskii mir,* no. 2–3 (1910): 33–47.

————. "Budushchnost' evreistva po Zombartu." *Novyi voskhod,* no. 16 (1912): 10–14.

————. "Byt' ili ne byt' Zaddikizmu v Iugo-zapadnom krae." In *Sobranie sochinenii,* 35–47. Chernigov, 1869.

————. "Chto nam delat' s russkimi evreiami?" *Voprosy evreiskoi zhizni,* 294–342; originally published in *Rassvet* (1879): 3–6.

————. "Kagal, ego istoricheskoe proiskhozhdenie i uchrezhdeniia magdeburgskogo prava: Po povoodu [povodu] 'Knigi kagala.'" *Den',* nos. 4, 5, 6, 11, 13, 14, 19, and 21 (1871).

————. *Il'ia Grigor'evich Orshanskii i ego literaturnaia deiatel'nost'.* St. Petersburg, 1901.

————. *Istoricheskie etiudy: Gilel', Akiba.* Odessa: Izd-vo Odesskago otdeleniia Obshchestva rasprostraneniia prosveshcheniia mezhdu evreiami v Rossii, 1898.

————. "Iz moikh vospominaniii." *Voskhod,* no. 4 (1895): 21–35.

————. "Iz moikh vospominaniji [vospominanii] (vysshaia komissiia grafa Palena po evreiskomu voprosu)." *Evreiskii mir,* no. 6 (1909): 22–44.

————. "K istorii obrazovaniia russkikh evreev." In *Voprosy evreiskoi zhizni,* 1–196; first published in *Evreiskaia biblioteka,* vols. 1–3 (1872–73).

————. "Le-shnei batei Yisrael," *Ha-pardes,* no. 1 (1892): 261–66.

————. "Mnenie komiteta odesskogo otdeleniia Obshchestva rasprostraneniia prosveshcheniia o evreiskoi narodnoi shkole." *Voskhod,* no. 16 (1902): 4–9.

————. "Natsionalizatsiia i assimiliatsiia." *Voskhod,* no. 5 (1902): 99–115.

Morgulis, M. "Nikolai Ivanovich Pirogov i ego otnoshenie k evreiskomu voprosu (po povodu ego piatidesiatiletnego iubileiia)," *Voskhod*, no. 5 (1881). In *Vosprosy evreiskoi zhizni*, 521–31.

———. "Ocherk ugolovnogo Suda evreev po talmudskomu pravu." In *Sobranie sochinenii*, 76–101.

———. "O Kagale (istoricheskii etiud)." *Russkii evrei*, nos. 46–52 (1882).

———. "Ob organizatsii evreiskoi obshchiny," *Evreiskaia nedelia*, nos. 8–9 (1910): 8–21.

———. "O professional'nom obrazovanii evreev v Odesse." In *Sbornik v pol'zu na[c]hal'nykh evreiskhikh shkol*, 389–90. St. Petersburg, 1896.

———. "O sovremennykh obshchestvennykh shkolakh evreev." *Voprosy evreiskoi zhizni*, 196–224; originally published in *Rassvet*, nos. 5–8 (1880).

———. "Preobrazovanie evreiskikh nachal'nykh shkol." *Budushchnost'*, 12 April 1902, 388–91.

———. "Samoosvobozhdenie i samootrechenie." *Voprosy evreiskoi zhizni*, 534–94.

———. *Sobranie sochinenii*. Chernigov, 1869.

———. "Sushchnost' iudaizma." *Voskhod*, no. 1 (1891): 75–79; no. 3 (1891): 3–17.

———. *Vopros, imenuemyi evreiskim*. St. Petersburg: Tip. Obshchestvennaia pol'za, 1906.

———. *Voprosy evreiskoi zhizni: Sobranie statei*. St. Petersburg: Tipo-lit. A. E. Landau, 1899.

———. "Vozmozhno-li i sleduet-li predostavit' evreiam pravo samoupravleniia obshchestvennymi delami?" in *Voprosy evreiskoi zhizni*.

Mosse, George. "Jewish Emancipation between Bildung and Respectability." In *The Jewish Response to German Culture: From the Enlightenment to the Second World War*, edited by Jehuda Reinharz and Walter Schatzberg, 1–16. Hanover, NH: University Press of New England/Clark University, 1985.

Nakhimovsky, Alice Stone. *Russian-Jewish Literature and Identity: Jabotinsky, Babel, Grossman, Galich, Roziner, Markish*. Baltimore: Johns Hopkins University Press, 1992.

Nathans, Benjamin. *Beyond the Pale: The Jewish Encounter with Late Imperial Russia*. Berkeley: University of California Press, 2002.

———. "Conflict, Community and the Jews of Nineteenth-Century St. Petersburg." *Jahrbücher für Geschichte Osteuropas* 44: 2 (Spring 1996): 178–216.

Novgorodtsev, P. I., and S. N. Bulgakov, eds. *Problemy idealizma: Sbornik statei*. Moscow: Izd-vo Moskovskogo psikhologicheskogo obshchestva, 1903.

Obshchestvo dlia rasprostraneniia prosveshcheniia mezhdu evreiami v Rossii. *Obshchestvo dlia rasprostraneniia prosveshchenia mezhdu evreiami v Rossii za piat'desiat let (kratkii istoricheskii ocherk)*. St. Petersburg, 1913.

Obshchestvo dlia rasprostraneniia prosveshcheniia mezhdu evreiami v Rossii. *Otchet Obshchestva dlia rasprostraneniia prosveshcheniia.* St. Petersburg, 1882–1913.

————. *Sovremennyi kheder po obsledovaniiu Obshchestva dlia rasprostraneniia prosveshcheniia v 1912.* St. Petersburg, 1912.

————. *Spravochnaia kniga po voprosam obrazovaniia evreev: Posobie dlia uchitelei i uchitel'nits evreiskikh shkol i deiatelei po narodnomu obrazovaniiu.* St. Petersburg, 1901.

Opalski, Magdalena, and Israel Bartal. *Poles and Jews: A Failed Brotherhood.* The Tauber Institute for the Study of European Jewry, no. 13. Hanover, NH: Brandeis University Press, 1992.

Orshanskii, Il'ia. "Russkoe zakonodatel'stvo o evreiakh." *Evreiskaia biblioteka* 3–5 (1872–74).

Papernyi, Vladimir. "Lev Shestov i russkaia kul'tura." In *Evrei v kul'ture russkogo zarubezh'ia: Sbornik statei, publikatsii, memuarov, i esse,* edited by Mikhail Parkhomovskii, vyp. 2, 122–40. Jerusalem: n.p., 1993.

Pipes, Richard. *Struve: Liberal on the Right, 1905–44.* Cambridge, MA: Harvard University Press, 1980.

Polishchuk, M. L. *Evrei Odessy i Novorossii: Sotsial'no-politicheskaia istoriia evreev Odessy i drugikh gorodov v Novorossii. 1881–1904.* Jerusalem: Gesharim; Moscow: Mosty kul'tury, 2002.

Pomialovskii, N. *Ocherki bursa.* St. Petersburg, 1860.

*Pomoshch' evreiam, postradavshim ot neurozhaia: Literaturno-khudozhestvennyi sbornik.* St. Petersburg: Tip. I. Gol'dberga, 1901.

Pozner, Solomon. *Evrei v obshchei shkole: K istorii zakonodatel'stva i pravitel'stvennoi politiki v oblasti evreiskogo voprosa.* St. Petersburg: Razum, 1914.

Proskurina, Vera. *Techenie Gol'fstrema: Mikhail Gershenzon: Ego zhizn' i mif.* St. Petersburg: Aleteiia, 1998.

————. "Tvorcheskoe samosoznanie Mikhaila Gershenzona," *Literaturnoe obozrenie* 8 (1990): 93–96.

*Protokol soveshchaniia komiteta obshchestva dlia rasprostraneniia prosveshcheniia mezhdu evreiami v Rossii s inogorodnymi chlenami 25–27 dekabria 1902 g.* (St. Petersburg, 1903).

Rappaport, Steven. "Jewish Education and Jewish Culture in the Russian Empire, 1880–1914." Ph.D. diss., Stanford University, 2000.

*Registy i nadpisi: Svod materialov dlia istorii evreev v Rossii.* 3 vols. St. Petersburg, 1897, 1901, 1903.

Rivesman, M. "Vospominaniia i vstrechi (1877–1915)." *Evreiskaia letopis'* 3 (1924): 71–85.

Rosenthal, Bernice Glatzer, ed. *Nietzsche in Russia.* Princeton, NJ: Princeton University Press, 1986.

Rosenthal, Herman. "The Martyrdom of the Jew." *The Outlook* (1911): 109–17.

————. "A Phase of the Russian Spy System." *Review of Reviews* (1911): 363–64.

Rosenthal, Herman. "Preface." In *The Land of Riddles (Russia of To-Day)*, by Hugo Ganz. New York and London: Harper and Brothers, 1904, iii–vii.

————. *Report on Japan, Corea and China*. St. Paul, 1893.

"Rosenthal, Herman." *The Jewish Encyclopedia: A Descriptive Record of the History, Religion, Literature, and Customs of the Jewish People from the Earliest Times to the Present Day*, 4: 478–79. 12 vols. New York and London: Funk and Wagnals Co., 1905.

Rosenthal, Leon, ed. *Toledot hevrat marbei haskalah beyisra'el be'erets rusiyah*. 2 vols. St. Petersburg, 1886–90.

Roskies, David G. "Introduction." In *The Dybbuk and Other Writings*, by S. A. Ansky, edited by Roskies, xi–xxxvi. New York: Schocken Books, 1992.

————. "S. Ansky and the Paradigm of Return." In *The Uses of Tradition: Jewish Continuity in the Modern Era*, edited by Jack Wertheimer, 243–60. New York: Jewish Theological Seminary of America, 1992.

Rozanov, Vasilii. "Levitan i Gershenzon." *Russkii bibliofil*, no. 2 (1916): 78–81.

Salmon, L. "Krizis evreiskoi samobytnosti i romany-manifesty G. I. Bagrova i L. O. Levandy." In *Evrei v Rossii: Trudy po iudaike. Istoriia i etnografiia*, edited by D. A. Eliashevich, vyp. 4, 284–314. St. Petersburg: Peterburgskii Evreiskii universitet, Institut issledovanii evreiskoi diaspory, 1997.

Seltzer, Robert Melvin. "Simon Dubnow: A Critical Biography of His Early Years." Ph.D. diss., Columbia University, 1970.

Serman, Ilya. "Spory 1908 goda o russko-evreiskoi literature i posleoktiabr'-skoe desiatiletie." *Cahiers du monde russe et sovietique* 36: 2 (April–June 1985): 167–74.

Shaw, Peter W. "The Odessa Jewish Community, 1855–1900: An Institutional History." Ph.D. diss., The Hebrew University, 1988.

Shestov, L. *Afiny i Ierusalim*. In *Sochineniia v 2 tomakh*. Edited by A. Akhutin. Moscow: Nauka, 1993.

————. *Apofeoz bespochvennosti: Opyt adogmaticheskogo myshleniia*. St. Petersburg: Obshchestvennaia pol'za, 1905. Reprint, Leningrad: Izd-vo Leningradskogo universiteta, 1991.

————. *Dobro v uchenii Gr. Tolstogo i Nitshe: Filosofiia i propoved'*. St. Petersburg: Tip. M. M. Stasiulevicha, 1900.

————. *Dostoevskii i Nitshe: Filosofiia tragedii*. St. Petersburg: Tip. M. M. Stasiulevicha, 1903.

————. "Gefsimanskaia noch' (filosofiia Paskalia)." *Sovremennye zapiski*, no. (March–June) and no. 20 (July–September) (1924). Reprinted in Shestov, *Sochineniia v 2 tomakh*, 2: 278–324.

————. *Nachala i kontsy*. St. Petersburg: Tip. M. M. Stasiulevicha, 1908.

————. *Shekspir i ego kritik Brandes*. St. Petersburg: Tip. M. M. Stasiulevicha, 1898.

————. *Sola Fide – Tol'ko veroiu: Grecheskaia i srednevekovaia filosofiia. Liuter i tserkov'*. Paris: YMCA-Press, 1966.

————. *Sochineniia v 2 tomakh*. Edited by A. Akhutin. Moscow: Nauka, 1993.

Shestov, L. *Vlast' kliuchei: Potestas Clavium.* Berlin: Skythen Verlag, 1923.

Shteinberg, Aron. *Druz'ia moikh rannikh let: 1911–28.* Edited by Georges Michel Nivat. Paris: Sintaksis, 1991.

———. *History as Experience: Aspects of Historical Thought—Universal and Jewish. Selected Essays and Studies.* New York: Ktav, 1983.

———. *Sistema svobody F. M. Dostoevskogo.* Berlin: Skify, 1923. Reprint, Paris: YMCA-Press, 1980.

Skabichevskii, A. M. *Istoriia noveishei russkoi literatury, 1848–1903 gg.* 5th ed. St. Petersburg: Obshchestvennaia pol'za, 1903.

Slezkine, Yuri. *The Jewish Century.* Princeton, NJ: Princeton University Press, 2004.

Sliozberg, G. *Baron G. O. Gintsburg: Ego zhizn' i deiatel'nost'.* Paris, 1933.

———. "Baron G. O. Gintsburg i pravovoe polozhenie evreev." In *Perezhitoe,* 2: 94–115. St. Petersburg, 1901–11.

———. *Dela minuvshikh dnei: Zapiski russkago evreia.* 3 vols. Paris: Komitet po chestvovaniiu, 1933.

———. *Dorevoliutsionnyi stroi Rossii.* Paris, 1933.

———. *Iubileinyi sbornik.* N.p., n.d.

———. *Pravovoe i ekonomicheskoe polozhenie evreev v Rossii (iz materialov po evreiskomu voprosu).* St. Petersburg: Levenstein, 1907.

———. "Ravvinskaia komissia." *Novyi voskhod,* no. 10 (11 March 1910): 15.

Slobin, Greta N. "Heroic Poetry and Revolutionary Prophecy: Russian Symbolists Translate the Hebrew Poets." *Judaism: A Quarterly Journal of Jewish Life and Thought* 51: 4 (Fall 2002): 408–18.

Slutsky, Yehuda. *Haitonut hayehudit-rusit bemeah ha-19.* Jerusalem: Mosad Bialik, 1970.

———. "Takanon havot ha-tsava ha-kallit 1874 ve-ha-yihudim." *He'avar* 21 (1975): 3–18.

Sorin, Gerald. *A Time for Building: The Third Migration, 1880–1920.* Baltimore: Johns Hopkins University Press, 1992.

Sosis, I. "Period obruseniia: Natsional'nyi vopros v literature v kontse 60-kh godov i nachala 70-kh godov." *Evreiskaia starina,* no. 2 (April–June 1915): 129–46.

Stanislawski, Michael. "Jewish Apostasy in Russia: A Tentative Typology." In *Jewish Apostasy in the Modern World,* edited by Todd M. Endelman, 189–205. New York: Holmes and Meier, 1987.

———. *Tsar Nicholas I and the Jews: The Transformation of Jewish Society in Russia, 1825–1855.* Philadelphia: Jewish Publication Society of America, 1983.

———. *Zionism and the Fin de Siècle: Cosmopolitanism and Nationalism from Nordau to Jabotinsky.* Berkeley: University of California Press, 2001.

Stasov, Vladimir, ed. *M. M. Anotokol'skii: Ego zhizn', tvoreniia, pis'ma, i stat'i.* St. Petersburg, 1905.

Stasov, Vladimir, ed. "Po povodu postroiki sinagogi v S.-Peterburge." *Evrei-skaia biblioteka*, no. 2 (1872): 453–73.

Stasov, Vladimir, and Baron David Guenzburg. *Ornementation des anciens manuscripts hébreaux*. Berlin: S. Calvary and Co., 1905.

Teitel, Ia. *Iubileinyi sbornik, 1851–1931*. Ed. N. L. Aronson. Paris-Berlin, 1931.

———. *Iz moei zhizni: Za sorok let*. Paris: Ia. Povolotskii, 1925.

Timberlake, Charles E. "The Zemstvo and the Development of a Russian Middle Class." In *Between Tsar and People: Educated Society and the Quest for Public Identity in Late Imperial Russia*, edited by Edith W. Clowes, Samuel D. Kassow, and James L. West, 164–82. Princeton, NJ: Princeton University Press, 1991.

Timenchik, R. "Russko-evreiskaia literatura." In *Kratkaia evreiskaia entsiklopediia*. 10 vols. Jerusalem: Obshchestvo po issledovaniiu evreiskikh obshchin, Hebrew University, 1996.

Timenchik, R., and Zoia Kopel'man. "Viacheslav Ivanov i poeziia Kh. N. Bialika." *Novoe literaturnoe obozrenie*, no. 14 (1995): 102–15.

Tolstoi, I., and Iu. Gessen. *Fakty i mysli: Evreiskii vopros v Rossii*. St. Petersburg: Obshchestvennaia pol'za, 1907.

Trotskii, Il'ia. "Evrei v russkoi shkole." In Frumkin, Aronson, and Gol'denveizer, *Kniga o russkom evreistve*, 353–64.

———. "Samodeiatel'nost' i samopomoshch' russkogo evreistva." In Frumkin, Aronson, and Gol'denveizer, *Kniga o russkom evreistve*, 473–502.

Trunk, I. "Istoriki russkogo evreistva." In Frumkin, Aronson, and Gol'denveizer, *Kniga o russkom evreistve*, 16–39.

Tsinberg, S. *Istoriia evreiskoi pechati v Rossii v sviazi s obshchestvennymi techeniiami*. Petrograd: Tip. I. Fleitmana, 1915.

Urussov, S. *Memoirs of a Russian Governor*. London: Harper and Brothers, 1908.

Veidlinger, Jeffrey. "From Shtetl to Society: Jews in 19th-Century Russia." *Kritika: Explorations in Russian and Eurasian History* 2: 4 (Fall 2001): 823–34.

———. "Jewish Cultural Associations in the Aftermath of 1905." In *The Revolution of 1905 and Russia's Jews*, edited by Ezra Mendelsohn and Stefani Hoffman, 199–211. University of Pennsylvania Press, 2007.

Vinaver, M. *Istoriia vyborgskogo vozzvaniia (vospominaniiu)*. Petrograd, 1917.

———. "Kak my zanimalis' istoriei." *Evreiskaia starina*, no. 1 (1909): 41–54. Reprinted in *Evrei v Rossiiskoi imperii XVIII–XIX vekov: Sbornik trudov evreiskikh istorikov*, edited by Aleksandr Lokshin, 65–78. Moscow: Evreiskii universitet; Jerusalem: Gesharim Press, 1995.

———. *Nedavnee: Vospominaniia I kharakteristiki*. 3rd ed. Paris, 1926.

Vishniak, M. *Dan' proshlomu*. New York: Izd-vo im. Chekhova, 1954. Quoted in R. Timenchik. "Russko-evreiskaia literatura."

Vital, David. *Zionism: The Formative Years*. New York: Oxford University Press, 1982.

Volkspartei. *Evreiskaia Narodnaia Partiia*. St. Petersburg: Evreiskaia Narodnaia Partiia, 1907.

Volynskii, A. "Bytopisatel' russkogo evreistva: Kriticheskii obzor beletristicheskikh proizvedenii L. O. Levandy." *Voskhod*, no. 1–2 (1889): 1–26.

Wagner, Richard. "Das Judentum in der Musik." *Neue Zeitschrift für Musik* (1850).

Walicki, Andrzej. *The Slavophile Controversy: History of a Conservative Utopia in Nineteenth-Century Thought*. New York: Clarendon, 1975.

Wengeroff, Pauline. *Rememberings: The World of a Russian-Jewish Woman in the Nineteenth Century*. Edited by Bernard D. Cooperman. Translated by Henny Wenkard. Potomac: University Press of Maryland, 2000.

Zeltser, A., and I. Lurie, "Moses Berlin and the Lubavich Hasidim: A Landmark in the Conflict between Haskalah and Hasidim." *Shvut: Studies in Russian and East European Jewish History and Culture* 5 (21) (1997): 32–54.

Zipperstein, Steven J. *Elusive Prophet: Ahad Ha'am and the Origins of Zionism*. Berkeley: University of California Press, 1993.

———. *The Jews of Odessa: A Cultural History, 1794–1881*. Stanford, CA: Stanford University Press, 1986.

———. "The Politics of Relief: The Transformation of Russian Jewish Communal Life During the First World War." In *The Jews and the European Crisis, 1914–21*, edited by Jonathan Frankel, 22–40. Studies in Contemporary Jewry, vol. 4. New York: Oxford University Press, 1988.

———. "Transforming the Heder: Maskilic Politics in Imperial Russia." In *Jewish History: Essays in Honor of Chimen Abramsky*, edited by A. Rapoport-Albert and S. Zipperstein, 98–106. London: P. Halban, 1988.

Zweifel, Eliezer. *Shalom 'al yisra'el*. Zhitomir, 1868.

# Index

*Note:* All writings are listed under their author.